A Personalist Jurisprudence, The Next Step

A Personalist Jurisprudence, The Next Step

A Person-Centered Philosophy of Law for the Twenty-First Century

Samuel J.M. Donnelly

Foreword by

Hon. Joseph R. Biden, Jr.
United States Senator from Delaware

CAROLINA ACADEMIC PRESS
Durham, North Carolina

ISBN 0-89089-156-7
LCCN 2002117308

Carolina Academic Press
700 Kent Street
Durham, NC 27701
Telephone (919) 489-7486
Fax (919) 493-5668
www.cap-press.com

Printed in the United States of America

To Mary Ann

Contents

Foreword   XI
Acknowledgments   XV

Chapter I   Introduction   3

   1. A Person Centered Jurisprudence   3
   2. The Personalist Judge   5
   3. Intellectual Method   10
   4. The Uses of Rights   13
   5. The Personalist Agenda   14
   6. An Interpretation of Law   16
   7. Central Ideas and Themes   18
     a. Rights   18
     b. The Common Good   19
     c. Method   21
     d. Legitimacy   21
     e. Interpretation   23

Chapter II   The Common Law Tradition   25

   1. Introduction   25
   2. The Great Quarrel over Method   28
   3. Critique and Reconstruction of Method   34
   4. The Common Law   41
   5. Legislation   50
   6. A Central Role for Dispute Settlement   60
   7. Legitimacy   65
     a. The Meaning of Legitimacy   65
     b. The Legitimacy of Personalist Method   68

Chapter III   Personalist Theory   71

  1. Introduction   71
  2. Action   74
  3. The Quarrel over Method: A Role for the Person   78
  4. Horizons   83
  5. Principles   87
  6. Insight   91
  7. Critique of Method   94
  8. The Common Good   99
  9. Horizons and Conversation in a Pluralist Society   103
 10. Rights   107
 11. Conclusion   111

Chapter IV   Constitutional Interpretation   115

  1. Introduction   115
  2. Interpreting a Written Document   120
  3. Method   122
  4. A Deliberating Society   123
  5. Rights Theory and Constitutional Interpretation   130
  6. Conversing with Tradition: Legal Classicism   137
  7. Deciding *Brown*   144
  8. The Great Quarrel over Method   153
    a. Conservative Theories   153
    b. Some Liberal Theories   161
    c. Other Liberal Theories   165
  9. Principles, Pluralism and Conversation   169
 10. Unenumerated Rights—Substantive Due Process   171
 11. Interpreting the Eighth Amendment   188
 12. Conclusion   195

**Chapter V   Justification, Legitimacy and
Moral Judgment**   197

  1. Introduction   197
  2. Justification   199
  3. Human Rights   210
  4. The Common Good   221

5. Method 227
6. Moral Judgment 233
7. Legitimacy 239
8. Authority, Legitimacy and the Use of Force 244

Chapter VI   The Language and Uses of Rights:
Relating the Multiple Players in the Game of Law
across Horizons 247

1. Introduction 247
2. Interpretation 249
3. Contrasting Visions 251
4. The Language and Uses of Rights 254
   a. Rights as Remedies, the Predictive View of Law 254
   b. Rights as Conclusions in a Legal System 255
   c. Rights as Reasons; Rights as Trumps 255
   d. Rights as Goals; Rights as Means 257
   e. Rights as Resources 258
   f. Anti-Rights Rhetoric and the Use of Rights 259
   g. Analyzing Horizons and Points of View:
      Understanding the Various Uses of Rights 260
5. Obligation 263
6. The Task of the Law Reform Litigator 267
7. Conversation: Communication across Horizons 270
8. Conclusion 272

Chapter VII   The Personalist Agenda 273

1. Introduction 273
2. Conversation; Continued Development of Theory 276
   a. Have a Conversation with This Book 276
   b. Method; Construction and Reconstruction 277
   c. The Personalist Interpretation of American Law:
      A Perennial Philosophy of Law 278
   d. The Personalist Scholar 279
3. The Role of the Practicing Attorney 280
4. Law Reform 283
5. Social Science and Law 289

6. Personalist Theory and Reform of Particular
   Legal Fields   293
7. Rethinking Criminal Justice   294
8. Conclusion   306

Concluding Postscript   307
Index   311

Foreword

Senator Joseph R. Biden, Jr.

Oliver Wendell Holmes, Jr. famously remarked that the life of the law is not logic, but experience. After close to forty years as a law professor and practitioner, Sam Donnelly knows this to be true. The central theme of his book is that the law is primarily about persons and their relations, a theory which he labels "personalism." Under this "person-centered" interpretation, he offers not simply another definition of "the law," but expounds a vision of the law as an activity engaged in by a variety of players, including judges, advocates, scholars and the general public. I am attracted to Donnelly's thesis on many levels, but perhaps most because I believe that it has the power to enhance the legitimacy of law. Why? Because it is grounded in respect and concern for each and all persons and is continually open to the needs, interests and circumstances of all members of a democratic society. Without a strong and abiding respect to the law and its institutions, no democracy can thrive and survive.

Donnelly offers two insights that caught my attention. First, he argues convincingly that the central achievement of twentieth century jurisprudence was the gradual recovery "of a role for the person." By this Donnelly means recognition of the great American ideal that each person is worthwhile and entitled to government protection of our lives, liberties and property. Second, he maintains that recent schools of constitutional interpretation—whether conservative or liberal—both often avoid the robust debate and difficult interpretative work needed to best unpack Constitutional concepts.

"Personalism" offers an interpretation of and reflections on American law. At its core, Donnelly argues, personalist theory maintains that respect for the human dignity of each person, as well as protection of the common good, is the core American insight which has emerged (albeit episodically) over two centuries. Hence, the personalist judge offers a theory of our Constitution as an ongoing action designed to promote that ideal. While a personalist judge would prefer to ground his rulings in constitutional concepts, this judge recognizes that in some cases he may be handicapped by the law's "limited vision" of some great national dispute. Personalist theory accepts such limitations, recognizing that the articulable principles that undergird landmark rulings may only be apparent in hindsight.

Donnelly points to the Warren Court's landmark ruling in Brown v. Board of Education of Topeka, Kansas as such an example. He applauds the Court's use of "means-end reasoning" to achieve our national ideals in public education. In so doing, the Court took giant steps to restore "a role for the person" in American jurisprudence. The central theme of Chief Justice Earl Warren's opinion was that the law evolves and should change to keep pace with significant cultural and sociological developments. While legal scholars have tried to read back into Warren's opinion a discussion of deliberation on the concept of equality or equal protection, Donnelly is willing to concede that the Brown decision is devoid of any principled analysis (in the Wechslerian sense) in support of the Court's position. Yet, far from concluding that Brown's reasoning is morally and intellectually bankrupt, Donnelly maintains that it is Warren's personalist-oriented approach which gives it its unsurpassed moral force. "Indeed, the result in Brown could be supported by ultimate legitimacy, that is, by reasons that have the possibility of being acceptable to all persons at all times because they are based on respect and concern for each person."

In his most provocative and original of insights, Donnelly takes both conservatives and liberals to task over their respective views of constitutional interpretation. Conservative thinkers want to preserve in stone the founding generation's supposed interpretation of the drafters' deliberately written general provisions. In contrast, liberal thinkers often want to advance political goals by arguing for decisions supported by their favored narrow principles. Ironically, both methods evidence a "refusal to deliberate" on the moral concepts contained within the Constitution, to discuss competing reasons or consider competing interests. Donnelly describes "the great quarrel over method" as becoming "particularly acrimonious" when these opposing constitutional camps discuss constitutional interpretation. Having served as Chairman of the Senate Judiciary Committee and chaired six Supreme Court nomination hearings, I can assure the reader that such debates over constitutional interpretation are, to say the least, heated.

Donnelly cites Judge Robert Bork's jurisprudence as an example of a conservative judicial philosophy that rejects the personalist approach.

Bork's emphasis on "established constitutional values" permits him to oppose the recognition of new unenumerated rights, whether by development of the due process or equal protection clauses or under the Ninth Amendment. For example, in considering the Fourteenth Amendment, Bork seeks to uncover "the values held by the generation which adopted the Fourteenth Amendment." Thus, for example, Bork opposes Shelley v. Kraemer because he does not believe that its finding of state action in the enforcement of a racially-restrictive covenant can be supported by a principle that will be neutrally applied in all situations. Rather, Bork attempts, in his own words, to "develop the values of the Constitution's drafters in a principled way" by limiting his analysis to what he thinks the founder's intended, even where the textual language supports a more expansive reading. In doing so, however, Donnelly argues that Bork avoids the hard and controversial work of deliberating on and explaining the great moral concepts in the Constitution.

Lest the reader think that Donnelly just likes to pick on conservatives, he next turns his critical analysis to liberal scholars who do the same thing in different analytical garb. For example, he criticizes Professor John Hart Ely for his "ingenious attempt to justify the work of the Warren Court," which "while offering a theory of judicial restraint, is an example of a liberal theory which produces liberally desirable political results while purporting to restrain judicial activism." Likewise, he questions Professor Laurence Tribe's model of an "aspirational penumbra" of uncertain constitutional dimensions. Donnelly maintains that Tribe's paradigm, like Ely's, allows him to avoid deliberation of contested constitutional concepts and instead to offer "a formula for judicial restraint which supports results admired by liberal activists."

Having rejected what he considers the extremes of right and left, Donnelly endorses the approach of a "personalist judge" who uses means-end reasoning to promote constitutional goals and to enhance protected primary social goods. He cites Justice William Brennan's opinion in New York Times v. Sullivan as a good model for a personalist judge. There, Brennan modified the common law of libel by holding that a public official suing a newspaper for libel must show malice in addition to the elements of the common law action. This holding balanced the interests of Commissioner Sullivan and other public officials in their reputations against the freedom of the press of The New York Times and the black ministers who published the allegedly libelous advertisement. According to Donnelly, this is an example of a personalist judge at his best, forcefully pressing a "sparkling vision of concern for the human dignity of each person."

After almost thirty years in the United States Senate, I have been called on to consider the nomination for each of our nine Supreme Court Justices, as well as chair numerous Supreme Court nomination hearings. Virtually every nomination has witnessed a "quarrel over method," to use Donnelly's phrase—a robust debate over the judicial philosophy of the nominee. I think Donnelly's work may well be an invaluable guide in considering what counts most in a Supreme Court justice; nominees who fall into the "personalist camp", and evidence, in his words, "a theory of our Constitution and a method for interpretation which will be in accord with his commitment to afford all persons deep respect and concern and try to understand persons, their needs and their horizons."

Acknowledgments

My profound thanks go first to Mary Ann Abend Donnelly, J.D. Harv. 1962, who as lawyer, teacher, scholar and lover of the law I imagined as the ideal reader. Also she has lived with this book as long as I have. Thank you Senator Joseph Biden for graciously writing the Foreword to this book. Then I thank Prof. Edward Walsh, who taught me how to write; Dr. Quentin Lauer, S.J., who introduced me to and shared with me his fascination with philosophy, Dr. Robert Johann, who introduced me to the thought of John Macmurray, and Dr. Gerald McCool, S.J., who taught me about Bernard Lonergan, S.J. Joining the personalism of John Macmurray and others with a critique of method inspired by Lonergan is the central insight of this book. I thank Prof. David Granfield, O.S.B., for yet more immediate inspiration. I thank also the Hon. Nathan Jacobs, Associate Justice of the New Jersey Supreme Court, who introduced me to judicial decision making and my colleagues particularly Dr. Richard Schwartz, Dr. William Wiecek and Dr. Michael Barkun whose conversation, scholarship and friendship contributed to the inspiration for this book. I thank Prof. George Christie for a very important (to me) note in his book (George C. Christie and Patrick H. Martin, Jurisprudence, Text and Reading on the Philosophy of Law, Second Edition, West (1995)). My secretaries, most especially Teia Johnson and Clair Doerle, and Margaret Smith, Lynn Oatman and Heather Fitzpatrick, were a great and indispensable help and I am profoundly grateful. The Loyola of Los Angeles Law Review published the article which led to this book and in adapted, rearranged and rewritten form became Chapter 3 of this book (S. Donnelly, Towards a Personalist Jurisprudence; Basic Insights and Concepts, 28 Loyola, Los Angeles L.Rev. 547 (1995)). The University Press of America published an earlier book (The Language and Uses of Rights: A Biopsy of American Jurisprudence in the Twentieth Century (1994)), which in partial, adapted and rewritten form became Chapter 6 of this book. I thank the Loyola of Los Angeles Law Review and the University Press of America. A number of research assistants have contributed to this book: Mr.

Peter Anthopolos, Ms. Michelle Saporito, Mr. Mark Hancock, Ms. Dianna Morris, Mr. Stuart Cohen, Ms. Stephanie Seeley, Mr. Brian Phillips, Ms. Melissa Mitchell, Ms. Lisa Christensen and Mr. A.J. Monaco. Thank you research assistants for your great and indispensable help. Finally my profound thanks to Anonymous who was the most important inspiration for this book.

Copyright Permissions

Chapter 3 is an adapted and revised version of my article: Samuel J.M. Donnelly, Towards a Personalist Jurisprudence: Basic Insights and Concepts, 28 Loy.L.A. L.Rev 547 (1995) and is reprinted with the permission of the publisher, Loyola of Los Angeles Law Review.

Chapter 6 is revised and adapted from the University Press of America book, Samuel J.M. Donnelly, The Language and Uses of Rights: A Biopsy of American Jurisprudence in the Twentieth Century (1994), and is reprinted with the permission of the publisher.

A Personalist Jurisprudence, The Next Step

CHAPTER I

Introduction

1. A Person Centered Jurisprudence

During the nineteenth century it was customary to offer definitions of law. John Austin defined law as the command of the sovereign backed by sanctions.[1] Later Oliver Wendell Holmes, Jr., described law as the predictions of what courts would, in fact, do.[2] During the twentieth century defining law has been less popular. American Pragmatists such as Roscoe Pound and Karl Llewellyn preferring to emphasize what went into rather than what was not part of law refrained from offering any definition.[3] In mid-century, H.L.A. Hart offered an elucidation rather than a definition of law. He argued that law should be perceived as a system of rules.[4] The American Pragmatist tradition from Holmes to Richard Posner in contrast tended to understand law as an activity with the judge as an important central actor.[5]

---

1. *See* JOHN AUSTIN, THE PROVINCE OF JURISPRUDENCE DETERMINED AND THE USES OF THE STUDY OF JURISPRUDENCE (H.L.A. Hart ed.) 13–14, 350 (1954); *see also,* SAMUEL J.M. DONNELLY, THE LANGUAGE AND USES OF RIGHTS: A BIOPSY OF AMERICAN JURISPRUDENCE IN THE TWENTIETH CENTURY ix (1994) (hereinafter, "THE LANGUAGE AND USES OF RIGHTS"); *but see,* H.L.A. HART, THE CONCEPT OF LAW 18–25 (1961).

2. *See* Oliver Wendell Holmes, Jr., *The Path Of The Law* 10 HARV. L. REV. 457, 461 (1897).

3. *See* Samuel J.M. Donnelly, *Book Review,* 3 HOFSTRA L. REV. 915–16 (1975).

4. *See generally* HART, THE CONCEPT OF LAW, *supra* note 1 at 77–96 (Offering an important clarifying concept, that a legal system is composed of the union of primary rules of obligation and secondary rules about primary rules such as rules of recognition, change, and adjudication).

5. *See* Holmes, *The Path Of The Law, supra* note 2 at 457 ("[W]hen we study law we are not studying a mystery but a well known profession. We are studying what we shall want in order to appear before judges, or to advise peo-

A principal theme of this book is that law is primarily about persons and their relations. Rather than a definition it offers a vision of law as an activity engaged in by a variety of players including judges, advocates for the plaintiff and defendants, law reformers, scholars and perhaps all of us.[6] In the American tradition the theory of personalism offered here has a central role for the judge.

The vision and the theory elaborating it are offered as part of "the grand conversation of anglo-american jurisprudence." As an arbitrary starting point for that conversation one could select 1880 and the publication by Oliver Wendell Holmes, Jr., of a series of lectures entitled *The Common Law*.[7] During the twentieth century one could designate H.L.A. Hart as host of the salon and catalyst for the discussion.[8]

Hart engaged in conversation with the thought of Holmes and the pragmatists who followed him, with Lon Fuller, Ronald Dworkin and many others. At times the conversation became an angry exchange. One could recall for example the debate between Karl Llewellyn and Roscoe Pound which began with Llewellyn's article, "A Realist Jurisprudence, The Next Step"[9] and some of the more recent criticisms of the Critical Legal Studies Movement. What could be described as "the great quarrel over method" becomes particularly acrimonious when discussing constitutional interpretation.

A central achievement of twentieth century jurisprudence, it will be argued, was the gradual and perhaps piecemeal recovery of a role for

---

ple in such a way as to keep them out of court..."); *see also*, R. POSNER, THE PROBLEMS OF JURISPRUDENCE 456–57 (1990) ("[L]aw is better, though not fully, described as the activity of the licensed professionals we call judges, the scope of their license being limited only by the diffuse outer bounds of professional propriety and moral concessions. Holmes was right on track in proposing the prediction theory of law, which is an activity theory; his critics have been too quick to dismiss it...").

6. *See* DONNELLY, THE LANGUAGE AND USES OF RIGHTS, *supra* note 1 at ix–xi (Much of this passage is adapted from THE LANGUAGE AND USES OF RIGHTS).

7. OLIVER WENDELL HOLMES, JR., THE COMMON LAW (1897).

8. *See generally* DONNELLY, THE LANGUAGE AND USES OF RIGHTS, *supra* note 1 at 83 ("[O]ne aspect of the art as practiced by Hart is to accept insights developed by other thinkers, rescue those insights from the competing view of legal philosophy and transform them so that these insights can become part of Hart's understanding of law...").

9. Karl Llewellyn, *A Realist Jurisprudence—The Next Step*, 30 COLUM. L. REV. 431 (1930); *see also* Donnelly, *Book Review*, *supra* note 3.

the person. The subject of large portions of the discussion has been judicial method. A central focus for the theory of personalism in law will be the judge as person seeking to understand his world and to develop an appropriate method. During the twenty-first century a logical next step would be the development of a person-centered jurisprudence.

Personalism offers an interpretation of and reflections on American law. In conversation with current methodologies and thought personalism from age to age can construct and reconstruct methods for deciding common law cases, and for statutory and constitutional interpretation. As a theory of our law personalism does not abandon or rewrite the common law tradition. Because a personalist thinker recognizes his own limited knowledge and understanding and is fascinated with and committed to the value of each person, he or she must remain in conversation with and learn from competing views.

2. The Personalist Judge

When reading this book one should imagine two sorts of personalist thinkers, one a common law judge and the other a legal scholar or philosopher. An interesting thought experiment would be to imagine oneself as a common law judge contemplating issues and ideas posed while reading this book. For reasons which will become clear, that would be a particularly useful point of view from which to read and participate in a conversation with this book and the common law tradition.

Martin Heidigger describes a person as being thrown into a world.[10] That metaphor may describe aptly not merely the experience of our youth when we began to sort out the world but also our law school education. During the first year of law school we plunge into the swimming pool of law, pretend that we can swim and then find that we can manage. A common law judge must have a similar experience when first appointed or elected. Although previous experience including work as an attorney is relevant, the world a new judge finds herself in is altogether new.

---

10. *See* MARTIN HEIDEGGER, IDENTITY AND DIFFERENCE 34–35 (J. Stambaugh trans., 1969); Samuel J.M. Donnelly, *Towards A Personalist Jurisprudence: Basic Insights And Concepts*, 28 LOYOLA OF L.A. L. REV. 547, 572 (1995) (hereinafter, "*Towards A Personalist Jurisprudence*") (This passage is adapted in part from *Towards A Personalist Jurisprudence*).

While reading the following chapters one could imagine a common law judge growing in sophistication perhaps while advancing in his career. Chapter 2 describes a personalist judge as one who recognizes his own limited although growing knowledge and understanding, and is fascinated by and committed to respect and concern for each person. While that is a modestly idealistic image, a number of judges approximate that description and others reveal some of the traits listed. We all recognize that some judges are seriously at odds with that modest ideal. The personalist judge as described in chapter 2 is neither a hero nor an analytical giant. One hopes that he resembles some garden-variety common law judges. In contrast the judge portrayed in chapter 3 has a philosophical inclination and an inquiring mind. Some of our best judges have been important jurisprudential thinkers. When new to the bench they experience intellectual excitement as they joyously but with a sense of responsibility begin to sort through their world. Chapter 3 builds on chapter 2 and defines the more intellectually curious judge as one committed to respect and concern for each person. Fascinated with others and with the intellectual possibilities of his new world he continues to recognize his own limited but growing knowledge and understanding. In chapter 4 as the exploration continues one can imagine the successful personalist judge now appointed to the United States Supreme Court. William Brennan could serve as a possible real world model for the ideal and more abstract portrait offered here of that judge.

Following this "Introduction" then, chapter 2 will offer a personalist interpretation of the common law tradition. During the twentieth century the great quarrel over method signals the importance of an appreciation for the differences in method to understand and interpret our law. Ronald Dworkin echoing others argues that common law method primarily should offer a justification for the public use of force.[11] Contrary to Dworkin, however, a focus on dispute settlement as the central function of our courts better describes what the courts do while offering a stronger foundation for drawing a relation between judicial decisions and respect and concern for persons. Dworkin argues that a legitimate decision is derived from principles which best justify the authoritative decisions of the past.[12] Again contrary to Dworkin the second chapter argues that a decision is legitimate when supported by ar-

---

11. *See* RONALD DWORKIN, LAW'S EMPIRE 190 (1986).
12. *See id.* at 190–95; and *see* RONALD DWORKIN, TAKING RIGHTS SERIOUSLY 110–15 (1978).

guments that a judge can expect reasonably to be acceptable to all persons including those particularly affected by his decision. Chapter 2 offers a preliminary understanding that a theory of legitimacy should explore the conditions for acceptance of law rather than the justified use of force.

Primarily the second chapter offers a critique and reconstruction of common law method grounded in the common sense of an average judge who is committed to persons. In the twenty-first century a personalist judge would find both Dworkin's high idealism and pragmatic instrumentalist decision making techniques attractive, helpful and inadequate. When reconstructing common law method a personalist judge should attempt to meld that high idealism with the down to earth respect for persons offered by pragmatic development of traditional common law reasoning. Chapter 2 illustrates that reconstruction by discussing method in the decision of common law cases and the interpretation of statutes. The argument is that the reconstructed method offers means for deciding cases that are legitimate and which enhance the settlement of disputes. A personalist method as preliminarily described in this chapter, it is argued, is one of a number of legitimate methods for deciding cases but has the capacity to enhance legitimacy. Personalist method from age to age can combine the better insights of competing methods. At the moment, it not only should merge personalist aspects of Dworkin and pragmatic-instrumentalist thought but also should be open to insights from post-modern thought.

More abstractly theoretical than chapter 2, chapter 3 offers a series of related insights and concepts which could be described as a theory of personalism in law. As an interpretation of law it is an alternative to legal pragmatism or to Dworkin's theory of law as Integrity.[13] Central to that theory is the judge's recognition of himself as one who acts. Following the Scottish philosopher, John Macmurray, the person or the

---

13. *See generally* DWORKIN, LAW'S EMPIRE, *supra* note 11 at 225–75 (Arguing that there are two distinct interpretations of law, Conventionalism and Pragmatism, and offering a third, Integrity. Conventionalism requires judges to study law reports and parliamentary records to discover what decisions have been made by institutions conventionally recognized to have legislative power. Pragmatism requires judges to think instrumentally about the best rules for the future. Dworkin's Law as Integrity is more relentlessly interpretive than either Conventionalism or Pragmatism, as Integrity asks judges to continue interpreting the same material that it claims to have successfully interpreted itself.)

judge understands himself as related to others through action.[14] In contrast to pragmatist theory which often understands law as action, the personalist theory of persons related to each other through action will provide a foundation for a comprehensive theory of law which in turn will support a theory of strong rights as well as dispute settlement.[15] Our intellectually curious judge in conversation with the common law tradition and twentieth century American jurisprudence will recognize the importance to his own decision making of the great quarrel over method. He also will recognize the gradual and partial recovery of a role for the person during that debate. A critical examination of method in relation to the judge's self-understanding and his commitment to persons, then, becomes important. An important personalist concept is "horizons."[16] A judge committed to persons who recognizes his own limited knowledge and understanding and hence his horizons will develop as part of his decision making process methods for crossing horizons. Principles either as means for organizing law or as reflecting our great ideals must be understood in relation to the problem of horizons. One important method for understanding foreign horizons is to locate and weigh relevant interests. In personalist theory, then, principled reasoning must be related to interest analysis.

Principles, at times, reflect our great ideals. A judge or scholar committed to persons can construct a theory of the common good which will support those great ideals. Chapter 3 drawing on Macmurray's understanding of persons related through action will offer a theory of the common good as persons acting together.[17] Inspired by John Rawls' concept, primary social goods,[18] chapter 3 will describe those goods as those necessary to participation in society, that is, in the common action. There are also goods we hold in common and which promote the interaction of persons in society. In contrast to the primary social

---

14. *See* JOHN MACMURRAY, THE SELF AS AGENT (1957) (volume 1 of Professor Macmurray's Gifford Lectures given under the title The Form of the Personal); and *see* JOHN MACMURRAY, PERSONS IN RELATION (1961) (volume 2 of Professor Macmurray's Gifford Lectures given under the title The Form of the Personal).

15. *See* Donnelly, *Towards a Personalist Jurisprudence*, *supra* note 10 at 554–55, 584–92.

16. *See id.* at 572–79.

17. *See id.* at 584–92.

18. *See* JOHN RAWLS, A THEORY OF JUSTICE 396–99, 433–39, 447 (1971); *and see* Donnelly, *Towards a Personalist Jurisprudence*, *supra* note 10 at 587–88.

goods we could call these the common goods. A common legal discourse, for example, is a common good whose benefit we share and which promotes the interrelation of persons in our society. A personalist theory of rights would protect persons from exclusion from the common action by deprivation of the primary social goods. Principles grounded in that theory and the theory itself must be understood in relation to action and horizons. In constructing his decision making method, a personalist judge must recognize his limited knowledge and understanding and that his theory, including his understanding of the primary social goods, was developed within his own horizons. As a judge in a pluralist society, that is, one composed of multiple horizons, he must provide horizon crossing techniques in his decision making method. He must seek to understand the relevant interests and needs of those in foreign horizons and relate them through interest balancing to his principles and his theory of primary social goods. Central then to personalist theory is an understanding of a judge related to others through action. His commitment to others and his recognition of his own limited knowledge and understanding becomes a basis for critically assessing method.

Chapter 4 will offer a method for constitutional interpretation. Personalist theory as described in chapters 2 and 3 provides a foundation for constructing a theory for constitutional interpretation. Arguably our Supreme Court charged by our Constitution with deciding cases and controversies is at the apex of a great dispute settlement institution. A central concept is a deliberating society. The founding generation, it will be contended, admired the virtue of deliberation and would desire the Court to deliberate concerning the great general standards which they intentionally included in our Constitution. While law surely is part of the political process, it offers an alternate means, rational discussion and argument, for addressing the great issues. Our court system, a great dispute settlement institution, relates segments of our pluralist society through rational argument. Because the personalist theory of a deliberating society refers to the court system and our legal culture as important vehicles for deliberation, this understanding of a deliberative society differs from that of Cass Sunstein as chapters 4 and 5 will explain.

The method offered includes aspects of Dworkian idealism with less emphasis on theoretical consistency and more on means-end reasoning, balancing interests and understanding opposing positions as well as the concrete circumstances of those appearing before the Court. It may resemble more the method employed by Justice William Brennan in *New York Times v. Sullivan*[19] combined with his mature theory that our post Civil War Constitution presents a sparkling vision of concern for the human dignity of each person.[20]

Quarrels over constitutional method are often acrimonious. Conservative thinkers want to preserve in amber the founding generation's supposed interpretation of the drafters' deliberately written general provisions. Liberal thinkers often want to advance political goals by arguing for decisions supported by their favored narrow principles. Chapter 4 will describe both methods as refusals to deliberate.

Chapter 4 in contrast offers a vision of the Supreme Court as the center of a great dispute settlement institution in a deliberating society. In the personalist tradition one can recognize a great American ideal that each person is worthwhile and entitled equally to government protection of our lives, liberties and property. The Supreme Court when interpreting our Constitution is engaged in on-going action designed to promote that ideal. In constructing a personalist method for constitutional interpretation it would be appropriate then to draw on both Dworkian idealism and pragmatic instrumentalist techniques, including means-end reasoning for pursuing our ideals.

The chapter will have a discussion of a series of cases including *Brown v. Board of Education of Topeka, Kansas*[21] and *New York Times v. Sullivan*[22] and will conclude with a discussion of substantive due process.

A basic argument of chapter 4 is that personalist method is legitimate and at times can appeal to what will be described as ultimate legitimacy. All great decisions and all methods incur legitimacy costs. However, some competing methods, both conservative and liberal, it will be argued, incur greater legitimacy costs.

3. Intellectual Method

Chapter 5 continues the critique of intellectual method in law. The great quarrel over intellectual method in modern and post modern

---

19. *Compare* New York Times v. Sullivan, 376 U.S. 254 (1963).

20. *See* William T. Brennan, Jr., *The Constitution of the United States: Contemporary Ratification*, in INTERPRETING THE CONSTITUTION: THE DEBATE OVER ORIGINAL INTENT 23, 28–29 (J.Rakove ed. 1990).

21. Brown v. Board of Education, 347 U.S. 483 (1954).

22. New York Times, 376 U.S. at 254.

thought has affected and confused our understanding of legal method. Over the past thousand years one method or another has attracted attention and dominated intellectual discussion. In the late middle ages and during the Renaissance logic and the mathematical methods were dominant. The scientific method struggled for acceptance and became for many the method of choice. In the twenty-first century we distinguish between the hard physical sciences and the soft social sciences. However, common sense method which could be described as the self-correcting process of learning through living still governs our day to day decisions.[23] Many current methodologies would be described as specialized common sense methods including historical scholarship, literary interpretation, theology and law.

In law, practitioners, scholars and judges depending on their education or inclinations bring differing understandings of intellectual methods to their critique of law. Economics, ethics, and logic all contend for dominance. Oliver Wendell Holmes, Jr., however, was probably correct when he argued that the life of the law is not logic but experience,[24] and supported a more sophisticated version of the common law methods. Roscoe Pound once explained: "Some think that law is economics, and there is a great deal to be said for this; others think that law is ethics, and some think that law is social engineering. They are all wrong. Law is all of these."[25] Chapter 5 will contend that law can be described best as using a sophisticated specialized common sense method. In the modern era an educated person can draw on multiple methodologies to enlighten his common sense and make it more sophisticated.

Judge Richard Posner in *The Problems of Jurisprudence* contends that law employs a variety of techniques of practical reason including analogy and distinction and means-end reasoning.[26] He would prefer, of course, that judges rely strongly on economic analysis. Posner argues that the normal common law reasoning, interpretation, and justification by philosophical reasoning all fail to adequately justify legal decisions. Rather than a rigorous justification, he argues, a judge should

---

23. *See* BERNARD LONERGAN, INSIGHT: A STUDY OF HUMAN UNDERSTANDING 44, 396–98, 425 (3d ed. 1970); *and see* D. TRACY, THE ACHIEVEMENT OF BERNARD LONERGAN 104–32 (1970).

24. *See generally* HOLMES, JR., THE COMMON LAW, *supra* note 7 at 1–38; and Holmes, Jr.,*The Path of the Law, supra* note 2.

25. *See* Donnelly, *Towards a Personalist Jurisprudence, supra* note 10 at 1.

26. *See* RICHARD POSNER, THE PROBLEMS OF JURISPRUDENCE 105–08 (1990).

offer a reasonable explanation for his decision.[27] In the neo-pragmatist tradition Posner expresses a broad skepticism concerning ideals and all forms of reasoning including those regularly used in the common law.[28]

In contrast, Ronald Dworkin requires his ideal Judge Hercules to justify his decisions rigorously under the principles which offer the best justification for extant law.[29] Dworkin would consider Posner's legal pragmatism morally and intellectually bankrupt and would argue that it is not capable of taking legal rights seriously.[30]

Dworkin's rigorous justification, chapter 5 will argue, prevents crossing horizons, understanding the needs and interests of persons and therefore raises issues of legitimacy in our pluralist society. Neo-pragmatism is excessively skeptical and because it has difficulty in grounding decisions in society's ideals is not capable of taking strong rights seriously.

Persons involved in disputes in our pluralist society, chapter 5 will argue, are entitled to a decision consistent with our ideals but based on sophisticated common sense by a judge who attempts to cross horizons and understand their needs and interests. Legitimacy requires an opinion which describes that process and using common sense and traditional legal reasoning offers a reasonable explanation. Judges with limited but growing knowledge and understanding, committed to respect and concern for persons, can be expected to adhere to those requirements of legitimacy but not to Dworkin's rigorous justification. The proposed standard of legitimacy is appropriate for dispute settlement, keeping the peace and for respecting persons.

Contrary to Posner and Dworkin, the common law's use of a sophisticated specialized common sense method is reliable and legitimate. A personalist interpretation and development of that method will enhance its legitimacy.

Chapter 5 is entitled, "Justification, Legitimacy and Moral Judgment." It is noted there that this is not a book about international law, human rights, or moral judgment. Nevertheless, on both constitutional and common law issues personalism offers positions grounded in strong adherence to human rights and takes a non-skeptical stance on moral judgment. Since the principal purpose of this book is to construct a person centered jurisprudence and method for judicial decision

---

27. *See id.* at 130–35.
28. *See id.* at 247–55.
29. *See* DWORKIN, LAW'S EMPIRE, *supra* note 11 at 238–39.
30. *See id.* at 95, 154–160.

making and argue for their legitimacy one should recognize that there is no obligation to justify the strong position on human rights and the non-skeptical stance on moral judgment. Rather one must show that those positions are legitimate as part of judicial decision making and an interpretation of American law. Arguably a strong human rights position enhances the legitimacy of personalist theory and method as does the non-skeptical stance on moral judgment. To round out personalist theory chapter 5 offers a brief discussion of moral judgment and human rights.

4. The Uses of Rights

Chapter 6 shifts point of view from the judge and his decision making to the multiple uses of rights and the language of rights in our complex pluralist society. To understand adequately the language of rights, it will be contended, one must recognize the point of view from which a statement about rights is made. One can perceive rights from the perspective of a litigator, a law reformer, a judge, a scholar describing law or in the alternative prescribing for judges or legislators and from a variety of other points of view. In modern jurisprudence writers have described rights as predictions that courts will afford remedies, as conclusions drawn within a system of rules, as claims such as those made in legal arguments, as criticism, as reasons for decisions, as trumps which will prevail over competing reasons, as goals to be pursued, as resources for conducting a campaign of law reform, as ideological, and as rhetoric.[31] Chapter 6 will argue that any statement concerning rights must be understood as made from a point of view and within a horizon. One can unify the discussion regarding the language of rights by understanding rights in relation to obligation. For example, a judge who recognizes no obligation and decides by whim is not capable of taking rights seriously. Litigants appearing before him cannot predict reasonably that he will recognize their rights or afford a remedy. In contrast a litigant before Dworkin's Judge Hercules can predict that he will recognize a claim of right if it falls within his established theory. One appearing before a personalist judge can expect an effort to understand his interests and to relate that understanding to respect and concern for persons and an expanding theory of the great rights.

---

31. See DONNELLY, THE LANGUAGE AND USES OF RIGHTS, *supra* note 1 at 11–43.

Chapter 6 will offer a vision of law as an activity engaged in by a variety of players. Rights discourse, the use of the language of rights by those engaged in the activity of law, is employed to establish, talk about, fight about and change relations between persons. Rights are tools used in law to conduct and settle great disputes.[32] A personalist as judge will relate his understanding of rights to his respect and concern for persons. A personalist as litigator or law reformer may use rights to hammer on foreign horizons and to urge society to recognize his clients as persons.

The principal purpose of Chapter 6 is to understand rights as used in the ordinary legal discourse of the many participants in our legal culture. Because every statement about rights is made within a horizon and from a point of view there are multiple different understandings and usages of rights discourse. From the base of a strong commitment one can perceive rights as entitlements but that does not capture the great diversity of usages of rights discourse. Understanding how people use rights discourse to relate to each other is an appropriate concern for the personalist agenda.

Responding to that concern offers an appropriate occasion to discuss personalist theory and the role of actors other than the judge. Chapter 6, then, also undertakes to offer a portrait of law as a culture in which multiple players use the language of law and the language of rights to talk about, fight about, establish and change human relations, to in other words, carry forward the on-going argument about society and human relations that constitutes society.

An occasion is taken at the beginning of the chapter to discuss the art of interpretation. The chapter, then, interprets law to show the interaction of a multiplicity of players.

5. The Personalist Agenda

Again in chapter 7, "The Personalist Agenda," the discussion changes point of view, to that of a scholar engaged in personalist jurisprudence. After the end of the twentieth century that scholar can look back at the grand conversation during the past hundred and twenty years of Anglo-American jurisprudence. Holmes is a great overarching figure while H.L.A. Hart could be described as the host of the salon. Recognizing the

---

32. See id. at 58–64, 89–109.

partial and piecemeal recovery of a role for the person in twentieth century jurisprudence and analysis of method should enhance that discussion for a personalist philosopher. Using a personalist critique of method he or she may engage the past and the future in conversation, learning from competing understandings of law and emphasizing personalist insights.

Like the personalist judge, the scholar should recognize his own horizons and his own limited knowledge and understanding. One then can engage in a personalist conversation with Rawls, Dworkin, Posner, Kennedy, Unger, the critical legal studies movement in general, with feminism, and with critical race theory. Indeed, one could engage heavily in law and economics, feminism, critical legal studies, law and literature, or critical race theory while emphasizing the personalist aspects of the thought one is exploring. In doing so, indeed, in engaging in any jurisprudential conversation, it would of course be important to be aware of the impact of one's thought on persons and their relationships, to be conscious of the phenomenon of horizons and of the perception of theories of the good within horizons. Recognizing the importance of crossing horizons and understanding and protecting rights as perceived in foreign horizons is more critical when one is developing an ideologically supported full theory of the good. Carrying forward the conversation with other thinkers and schools of thought is perhaps the most significant way of doing personalist jurisprudence while contributing to the development of American thought.

For a private attorney with personalist commitments law reform should be high on the agenda for the twenty-first century. An analysis of the use of rights as tools in law reform is presented in chapter 6. Chapter 7 then offers further personalist insights into law reform and also for the practicing attorney. Social Science studies have an important role in law reform and for personalist theory. Personalist method for judicial decision making requires a judge to cross horizons by use among other means of impact and interest analysis. Social Science studies are an important means in impact and interest analysis and for law reformers to call attention to oppression while persuading judges and society to cross horizons. Chapter 7 places high on the personalist agenda for the twenty first century the task of relating social science more closely to law.

For the scholar the construction of personalist theories of particular fields may be an important tool for law reform. Criminal law is a field in which reform is seriously required. As an illustration chapter 7 concludes with a brief sketch of a personalist theory of criminal justice. Developing that theory and theories in other particular fields of law is a personalist task for the twenty first century. Actually reforming criminal justice is a yet more important and difficult task and requires among other means the tools discussed in chapter 6 and earlier in chapter 7.

While the book will conclude with chapter 7 there will be an appendix discussing sources and indicating some origins for the personalist tradition both in Europe and America. This appendix will appear not in this book but on the Syracuse University College of Law website (Website: http://www.law.syr.edu/faculty/donnelly/apersonaljurisprudence/). One should note that while this book is inspired by personalist tradition and by insights from personalist thought, it is a creative construction of a theory of personalism in law and a method for judicial decision making. The reader should not expect a simple report of personalist thought and an application of an extant theory to law. Rather personalist insights are in conversation with the history of American jurisprudence to construct a personalist interpretation of American law. An important suggestion for both personalist thought and American law is the incorporation of a critique of intellectual and legal method. The appendix will discuss the sources for the proposed personalist critique of method. When subsequent chapters refer to personalist theory, it is the theory constructed and offered in this book.

6. An Interpretation of Law

As an interpretation of law, then, personalism offers an interrelated set of insights, concepts and principles which constitute a coherent theory. At the center of the theory is the personalist judge who perceives himself as a person of limited but growing knowledge and understanding, who is committed to respect and concern for each person and who wants to grow in his understanding of people. One could imagine that judge introspectively reflecting on his own stream of consciousness. He would recognize the need to critique and develop his own general intellectual method and his method for judicial decision making. He also would recognize his own horizons and the need to develop as part of his method means for crossing horizons. He would recognize himself as one who acts and who is related to others through his action.

The concepts, insights and principles offered as a personalist theory of law can be organized around the judge's introspective analysis and reconstruction of his own method and his ongoing relations with others. The inward and outward looking aspects of personalist theory are closely related. When constructing method the judge as one engaged in action is concerned not only with his own intellectual process but also with understanding the impact of his action on others and with creating tools for appropriate action.

Introspectively, then, but with a concern for interpersonal action a personalist judge would critique and recreate his general intellectual methods, his methods for deciding common law cases and for interpreting statutes and the United States Constitution. While critically creating those tools the judge through action including the action of his decisions would be in relations with others. His commitment to others would be a ground for his critique of method, his choice of combining pragmatic instrumentalist technique with Dworkian idealism and an openness to post modern thought. As one who acts he would perceive the Supreme Court when interpreting the United States Constitution as participating in the great common action of society and as pursuing by appropriate means the great American ideal that each of us is worthwhile and that no one should be excluded from society's common action. Dispute settlement is the central aspect of our courts' work not only historically but because it is concerned with establishing, reestablishing and changing human relations. The test of legitimacy is not justification of the public use of force but the acceptability of the reasons offered for resolutions of particular disputes. A reason has ultimate legitimacy when it has the capacity of appealing to all persons at all times. A judge resolving disputes in a pluralistic society, that is one composed of multiple horizons must adhere to his ideals but with a recognition of his horizons, that is, his limited knowledge and understanding. When offering principles which reflect his ideals as reasons for his decisions he must join principled analysis with an understanding of interests and other means for crossing horizons.

The personalist interpretation of law then offers a coherent theory, a set of interrelated concepts, insights and principles. One argument in the book is that personalist method as well as other common law methods is legitimate and can enhance the legitimacy of decisions. Because it is continually open to new thought and new human needs it can enhance and maintain the legitimacy of the common law as society changes. Using Dworkin's test for an appropriate interpretation, personalist method and theory has good institutional fit with the common law tradition and can make the most that now can be made of our tradition.[33]

---

33. *See* DWORKIN, LAW'S EMPIRE, *supra* note 11 at 227–32; *and see* DWORKIN, TAKING RIGHTS SERIOUSLY, *supra* note 12 at 81–130.

7. Central Ideas and Themes

Some central ideas run through and are developed in different ways by several chapters. Among these are rights, human rights and their relation to a personalist theory of the common good. Because personalism in law offers a consistent theory interrelating a set of concepts, insights and subtheories, the discussion of method which also runs through several chapters and interpretation are related to the analysis of rights and the common good and in turn to legitimacy. The central argument of the book is that the personalist interpretation of American law and decision making method is legitimate. A basic reason for that legitimacy is that personalism respects each person and all persons and grounds a theory of rights as related to the common good and to decision making method in that deep respect and concern. A brief overview of those central ideas and an indication of the chapters developing them may be helpful. In particular an outline of some themes of personalist rights theory may show the linkage between the discussion in several chapters.

a. Rights

The personalist theory of human rights is grounded in the personalist commitment to afford each person and all persons deep respect and concern and in the personalist theory of the common good.

Chapter 3 proposes a personalist theory of the common good as persons acting together and explains those actions contrary to the common good as any which tend to destroy the common action or eliminate any individual from participation in that action. Chapter 3 defines the primary social goods as those necessary or important to participation in this society or any society. The great rights are those which protect each person's share of the primary social goods.

In chapter 4, "Constitutional Interpretation," the theory of rights developed in chapter 3 is applied when interpreting the United States Constitution and in offering theories of contested moral concepts found in the Bill of Rights and the Fourteenth Amendment.

In chapter 5, "Justification, Legitimacy and Moral Judgment," arguments are offered to support the personalist commitment to afford all persons deep respect and concern and to defend the legitimacy of that position. To round out personalist theory several controversial questions concerning human rights are addressed including whether rights are universal and whether they are absolute. In offering positions on these issues chapter 5 draws on both the personalist commitment to each and all persons and the personalist theory of the common good.

In chapter 6 rights are described as tools used in the conduct of our profession to carry forward the argument about society which constitutes society, to establish, change, converse and fight about human relations. Personalist theory perceives law and rights as part of law as means for relating persons directly or indirectly in society. Rights also are language and discourse. Language itself is an activity which is inescapably interpersonal. Rights discourse, as one of the regular ways in which lawyers conduct our profession can be understood better under the personalist theory as outlined in chapter 3 as action relating persons. Under the theory of the common good rights discourse can be linked to a personalist understanding of the primary social goods. When a law reform attorney seeks to advance his client's share of the primary social goods and to insist on his right to participate in society he is seeking recognition under personalist theory for his client as a person.

While in our pluralist society composed of multiple horizons there are many different understandings of and positions on rights, striving to understand statements about rights in relation to the speaker's perception of his obligation may provide a basis for analyzing his use of the language of rights. A personalist judge is committed to afford all persons and each person deep respect and concern. His understanding of rights, then, should be linked to that obligation and to the personalist theory of the common good.

In chapter 7, there is a discussion just before concluding of criminal justice. The theory of criminal justice proposed and outlined there is grounded in the personalist commitment to all and each person and the common good. That part of chapter 7 illustrates the manner in which fundamental personalist theory can provide a basis for critical analysis and reconstruction of theories for particular fields of law.

Rights theory grounded in more fundamental personalist commitments and theory is elaborated, then in several chapters.

b. The Common Good

The personalist theory of the common good is related closely to the understanding of rights. Chapter 3 when offering a personalist theory and interpretation of American law includes a theory of the common good and an explanation of rights as designed to protect the primary social goods. The primary social goods are those necessary or important to participation in this society or any society. One affords each person deep respect and concern by protecting his or her fundamental right to participate in the common action of society, the common good. Since individuals are more fully persons in interaction with others, a denial of the right to participate in society or of the means for doing so is a fundamental assault on human dignity.

In chapter 4 the theory of rights as related to the primary social goods and hence to the common good is applied to constitutional interpretation. When interpreting the Constitution principles as reasons for decisions based on individual rights must be reconciled with policies as reasons for decisions based on group goals. Some policies are derived from a desire to promote the common good, that is, those things which we share in common, that promote and enable our interaction in society.[34] Actions contrary to the common good include those which would prevent any person from participating in the common good and those which tend to interfere with the common action. The goods we share in common, the common goods, would include institutions such as our court system and our legal culture which enable interaction in society and other goods which enhance common action and serve all. Policies as designed to promote those institutions and common goods are related to respect and concern for all persons interacting.

In chapter 5 when discussing the foundations both for a theory of rights and for the common good, the question of whether rights are absolute is confronted. In analyzing that question the personalist commitment both to the individual and to the common good is relevant.

In chapter 7 the personalist theory of the common good provides a basis for critiquing the goals of criminal punishment and developing an integrated theory of criminal justice.

The personalist theory of the common good, then, is linked to the theory of rights and to further development of personalist theory. To understand the relation between rights theory, the common good and judicial decision making, however, requires reflection on method.

---

34. *See* David Hollenbach, *Justice, Peace and Human Rights American Catholic Social Ethics in a Pluralistic World*, New York Crossroad (1988); *Claims in Conflict, Retrieving and Renewing the Catholic Human Rights Tradition* New York Paulist Press (1979).

c. Method

Method and the critique of method are central to the personalist interpretation of American law. In conversation with the common law tradition chapter 2 offers a reconstruction of judicial decision making method by melding Dworkian idealism, pragmatic contributions to judicial method and some post-modern insights. In chapter 4 a similar method for constitutional interpretation is constructed from the great quarrel over method. In chapter 5 there is a discussion of the multiple intellectual methods available to us today and the implications of that for construction of legal method and for addressing questions such as those raised by the skeptical challenge to legal reasoning.

Personalist theory offers criteria for assessing the decision making method one would recommend to a judge. "To the extent that a particular understanding of judicial method overlooks the judge as person or fails to insist upon persons and their relations in the situation before the court, that understanding of method is less satisfactory."[35] In contrast, a method is more satisfactory to the extent that it emphasizes the role of persons.

Because personalist method is constructed in conversation with the common law tradition and the tradition of constitutional interpretation and draws on and relates existing methodologies it is a legitimate method for judicial decision making.

d. Legitimacy

Legitimacy is a multilayered concept. *Webster's New World Dictionary* describes legitimacy as "the quality or state of being legitimate."[36] Its meaning then depends on the definition of legitimate which has multiple alternate usages, as in, for example, a legitimate offspring. After setting forth that usage, the dictionary offers a second definition, "sanctioned by law or custom; lawful, allowed," and a fourth, "reasonable, logically correct; as, a legitimate inference."[37]

When discussing law, legal thinkers from time to time offer theories of legitimacy. In chapter 5, Ronald Dworkin's theory of legitimacy is contrasted with Cass Sunstein's. On a simple level the dictionary defini-

---

35. *See* Donnelly, *Towards a Personalist Jurisprudence, supra* note 10 at 568.
36. Webster's New World Dictionary 772 (3d ed. 1994).
37. *Id.* at 772.

tion is relevant. A judicial decision is legitimate when it is lawful, when it is in accordance with law. The common law, however, in its 800 year history has regularly developed and changed as have the methods judges use when deciding cases. Constitutional law in its shorter history has followed a similar pattern. A judicial decision is legitimate, then, when it is made in accord with the customs and practices of the common law or within the tradition of constitutional interpretation.

Legitimate argument for a decision or a position confers power, the power to persuade, or the freedom to make future important decisions. The legitimacy power of a decision is related not merely to its acceptability but also to its persuasiveness, its ability to become acceptable.

Drawing on H.L.A Hart's concern for acceptance of law by the people,[38] chapter 2 argues that a decision and the arguments supporting it are legitimate when it is reasonable to expect they will be acceptable. Arguably, however, Lon Fuller was correct when he urges us to look to the conditions which enhance the acceptability of law.[39] A personalist would argue that grounding a decision in respect and concern for each person and in an effort to understand persons and their needs and interests generally will enhance the acceptability of law and that decision. Chapters 2 and 5 develop that argument further.

Contrarywise, some methods and decisions which are legitimate because they are within our legal traditions may incur legitimacy costs by lessening the likelihood of acceptance. Pacemaking decisions often incur risks and perhaps legitimacy costs. Chapter 4, "Constitutional Interpretation," however offers the argument that some decisions, disputable in their time, appeal to ultimate legitimacy because they have the capacity of appearing reasonable to all persons in all times. A decision would have that quality if it is based on a profound respect and concern for each person.

The purpose of this book is to construct a person centered interpretation of American law and a personalist method for judicial decision making and to argue for their legitimacy. The essence of the argument is that the decision making method is in the mainstream of our common law and constitutional law traditions and has the power to en-

---

38. *See* HART, THE CONCEPT OF LAW 238–76, *supra* note 1.

39. LON FULLER, THE MORALITY OF LAW (1964); *see also* Lon Fuller, *Positivism and Fidelity to Law—A Reply to Professor Hart*, 71 HARV. L. REV. 630 (1958).

hance the legitimacy of law because it is grounded in respect and concern for each and all persons and is continually open to the needs, interests and circumstances of each and all. In contrast some competing methods incur various legitimacy costs.

Arguably the personalist interpretation of American law consolidates insights regarding persons and law which have accumulated in multiple theories over the course of the twentieth century and offers a sound and legitimate next step for theoretical development during the twenty-first century.[40]

e. Interpretation

Chapter 6 begins with a discussion of the art of interpretation and argues that in part it consists of an exchange of insights and moments of understanding, of human experience. A contention is made there that Ronald Dworkin who makes interpretation the center of his legal theory and Richard Posner who has little use for interpretation both overlook the exchange of human experience as central to interpretation.

The personalist interpretation of American law unfolds over the seven chapters of this book and continues in chapter 2 with the common law tradition. While that chapter begins the construction of a personalist decision making method, the law trained reader should find there much that is familiar.

A basic argument in this book is that the construction of a personalist jurisprudence makes sense as the next step in American legal thought. From hindsight one feature of Anglo-American Jurisprudence during the twentieth century was the gradual and piecemeal recovery of a role for the person in law. Chapter 2 begins to construct a theory and a method which organizes and makes explicit that emphasis on the person.

---

40. One also should note and compare the legitimacy theory of Jürgen Habermas. *See generally*, JÜRGEN HABERMAS, BETWEEN FACTS AND NORMS: CONTRIBUTIONS TO A DISCOURSE THEORY OF LAW AND DEMOCRACY (1998). Compare *Fifth Annual Legal Theory Symposium: Exploring Habermas on Law and Democracy*, 76 Denver University L. Rev. 927 (1999).

CHAPTER II

The Common Law Tradition

1. Introduction

James Boyd White described our common law as an inherited culture[1] which has been more than eight hundred years in the making. Judges in the common law tradition use different methods for deciding cases and developing law than those in the European Civil Law. Since the Middle Ages common law method has changed regularly while retaining a family resemblance to previous methods.

In the grand conversation of twentieth century Anglo-American jurisprudence discussion of and creation of method has been an important focus for many thinkers. A purpose of this chapter is to portray briefly and to enter into a conversation with the common law tradition and some of its many methods, and then to argue that to understand method one should give a central role to dispute settlement.[2]

This chapter will offer a preliminary sketch of a personalist method for judicial decisions. For this purpose a personalist judge may be described as one who recognizes herself or himself as a person of limited but growing knowledge and understanding, who is committed to respect and concern for each person, and who is fascinated with human beings. A personalist method is one which reflects the commitments and understanding of a personalist judge. More particularly in late

---

1. *See* JAMES BOYD WHITE, HERACLES' BOW: ESSAYS ON THE RHETORIC AND POETICS OF THE LAW 32–35 (1985).
2. *See* SAMUEL J. M. DONNELLY, THE LANGUAGE AND USES OF RIGHTS 11–46 (1994); and *see generally* KARL LLEWELLYN, THE COMMON LAW TRADITION: DECIDING APPEALS (1960).

twentieth century America a personalist judge would find both the conflicting theories of pragmatic instrumentalism and Ronald Dworkin[3]
helpful but inadequate. At this moment in legal history a merger of insights from both would form a framework for personalist method.

What this chapter proposes to discuss then are the practical relations
between human persons and the law. An effort will be made to simplify
this very complex discussion. Ultimately, however, simplicity results
from a recognition that the law concerns persons and their relations.
The commitment to respect, understand and be concerned for persons
when joined to an understanding of legal method sheds a simple and
clear light on many complexities. For example, it makes possible the
joining of insights from pragmatic instrumentalism and Dworkian
thought.

A modest argument will be offered that a personalist method as described preliminarily in this chapter will enhance the legitimacy of a
judge's decision making and has greater capacity to do this than pragmatic-instrumentalism or Dworkin's method. Personalist method will
be described in greater depth in chapter 3.

This chapter will include a sketch of common law methods and personalist method for deciding cases and interpreting statutes. While
methods for constitutional interpretation will be mentioned, chapter 4
will address that great quarrel and offer a personalist theory.

This chapter, then, has the modest purpose of offering a preliminary
sketch of personalist method, of arguing for its legitimacy and that it
offers a more adequate way of deciding common law cases and interpreting statutes than pragmatic instrumentalism or the methods offered by Ronald Dworkin.

The reader may want to accept the suggestion made in chapter 1 to
read the following discussion while imagining that he or she is an ordinary common law judge with personalist inclinations attending a somewhat advanced continuing legal education presentation for judges on
judicial decision making method. In that event the presentation would
begin as does this chapter in part two with an overview of the great
quarrel over method beginning in the late nineteenth and continuing
throughout the twentieth century. Despite his lack of philosophical inclination our ordinary judge would find that much of the discussion of
method is found in the writings of legal philosophers. Part two will pre-

---

3. *See generally* RONALD DWORKIN, LAW'S EMPIRE (1986).

sent the contrasting visions of law as a system of rules or as an activity in which we engage. More importantly it will sketch the history of pragmatic instrumentalist method which has dominated judicial decision making since mid-twentieth century and explain Ronald Dworkin's criticism of that method. Focusing primarily on the contrast between Dworkin's proposed method and pragmatic instrumentalism will simplify the discussion while illustrating the importance of method and our differences over method. Our ordinary common law judge may then recognize the need to reconstruct method including his own decision making process. Recognizing the gradual recovery of a role for the person during our twentieth century quarrel over method may provide a valuable clue for that reconstruction to our ordinary judge with personalist inclinations. Part three then will begin the critique and reconstruction of method. It will continue the critical evaluation of Dworkin and pragmatic instrumentalist method and argue that the personalist aspects of each method should be extracted and melded to create a new method.

Parts four and five will argue that the proposed personalist method has good institutional fit with traditional common law methods for deciding cases and interpreting statutes. Part four will include a reflection on the complexities of developing and changing case law using the evolution of products liability as an example. Part five among other matters will reflect on interpreting statutory language in the varied cultural contexts presented by time and geography. Lon Fuller in his well-known exchange with H. L. A. Hart called our attention to that problem.[4] In postmodern thought the perception by the judge of law and legal language in cultural contexts has presented significant problems for our understanding of law. The simple melding of the personalist aspects of Dworkian and pragmatic instrumentalist method may not sufficiently address those problems. Recognizing that will provide an opening for a more profound discussion of personalist method in chapter 3.

To continue the critique and reconstruction of method part six will argue that dispute settlement rather than regulation or the justified use of force should be the central focus for judicial decisions. The chapter will conclude in part seven with a preliminary argument for the legitimacy of the proposed reconstructed method.

---

4. *See generally* Lon Fuller, *Positivism and Fidelity to Law—A Reply to Professor Hart*, 71 HARV. L. REV. 593 (1958).

The discussion then should begin in part two with the great quarrel over method.

2. The Great Quarrel over Method

One could understand portions of twentieth century jurisprudence as a great quarrel over method. As host of the salon H. L. A. Hart tried to engage some of the participants in conversation. The American Pragmatists inspired by Oliver Wendell Holmes, Jr. were his initial choice for conversation partners.[5] In pursuing his own project of offering great clarifying concepts Hart described law as a system of rules.[6] Holmes, in contrast, understood law as an activity, as a "well-known profession" which we all practice.[7] At the center of that activity is the principal actor, the judge.

In his famous book, *The Common Law*,[8] which began as a set of lectures given in 1880 at the Harvard Law School, Holmes arguably was confronting Christopher Columbus Langdell who then was dean of that school. Langdell like Hart perceived law as language and system, as a system of rules and principles.[9] Langdell was a leader in a much needed organization of common law cases around principles and rules. His efforts which Holmes joined[10] culminated ultimately in the Restatements of Law as well as the great organizing treatises of the late nineteenth and early twentieth century. Langdellians arguably wanted to reconstruct

---

5. *See generally*, H.L.A. Hart, *Positivism and the Separation of Law and Morals*, 71 Harv. L. Rev. 593 (1958); *Definition and Theory in Jurisprudence*, 70 Law. Q. Rev. 37 (1954).

6. *See* H.L.A. Hart, The Concept of Law 77–96 (1961) (Defining law as a union of primary rules of obligation and secondary rules about primary rules, such as rules of recognition, change, and adjudication. This great "clarifying concept" that Hart offers concerns the interplay between primary and secondary rules, thereby offering a paradigm to describe law "wherever it may be found.")

7. *See* Oliver Wendell Holmes, Jr., *The Path of the Law*, 10 Harv. L. Rev. 457, 461 (1897).

8. Oliver Wendell Holmes, Jr., The Common Law (1881).

9. *See* Richard Posner, The Problems of Jurisprudence 14–15 (1990).

10. *See id.*; and *see generally* Samuel J.M. Donnelly, *The Fault Principle: A Sketch of its Development in Tort Law During the Nineteenth Century*, 18 Syr. L. Rev. 728 (1967).

the common law as a closed logical system.[11] Stated simplistically one could transform the accumulating case law into a closed logical system by extracting principles from past decisions and then deciding future cases by deduction and only by deductions from those principles.

In the opening pages of *The Common Law* Holmes arguably confronting Langdell contends that the life of the law has not been logic but experience and that the felt necessities of the time have a great deal more to do with judicial decisions determining the content of the law than the syllogism.[12] Throughout *The Common Law* Holmes demonstrates that judges from age to age have adapted the law to the convenience and needs of their own times.

One could perceive the history of American legal thought in the twentieth century as a long and continuing argument between those who perceive law with Langdell as language and system and those who favor Holmes' understanding of law as an activity centering on judges and directed toward the achievement of social purpose.

One also could perceive that history as a continuing argument and discussion regarding legal method particularly the method which judges use to decide cases. Among those who claim Holmes as their intellectual ancestor are the legal pragmatists who would include such varied thinkers as Roscoe Pound, Karl Llewellyn[13] and his fellow legal realists and more recently Judge Richard Posner.[14] Despite their large differences and their quarrels with each other one can trace certain themes through the writings of the legal pragmatists. All have a distaste for what Posner calls overarching theory[15] and with Holmes a suspicion of principle. Holmes despite his effort during his youth to organize law around principles is renown for his statement in *Lochner v. N.Y.* that general propositions do not decide concrete cases.[16] Beyond that and a preference for the more concrete decision making of the ancient common law the legal pragmatists proposed a number of creative contributions to judicial methodology.

---

11. *See id.*

12. *See* HOLMES, JR., THE COMMON LAW, *supra* note 8 at 1 ([T]he life of the law has not been logic: it has been experience...).

13. *See generally* Samuel J.M. Donnelly, *Book Review*, 3 HOFSTRA L. REV. 899 (1975).

14. *See* POSNER, PROBLEMS OF JURISPRUDENCE, *supra* note 9 at 454–69.

15. *Id.* at 460 ("[S]eventh, there are no overarching concepts of justice that our legal system can seize upon to give direction to the enterprise...").

16. Lochner v. New York, 198 U.S. 45, 76 (1905) (Holmes, J., dissenting).

Roscoe Pound proposed social engineering one aspect of which was impact and interest analysis.[17] A judge or a legislator should endeavor to locate the interests affected by his decision or statute and then estimate the potential impact on those interests. Over the years social science information may accumulate supporting or questioning that estimate. In view of that information the courts or the legislature may revise the past rule.[18] Karl Llewellyn contrasted his proposed "grand style of the common law" with its openness to reason, purpose and situation sense and an emphasis on case by case development of the law with the Langdellian strict style and its tendency to treat law as a closed logical system.[19] Posner is a leading proponent of law and economics.[20]

In the late twentieth century Ronald Dworkin attacked legal pragmatism in essence accusing it of moral and intellectual bankruptcy and arguing that judges following pragmatic methodology could not take legal rights seriously.[21] Dworkin, himself, in contrast to the pragmatists offered a principled understanding of law grounded in a consistent general theory of the common law or constitutional law.[22] Because the pragmatists are concerned with the future or, as Holmes put it, with social advantage and are not tied to authoritative positions from the past, Dworkin argues that they pay lip service to legal rights and treat them only "as if" they exist.[23] Dworkin in contrast would offer the best theory of the authoritative positions of the past as a foundation for future decisions.[24] He offers two tests of an appropriate theory: (i) Does it have good institutional fit with our law, its structure, our history and our culture? And (ii) Whether the theory makes the most, including the most morally that can now be made of our law or our constitution.[25]

---

17. *See* Roscoe Pound, An Introduction to the Philosophy of Laws 42–45 (rev. ed. 1945).

18. *Id.*

19. *See* Samuel J. M. Donnelly, *Principles, Persons, and Horizons: A Friendly Analysis of What Dworkin Has Overlooked*, 26 St. Louis U. L. J. 217 at 232–34 (1982); *see also* Llewellyn, The Common Law Tradition, *supra* note 2.

20. *See generally* Richard Posner, Economic Analysis of Law (1972).

21. *See* Dworkin, Law's Empire, *supra* note 3 at 151–75.

22. *See generally id.*at 225–75; *see also* Ronald Dworkin, Taking Rights Seriously 81–149 (1978).

23. *See supra* note 21.

24. *Id.*

25. *See* Dworkin, Taking Rights Seriously, *supra* note 22 at 110–30; *See also* Dworkin, Law's Empire, *supra* note 3 at 230–31.

Arguably adherence to the great legal principles, particularly important constitutional principles which are closely related to human rights, is important for taking rights seriously. Arguably, then, legal pragmatists with their suspicion of principles may have difficulty in respecting constitutional and other rights.

Contrarywise, a judge who adheres rigorously and consistently to a general theory of past decisions may have difficulty relating his decisions to current needs, to what Holmes called the felt necessities of the time. Correspondingly he may have difficulty listening to people's current needs and hence to their demand for rights related to those needs.[26] For one concerned with judicial decision making method two related questions then are posed. First, if the distaste for principle and overarching theory in legal pragmatist thought renders it vulnerable to Dworkin's criticism, could one amend pragmatist decision making method to correct that defect? In the alternative could one appropriate aspects of legal pragmatist method for the purpose of improving Dworkin's prescriptions for judicial decision making?[27]

An important purpose of this book is to offer a critique and reconstruction of legal method including methods for judicial decision making. Joining insights from Holmes, Pound and Llewellyn with a role for high principle related to important human rights and interests will be an essential aspect of that reconstruction.

Arguably the Warren Court's decision in *Brown v. Board of Education of Topeka, Kansas*[28] was the high point of pragmatic instrumentalist method in constitutional decision making. Disturbed by the Warren Court, Herbert Wechsler criticized *Brown* because the court could not support its decision by neutral principles of Constitutional law.[29] Conservative theories initially inspired by critics of the Warren court resisted development of constitutional provisions.[30] Ronald Dworkin's criticism of strict construction as an incoherent position may be perti-

---

26. *See* Donnelly, *Principles, Persons, and Horizons, supra* note 19 at 280–84.

27. *See generally id.*

28. Brown v. Board of Education of Topeka, Kansas, 347 U.S. 483, (1954).

29. *See generally* Herbert Wechsler, *Toward Neutral Principles of Constitutional Law*, 73 HARV. L. REV. 1 (1959).

30. *See generally* ROBERT BORK, THE TEMPTING OF AMERICA: THE POLITICAL SEDUCTION OF THE LAW (1990); and ANTONIN SCALIA, A MATTER OF INTERPRETATION: FEDERAL COURTS AND THE LAW (1997).

nent in assessing the more sophisticated theories of original intent and textualism-originalism.[31] Along with the majoritarianism found in many Burger Court opinions[32] these conservative theories of apparent restraint could be described as refusals to deliberate concerning the great constitutional principles. Defenders of the Warren Court also developed theories of restraint. John Hart Ely argued that the Warren Court intervened primarily to correct flaws in process including those resulting in exclusion from participation in our democratic society.[33] In *Taking Rights Seriously* Ronald Dworkin offers a highly principled theory of constitutional interpretation and judicial decision making which he develops further in *Law's Empire,* for the purpose of justifying the decisions of an activist court.[34] Although Dworkin rejects the pragmatic instrumentalism often a characteristic method in Warren Court decisions he believes his more restrained and principled methods would support many of the Court's conclusions.

The quarrels over methods for constitutional interpretation are more complex than those concerning judicial development of the common law partly because a series of strong conservative methods are added to the confrontation between principled decision making and pragmatic instrumentalism. Nevertheless the insights developed in reconstructing common law method may provide clues for reconstructing constitutional interpretation. A further purpose is to offer that reconstruction while criticizing a number of the conservative and some liberal methods as a refusal to deliberate concerning the great constitutional principles. Chapter 4 will offer further discussion, including a critique and proposed reconstruction of methods for constitutional interpretation.

David Granfield in his book, *The Inner Experience of Law, a Jurisprudence of Subjectivity,*[35] offered another way of characterizing the struggles during the twentieth century over methods for judicial decision making. Rather than a series of attacks on Langdellian formalism,

---

31. *See generally* Scalia, *supra* note 30; *see also* Dworkin, Taking Rights Seriously, *supra* note 22 at 131–49.

32. *See for example* Gregg v. Georgia, 428 U.S. 153, (1976).

33. *See generally* John Hart Ely, Democracy and Distrust: A Theory of Judicial Review (1980).

34. Compare Dworkin, Taking Rights Seriously, *supra* note 22 at 147–49, with Dworkin, Law's Empire, *supra* note 3 at 369–73 (Which demonstrates that even the analytical mind may shift with the political wind).

35. David Granfield, The Inner Experience of Law (1988).

Granfield argues that the proliferation of methods represent a gradual piecemeal recovery of a role for the person in law.[36] Following Holmes' openness to human experience and social advantage, Roscoe Pound's social engineering sought to satisfy the multiple demands which people make on law by attempting to identify and reconcile their competing interests while assessing the impact of legal decisions on those interests.[37] In their youth during the twenties and thirties Legal Realists such as Karl Llewellyn and Jerome Frank sought to predict what judges with their human quirks and influenced by their political, social and cultural backgrounds would in fact do.[38] In the process they stumbled across judges as human beings. Lon Fuller in many writings was concerned not merely with the morality that makes law possible but with reciprocal relations between government and the governed and between human persons.[39] Ronald Dworkin grounds his theories in equal respect and concern for all persons or in political friendship.[40] The critical legal studies movement claimed legal realism as its intellectual ancestor and its goal as support for the cause of humanity.[41] Feminist jurisprudence not only attacks patriarchal structures in society and law but seeks to transform society and make it more caring.[42]

One aspect or another of the person in law has been recognized and emphasized by our proliferating understanding of law. One could draw an analogy·with the children's story from India where four blind men attempted to describe an elephant. One holding the elephant's tail said it was a rope. Feeling the ear another disagreed and claimed it was a fan. The third examining the leg said it was a log. Patting the body,

---

36. *See* Samuel J.M. Donnelly, *Towards a Personalist Jurisprudence: Basic Insights and Concepts*, 28 LOYOLA OF L.A. L. REV. 547, 556–58 (1995).

37. *See id.* at 566–67 (This passage is adapted from the cited paragraph).

38. *See* Karl Llewellyn, *A Realist Jurisprudence—The Next Step*, 30 COLUM. L. REV. 431 (1930); *see also* JEROME FRANK, COURTS ON TRIAL: MYTH AND REALITY IN AMERICAN JUSTICE 146–56 (1973); and *see* Donnelly, *Book Review*, *supra* note 13 at 901.

39. *See generally* LON FULLER, THE MORALITY OF LAW (1964).

40. *See* DWORKIN, TAKING RIGHTS SERIOUSLY, *supra* note 22 at 182; *see also* DWORKIN, LAW'S EMPIRE, *supra* note 3 at 195–216.

41. *See* Donnelly, *Towards a Personalist Jurisprudence*, *supra* note 36 at 556–57 (This passage is adapted from *Towards a Personalist Jurisprudence*).

42. *See generally* Leslie Bender, *From Gender Difference to Feminist Solidarity: Using Carol Gilligan and an Ethic of Care in the Law*, 15 VT. L. REV. 1 (1990).

the fourth said it went on and on forever.[43] American thinkers, examining the role of the person in law have recognized one or another of the multiple ways in which people and law interact. Because of these partial insights our theories of jurisprudence conflict and present a series of puzzles.[44]

There is then a need to consciously reflect on and reconstruct method, a need which the judge attending our continuing legal education program should recognize as important for his or her own decision making process. David Granfield's recognition that we have gradually recovered a role for the person in our great quarrel over method may provide a clue for that reconstruction. Part three will argue that neither Dworkian method nor pragmatic instrumentalism afford adequate respect and concern for those affected by judicial decisions. The reconstruction of judicial method will begin with a suggestion for relating those aspects of each method more significantly concerned for persons. Part three will begin with an intriguing technique employed by Duncan Kennedy for examining one's own decision making process.

3. Critique and Reconstruction of Method

In a uniquely balanced article, "Freedom and Constraint in Adjudication: A Critical Phenomenology,"[45] Duncan Kennedy offers a joyous but humorously cynical challenge to more solemn views of the common law tradition. He also describes an intriguing method for examining a judge's decision making process, which he calls a critical phenomenology. Kennedy characterizes himself in this published fantasy as a Federal District Judge presented with a labor dispute. City bus drivers on strike have determined to prevent scabs from driving the busses by lying down in front of them. Because of the perceived inadequacy of local law enforcement the company seeks a labor injunction under federal law. Kennedy then reports and critically examines his decision making process and the stream of consciousness which accompanies it.

---

43. *See* Donnelly, *Towards a Personalist Jurisprudence, supra* note 36 at 558.
44. *Id.* (This passage is also adapted from *Towards a Personalist Jurisprudence*).
45. Duncan Kennedy, *Freedom and Constraint in Adjudication: A Critical Phenomenology*, 36 J. LEGAL EDUC. 518 (1986).

His initial impression that the law is on the company's side is at odds with his own goals or what he calls "How I Want To Come Out (HI-WTCO)."[46] His description of his stream of consciousness follows his struggle with the law through several stages including "playing around with the rule" and "racking his brain."[47] In despair because he is unable to shape the law to conform to his own political position that the workers should control the means of production, he has a sudden insight or "breakthrough."[48] The case, he perceives, can be recharacterized as a First Amendment freedom of speech case rather than one concerning a labor injunction. By lying in front of the busses the workers are engaged in symbolic speech. An injunction, then, would be a prior restraint prohibited in freedom of speech cases. By recharacterizing the case Duncan Kennedy is able to achieve his political agenda while offering good legal arguments for his position.

Kennedy, as a member of the Critical Legal Studies movement, argues a classic movement position that the materials of the law, the common law tradition, can and should be manipulated to advance one's political agenda.[49] Ronald Dworkin in *Law's Empire* offers a position which he calls law as integrity[50] in seeming contrast with that of Kennedy. On examination, however, there are some remarkable resemblances between Kennedy's decision making method and that which Dworkin prescribes for his ideal, Judge Hercules.

Judge Hercules when he first comes to the bench is to frame a consistent general theory which will offer the best explanation of our constitution, and our common law. That theory should have good institutional fit with our law, the structure of our government, our history and our culture. Nevertheless it should offer an interpretation which makes the most, including the most morally, that now can be made of our government and laws. Integrity, as Dworkin understands it, requires Judge Hercules to decide cases on the basis of principles which are rigorously consistent with his general theory. Law as integrity, according to Dworkin, holds that people have as legal right whatever rights are sponsored by the principles that provide the best justification of legal practice as a whole.[51]

---

46. *Id.* at 519–21.
47. *Id.* at 523.
48. *Id.* at 525.
49. *Id.* at 542.
50. *See* DWORKIN, LAW'S EMPIRE, *supra* note 3 at 225–75.
51. *Id.* at 225.

Kennedy has a firm grasp of the judge as a thinking and feeling person who is puzzling through the case before him. Dworkin reveals an understanding of the judge as a moral and conceptual thinker but his report of Judge Hercules' analytical process is more narrow than Kennedy's critical phenomenology. Judge Hercules is an analytical giant but apparently has no feelings or relevant social, cultural or political background. Hercules frames a general theory but does not grow intellectually or morally as he struggles over a life time with decisions in multiple cases.

Nevertheless the positions of Dworkin and Kennedy have several resemblances. Neither is concerned with the concrete circumstances of the parties. Kennedy does not discuss the circumstances of the bus strike; he simply assumes from his ideological position that advancing worker control of the means of production is the most suitable and advantageous result for society or for his own political cause. Dworkin's Judge Hercules will decide cases on the basis of applicable principles which offer the best explanation of the relevant law but without apparent examination of the parties' needs, interests or circumstances.[52] One can argue that Judge Hercules' grand theory and the principles supported by it is simply another ideological position. Hercules' political positions, one could argue are perhaps more analytically complex than those of Kennedy but not less political or less ideological.

Dworkin could reply that Hercules' general theory must have good institutional fit. Kennedy, however, for the purpose of enhancing his legitimacy power wants to support his holding by good legal arguments. Both institutional fit and good legal arguments acceptable within the common law tradition are notes of legitimacy.

Dworkin also requires Judge Hercules to offer a general theory which will make the most including the most morally that now can be made of the law. Such a general theory could be grounded in political friendship[53] or in the principle, afford all persons equal respect and concern.[54] That note is missing in Kennedy's thought although he would claim that his ideology is designed to advance the cause of humanity. Later it will be argued that grounding one's decision in respect and concern for each person is a major note of legitimacy because rea-

---

52. *See* Donnelly, *Principles, Persons, And Horizons, supra* note 19 at 234.
53. *See* DWORKIN, LAW'S EMPIRE, *supra* note 3 at 195–216.
54. *See* DWORKIN, TAKING RIGHTS SERIOUSLY, *supra* note 22 at 180–83.

sons for a decision which are so grounded are capable of appealing to all persons at all times.

Nevertheless, Dworkin's Judge Hercules would offer such reasons in an abstract, principled, almost Langdellian form. In *Law's Empire* Dworkin attacks legal pragmatists because they reject overarching theory, are suspicious of principle and treat legal rights only "as if" they existed.[55] Pragmatists according to Dworkin seek the decision which will be best for the future rather than respecting legal rights grounded in principles offering the best explanation of the law.

During the grand conversation of American Jurisprudence, however, pragmatists have creatively designed a number of decision making tools designed to grapple with the interests, concrete relations and circumstances of those affected by a judicial decision. These would include Roscoe Pound's impact and interest analysis and Karl Llewellyn's situation sense. Dworkin does not address the interests and concrete circumstances of the parties to a case. Arguably, then, he overlooks this aspect of respect and concern for persons.[56]

William James once contended that the only reason for recognizing a claim is because it is made. Influenced perhaps by that argument Roscoe Pound wanted to recognize as many competing interests as possible. A judge or a legislator should inquire using a lawyer's issue spotting skill what interests are likely to be affected by a proposed rule. A judge can reconcile competing interests by asking which interest is more seriously affected by his decision or by creating a rule designed to protect both interests.[57]

William Twining's biography, *Karl Llewellyn and The Legal Realist Movement*,[58] contains one of the best descriptions of Llewellyn's situation sense.[59] A judge using situation sense should refrain from legally characterizing a case until he has attempted to understand the parties' relationship, and the values they or their group would bring to the problem. The judge should try, then to describe the life situation in

---

55. *See supra* note 21.

56. *See generally* Donnelly, *Principles, Persons, And Horizons, supra* note 19.

57. *See generally* Roscoe Pound, *A Theory Of Social Interests*, 1920 PUBLICATIONS OF THE AM. SOC. SOC'Y. 16 (1921).

58. WILLIAM TWINING, KARL LLEWELLYN AND THE REALIST MOVEMENT (1973).

59. *Id.* at 226–27.

narrow terms. Only then should he apply legal categories to the case.[60] In the grand style of the common law judges study previous precedent to determine the life situation which supplies the context for the holding. If the reason for the holding in that life situation applies to the situation before the judge then the rule of the previous case applies.[61]

Arguably a judge determined to afford the parties before him and others affected by his decision deep respect and concern must assess the impact of his decision on relevant interests and should be concerned with the relations of persons in the situations which appear in the case. Dworkin's Judge Hercules does none of that. Therefore this analytic giant who constructs grand theories is not capable of affording real persons respect and concern. This lack of concern for real persons in concrete situations marks a serious inconsistency in Dworkin's thought.[62]

Dworkin's analysis of the role of principles and policies in judicial decision making provides a foundation, however, for suggesting revisions in his method. Dworkin defines principles as reasons for decisions based on individual rights. Policies in contrast are reasons for decisions based on group goals.[63] Principles in the judicial reasoning process should trump considerations of policy. Freedom of speech, for example, should prevail despite it's interference with a national policy of conducting a war effort. Typically, Judge Hercules should base all of his decisions on principle rather than policy. In common law decisions Judge Hercules should respect the gravitational weight of precedent. He should form the best theory of the precedent. Litigants, then, have a legal right to a decision based on principle rather than policy.[64]

One could amend Dworkin's method by recognizing as he does from time to time that there are strong and weak rights. A litigant has a right even a weak right according to Dworkin if it counts in the argument.[65] A right based primarily on precedent could be described as a weak legal right in contrast to strong constitutional rights closely related to our

---

60. *See* Donnelly, *Principles, Persons, and Horizons, supra note* 19 at 228–29; *see also Donnelly, Book Review, supra note* 13 at 910–11.

61. *See* Donnelly, *Book Review, supra* note 13 at 912–13; and *see generally* LLEWELLYN, THE COMMON LAW TRADITION, *supra note* 19.

62. *See* Donnelly, *Principles, Persons, and Horizons, supra* note 19 at 252–53.

63. *See* DWORKIN, TAKING RIGHTS SERIOUSLY, *supra* note 22 at 90.

64. *See id.* at 115; *see also* DWORKIN, LAW'S EMPIRE, *supra* note 3 at 243.

65. *See* DWORKIN, TAKING RIGHTS SERIOUSLY, *supra* note 22 at 91.

important national ideals. Not only do stronger rights trump weaker rights but strong policies, one could argue, trump weak rights. Pursuit of a national war effort could trump legal rights based simply on precedent as opposed to those grounded in the First Amendment.

Recognizing that strong policies prevail over weak rights provides sufficient flexibility in Dworkin's method to accommodate impact and interest analysis, situation sense and other pragmatic instrumentalist decision making techniques. For example, when a litigant urges a right based on precedent that assertion counts in the argument but may not prevail if the judge's balancing of competing interests persuades him that the relevant precedent should be distinguished or overruled. In contrast, however, the great constitutional rights would trump competing policies.

The great flaw in pragmatic instrumentalist method is its rejection of overarching theory.[66] For this reason it cannot ground its understanding of law, society or government in a strong intellectual as distinguished from an emotional or practical commitment to persons. The great strength of legal pragmatism is its openness to new solutions, to problem solving and to the needs of people some newly discovered.

Robert Summers has suggested a method for relating classic pragmatic means—goal reasoning to general theory[67] thereby compensating pragmatism's great weakness and taking advantage of its great strengths. Legal pragmatism is renown for its concern with means and for its use of means-goal reasoning. Nevertheless there is little discussion of goals or choice of goals in pragmatist thought. Summers has argued that the choice of goals could be based on a general theory.[68] That general theory could be tied to political friendship or to a commitment to respect and concern for each person. Use of pragmatic instrumentalist decision making technique grounded in such a theory would support the great rights while remaining open to new claims and the newly discovered needs of persons. Interest balancing and a concern for relating law to the human situation could be grounded in theory and principle. Rights at times, then, would be goals to be pursued by appropriate means.[69]

---

66. *See* POSNER, PROBLEMS OF JURISPRUDENCE, *supra* note 9.

67. *See* ROBERT SAMUEL SUMMERS, INSTRUMENTALISM AND AMERICAN LEGAL THEORY 272–81 (1982).

68. *Id.* at 269.

69. *See generally id.* at 61–80.

Summarizing, then, a personalist judge could amend both Dworkin's proposed method and pragmatic instrumentalism. The proposed amendments would be for the sake of respect and concern for each person. One could incorporate into Dworkin's method the practical down to earth respect and concern afforded each person by pragmatic instrumentalist techniques through a more careful analysis of strong and weak rights. One could graft Dworkin's high idealism to pragmatic instrumentalist method by providing a personalist foundation for the choice of goals. Either would provide a beginning outline for personalist method.

The next two parts will illustrate personalist method more particularly while relating it to and entering into conversation with the common law tradition for deciding cases and interpreting statutes. Part four will compare both Dworkian method and pragmatic instrumentalism with the common law tradition and continue to argue for combining the personalist aspects of each method. It will conclude with an overview of the development of products liability law from *MacPherson v. Buick Motor Co.*[70] to *Henningsen v. Bloomfield Motors, Inc.*[71] and *Greenman v. Yuba Power Products, Inc.*[72] for the purpose of illustrating the greater complexity of modern common law decision making. It will be argued that Dworkian method cannot account for the changes of vision and paradigm illustrated by that series of cases while personalist theory can. Part five will compare Dworkin's theory of statutory interpretation with pragmatic instrumentalism and offer a personalist method for interpreting statutes. Statutory interpretation will be illustrated by H. L. A. Hart's imaginary statute prohibiting vehicles in the park.[73] Commenting on that statute Lon Fuller once remarked that the word vehicle must be understood not only in relation to the word, park, but also to the use of parks in our culture.[74] Part five, after reviewing statutory interpretation, will argue that the understanding of statutory language will be affected by our culture and the judge's vision. While Dworkin's theory cannot account for that phenomenon, personalist

---

70. MacPherson v. Buick Motor Co., 111 N.E. 1050 (N.Y. 1916).

71. Henningsen v. Bloomfield Motors, 32 N.J. 358, 161 A.2d 69 (1960).

72. Greenman v. Yuba Power Products, Inc., 59 Cal.2d 57, 27 Cal.Rptr. 697, 377 P.2d 897 (1963).

73. *See* H.L.A. Hart, *Positivism and the Separation of Law and Morals*, 71 HARV. L. REV. 593, 606–15 (1958).

74. *See* Fuller, *Positivism and Fidelity to Law, supra* note 4 at 661–64.

theory can. Nevertheless that discussion will illustrate the need for the more complex personalist theory offered in chapter 3.

4. The Common Law

If one dates the common law from the Assize of Clarendon, in 1166,[75] which is a convenient starting date, then it is more than 800 years old. S.F.C. Milsom comments that if Sir John Fortesque, Chief Justice of King's Bench during the fourteenth century, were to attend the courtroom of Oliver Wendell Holmes, Jr., he would find much that is familiar and vice versa.[76] Nevertheless, the common law has been transformed many times over the ages. Paradigms in the Kuhnian sense have arisen, have fallen and have been replaced by new paradigms and sub paradigms.[77]

For much of that history there were two principal common law courts, King's Bench and Common Pleas. The normal method of legal reasoning was to develop the law by analogy and distinction. Early in British history a case would be heard and not dismissed if its facts were analogous to other cases allowed under that writ or that form of action. The *Humber River Ferry Boat* case during the fourteenth century offers a fascinating example.[78] Courts had long recognized trespass vi et armis et contra pacem as a valid form of action. A law abiding knight alleged the ferry boatman hired to transport his horse across the Humber River had dumped, probably negligently, the horse from his raft. The horse drowned. On demurrer by the ferry boatman, the Court of King's Bench allowed the action.[79] By analogy to trespass vi et armis the court developed and recognized here the action of trespass on the case, perhaps describable as trespass on the good story.[80] Although there was no

---

75. *See* THEODORE F.T. PLUCKNETT, A CONCISE HISTORY OF THE COMMON LAW 19, 111–13 (5th ed., 1956).

76. *See* S.F.C. Milsom, *Reason in the Development of the Common Law*, 81 L. Q. R. 496 (1965).

77. *See* Donnelly, *Principles, Persons, and Horizons, supra* note 19 at 265–70.

78. The Humber River Ferry Boat Case 22 Ass. 94 (no. 41) (1348).

79. *See* Plucknett, *supra* note 75 at 469–71.

80. *Id.* at 468–72.

force or arms (as a precaution the knight had alleged a legal fiction "to wit with bows and arrows") the action was similar to although also different from the existing trespass writ. Nevertheless the policy of suppressing private violence was relevant; law abiding knights should be encouraged to bring their cases to court. The new form of action, trespass on the case, has been described as the fertile mother of the common law. For example, the foundations of our modern tort and contract law developed by analogy and distinction from the *Humber River Ferry Boat* case.[81] By the close of the nineteenth century, the courts had created much of our modern common law case by case over the centuries.

In the mid eighteenth century *Comyn's Digest* collected cases allowed by King's Bench and Common Pleas and organized them under the respective causes of action, for example, trespass vi et armis, trespass on the case, or assumpsit, the common law form of action for contract.[82] An attorney would argue that his action was allowable by analogy to one or more of the existing cases. In developing the law the wiser judges would base their analogy or distinction on a policy ground. Occasionally but seldom would the cases discuss what we would now describe as principle.

Roscoe Pound has described the early nineteenth century as the formative era of American law.[83] Karl Llewellyn reports that judges during that same period employed an early version of what he calls the grand style of judicial decision making.[84] British decisions prior to July 4, 1776 normally were considered binding precedent in American courts. Our early judges, however recognized that British law had to be adapted to changed American circumstances. In that early grand style judges openly developed the law using policy reasoning.[85]

During the first 700 years, then, British and American courts, using analogy and distinction often grounded in policy analysis, developed

---

81. *See generally* Plucknett *supra* note 75 at 371–73, 460–61, 468–71, 637–40; and S. F. C. Milsom, *Trespass from Henry III to Edward III*, 74 L. Q. R. 561 (1958).

82. *See* Roscoe Pound and Theodore F.T. Plucknett, History and System of the Common Law 303 (3rd ed. 1927).

83. *See generally* Roscoe Pound, The Formative Era of American Law (1938).

84. *See generally* Llewellyn, The Common Law Tradition, *supra* note 2.

85. *See id.*

our law freely. The strongly principled reasoning of a Dworkin or a Langdell, then do not have good institutional fit with most of our common law tradition. In contrast the various pragmatic instrumentalist methods beginning with Holmes and running through Pound and Llewellyn and represented by many current thinkers including Posner and Margaret Jane Radin do have good institutional fit.

Lawyers in the mid-nineteenth century faced a crisis. The common law forms of action were intellectually outmoded. By adding written opinions from the high courts in each of our states, which were growing in number, to those of the federal and the British courts, the volume of relevant precedent either binding or persuasive had become overwhelming. Without the aid of modern computers lawyers found it extraordinarily difficult to organize or understand the law. Abandonment of the forms of action and reorganization of the law around rules and principles became vitally important.[86]

During the late nineteenth and early twentieth century as that task was completed battles raged over whether our law should more closely resemble a closed logical system or should continue to develop as during most of its history with modest creativity and flexibility.[87] Current arguments at times reflect those battles of the past. In his common law decision making method Ronald Dworkin tends although not entirely towards the Langdellian closed logical system. Conservative thinkers insist contrary to 800 years of history upon strict adherence to precedent and avoidance of judicial creativity. Justice Antonin Scalia has difficulty with the common law method precisely because of its flexibility and leeway for judicial creativity which he would describe as anti-democratic.[88]

In our own modern global paradigm of the common law principle has an important role to play. Pragmatists and others who would reject understanding the common law as a closed logical system nevertheless often would recognize the organizing role of principle or use principles as guidelines.[89] For these purposes a principle could be described as a policy theme running through a series of cases. Principled reasoning could be related to typical pragmatic instrumentalist reasoning techniques such as the balancing of interests. A principle could be under-

---

86. *See* Donnelly, *The Fault Principle*, *supra* note 10.
87. *See generally* POSNER, PROBLEMS OF JURISPRUDENCE, *supra* note 9.
88. *See* SCALIA, *supra* note 30 at 12–14.
89. *See* LLEWELLYN, THE COMMON LAW TRADITION, *supra* note 2 at 36.

stood as declaring that a particular interest such as the interest in privacy is a protectable interest. That theme will run through all privacy cases but will not necessarily determine the outcome of those cases. In particular cases a court may perceive competing interests also protectable such as an interest in freedom of the press. The outcome in the particular case will turn on the appropriate balancing of the competing interests.[90]

Ronald Dworkin distinguishes principles from policies. Policies are reasons for decisions based on group goals or advantages. Principles are reasons for decisions grounded in individual rights. Typically common law judges according to Dworkin should decide cases on the basis of principle rather than policy.[91] A litigant has a right to a decision under a principle which best explains existing precedent.[92] In ordinary common law tort, contract or agency cases this method closely resembles the Langdellian tendency towards a closed logical system. Dworkin differs from Langdell because he would allow his ideal Judge Hercules to remake periodically his theory of the precedent discarding some precedent perhaps even some of his own under a theory of mistakes.[93] Dworkin also differs from Langdell because he requires Judge Hercules to offer a theory of the precedent which not only has good institutional fit but also makes the most including the most morally that now can be made of the law. Hercules, then, can modernize his understanding of law and relate it to current problems. Dworkin's method nevertheless relies heavily on inductive and deductive logic while rejecting incremental development of law. Principled reasoning, I once remarked, refuses to go at a pedestrian pace, it rides on horseback or refuses to go at all.[94] If Hercules perceives the current precedent as making the most that now can be made of the law he will adhere strongly to it and refuse to change. If current precedent, however, is out of accord with Hercules' fundamental views then he will change it rapidly by logical development from his theory. Unlike traditional common law and the pragmatic instrumentalist recreation of it Hercules will not develop the law on a case by case experimen-

---

90. *See* PAUL J. MISHKIN AND CLARENCE MORRIS, ON LAW IN COURTS: AN INTRODUCTION TO JUDICIAL DEVELOPMENT OF CASE AND STATUTE LAW 175 (1965).

91. *See* DWORKIN, TAKING RIGHTS SERIOUSLY, *supra* note 22 at 84.

92. *See id.* at 115; *see also* DWORKIN, LAW'S EMPIRE, *supra* note 3 at 312.

93. *See* DWORKIN, TAKING RIGHTS SERIOUSLY, *supra* note 22 at 118–23.

94. *See* Donnelly, *Principles, Persons, and Horizons, supra* note 19 at 237.

tal basis.[95] Dworkin's method, then has less institutional fit with traditional common law than pragmatic instrumentalism.

Personalism accepts the pragmatic instrumentalist developments of the common law method. For example, it accepts the use of principles as organizing themes and as guidelines in the decision of particular cases. It rejects the rigid Dworkian distinction between principle and policy and his requirement that courts normally decide common law cases on the basis of principle rather than policy. Reasons of principle as understood by Dworkin and reasons of policy both may be grounded in respect and concern for human persons. National or other group goals may be grounded in such humane policies as reducing malnutrition, allowing adequate compensation to injured workers or assuring proper housing for the poor. Promotion of these and similar policies may be anchored in respect and concern for each person. Pragmatic means end reasoning and related interest balancing are traditional and appropriate means for developing the common law while resolving disputes.

Principles, at times however, may not be adequately described as policy themes running through a series of cases. Some principles embody our great ideals, some of which are found in the United States Constitution and some in the common law. For example, courts have found protection for the right of privacy both in the common law and in the Constitution. A great national ideal may represent a good to be pursued by adequate means. Principles in the Dworkian sense of reasons based on individual right may be grounded in such national ideals. One can describe such rights as strong rights which often should trump competing reasons for decision.

Pragmatic instrumentalism because it rejects overarching theory cannot account adequately for strong rights. Personalism, however, offers a theory grounded in respect and concern for each person which will support strong rights. Because personalist thought recognizes that the judge is a person with limited but growing knowledge and understanding who is committed to respecting and attempting to understand other persons it also can offer a theory of common law courts with a central function of dispute settlement during which the judge appropriately balances and seeks to understand the conflicting interests. Personalism can support both a theory of strong rights and a theory of dispute

---

95. *Id.* at 234–37.

settlement which attempts to reconcile parties and interests. In conversation with Dworkin's thought personalism would recommend a theory of strong rights and weak rights, a role for policy, for balancing interests and attempting to understand persons. In conversation with legal pragmatism personalism would argue for an overarching theory grounded in deep respect and concern for each person and in a desire to understand persons which would support respect for strong rights while accepting pragmatic instrumentalist decision making technique.

The common law tradition, however, is more complex than so far portrayed. For example, from time to time new global paradigms or new subparadigms are established while old ones are abandoned.[96] Richard Posner remarks that these shifts in paradigm can only be described as a conversion, a change of vision.[97] Duncan Kennedy reports the recurring phenomenon of recharacterization which may be related to a change of vision.[98]

Classical examples of changes of subparadigm may be found in the history of products liability law and in important products cases such as *MacPherson v. Buick Motor Co.*,[99] *Henningsen v. Bloomfield Motors Co.*,[100] and *Greenman v. Yuba Power Products.*[101]

Judge Cardozo's decision in *MacPherson* has been the subject of extensive analysis and commentary. A traditional analysis attributes two distinct but converging methods of reasoning to Cardozo in *MacPherson.*[102] (i) New York had established a series of exceptions to the English rule found in *Winterbottom v. Wright*[103] that the user or consumer of a manufactured product could not sue the manufacturer for negligence. The manufacturer would be liable only in contract and only to a person in privity of contract with him. As the law of negligence developed during the late nineteenth century, New York in a series of cases gradually established a dangerous product exception to the rule of *Winterbot-*

---

96. *Id.* at 265–70.

97. *See* POSNER, PROBLEMS OF JURISPRUDENCE, *supra* note 9 at 148–53.

98. *See* Kennedy, *supra* note 45 at 523–25.

99. MacPherson, 111 N.E. at 1050.

100. Henningsen, 32 N.J. at 358, 161 A.2d at 69.

101. Greenman, 59 Cal.2d at 57, 27 Cal.Rptr. at 697, 377 P.2d at 897.

102. *See* LLEWELLYN, THE COMMON LAW TRADITION, *supra* note 2 at 430–37.

103. Winterbottom v. Wright, 10 Mees. & W. 109, 152 Eng. Rep. 402 (Exch. 1842).

tom.[104] That exception first applied to products such as poison which were inherently dangerous. Ultimately in *Devlin v. Smith*[105] the New York Court of Appeals held that a person without privity of contract could sue a manufacturer in negligence when injured by a product which was dangerous because it was badly made. In *MacPherson* Cardozo generalized that line of cases by finding that any negligently manufactured product could be dangerous and that a person injured by such a product could sue the manufacturer for negligence. (ii) In mid-nineteenth century, the time of *Winterbottom v. Wright* the modern law of negligence had just begun to develop. In 1854, *Brown v. Kendall*[106] had abolished the old fashioned distinction between trespass vi et armis and trespass on the case and held that a person would not be liable in tort for harm done unless he was at fault. Fault could be either intentional or negligent. By 1916, Cardozo in *MacPherson* was able to generalize from sixty years of development in the law of negligence to establish the corollary principle that one normally would be liable for harm caused by his negligent fault. A manufacturer, then, despite his contractual relations with his immediate purchaser, would be liable in negligence rather than contract to a third person injured by his negligently manufactured product. Cardozo, then, deduced that holding in *MacPherson* from the fault principle. Although newly recognized that principle had been developed over a sixty year period. Sometimes this second mode of reasoning in *MacPherson* is described as reasoning from the top down. However, Cardozo also had reasoned from the bottom up by generalizing from a long series of exceptions in New York to the rule of *Winterbottom v. Wright*. That series of exceptions had developed over time by analogy and distinction.

MacPherson v. Buick Motor Co. presents a classic example of early twentieth century post Langdellian common law reasoning. While building on previous decisions Cardozo uses the power of principle to establish firmly a new vision, namely, that manufacturers should be liable for harm caused by their negligence. Mid-nineteenth century judges still influenced by the forms of action and bewildered by the presence of contract and tort issues in the same case were not able to achieve that clarity of vision. The fault principle now articulated by Cardozo became the organizing principle of modern tort law. In prod-

---

104. *Id.*
105. Devlin v. Smith, 89 N.Y. 470 (1882).
106. Brown v. Kendall, 6 Cush. 292, 60 Mass. 292 (1850).

ucts liability Cardozo had established the core central achievement for a new subparadigm which would govern practice, the questions to be asked, the arguments to be made and the law suits to be brought for decades afterward.

In 1960 in *Henningsen v. Bloomfield Motors*,[107] Justice John Francis of the Supreme Court of New Jersey established a new subparadigm for products liability law. Manufacturers of automobiles normally provided ultimate purchasers with a New Car Warranty. Generalizing from the sales law regarding warranty Justice Francis allowed an action for breach of warranty against the manufacturer by personally injured ultimate users or consumers. That action would be available despite the absence of privity of contract. Arguably the manufacturer had contractual relations with and had made a warranty to the car dealer and perhaps to the purchaser of the car. Under contract theory that warranty would not be available to non-purchasers such as passengers in the car. Therefore, Justice Francis also recognized a broad implied warranty of safety made by a manufacturer at the time of marketing the product to all who would be affected by breach of that warranty. In a warranty action the plaintiff must prove breach of the warranty and the resulting injury. The plaintiff would not have to prove negligent manufacture.

Commenting on *Henningsen* Professor William Prosser, the author of a standard treatise on tort law[108] and the reporter for the *Restatement 2nd of Torts*,[109] argued that we should have strict liability in tort for defective and dangerous products and should establish that strict liability without a contact or warranty rationalization.[110] In *Greenman v. Yuba Power Products*[111] Justice Traynor of the California Supreme Court accepted Prosser's invitation and established a strict liability in tort action against a manufacturer of a defectively dangerous product for those injured by the product. In a strict liability action the plaintiff must prove the defect and his injury but need not prove negligence in manufacturing the product.

One could argue that *Henningsen* and *Greenman* use the same classic common law reasoning as *MacPherson* perhaps with a slightly greater emphasis upon policy. On the contrary, however, one could contend

---

107. Henningsen, 32 N.J. at 358, 161 A.2d at 69.

108. W. PAGE KEETON, PROSSER AND KEETON ON TORTS (5th ed., 1984).

109. RESTATEMENT (SECOND) OF TORTS (1958).

110. *See* William Prosser, *The Assault Upon the Citadel*, 69 YALE L. J. 1099 (1960).

111. Greenman, 59 Cal.2d at 57, 27 Cal.Rptr. at 697, 377 P.2d at 897.

that *Henningsen* and *Greenman*, particularly the latter, are typical mid-twentieth century pragmatic-instrumentalist decisions which seek to establish on policy grounds the best rule for the future. *Greenman*, in particular, one could argue, represents an effort to allocate loss and is supportable primarily by economic policy considerations. Both cases, then, are prime examples of judicial decisions as regulation rather than dispute settlement.

Nevertheless, *Henningsen* and *Greenman* established a new vision and a new subparadigm or perhaps two overlapping and at times conflicting subparadigms. Arguably the creative use of common law precedent and concepts as well as policy arguments made that new vision possible. The new subparadigms determined the structure and practice of products liability law for the remainder of the twentieth century.

One can argue that despite the regulatory aspects of *Henningsen* and *Greenman* the cases actually engaged in dispute settlement on a high level and established a pattern, the new subparadigm, for on going resolution of disputes between manufacturers and consumers of their products. Products liability lawyers representing injured consumers for half a century had contended while seeking more adequate verdicts for their clients that manufacturers were exploiting consumers of their products. The automobile while providing large benefits also increased the number of personal injuries. *Henningsen* and *Greenman* then contributed the settlement not only of the individual disputes presented in those cases but also of a nationwide dispute regarding the relations between manufacturers and those injured by their products.

Dworkin's interpretation of law as Integrity cannot account for the shift of paradigms and subparadigms, nor the related development of new visions. Because of its narrow focus on principles which best justify existing authority, law as Integrity cannot understand the relation between law, society and dispute settlement nor does it strive to understand the creativity of the common law judge. Legal realism and more modern schools of thought influenced by legal realism do account for and attempt to understand the mind of the judge.

Personalist theory, likewise, can account for and seek to explore a judge's creativity while offering an overarching theory which will support strong principles and a strong rights theory. Personalism because it is grounded both in a commitment to each and every person and fascination with human beings and the relations between them can account for and explore the multiple aspects of and connections between law, society, principles and the judge's mind.

5. Legislation

When confronted with the text of a statute the traditional common law turned conservative. Statutes in derogation of the common law, according to the old rubric of statutory interpretation, should be strictly construed.[112] Karl Llewellyn once mocked the rubrics of statutory interpretation arranging them in two columns one entitled "Thrust" and one entitled "Parry."[113] For example, the rubric just recited was listed under "Thrust" and under "Parry" was balanced by a competing rubric: Remedial statutes should be broadly construed.[114] As a principal drafter of the Uniform Commercial Code, however, even Llewellyn had an appropriate admiration for statutory text. William Twining in his biography, *Karl Llewellyn and The Legal Realist Movement*,[115] quotes a Llewellyn ode to statutory interpretation in which the following concern for attention to text is found:

> "The text lays out, the *text you see*, unyielding all perimeters; though slight penumbra there must be you'll find in force and quantity sharp, given verbal limiters."[116]

Nevertheless, the Llewellyn known for his wise common sense, for what he called horse sense, appears in the next two verses where he insists that a "purpose" is "what you need to understand the statutory oracle" and argues that purpose, however discerned is "what lends to *words* all guiding spirit."[117]

Legislative intent in the late twentieth century is a controversial tool for statutory interpretation. Justice Antonin Scalia argues perceptively that it is inappropriate to attribute an intention to a group of people.[118] A committee report explaining the purpose of a statute, for example, is not enacted by the legislature. Ordinarily such a report is drafted by staff and may be reviewed only cursorily by the committee chair. Whether all the legislators who voted for a statute had the same intention is doubtful and can only be the subject of speculation.

---

112. *See* Karl Llewellyn, *Remarks on the Theory of Appellate Decision and the Rules or Canons About How Statutes are to be Construed*, 3 VAND. L. REV. 401–06 (1950).

113. *Id.*

114. *Id.*

115. *See* KARL LLEWELLYN AND THE REALIST MOVEMENT, *supra* note 58.

116. *Id.* at 240.

117. *Id.*

118. *See* SCALIA, *supra* note 30 at 16–18, 29–37.

Ronald Dworkin offers a theory of statutory interpretation, consistent with his theory of law as Integrity, which avoids the just described misunderstandings of legislative intent. Judge Hercules, he argues, should construct a theory of the statute consistent with his theory of law and government. He should inquire under that theory of government what the legislature's duty was when it passed the statute in question. That duty, then, would become the legislative intent or purpose in enacting the statute.[119] Dworkin avoids the trap of treating committee reports or arguments on the legislative floor as the equivalent of enacted statutory language. He nevertheless attributes an intention to the legislatures.

Scalia would rely on the plain meaning of the statutory language. In his Tanner Lecture published under the title, *A Matter of Interpretation*, he describes himself as a textualist.[120] He distinguishes textualism from other conservative theories such as strict construction and original intent and argues for a sophisticated textualism. For example, one should understand the particular text in the context of the entire statute.[121]

Like Scalia and Llewellyn, Dworkin would have Judge Hercules begin by examining the statutory text. Both Dworkin and Scalia would avoid confusing committee reports with enacted language. Like Llewellyn, however, Judge Hercules would seek to discern the statute's purpose. Arguably Llewellyn's informal common sense and Hercules' analytical power often will discern the same purpose in a statute. The subsequent discussion will offer an intriguing example of that taken from a mid-twentieth century exchange.

In that discussion, I want to argue that courts engaged in statutory interpretation are performing a task which closely resembles common law dispute settlement. Common law development of precedent, an understanding of the interests of the parties, and the development of judicial vision are relevant in cases requiring statutory interpretation. In the mid-twentieth century, H.L.A. Hart in *The Concept of Law* defined formalism as the vice of juristic theory which denies or attempts to disguise the presence of choice in law.[122] In contrast to formalism he offered his understanding of legal and statutory language as open

---

119. *See* DWORKIN, TAKING RIGHTS SERIOUSLY, *supra* note 22 at 108; *see also* DWORKIN, LAW'S EMPIRE, *supra* note 3 at 313.

120. *See* SCALIA, *supra* note 30 at 23–25.

121. *Id.*

122. *See* HART, THE CONCEPT OF LAW, *supra* note 6 at 126.

textured. The price, he contended, of governing people by general rules is indeterminacy at the fringes. Typically, then, legal language has what he called a clear core meaning surrounded by a fringe of indeterminacy which he called the penumbral, shadowy or open-textured area of law.[123] To illustrate open texture he offered an imaginary statute prohibiting vehicles in the park. That statute became the subject of a fruitful intellectual exchange between Hart and his conversation partner, Harvard's Lon Fuller.[124]

I use that statute on the first day of class to introduce new law students to the common law tradition and its techniques of legal reasoning. Imagine, I suggest, a small central New York village whose town council enacts an ordinance which states: "There shall be no vehicles in the Park." Immediately after voting for the ordinance the council members depart for a fishing vacation at a remote Canadian lake. I then designate the members of the class as justices of the peace in the small village. Early Monday morning, that is, the first day of class, a conscientious police sergeant in the village charges a group of teenagers with riding bicycles in the Park in violation of the ordinance. The facts are conceded and the dispute centers on the appropriate interpretation of the legislative language: are bicycles vehicles prohibited in the Park by the ordinance. Class opinion is usually mixed. Some very helpfully to the discussion want to adhere to a dictionary definition of vehicle which they allege includes bicycles. As discussion proceeds they are asked to decide whether roller skates, baby carriages, and toy trucks in the sandbox are vehicles prohibited in the Park by the ordinance. Ultimately they are requested to contemplate the situation at the end of the summer when the town council returns from vacation to find the village in an uproar and mothers with baby carriages picketing town hall.

Others argue that the ordinance according to common sense was designed to protect the safety, the environment and the recreational uses of the Park. Opinion differs on whether bicycles violate the purpose of the ordinance. After arguing in support of their bicycle decision students are asked to decide that roller skate case.

---

123. *See* Hart, The Concept of Law, *supra* note 6 at 121–32; *see also* Hart, *Positivism and the Separation of Law and Morals*, *supra* note 73 at 607.

124. *See* Hart, The Concept of Law, *supra* note 6 at 125; and Hart, *Positivism and the Separation of Law and Morals*, *supra* note 73 at 607; and Fuller, *Positivism and Fidelity to Law*, *supra* note 4 at 667.

While discussing their roller skate decision students are asked whether they are bound by their bicycle decision. One can explain the common law doctrine of stare decisis in the context of keeping the peace in the village by settling disputes. If the justice of the peace allows bicycles in the Park on Monday, prohibits them on Tuesday, again allows them on Wednesday and so on for the rest of the summer, he will have failed to settle the dispute and keep the peace. Confused by the court decisions the police sergeant and the teenagers will continue their confrontation. To prevent that the court must adhere to its bicycle decision for a reasonable period of time.

Query whether the bicycle decision should influence the roller skate decision for similar reasons? Arguably confusion would result if the court permitted bicycles but prohibited roller skates and a fortiori baby carriages. If the court permits bicycles then by analogy the court also must permit roller skates and baby carriages. The policy reason supporting the analogy is that roller skates and baby carriages do not interfere more seriously than bicycles with the safety, environment, and recreational uses of the Park. However, justices of the peace who have prohibited bicycles may distinguish roller skates and baby carriages on the ground that they pose less serious dangers to the Park's safety, environment and recreational uses.

One, then, can understand the common law doctrine of precedent as being very helpful or necessary to the courts' function of dispute settlement. A court under this view makes law as a byproduct of the dispute settlement process. After a series of decisions, a scholar could write an article based on the holding of cases describing what items are prohibited or permitted in the Park. The courts make law because they adhere to their previous holdings. Nevertheless they must adhere to previous holdings for a reasonable time in order to settle disputes. Under this analysis, however, only a reasonable adherence to precedent is required.

Hart argued that in order to communicate at all general open textured legal language must have a clear undisputed core meaning. He contended that "motor vehicle" was the core meaning of the statute prohibiting vehicles in the park.[125] Courts then when presented with disputes must specify the meaning of the statute in the shadowy or penumbral area surrounding the core meaning and determine whether bicycles, roller skates or baby carriages are prohibited in the park.

---

125. *See* HART, THE CONCEPT OF LAW, *supra* note 6 at 123; and Hart, *Positivism and the Separation of Law and Morals, supra* note 73 at 607.

When interpreting a statute courts settle disputes very much as they do in common law cases.

Lon Fuller, Hart's conversation partner in the mid-twentieth century disagreed with Hart's analysis of the imaginary statute. The problems of the core, Fuller explained, are not different than the problem of the penumbra. Our understanding of the statutory language reflects our culture whether we are deciding a core case or one in the shadowy open-textured area. We must understand the word vehicle in the context of the statute and in relation to the uses of parks in our culture.[126]

Fuller offered a mild example when he wondered whether the statute would prohibit the Veterans of Foreign Wars from placing a jeep in the park as a monument.[127] More imaginative examples are available. Would the statute prohibit a police car from racing across the park to prevent a mugging or an ambulance from entering the park to save a heart attack victim? Those who favor purposive interpretation could argue that the use of these vehicles in the park is consistent with protecting the safety, environment and recreational uses of the park and therefore not prohibited. One could imagine that the statute was passed in 1880. In that event it probably was designed to prohibit horse drawn carriages. Contrary to Hart the core meaning of the statute is not motor vehicles. Rather as Fuller argues the meaning of legal language both in the core and the penumbra depends on our cultural context.

Hart, as already explained used his imaginary statute to attack the vice of formalism. In his statute a formalist court could insist as my students did on the dictionary definition of vehicle and understand the legislative language as broadly as conceivable to include bicycles, roller skates and baby carriages. In the alternative a formalist could argue for a minimalist interpretation confining the statute's meaning to motor vehicles. Formalism can deny the presence of choice in legal language by insisting on either the broadest possible understanding of legal language or the most narrow interpretation. Lon Fuller would not disagree with Hart's condemnation of formalism. Rather, he disagreed with Hart's compromise which could be described as an acceptance of formalism for the core meaning of legal language while allowing courts discretion in the shadowy or penumbral area.

Ronald Dworkin, Hart's successor in Oxford's chair of jurisprudence, praised Hart and disagreed with him in his inaugural lecture. A

---

126. *See* Fuller, *Positivism and Fidelity to Law, supra* note 4 at 661–69.
127. *Id.* at 663.

revised version of that lecture is recorded in chapter 4 of Dworkin's *Taking Rights Seriously*.[128] Dworkin contended that in hard cases which may resemble Hart's penumbral area cases courts should have weak as opposed to strong discretion.[129] The statutory standard should govern the court's decision not only in the core but also in the open-textured area.

A judge, according to Dworkin, should ask why a legislature would pass the statute in question under his understanding of the legislature's duty and role in government. A judge, for example, using that analysis could conclude that the town council prohibited vehicles in the park for the purpose of protecting its safety, environment and recreational uses. Rather than deriving that conclusion from common sense, however, Dworkin's judge would deduce it from his comprehensive theory of law and government. Using that analysis to interpret the statute the judge should find a statutory standard which explains both core and penumbral area decisions. The statutory standard governs throughout.[130]

In *Law's Empire* Ronald Dworkin attacks Hart's theory of legal language with its distinction between core and penumbra. That distinction Dworkin argued is an interpretation rather than a description of legal language.[131] Dworkin much prefers his own interpretation of law as Integrity. A court pursuing Integrity should decide cases according to principles which best justify extant authoritative decisions.[132] When interpreting a statute such as the one prohibiting vehicles in the park the court should ask what the legislature's duty should be when enacting such a statute. Probably Judge Hercules would reach the same conclusion as my students; the statute was or should have been enacted to protect the safety, environment and recreational uses of the park. Those, of course, are policy reasons which Dworkin considers appropriate grounds for legislative enactments. From the perspective of the court, however, those reasons lead to enunciation of the statutory standard: vehicles prohibited in the Park are those which harm the safety, environment or recreational uses of the Park. That standard will govern all cases arising under the statute whether Hart would describe those cases as core or penumbral. Judge Hercules has weak and not strong discretion when interpreting the statute. Using his own intellectual percep-

---

128. DWORKIN, TAKING RIGHTS SERIOUSLY, *supra* note 22 at 81–130.
129. *Id.* at 101–05.
130. *See generally* DWORKIN, LAW'S EMPIRE, *supra* note 3 at 313–54.
131. *Id.* at 45–53.
132. *Id.* at 225, 243.

tion Hercules locates the statutory standard. He is then bound by that standard in all his decisions. Contrary to Hart he does not freely specify the statute's meaning in each open-textured area case.[133]

One could use Dworkin's theory of statutory interpretation as applied to the statute prohibiting vehicles in the park to make more of his insistence on legal rights than was granted above in the discussion of common law decision making. Under an appropriate interpretation of the statute the children have a legal right to push doll carriages in the Park. The town council did not intend to prohibit doll carriages. When the conscientious police sergeant, using a crude formalist or plain meaning interpretation of the statute, arrests the children he is attacking outrageously and violating their legal rights. As Dworkin argues the children have a legal right to those uses of the Park which are supported by an interpretation which best justifies the statute.[134]

Nevertheless, the central function of the court when interpreting the statute is to settle disputes. As illustrated by the statute prohibiting vehicles in the Park, disputes arise in regard to administration of statutes. A significant number of these disputes regard different understandings of relevant statutory language. Litigants, however, bring these disputes to court because their interests are at stake. The legislature by enacting the statute protects or promotes certain interests. In complex social circumstances, however, it is not always clear what balance of interest the legislature intended.

For example, did the town council which passed the statute prohibiting vehicles in the park mean to prefer environmental, safety or recreational interests when these are in conflict? Or did the legislature under a general standard (which applied throughout) mean the court to implement the statute by effectuating the appropriate balance in each case? As in common law cases, courts presented with disputes under statutes must locate and balance relevant interests. In doing so they should be guided by the legislature's standard.

The court's understanding of the legislature's standard at times will be affected by the judge's political, social and cultural background. Unlike Judge Hercules the normal judge is a person of limited although perhaps growing knowledge and understanding. As in common law cases the judge's vision at times affects his holding.

---

133. *See* HART, CONCEPT OF LAW, *supra* note 6, with DWORKIN, LAW'S EMPIRE, *supra* note 3.

134. *See* DWORKIN, LAW'S EMPIRE *supra* note 3 at 152.

While statutes are different than the common law and are treated more conservatively even by pragmatists, H.L.A. Hart had a significant insight when he perceived the resemblance between common law rules and statutory standards.[135] Courts interpreting statutes like judges settling disputes under the common law rely on and develop precedent, locate and balance interests, and are affected or inspired by their vision and by their political, social and cultural background. In both statutory and common law cases the courts have a regulatory function; by adhering to previous precedent, they make law. Nevertheless, the dispute settlement function is central.

One can grant Dworkin's argument that the statutory standard governs throughout and then add insights from pragmatic instrumentalist and personalist thought. Judges interpreting statutes are human beings who have or lack vision. That vision affects their understanding of the statutory standard and the relevant interests. Nevertheless to resolve disputes they must locate and balance interests using their perception of the legislative standard and make law by adhering to precedent.

Interpreting the statute prohibiting vehicles in the Park, however, may be more complex than portrayed to this point. Imagine the statute is of modestly ancient vintage. Assume that until recently the Park was used primarily by older citizens who enjoyed walking in the Park and sitting in the sun on the benches conveniently provided. Recently as a result of housing developments on two sides of the Park parents with children primarily under twelve years of age have begun bringing their children to the Park and teenagers from a minority group are riding their bicycles there. After complaints from the elderly and the parents of young children the police ordered the teenagers to keep their bicycles out of the Park. The teenagers returned with skateboards which they use primarily on a hill with blacktop paths. The police then arrested the teenagers charging them with violation of the statute.

In resolving this dispute the court properly should weigh the interests of the minority teenagers in reasonable recreation against the interests of the elderly and parents of small children in peaceable use of the Park. An administrative agency could resolve the dispute by reserving one segment of the Park for skateboard use. While a court does not have that resource one could imagine a pragmatic court developing a subrule regarding reasonable use of the Park. The rule would allow

---

135. *See* Hart, THE CONCEPT OF LAW, *supra* note 6 at 120–22.

skateboards while confined to portions of the park not frequently used by pedestrians and children. One also could imagine a legislature passing a statute directing the courts to develop its standards by reasonable additional rules. Indeed one could argue that a normal expectation is that courts settling disputes under statutes or the common law will develop subrules reflecting the statutory or other existing standards to resolve new but unforeseen difficulties. A court could develop a statute in the manner just described while adhering throughout its process, as Dworkin desires, to the statutory standard. In the pragmatic-instrumentalist tradition while adhering to the statutory standard a court could understand protection of the environment, safety and recreational uses of the Park as legislative goals to be served by adequate means such as subrules regarding reasonable use.

In some cases, a court may find it necessary to balance the competing interests in protecting the environment and safety of the Park while allowing reasonable recreational uses. When effectuating that balance a judge even if he is Judge Hercules may find his perception affected by his political, social and cultural environment. Indeed one could imagine that the judge grew up as a member of the minority group or that he spends his weekends caring for his elderly mother who enjoys sitting in the park although perhaps not that Park. In other words the judge is a person of limited although perhaps growing knowledge and understanding whose perception of the statutory standard and the parties will be affected by his personality and his horizons.

The argument in the chapter is that a personalist method has a greater capacity for addressing and resolving the questions and problems presented by judicial settlement of disputes than competing methods. A personalist judge is one who recognizes himself or herself as a person of limited but growing knowledge and understanding, who is committed to respect and concern for each person, and who is fascinated with human beings. A personalist method is one which reflects the commitments and understandings of a personalist judge. In the global paradigm of early twenty-first century American common law, a personalist judge would seek to combine pragmatic-instrumentalist decision making technique with a commitment to and deliberation concerning the great ideals of our society and law. Some of these ideals become the foundation for strong rights which will trump strong policies in the judicial reasoning process. Insights from Ronald Dworkin's thought would be helpful in understanding those ideals and strong rights.

When interpreting statutes a personalist judge adjudicating a dispute again would use pragmatic instrumentalist techniques. Like Llewellyn he would start with the text and seek a purpose. Often that purpose will be a set of interests which the legislature wants to protect or advance. The competing interests of the parties must be understood, weighed and balanced. The judge will use means-end reasoning to serve the legislative goals perhaps while devising subrules which will resolve disputes while promoting the goals. Dworkin is persuasive that the legislative standard should govern throughout. Using that standard, however, is compatible as shown above, with the use of the pragmatic-instrumentalist techniques just listed. Dworkin's method for finding the legislature's purpose also is impressive and would be used as well as common sense methods for understanding that purpose. Legislative history is less important than statutory language and would be consulted only to understand the statute's context and goals. Context may include the discourse community which will use the statute. For example, familiarity with the community of commercial lawyers may be necessary to understand the meaning of the Uniform Commercial Code. Familiarity with administrative law and practice and the context of the regulated industries may be a necessary prelude to understanding the meaning of a regulatory statute.

Dworkin's thought, however, does not address the judge's perception of legislative goals and the interests of parties. Some pragmatic thought does. Personalist method because its ideal judge is fascinated with and seeks to understand persons is capable of exploring the judge's perception. Personalist method can meld pragmatic instrumentalist techniques with aspects of Dworkin's method and beyond that can absorb insights concerning language and human imagination from post-modern thought.

Personalist method when applied to common-law decision making or statutory interpretation has good institutional fit. Like other methods currently in use it bears a family resemblance to traditional common law methods. Engaging in conversation with current methods personalism extracts and melds insights related to understanding and respecting persons in the process of settling disputes. Personalism also makes the most that now can be made of the common law tradition because it can construct and reconstruct methods which reflect the best of current thought. A personalist judge would accept insights from recent thinkers in so far as doing so would enhance his self-understanding, his effort to understand others, and his respect and concern for parties who appear before him, and others affected by his decisions and his regard for their rights.

Personalism is able to reconstruct method from time to time while extracting insights from competing thought because it is committed to respect, understand and be concerned for persons. That commitment becomes the test for critiquing and extracting insights from competing methods as illustrated in this chapter by discussion of Dworkian and pragmatic-instrumentalist decision making. That criteria makes possible the combination of personalist insights from both methods. For a more satisfactory method, however, additional insights are required. Among other matters one must address the judge's limited but growing knowledge and understanding, that is, his horizons and his vision, and add techniques for crossing and transcending horizons.

6. A Central Role for Dispute Settlement

Different thinkers offer competing versions of the function of judicial decision making. Ronald Dworkin who in this respect agrees with Holmes sees it as a process for justifying the use of force.[136] Harry Wellington discussing constitutional decisions perceives two aspects, dispute settlement and regulation, that is, establishing new rules for the future.[137] Wellington believes regulation is the more important function of constitutional decisions. One also could argue that dispute settlement is the central function of the court system, that the establishment of a new rule is a related but secondary function, an important byproduct and part of the settlement of disputes, and that force is not central but a significant tool helpful in securing the peaceful settlement of disputes.

When reconstructing judicial method with an emphasis upon respecting and understanding persons, interpreting our courts' function as dispute settlement, rather than regulation or justifying the use of force offers a more powerful tool for discussing the multiple relations between persons and decision making.

Whether one can offer a rigorous justification for a judicial decision as an application of public force will be the subject of chapter 5.

---

136. *See* DWORKIN, LAW'S EMPIRE, *supra* note 3 at 110.
137. *See* HARRY H. WELLINGTON, INTERPRETING THE CONSTITUTION: THE SUPREME COURT AND THE PROCESS OF ADJUDICATION 3–19 (1990).

Richard Posner denies that possibility and prefers to describe a judicial opinion as a reasonable explanation of a decision.[138] Ronald Dworkin contends that pragmatists such as Posner are incapable of taking rights seriously and ties his own understanding of rights to a rigorous theoretical justification of past decisions.[139] It is precisely that rigorous theory, however, that prevents Dworkin's Judge Hercules from attending to the needs and circumstances of parties to the case. It also prevents Dworkin from reflecting on Hercules' limited knowledge and understanding, on his feelings and emotions and his moral growth. To Dworkin Hercules is an analytic giant who decides cases on the basis of his great theory.[140]

Oliver Wendell Holmes, Jr., as a civil war hero, is renown for his fighting faith. He probably perceived law as a controlled fight or struggle over competing interests and ideals.[141] He certainly saw force as an ultimate arbiter in society. When advising clients such as his famous bad man he would want to anticipate and avoid adverse use of public force.[142] Like Holmes, Ronald Dworkin perceives the public use of force as fundamental to law. A judicial decision, he argues, should justify that public use of force.[143]

Without denying Holmes' insight or the importance for law of public force personalist theory chooses dispute settlement rather than the justified use of force as central to the work of our courts.

A theory in which dispute settlement is central to the work of our courts can account and provide a role for force and Holmes' fight theory. Force is indeed a necessary backup for a court's decision. From a litigant's perspective a lawyer is fighting to advance the interests of his or her client. A primitive method for keeping the peace is to channel disputes into controlled combat. If that function continues today, how-

---

138. *See generally* POSNER, PROBLEMS OF JURISPRUDENCE, *supra* note 9 at 130.

139. *See* DWORKIN, LAW'S EMPIRE, *supra* note 3.

140. *See* Donnelly, *Principles, Persons, and Horizons, supra* note 19 at 222–25.

141. *See generally* CATHERINE DRINKER BOWEN, YANKEE FROM OLYMPUS 389–92; and Abrams v. United States, 250 U.S. 616, 630 (1919) (Holmes, J., dissenting) ("[B]ut when men have realized that time has upset many fighting faiths, they may come to believe that even more than they believe the very foundations of their own conduct that the ultimate good desired is better reached by free trade in ideas…").

142. *See* Holmes, *The Path of the Law, supra* note 7 at 459.

143. *See* DWORKIN, LAW'S EMPIRE, *supra* note 11 at 218–19.

ever, we bring disputes to a forum where rational argument is the ideal weapon.

H.L.A. Hart when refuting John Austin's theory that law is the command of the sovereign backed by sanctions analogized that view to a vision of a gunman written large.[144] One does not have an obligation to obey the law, he explained, because one is obliged to do so by the threat of force.[145] In contrast to force, Hart called attention to acceptance of law by the people.[146] While force should not be overlooked the acceptance and hence the legitimacy of law is more central to the historic function of keeping the peace.

Historically the contribution of the courts to keeping the peace has not been force but dispute settlement. An important aspect of the rule of law is that one should bring one's disputes to court and abide by the results rather than fighting in the streets.

Modern law students are trained to make good rules as legislators, administrators, when drafting contracts or in judicial holdings. Not surprisingly then some find the regulatory aspects of judicial decisions the most interesting. Again a theory with a central role for dispute settlement should account for the rule making regulatory function of the courts. A judge cannot settle a dispute adequately without anticipating future disputes and making a rule which will continue to keep the peace. To make such a rule a judge should anticipate future problems and account for and balance competing interests. Those who perceive judicial decisions as applications of pre-existing rules or principles miss this aspect of dispute settlement.

Courts, of course, make law. Arguing, however, that regulation is their principal function rather than a by-product of dispute settlement raises large questions and difficulties under most versions of democratic theory. It also focuses the court's attention on the legislative question of what is the best rule for the future[147] rather than understanding the parties to the dispute and their relationships. A judge who focuses on the parties and others who will be affected by the decision is more likely to frame a rule which will settle the dispute by improving relations between the relevant parties.

---

144. *See* Hart, The Concept of Law, *supra* note 6 at 18–25.
145. *See id.* at 79–86.
146. *See id.* at 97–100.
147. *See* Dworkin, Law's Empire, *supra* note 3 at 155–60.

Recognition that dispute settlement is the primary function of the courts allows the melding suggested above of high principles grounded in deep respect and concern for each person with pragmatic instrumentalist openness to human need and the techniques developed for locating and understanding those needs.

One can argue that common law respect for precedent has a dispute settlement function. A judge who changes his holding every time the same question comes before him has not settled the dispute. For that purpose he must adhere to his decision for a reasonable period of time. A litigant's legal right to have a decision according to precedent counts in the argument but is a weak right. Rather a litigant has a right to be listened to and heard as he describes his perceived wrongs, his proposed remedies and the relation between his story and the common law tradition. A judge having listened to the opposing stories after attempting to understand the relation and situation of the parties should describe their interests in more general terms and balance those interests. Drawing on the resources of the common law tradition he then should frame a rule which will resolve the dispute and provide a continuing satisfactory solution for similar type situations in the future.[148] Understanding the central function of the courts as dispute settlement rather than the application of preexisting rules provides the parties with a right to a judge who will listen, seek to understand their dispute and provide a reasonable solution which will further their relations and the future relations of similar parties.[149]

Again, understanding the central function of our courts as dispute settlement more closely resembles what our courts in fact do than the opposing views and therefore has what Dworkin describes as good institutional fit. Our courts do in fact settle disputes and in doing so pay some attention to the interests of the parties. Courts, of course, do establish new rules and therefore engage in regulation. As just argued, however, establishing new rules which courts adhere to under the doctrine of precedent is important to the settlement of disputes. Some disputes presented to courts, some great constitutional issues, for example, represent clashes between great interests and seriously divided opinion in our country. Each competing group is seeking through the judicial

---

148. Cf. Donnelly, *Book Review, supra* note 13 at 906–11.

149. Of course, a lawsuit does disrupt relations between persons. However, judicial intervention prevents us from settling disputes through private action and the use of force.

process rather than legislation a new rule which will favor its interests and views. Arguably the court's holding establishing that new rule is not simply regulation, that is, legislation by an alternate means but dispute settlement. The court system and the legal argument which it allows provides an alternative to the normal political process for arguing rationally and deliberating concerning important national disputes. The courts seek to establish a rule which will settle those disputes in a manner consistent with our great national ideals.

Understanding that process as the rigorous application of a consistent theory to justify that public use of force does not capture what the courts are engaged in nearly as well. In less important disputes, that has a Langdellian flavor long since abandoned by the courts. In the great dispute it misses the exchange of ideas and the process of reconciliation which can take place as rational arguments are made. It makes the peace keeping function of the courts turn on the justified uses of force rather than on dispute settlement through channeling serious national disputes into rational argument.

Understanding the central function of the courts as dispute settlement arguably makes the most morally that now can be made of our legal system. That explanation most closely reflects the multiple human relations in our society and allows the development of law in accord with changing human needs and relations. It allows a judge to perceive himself as a person of limited knowledge and understanding who matures morally as he seeks to understand persons while resolving disputes. Like Dworkian theory it can relate dispute settlement to our national ideals and to deliberation on those ideals.[150] Understanding judicial decision making as dispute settlement allows a melding of significant personalist insights from pragmatic instrumentalist and Dworkian theory.

---

150. Dworkin requires Judge Hercules to be arrogant and comprehensive of all that has taken place in the case before him. However, this arrogance does not allow judges to gain moral maturity because they have no emotional presence in the adjudication of the dispute. This absence therefore disallows the judge to struggle with himself and prevents him from understanding his own personal limitations. When forced to personify such an abstract and analytical machine, a judge is unable to make sound decisions because he cannot be expected to understand the limitations of the litigants who look to him for understanding and resolution.

In the next segment it will be argued that this personalist under-standing of law which recognizes dispute settlement as the central func-tion of our courts also has greater legitimacy.

7. Legitimacy

a. The Meaning of Legitimacy

Duncan Kennedy in "Freedom and Constraint in Adjudication: A Critical Phenomenology" explains that he would make good legal argu-ments in support of his decision as a judge in order to enhance his legit-imacy power.[151] Important decisions backed by good legal arguments are more likely "to stick" on appeal and to be followed in the future.[152] Moreover, if he regularly uses good legal arguments to support pace making decisions he will have a greater chance of succeeding in his po-litical agenda and successfully pursuing his career as an activist judge. Kennedy understands legitimacy in judicial decision making as linked to political power.

Ronald Dworkin's discussion of legitimacy in *Law's Empire* offers a contrasting vision.[153] Legitimacy, he argues, is related to the political obligation of citizens to obey the law. A judge's decision is legitimate when it enhances that obligation and strengthens the foundation for obedience to law. While recognizing that philosophers have struggled to understand why a person who has not agreed to do so had an obligation to obey the law, Dworkin would find that obligation in the political friendship that arises from community.[154] A judge enhances that politi-cal friendship by his decisions when he grounds them in principles, the principles which best explain the political practices and institutions of the community.[155]

While tough issues remain, Dworkin probably offers the best foun-dation for political obligation, grounding it in the respect and concern which arises from our association with our fellow citizens. The ques-tionable obligations of an outsider present the toughest problem to that

---

151. *See* Kennedy, *supra* note 45 at 527–28.
152. *Id.*
153. *See* DWORKIN, LAW'S EMPIRE, *supra* note 3 at 190–206.
154. *Id.* at 216–24.
155. *Id.*

solution and may require us to add a right to reasonable self defense. Nevertheless, even when exercising that right it may make sense to treat the outsider as if he were a willing member of the community entitled to respect and concern.

Arguably, however, Dworkin has several flaws in his understanding of legitimacy. First, rather than addressing the legitimacy of a judge's decision directly, he derives the notion of legitimacy from obligation and not the obligation of the judge but that of the people to obey the law. That is a point of view mistake. Rather, he should ask from the judge's point of view what is his obligation in making a decision. Although judges agree in their oath of office to follow the law, perhaps that obligation is more derived from community and the respect and concern which the judge should have for his fellow citizens. Secondly, Dworkin finds highly structured principled decision making central to the legitimacy of all judicial decisions. That conclusion is closely tied to and shares the same problems as Dworkin's theory of justification. His Judge Hercules trapped in an abstract, principled theory which offers the best justification for decisions from the past is unable to address the real needs and circumstances of the parties before him and others affected by his decision. For that reason his decisions often will be less acceptable to present litigants and relevant others than many pragmatic instrumentalist opinions.

In the course of their mid-twentieth century confrontation-conversation, H.L.A. Hart and Lon Fuller addressed acceptance of law.[156] Hart defined a valid, and we could argue, a legitimate, legal system as one accepted by the people.[157] He recognized various degrees of acceptance. Lon Fuller thought that definition would misfocus and make the inquiry less productive.[158] Rather, he suggested, we should inquire into the conditions which would make acceptance by the people possible and more probable.[159] Among those conditions, he argued, were the requirements of internal morality, the morality that makes law possible. For example where there is a complete failure to communicate the law, it is impossible for citizens to accept or obey it. If all laws are ex post facto, secret, or completely arbitrary there is a complete failure to com-

---

156. *See* Hart, *Positivism and the Separation of Law and Morals, supra* note 73 at 593, and Fuller, *Positivism and Fidelity to Law supra* note 4 at 630.

157. *See* HART, THE CONCEPT OF LAW, *supra* note 6 at 114–20.

158. *See* Fuller, *Positivism and Fidelity to Law, supra* note 4 at 633–35.

159. *See generally* FULLER, MORALITY OF LAW, *supra* note 39.

municate and a major violation of the internal morality of law. Fuller, like Hart, recognized degrees, here various levels of adherence to the internal morality of law.[160] In a related development, the Watergate prosecutor, Archibald Cox, argued that a morality of means rather than ends was vital to the functioning of a democracy.

For the purpose of further exploring the ideal of legitimacy for judicial decisions, we can extract from the Hart-Fuller debate the notion of acceptance of law and the conditions which make acceptance of law possible or more probable. A judge who has respect and concern for each person should offer reasons for his decision which show respect for those affected by his decisions. Not all persons will agree with his decisions. Inevitably in legal cases one party loses. Nevertheless if possible the reasons supporting a decision should be those which are acceptable to those affected by the decision or have a reasonable possibility of being acceptable.

Note that the proposal to explore legitimacy and its relation to acceptance of law is grounded in the judge's obligation to offer acceptable and ultimately legitimate reasons for his decision. In contrast Dworkin explores legitimacy in relation to the obligation of those affected by the decision to obey the law.

A variety of qualities would enhance the acceptability of an opinion. As Duncan Kennedy notes offering good legal arguments, that is, arguments which are acceptable within the common law tradition, will enhance the acceptability and legitimacy of a decision.[161] Because a judge has an obligation of respect for the institutions of his society and for his fellow actors in those institutions he should offer good legal arguments. Beyond that minimal requirement, however, a judge should demonstrate that he has listened to and made an effort to understand the parties and their circumstances. He should recognize, consider and weigh the interests of the parties and others affected by his decision. That again would be a bedrock requirement for a judge who perceives dispute settlement as central to judicial decision making and recognizes an obligation of respect and concern for all persons. Principles have proved important in organizing case law and coordinating the positions of courts and should be used and respected as part of the common law tradition. Principles at times reflect the great ideals of our society some

---

160. *See Id.* at 33–94.
161. *See* Kennedy, *supra* note 45.

related to important human rights. A judge committed to respect and concern for all must account for those principles in relevant decisions.

One can offer then a preliminary observation that a judge's decision is legitimate if it is supported and supportable by arguments which can be expected reasonably to be acceptable in the senses just described. Appropriately many of the competing methods in the common law tradition would meet that test of legitimacy. Perhaps even Duncan Kennedy's grab for power might qualify. Surprisingly one could question under that definition and describe as illegitimate some aspects of Dworkin's decision making method. His Judge Hercules does not examine the circumstances and interests of the parties and others affected by his decision. Listening is an important part of legitimate dispute settlement and Hercules' method has no role for listening. Perhaps that is why Dworkin avoids discussing the dispute settlement function of the courts while emphasizing the justified use of public force.

Nevertheless one can raise problems with the beginning general definition of legitimacy offered above. In our complex pluralist society one can ask to which of the many competing positions should an opinion appear acceptable? One traditional answer in our democratic culture is that it should be acceptable to a majority. In *Taking Rights Seriously* Ronald Dworkin brilliantly addressed the problem of majoritarianism in judicial decisions.[162] He noted that though useful majority rule when standing alone is only one aspect of democratic theory. In our tradition we have a growing awareness that each one of us is worthwhile and should be protected by our law. A theory of rights then, which will prevail over majority will is necessary to our understanding of democracy. Does that more developed understanding of democracy compel us to accept Dworkin's theory of legitimacy? That question should be addressed as we refine our theory of legitimacy by examining and arguing for the legitimacy of a personalist judge's decision making method.

b. The Legitimacy of Personalist Method

A personalist judge is one committed to deep respect and concern for each and every person, who recognizes himself as a complicated person with limited but growing knowledge and understanding, and who wants to understand and respect the complex human relations and cir-

---

162. *See* Dworkin, Taking Rights Seriously, *supra* note 22 at 131–49.

cumstances of the parties who appear before him and others affected by his decisions. He finds people fascinating as well as worthwhile.

In his decision making a personalist judge should observe the general conditions for legitimacy described above. Unlike Dworkin's Judge Hercules, he will consider the circumstances and interests of the parties as well as legal rights based on precedent and principle. In contrast however, to the pragmatist tradition he will offer a general theory of law which will support his decision making method as well as his decisions.

That general theory may be grounded both in a personal commitment to afford all persons deep respect and concern and in our national ideal that each one of us is worthwhile and entitled to government protection for our lives, liberty and property. The foundation for the general theory will be developed further in chapter 3 and applied to interpretation of the United States Constitution in chapter 4. One can argue that under Lockean theory the basic function of government is to protect each person's life, liberty and property.[163] Locke's reason for establishing governments also will support the negative liberties found in amendments to the United States Constitution and in the Fifth and Fourteenth Amendment due process clauses. Over our history we have gradually recognized the importance of not excluding anyone from the protection of government. That national ideal that each one of us is worthwhile also will support a theory of the common law and the central dispute settlement function of our courts. Under that national ideal some common law principles closely related to human dignity would support strong rights which would trump competing policies.

Contrary to Dworkin, it would not make sense to offer a theory of legitimacy which would compel us to conclude that all competing methods of decision making are illegitimate. One can argue, however, that the personalist method as sketched in this chapter is legitimate and that it will enhance the acceptability and legitimacy of judicial decisions. Personalist method by melding aspects of pragmatist and Dworkian method can do this in ways not available to either of those methods standing alone. Unlike pragmatism, personalism can offer an overarching theory grounded in respect and concern for each person which will support a theory of strong rights. Unlike Dworkin's Judge Hercules a personalist judge starts by inquiring into and attempting to

---

163. *See* JOHN LOCKE, TWO TREATISES OF GOVERNMENT 283–446 (Peter Laslett ed., 1960) (1690).

understand the circumstances and interests of the parties. Weak legal rights arising from precedent will yield to considerations arising from balancing interests. Overarching personalist theory grounded in a commitment to respecting and understanding persons will require that method as well as respect for strong rights. To respect rights, then, it is not necessary to adopt Dworkin's theory of rigid principles.

Personalist decision making method because it is grounded in the judge's commitment to respect and understand each person and in our national ideal that each one of us is worthwhile has the capacity of appearing reasonable to all persons at all times. Many litigants, of course, will continue to disagree with decisions adverse to them. And judges with limited knowledge and understanding will apply the method imperfectly.

Nevertheless, personalist theory can accept Dworkin's deeper understanding of democracy while avoiding his rigid principled understanding of legal rights. While honoring the great rights it offers a method for settling disputes which requires listening to persons, and understanding and reconciling their interests.

The next chapter will offer a deeper understanding of personalist theory and method than the general and preliminary one just described. Chapter 4 drawing on that deeper theory and on insights from the discussion here of the common law tradition and techniques for statutory interpretation will construct a personalist method for constitutional interpretation.

CHAPTER III

Personalist Theory

1. Introduction

The purpose of this chapter is to present a theory of personalism. A personalist theory is an interpretation of law and consists of a series of related insights and concepts. Personalism is not novel in philosophy or law. A number of European thinkers have offered theories of personalism.[1] In America, Alan Gewirth's valuable theory of personalism is developed differently than the theory described in this chapter.[2] Margaret Jane Radin, as a pragmatist and feminist also has offered significant personalist insights to the conversation about jurisprudence.[3]

John Macmurray, the Scottish philosopher, has offered a theory of persons related to each other through action. His books, *The Self As Agent*,[4] that is as one who acts, and *Persons In Relation*,[5] are a principal source for the personalism described in this chapter.[6] In the last chapter it was argued that a grasp of method is important to understanding the

---

1. *See* Samuel J.M. Donnelly, *Towards a Personalist Jurisprudence: Basic Insights and Concepts*, 28 Loy L.A. L. Rev. 547–50 (1995) referring to, Bernard Haring, Free and Faithful in Christ (1978); Bernard Haring, The Christian Existentialist (1968); Karol Wojtyla, The Acting Person (Tymiencia ed. & Potocki trans.) (1979); Bernard J.F. Lonergan, Insight: A Study of Human Understanding (3d ed.) (1970); Bernard J.F. Lonergan, Method In Theology (2d ed.) (1970); John Macmurray, The Self As Agent (1957); and John Macmurray, Persons In Relation (1961).
2. *See* Alan Gerwith, Reason and Morality *(1978)*.
3. *See* Margaret Jane Radin, *The Pragmatist and the Feminist, in* Pragmatism in Law and Society 127 (Michael Brint & William Weaver eds.) (1991).
4. *See* MacMurray, The Self As Agent, *supra* note 1.
5. *See* Macmurray, Persons In Relation, *supra* note 1.
6. *See generally*, Donnelly, *Towards a Personalist Jurisprudence, supra* note 1 (Much of this chapter is a rethinking of *Towards a Personalist Jurisprudence*).

common law and the debates in twentieth century jurisprudence. A jurisprudence whose principal focus is the judge's decision making process must offer a critical understanding of method. Introspective reflection on method, perhaps in the manner of Duncan Kennedy's critical phenomenology,[7] would be important to a judge's self-understanding as person. Relating a critical understanding of method, then, to Macmurray's theory of personalism is an important step in elaborating a personalist theory of law.

One engaged in personalist jurisprudence can fruitfully recall the judge newly appointed to the bench who plunges into a new world and begins to explore it. In this chapter that judge is intellectually curious and inclined to philosophical reflection. As a personalist judge he remains committed to respect and concern for each person and retains his fascination with people. While perhaps brighter than the ordinary judge, unlike Ronald Dworkin's ideal, Judge Hercules, he is not an analytical giant.[8] He recognizes his own limited although growing knowledge and understanding.

Following Macmurray the judge will recognize himself as one who acts. Part two of this chapter immediately following this introduction will present that central concept of personalism, the person—or judge—as one who acts, and will discuss the significance of that concept for jurisprudence. As a thinker in conversation with American jurisprudence our intellectually curious judge will recognize the importance of the debate about method and the piecemeal recovery of a role for the person during that debate. Part three, in brief conversation with the history of American jurisprudence, will present the recognition of the role for the person and a critical examination of method as significant in that history and in personalist theory. While reflecting on method and his own decision making process, a judge may recognize the phenomenon I will describe as "horizons." Part four will elucidate the personalist concept, horizons, and its role in a personalist understanding of method. A judge committed to persons who recognizes his own limited knowledge and understanding and hence his horizons will develop as part of his decision making process methods for crossing horizons. A judge meditating on the common law tradition also will encounter principles and the quarrel over their function. Part five will

---

7. Duncan Kennedy, *Freedom and Constraint In Adjudication: A Critical Phenomenology*, 36 J. Legal Educ. 518 (1986).

8. *See* RONALD DWORKIN, LAW'S EMPIRE 238–40 (1986).

offer a personalist theory of the role of principles. Principles must be understood in relation to the problem of horizons and the methods for horizon crossing. One important method for understanding foreign horizons is to locate and weigh relevant interests. In personalist theory then principled reasoning must be related to interest analysis.

A judge who in particular cases introspectively examines his own decision making process will discover the phenomenon described here as insight. The Legal Realist discovery of insight which Jerome Frank called "the Gestalt"[9] and Karl Llewellyn hunching[10] was a high point in the recovery of a role for the person in law. Part six will discuss insight, its relation to decision making in particular cases, to horizon crossing and principled reasoning.

Part seven will discuss methods as such and present a personalist critique and critical analysis of method. Arguably one can critique the multiple common law methods by examining the extent to which they recognize a role for the person, for principles as related to our great ideals and for the self-understanding of the judge as it relates to his decision making in particular cases. On a deeper level, the recognition of multiple intellectual methods, the mathematical, the logical, the scientific, the common sense, is a way of understanding the complexities of modern thought and the manner in which that thought affects our understanding of law. Law will be described as employing a sophisticated, specialized common sense method. Judges familiar with other methods may use them to enlighten their common sense. That analysis of common law method supports Holmes in his declaration that the life of the law has not been logic but experience[11] while rejecting the rigid use of logic by Dworkin or Langdell and a Posnerian substitution of economic analysis for common law reasoning.[12] Ultimately a personalist method

---

9. *See* Samuel J.M. Donnelly, *Book Review*, 3 HOFSTRA L. REV. 899, 909 (1975) (reviewing, WILLIAM TWINING, KARL LLEWELLYN AND THE REALIST MOVEMENT (1973), and DAVID WIGDOR, ROSCOE POUND: PHILOSOPHER OF LAW (1973)), referring to, JEROME FRANK, COURTS ON TRIAL 165–85, 170–71, 175–79 (1950).

10. *See id.*, referring to Hutcheson, *The Function of the 'Hunch' in Judicial Decision*, 14 Cornell L.Q. 274 (1979).

11. *See* OLIVER WENDELL HOLMES, JR., THE COMMON LAW at 1 (1881) ("[T]he life of the law has not been logic; it has been experience…").

12. *See generally*, Dworkin, Law's Empire, *supra* note 8; and, RICHARD POSNER, THE PROBLEMS OF JURISPRUDENCE (1990).

must offer a theory of our great ideals as related to understanding of and respect and concern for persons. That is the function of part eight.

Drawing on Macmurray's theory of persons in relation through action and as indirectly related through the common action of society, part eight will offer a theory of the common good as persons acting together. In turn that theory can provide a foundation for a theory of rights, for understanding law and interpreting the United States Constitution. Part nine then will offer an outline of that theory of rights. Rights theory will be developed further in chapter 4 on "Constitutional Interpretation" and chapter 6 which offers a personalist understanding of the language of rights as employed in litigation and adjudication. In personalist theory rights, constitutional interpretation, and fundamental theory must be understood as used in the course of decision making by a judge who has limited knowledge and understanding and who is committed to crossing the multiple horizons in our pluralist society. Part ten, then, will discuss "Pluralism, Horizons and Rhetoric," in relation to rights and fundamental theory.

Parts eleven and twelve will summarize and reflect on the personalist theory presented in this chapter. Whether developed over time by a personalist judge reflecting on his world or by a scholar perhaps adopting the perspective of a judge as part of a thought experiment, a personalist theory is concerned with action and the relation of persons through the common action of the law.

It is appropriate then to begin this presentation of personalist theory in Part two with a central concept, the person, or the judge, as one who acts.

2. Action

Oliver Wendell Holmes, Jr., in The Path of the Law, described law as a well-known profession which we practice.[13] About a hundred years later in *The Problems of Jurisprudence*, Richard Posner insisted that law is action.[14] There is then a continuing tradition in American Pragmatism that law is human action, a profession, practice, decision making.

---

13. Oliver Wendell Holmes, Jr., *The Path of the Law,* 10 HARV. L. REV. 457, 461 (1897).

14. *See,* POSNER, *supra* note 12 at 225.

Pragmatism, here, contrasts with the alternate tradition associated with Langdell, with H. L. A. Hart, and with Dworkin that law is a system of rules.[15]

Personalism has a vision of law more deeply grounded but essentially the same as American Pragmatism. John Macmurray in *The Self As Agent* describes the person as one who acts.[16] In *Persons in Relation* he explains that persons are best understood as acting together.[17]

Modern philosophy may be described as beginning with Reneé Descartes' *cogito ergo sum*, I think therefore I am.[18] That formula, or perhaps that flash of insight, locates the thinker as an isolated individual. In contrast, personalism emphasizes action rather than thought. Reflection or thought is for the sake of action. To make thought primary rather than secondary in our self-understanding isolates us from the world, from relations with others, and in our philosophical history puts in question the existence of others and the external world. Action, however, involves relations between persons, and with the physical objects which impede or advance our action. Macmurray insists that persons are understood best in relation to the other persons.[19] Communication, for example, which is so important to our self-understanding and to the development of our thought, is an interpersonal phenomenon. Society is a set of interrelations or common actions. It is difficult to understand ourselves absent our relations with others and the common actions which we perform with them. In the preface to *Persons in Relation*, Macmurray explains:

> "The effect of transferring the centre of reference to action, and at the same time its sufficient justification, is that man recovers his body and becomes personal. When he is conceived as agent, all of his activities, including his reflective activities, fall naturally into place in a functional unity. Even his emotions, in-

---

15. See H.L.A. HART, THE CONCEPT OF LAW 77–96 (1961) (Offering a definition of law as a union of primary rules of obligation and secondary rules of recognition, change, and adjudication); but *see* DWORKIN, LAW'S EMPIRE, *supra* note 8 (Where Dworkin argues that law is more properly perceived as a system of rules and principles).

16. *See* MACMURRAY, THE SELF AS AGENT, *supra* note 1.

17. *See* MACMURRAY, PERSONS IN RELATION, *supra* note 1.

18. *See* RENE DESCARTES, MEDITATIONS ON FIRST PHILOSOPHY (George Heffernan ed. & trans., 1990).

19. *See* MACMURRAY, PERSONS IN RELATION, *supra* note 1 and MACMURRAY, THE SELF AS AN AGENT, *supra* note 1.

stead of disturbances to the placidity of thought, take their place as necessary motives which sustain his activities, including his activity of thinking. For our present purpose, however, the result which concerns us especially is that it ends the solitariness of the 'thinking self', sets man firmly in the world he knows, and so restores him to his proper existence as a community of persons in relation. It is the purpose of this book to show how the personal relation of persons is constitutive of personal existence; that there can be no man until there are at least two men in communication."[20]

In law defining the person as one who acts and society as acting together would lead us with Holmes to understanding law as a profession which we practice and to perceive the system of rules as a means of communication, an adjunct and aid to action. "Defining the person as one who acts provides a foundation for exploring the decision-making method of the judge as one who acts and decides."[21] In American jurisprudence, including that of Ronald Dworkin whose ideal jurist, Judge Hercules, is an analytic giant, thinkers traditionally have concentrated on the judge, his role, his decision making process, how to predict his decisions and how he ought to decide.

For a theory of personalism in law a focus on the judge as one who acts and decides offers a number of advantages. Historically in American thought it has invited an examination of the judge's decision making process. Our sophisticated, philosophically inclined judge, recognizing himself as one who acts and decides, reasonably would respond by an introspective analysis of his own decision making process. He should recognize that this turn to himself as subject implies that he is a person reflecting on how he makes his decisions, that is, how he acts towards others, those affected by his decisions. As one who acts or decides he is related to others through his actions. An important step for personalism in law is to relate a critical understanding of method to Macmurray's theory of personalism which offers an analysis of persons related through action. Our philosophically inclined judge introspectively reflecting on his own decision making process is on the verge of discovering such a critical analysis of method. That moment of discovery provides an opportunity to explore the relation between legal rules and principles and persons. As I have argued previously: "An important task in American legal theory is to relate abstract principles grounded, as

---

20. *See* MacMurray, Persons In Relation, *supra* note 1 at 12.
21. *See* Donnelly, *Towards a Personalist Jurisprudence, supra* note 6 at 554.

Dworkin recommends, in friendship or deep respect and concern for the other, to a more concrete understanding of human persons acting together in real life situations. The personalist understanding of the judge as a person in relation to other persons through his actions and who should appropriate his own decision-making method through introspective analysis, provides an opportunity for exploring the relationship between abstract principles and concrete interpersonal relations."[22]

A focus on the judge as actor provides a further advantage for personalism in law. A judge who perceives herself as a person whose decision making process is worth examining is more likely to perceive others as persons including the parties in cases. In action, as Macmurray explains, one cannot understand oneself as isolated.[23] Action always is in relation to some person or something. Macmurray contends that one who acts, for example, by intentionally touching an object will encounter resistance and will perceive the object which is resisting. As one who intends the action he will perceive himself as a subject. By experimenting he will perceive that at times the resistance he encounters is intentional and therefore by analogy to his own action is the resistance of a subject. When engaged in some action he will perceive himself as an actor and a subject and himself as the object of another subject. Interacting with others he can understand himself as both subject and object; he can characterize himself as both "I," the one who acts, and as "You," the object of another's action. In action, including the action of a judge persons are perceived and given together. In action between persons there is an I and a You, persons or subjects who understand one another as acting intentionally while they are objects of each other's acts.[24] Macmurray remarks:

> "We know existence by participating in existence. This participation is action. When we expend energy to realize an intention we meet a resistance which both supports and limits us, and know that we exist and that the Other exists, and that our existence depends upon the existence of the Other."[25]

Central to a theory of personalism in law, then, is an understanding of the judge as one who acts and who understands himself through his

---

22. *Id.*

23. *Id.* at 554–55; referring to MACMURRAY, PERSONS IN RELATION, *supra* note 1 at 64–85.

24. Donnelly, *Towards a Personalist Jurisprudence, supra* note 6 at 555; referring to MACMURRAY, PERSONS IN RELATION, *supra* note 1 at 27–28.

25. *Id.*; quoting MACMURRAY, PERSONS IN RELATION, *supra* note 1 at 16–17.

action as a person in relation to other persons. Reflection on method, then, is reflection on action, and on action which relates persons. The personalist emphasis on action will join personalist jurisprudential thought to the mainstream of American legal philosophy with its central focus on the judge and his decision making process. It would lead a personalist thinker to consider law primarily as an activity and only secondarily as a system of rules. That activity is an ongoing action which relates persons in society.

Our philosophically inclined judge reflecting on his own decision making method should then critique and improve that method because it is action which relates and affects persons.

3. The Quarrel over Method: A Role for the Person

Our philosophically inclined judge reflecting on his own decision making process as action relating persons would appropriately begin to read voraciously thereby entering into conversation with the common law tradition and those who have examined it philosophically. Reading in the history of American jurisprudence he would encounter what we have described as the great quarrel over method.

Modern method, he would find, begins with the late nineteenth century effort to organize the common law around principles and rules and hence with the confrontation between those two important laborers in that field, Oliver Wendell Holmes, Jr. and Christopher Columbus Langdell. We have reviewed in the last chapter the contrast between their two opposing visions, law as a closed logical system, and law as action centered on the judge, a well-known profession which we practice. From his personalist base our philosophically inclined judge already has made his choice between those two visions. Law understood as a system of rules is secondary and in service of law as action.

During the 1920s and 1930s Holmes' followers, the American Pragmatists in law laid the foundation for the triumph of pragmatic instrumentalist method during the 1950s in such cases as *Brown v. Board of Education of Topeka, Kansas*.[26] Both Karl Llewellyn and Roscoe Pound, despite their differences, were important in that development. Roscoe

---

26. Brown v. Board of Education of Topeka, Kansas, 347 U.S. 483, (1954).

Pound's social engineering gave us such devices as impact and interest analysis which could help a judge understand and assess how people and their interests are affected by his decisions. Like Holmes, Pound believed that judges should address social advantage. In contrast, legal realists such as Llewellyn and Jerome Frank wanted to predict what courts would in fact do. Llewellyn distinguished paper rules including statutes, opinions and restatements from real rules which were the prophesies of what courts would do.[27] Having accepted the predictive point of view of Holmes, Llewellyn and Frank found that judges were hard to predict because like all of us they are strange human beings affected by their political, social and cultural backgrounds and perhaps by weird quirks. Moving from the critical mode of their youth to what could be described as a more mature creative mode Llewellyn and Frank began to develop methods for judicial decision making rather than means for predicting judicial action.[28] Llewellyn offered his understanding of the grand style of the common law with its emphasis on case by case development of law and openness to sense, reason and results. A judge using the grand style should employ situation sense, a concrete assessment of the parties' circumstances and relations in determining whether rules from previous cases should apply analogously to the changed patterns of human relations he finds in the dispute before him.[29] Jerome Frank contrasted the flat law of formalism with three dimensional law where a fully human judge uses the rule and language element to address the complex human relations in the situation before him.[30]

Reflecting on American Pragmatism in law during the early twentieth century our personalist judge would be struck by the conscious emphasis on methods for judicial decision making, Pound's social engineering with his impact and interest analysis, Llewellyn's grand style and situation sense, Frank's three dimensional law. He also would be struck by the realist discovery that judges are human, a phenomenon

---

27. *See* Karl Llewellyn, *A Realist Jurisprudence — The Next Step,* 30 COLUM. L. REV. 431 (1930).

28. *See* Donnelly, *Book Review, supra* note 9 at 901; referring to KARL LLEWELLYN, THE COMMON LAW TRADITION: DECIDING APPEALS 213 (1960); and Frank, *supra* note 9 at 247, 292, 316.

29. *See id.* at 906; referring to Karl Llewellyn, *On the Current Recapture of the Grand Tradition,* 9 U. CHI. L.S. RECORD 6 (1960*),* KARL LLEWELLYN, JURISPRUDENCE 215, 222 (1962), and LLEWELLYN, THE COMMON LAW TRADITION, *supra* note 28 at 268.

30. *See* Frank, *supra* note 9 at 146–56.

they may have stumbled into during their youth while attempting to predict judicial decisions. When Frank became a judge of the Second Circuit and Llewellyn, the principal drafter of the Uniform Commercial Code arguably their point of view shifted from the perspective of one predicting court decisions to that of the lawmaker. From that new point of view they sought to account for a human judge wrestling with human problems. Llewellyn's grand style and situation sense could be described as an effort to create method or craftsmanship for such a judge.[31]

For our philosophically inclined personalist judge this would be a high point in reviewing the great quarrel over method. The legal realist explicit discovery of and emphasis on the human dimensions of law must be appropriated in personalist theory and incorporated in personalist decision making method. An important aspect of this realist achievement is the connection between the discovery that judges are human and the creation of decision making method. Our personalist judge would be impressed by and would want to imitate and perhaps copy that connection between method and the humanity of a judge grappling with human problems.

Continuing to follow the great quarrel over method our philosophically inclined judge would recognize the reaction during the late 50s and 60s as found in Herbert Wechsler's desire for neutral principles,[32] the Hart and Sacks analysis of Legal Process[33] and H. L. A. Hart's effort to incorporate pragmatist insights into an understanding of law as a dynamic system of open textured rules.[34] The criticism of American Pragmatism in law culminates in Ronald Dworkin's argument that pragmatist method is not capable of taking legal rights seriously.[35]

Since Dworkin's criticism of pragmatism in law is grounded partially in foundations shared by personalism a personalist judge must consider that analysis. Dworkin would ground his understanding of law in political friendship or in equal respect and concern for each person. In *Law's Empire*, he challenges legal pragmatism because it is unable to take legal

---

31. *See* Donnelly, *Book Review, supra* note 9 at 905–06.

32. *See generally* Herbert Wechsler, *Toward Neutral Principles of Constitutional Law,*73 HARV. L. REV. 1 (1959).

33. *See generally* HENRY HART, JR. & ALBERT SACKS, THE LEGAL PROCESS: BASIC PROBLEMS IN THE MAKING AND APPLICATION OF LAW (William Eskridge, Jr. & Philip Frickey eds. 1994).

34. *See generally* HART, THE CONCEPT OF LAW, *supra* note 15.

35. *See* DWORKIN, LAW'S EMPIRE, *supra* note 8 at 151–75.

rights seriously.[36] That alleged inability to respect legal rights was reviewed and assessed in the last chapter. There it was argued that pragmatists in law because they reject overarching theory are unable to ground their attention to persons in a fundamental respect and concern for each person. Dworkin argues, perhaps inaccurately, that because pragmatic decision makers want decisions and rules which are the best for the future, they pay lip service to legal rights, treating them only "as-if" they exist.[37] Rather, the lack of overarching theory and fundamental principle in pragmatic thought makes it difficult to provide a firm foundation for the great rights and the principles which reflect our great ideals. Dworkin's method provides a stronger foundation for the great rights. Nevertheless, as argued in the last chapter, his rigid theoretical development of law prevents his ideal Judge Hercules from affording actual persons deep respect and concern.

In the last chapter a garden variety judge committed to respect and concern for each person encountered in greater detail the contrast just sketched between pragmatic instrumentalism and Ronald Dworkin. In conversation with current thought regarding the common law tradition it was argued that a judge committed to persons preliminarily would reconstruct his decision making by combining those aspects of pragmatic instrumentalist and Dworkian method that related best to respect and concern for persons. Our more philosophically inclined personalist judge would accept that conclusion at the same preliminary stage for similar reasons. Having read voraciously and entered into conversation with American jurisprudence and the common law tradition he would find that reconstruction the best currently available method. As explained earlier in this part he would discover in the course of his reading the great quarrel over method. Because method related to understanding and respecting persons would be important to him he would engage in the reconstruction described in chapter 2.

While engaged in conversation with American jurisprudence our philosophically inclined judge also would encounter what David Granfield has described as the piecemeal recovery of a role for the person in law.[38] In reaction to Langdellian formalism, the tradition of American

---

36. *See id.* at 206–15; *see also* RONALD DWORKIN, TAKING RIGHTS SERIOUSLY 272–78 (1977).

37. *See* DWORKIN, LAW'S EMPIRE, *supra* note 8 at 154–55.

38. *See* Samuel J.M. Donnelly, *Book Review*, 36 AM. J. OF JURIS. 239 (1991), referring to DAVID GRANFIELD, THE INNER EXPERIENCE OF LAW: A JURISPRUDENCE OF SUBJECTIVITY 20–29, 33–35 (1988).

Pragmatism in law, although not exclusively, has been responsible for much of that recovery. A review of our sketch in this part of the quarrel over method would reveal a number of instances. Again the high point in recovering a role for the person would be the Legal Realist recognition that judges are human. They made this discovery while attempting to predict, but later from the perspective of the law maker began to develop methods for a human judge to use law to relate to situations with complex human relationships. Dworkin's grounding of principles in political friendship, however, represents a further stage in the piecemeal recovery of a role for the person in law. The Critical Legal Studies movement which has claimed the Legal Realists as intellectual ancestors also represents a further stage in that recovery. Influenced by post-modern thought as well as by Existentialism and American Pragmatism, the Critical Legal Studies Movement, emphasized and gave new depth to our understanding of the multiple influences on a judge's decision making process and on the difficulties of attributing an explicit meaning to a legal text. With a desire for reform, perhaps radical reform, the Crits argued that our law and judicial decisions reflected not only our political, social and cultural background but the interests of the dominant classes in society. Law could be described as reflecting an ideology grounded in those dominant interests. Deconstruction as employed by the Crits was designed not only to demonstrate that ideological bias but to show that law is malleable. Law, according to the Crits, can and ought to be molded and reshaped for political purposes to new ideological goals, to avoid oppression and to promote the cause of humanity.[39]

As those influenced by the Critical Legal Studies movement proliferated and developed into separate ideological groups including Feminism and those concerned with Critical Race Studies it became apparent that their insights were helpful in understanding how law impacted various groups in society, and how those groups as well as the dominant tradition perceived law.[40]

Since he is committed to understanding and respecting persons, our philosophically inclined judge reflecting on the great quarrel over

---

39. See SAMUEL J. M. DONNELLY, THE LANGUAGE AND USES OF RIGHTS: A BIOPSY OF AMERICAN JURISPRUDENCE IN THE TWENTIETH CENTURY 5–6 (1994), referring to Kennedy, *supra* note 7; Roberto Unger, *The Critical Legal Studies Movement*, 96 HARV. L. REV. 563 (1983).

40. *See* for example Robin West, *Jurisprudence and Gender*, 55 U. CHI. L. REV. 1 (1988); MARTHA MINNOW, MAKING ALL THE DIFFERENCE: INCLUSION, EXCLUSION, AND AMERICAN LAW (1990).

method would recognize the need to account for the insights of Ronald Dworkin and the Critical Legal Studies Movement in framing his own method for judicial decision making.

At the end of the twentieth and the beginning of the twenty-first centuries a personalist reconstruction of judicial decision making method would begin with the combination of personalist insights from pragmatic instrumentalist and Dworkian method described in chapter 2. Beyond that his reflections on the continuing quarrel over method, on perception, language and general intellectual method would lead our philosophically inclined judge to add a series of distinctively personalist elements, concepts and insights to his decision making method. The next several parts of this chapter will discuss several of those insights and concepts culminating in part seven with a personalist critique and critical analysis of method. Next in part four, the concept of horizons and its role in a personalist understanding of method will be presented. The metaphor of horizons and methods for crossing horizons will account at least in part for the problems of perception and oppression called to our attention by the Critical Legal Studies movement and will be a basis for a personalist methodological response to those problems.

4. Horizons

Horizons is a concept and a metaphor employed by such thinkers as Heidegger, Gadamer and Lonergan to reflect on our limited knowledge and understanding and our encounter with other cultural contexts.[41] It is relevant when discussing how to interpret texts including a Shakespearean play or the United States Constitution. A modern scholar attempting to understand an ancient text should recognize that the horizon in which it was originally produced or read was different than his own.

Horizons as a metaphor draws on a physical analog, the circle that marks the limit of our vision when we gaze around and across the land-

---

41. *See* Donnelly, *Towards a Personalist Jurisprudence, supra* note 1 at 572, referring to MARTIN M. HEIDIGGER, IDENTITY AND DIFFERENCE 34–35 (J. Stamburgh trans. 1969), and DAVID TRACY, THE ACHIEVEMENT OF BERNARD LONERGAN 104–32 (1970) (much of the following passage is adapted from *Towards a Personalist Jurisprudence*).

scape.[42] From my office window at Syracuse University where I teach I can see the circle of small hills which surround our modest sized Central New York city. The hills lie on the horizon, the limit of my vision. About a half hour drive beyond those hills one may find Skaneateles Lake where I have spent some pleasant summer days. Skaneateles is a splendid jewel, one of the Finger Lakes, a remains of the glaciers which covered Central New York during the Ice Age. In the summer by the lake my mood, my surroundings, my activities are different than in the city, or at the university. While at the lake I cannot see the university or the city; my physical horizons and correspondingly my cultural horizons are different. At the university I cannot see the lake although I have fond memories. Perhaps more significantly I can take my car from the University parking lot and drive to the lake. I can cross from one physical horizon to another. At the same time my vision, what I can see, will change as indeed will my mood and my outlook on life.

Our philosophically inclined judge could use the metaphor, horizons, to reflect on his own extensive experience. Metaphorically he has crossed many horizons in his lifetime. He has traveled and encountered foreign cultures. During his junior year in college he studied in Paris and mastered a new language. College itself took him from his small city to a wider arena. He studied literature, philosophy and economics. Each introduced him to worlds he was not familiar with before. During his first year of law school he found himself in a very strange world which he gradually mastered. Later in practice he mastered the foreign horizons of several industries.

As one becomes familiar with new cultural or intellectual horizons one understands practices, ideas, ways of doing things that one did not understand or perhaps was unaware of before. Horizons, however, both create and confine vision. During law school our judge gradually lost interest in areas that excited his curiosity during college. One heavily engaged in economics or holding a highly structured moral theory may have difficulty recognizing or raising policy or moral questions not covered by one's theory. Horizons are the result of past achievements and may allow a person to see problems, ask questions and pursue answers which others would not see, ask or pursue. Likewise one's horizon may conceal issues, outlooks, explorations which would excite persons with

---

42. *See id.* at 573, quoting LONERGAN, METHOD IN THEOLOGY, *supra* note 1 at 235–36.

other horizons. A tax lawyer unless he is a tax litigator may profess ignorance of and a profound lack of interest in a question of evidence which would fascinate a trial lawyer. Some lawyers would not pursue articles describing a new discovery in particle physics while scientists may ignore with pleasure a recent United States Supreme Court decision. "Horizons then are the sweep of our intersts [sic] and of our knowledge; they are the fertile source of further knowledge and care; but they also are the boundaries that limit our capacities for assimilating more than we already have attained."[43]

Our philosophically inclined judge reflecting on his own extensive experience would find the metaphor of horizons helpful in perceiving the limitations of his own knowledge and perceptions. Being committed as a personalist to respect and concern for persons and to the attempt to understand them and their circumstances, he would desire to cross horizons. On a previous occasion I argued:

> "A judge who wants to take rights seriously will provide means in his decision making methodology for both transcending and crossing horizons. Horizons are established by various processes for learning, by the devices and techniques which accompany these processes, and by the information and ways of acting which are the results of their use. Horizons can be transcended or crossed by using similar learning processes to establish new, different, or more encompassing horizons and may be accompanied by techniques for restraining the vision-blocking characteristics of one's present horizons."[44]

One may cross horizons in the same way as one establishes them. Physically one can go there, fly to Paris, take a car to the summer cottage on the lake. Intellectually one can study economics, philosophy or anthropology. A judge familiar from his practice with several industries may cross with his acquired skill and understanding into the horizon of a new industry with the help of counsel perhaps with the aid of Brandeis briefs. Transcending horizons differs from crossing:

> "A higher theory, including a higher moral theory, may provide one with a broader view which would include both accep-

---

43. *See id.* at 574, quoting LONERGAN, METHOD IN THEOLOGY, *supra* note 1 at 254, n.250.

44. *See id.* at 575, quoting Samuel J. M. Donnelly, *Principles, Persons, and Horizons: A Friendly Analysis of What Dworkin Has Overlooked*, 26 ST. LOUIS U. L.J. 217, 256–260 (1982).

tance of one's own previous theoretical or moral views and those of others. When a judge with a particular political, moral, or cultural background puts on the judicial robe and mounts the bench, he may perceive a duty of fairness to those with other backgrounds which he would not have accepted as readily before his appointment to the judiciary. The new judge with a commitment to fairness has transcended his previous horizons. It also would be helpful if he would cross horizons by enlarging his understanding of the great variety of human situations."[45]

Crossing or transcending horizons, of course, may establish new horizons which both will create and confine vision. A judge who studies Immanuel Kant or Ronald Dworkin like Judge Hercules may develop a comprehensive vision of life and law which will transcend previous political, social or cultural horizons but which may prevent him from understanding the concrete problems of some litigants. A personalist judge then must have a method which provides for repeatedly crossing horizons.

One should recognize that there is a philosophical dispute concerning our ability to cross horizons. Gadamer argues that a historian interpreting a text from the past cannot fully recapture the horizon of the author; ultimately his own horizon merges with his attempts to understand the past.[46] Others would contend that we can never fully cross into the horizons of a foreign culture. As Rudyard Kipling put it "east is east and west is west and ne'er the twain shall meet."[47] Nevertheless it is apparent that in our complex culture we regularly cross at least partially into unfamiliar horizons. Litigation lawyers, for example, often make an effort to understand medicine and the practice of physicians.

In the pragmatic instrumentalist tradition as described in chapter 2, Pound, Llewellyn and others have developed decision making techniques which could be described as methods for crossing horizons. These would include impact and interest analysis and situation sense. Deconstruction, that favorite device of the Critical Legal Studies Movement, could be described as a means for breaking down established horizons and overcoming their vision blocking effects.

Reflecting on his own limited knowledge and understanding our philosophically inclined personalist judge would recognize the need to cross and transcend horizons. Because he is committed to respect and

---

45. *See id. at 577.*
46. ROUTLEDGE ENCYCLOPEDIA OF PHILOSOPHY 828–30 (Edward Craig, ed., 1998)
47. *See* Rudyard Kipling, The Ballad of the East and West.

concern for persons and to the attempt to understand them and their interests he would provide means for crossing horizons as a regular feature of his decision making method.

Part five will illustrate the manner in which horizon crossing techniques can be incorporated with decision making method while discussing the role of principles.

5. Principles

American legal thought and indeed general intellectual method has been ambivalent towards the role of principles in decision making. Oliver Wendell Holmes, Jr. expressed the unease of American thought regarding principles in a letter to Sir Frederick Pollock: "I always say that the chief end of man is to frame general propositions but that no proposition is worth a damn."[48]

In our present understanding of the common law tradition, one normally could define a principle as a policy theme running through a series of cases. That definition of principle was accepted and used in chapter 2, our conversation with the common law tradition. Principles, however, also reflect the great ideals of our society. The principles of justice as described by John Rawls are great ethical ideals or commitments.[49] Immanuel Kant's categorical imperative, act in such a way that you could wish all persons would act in the same way, is a fundamental ethical principle.[50] Ronald Dworkin's principle, afford all persons equal respect and concern, resembles it.[51]

Our philosophically inclined personalist judge would encounter the dispute over principles during his review of the great quarrel over method. Because he is committed to respect and concern for all persons he would honor principles which reflect that commitment or the ideals derived from it. He would recognize the important role of principles in

---

48. See Donnelly, *Book Review, supra* note 9 at 239, referring to GRANFIELD, *supra* note 32 at 10–11, quoting Holmes-Pollock Letters vol. 2, p. 59 (M. Howe ed. 1961).

49. *See generally* JOHN RAWLS, A THEORY OF JUSTICE (1971).

50. *See* IMMANUEL KANT, THE METAPHYSICAL ELEMENTS OF JUSTICE 100 (J. Ladd trans. 1965) (For a discussion of the categorical imperative in the context of crime and punishment.).

51. *See* DWORKIN, TAKING RIGHTS SERIOUSLY, *supra* note 36 at 177–83.

ethical discourse. Likewise, as noted in chapter 2, he would understand and accept the organizing role which principles serve in modern, post-Langdellian common law.

Principles, however, have the power to create horizons particularly when used systematically and rigorously. An insight incorporated in a principle has the capacity to attract attention or command support and to allow us to perceive a moral or policy issue more clearly. By focusing attention a principle also has the capacity to divert us from other factors relevant to a decision. Principles which establish horizons can block as well as create vision.

Ronald Dworkin's proposed method explained first in *Taking Rights Seriously* and then modestly revised in *Law's Empire* would attract our philosophically inclined personalist judge because it offers a principled interpretation of law grounded in political friendship or equal respect and concern for each person. As argued in the last chapter, however, Judge Hercules' rigid principled decision making would prevent him from addressing or understanding the actual needs of the parties who appear before him. Now it can be argued that Hercules' consistent theory of constitutional or statutory interpretation, and common law development, with the rigidity required by Dworkin under his interpretation of law as Integrity, creates a horizon which confines vision. Hercules' theory may allow him to transcend his political, social and cultural horizons. The theory, itself, however, establishes a new horizon. Because Dworkin has no place in his understanding of law for horizon crossing Judge Hercules often will ignore human interests and needs.

In this respect Dworkin resembles those who accept a political ideology which they desire to advance in all their judicial decisions. That political ideology may or may not be relevant to the needs and interests of the parties or others affected by the decision. An ideology can create a horizon which blocks vision while focusing perception. One who consciously holds an ideology and does not employ horizon crossing will ignore human needs and interests. This will be true even if one accepts an ideology for the purpose of promoting the cause of humanity.

Reflecting on the common law tradition and his own decision making process our philosophically inclined personalist judge would recognize both the relation of the principles to important ideals and their vision blocking characteristics. His understanding of horizons would contribute to his perception of the problem and would offer a potential solution. Principled decision making, when relevant, must be coupled with the deliberate use of horizon crossing devices.

Pragmatic instrumentalists such as Pound or Llewellyn could be described as inventors of horizon crossing techniques. Pound's social engineering included a role for impact and interest analysis. Chapter 2 argued that a personalist judge should join principled decision making with impact and interest analysis. After discussing the problem of horizons our philosophically inclined personalist judge would perceive impact and interest analysis as a means for crossing horizons. Before reaching a holding he should locate the relevant interests and assess the impact of his proposed holding on those interests. If a principle is applicable to a case, the judge could describe that principle as indicating that a relevant interest is important or protectable under the law. After weighing that interest against competing interests the judge will determine whether the principle should control his holding.

This combination of principled reasoning with interest analysis will prevent the principle from rigidly controlling the judge's vision or decision. Seeking out the relevant interests would be a way of inquiring into human needs in a foreign horizon.

Karl Llewellyn's situation sense had a role in his understanding of the grand style of the common law, a style of decision making emphasizing the traditional case by case development of law. A judge, Llewellyn contended, should understand the rule or holding of a previous case in relation to the type or life situation presented by the facts. He should size up the situation in the facts before him trying to describe them in terms of a recurrent pattern or type. If the reasons for applying the rule in the type situation of the previous case apply in the different although perhaps similar situation before him, then the rule should apply.

William Twining, in *Karl Llewellyn and The Legal Realist Movement*, offers an analysis and restatement of situation sense.[52] Through situation sense one can acquire an understanding of group relations, patterns of behavior and values. A judge, then, can use situation sense as a means for crossing into and trying to understand a foreign horizon, that of a different ethnic group, or of an unfamiliar industry, to offer two examples.

Our personalist judge learning from but not following Llewellyn's somewhat primitive grand style could use situation sense while developing a relevant principle. He should not use the principle as the gen-

---

52. *See* Donnelly, *Book Review, supra* note 9 at 907, referring to WILLIAM TWINING, KARL LLEWELLYN AND THE REALIST MOVEMENT 226–27 (1973).

eral premise of a syllogism. Rather he should examine the situation before him, attempting to understand the pattern of relations and then ask whether it makes sense to apply the principle. Perhaps he will decide that the principle is applicable but requires further development and adaptation.

Our personalist judge should use principles in conjunction with these or other horizon crossing techniques perhaps including in appropriate circumstances, deconstruction. Principles at times reflect our great national ideals. Rigorously and systematically applied principles, however, can lock a judge within a horizon. The use of interest analysis, situation sense or other horizon crossing methods in conjunction with the development or application of a principle could overcome the principle's vision blocking characteristics.

A dramatic event, a traumatic experience, a world shaking catastrophe could disturb our established understanding and enlarge or change our horizons. Richard Posner notes that a judge or the law may have a conversion experience.[53] Arguably the Second World War and the Holocaust changed our horizons and our principles sufficiently to allow the Supreme Court's decision in *Brown v. Board of Education of Topeka, Kansas*[54] and the subsequent desegregation movement. One can also imagine a slower, less dramatic conversion with its consequent change of horizons and principles.

As our personalist judge crosses multiple horizons and gathers experience he may discover deeper foundations for his previous principles but in contrast he may acquire a new vision. With his concern for the vision creating and vision blocking aspects of horizons, a personalist judge should be prepared to reassess his principles.

Continuing his introspective analysis of his own decision making experience our philosophically inclined personalist judge would encounter the phenomenon we will call "insight" but Llewellyn called "hunching" and Frank a lightening "gestalt."[55] Again, our judge would want to understand insight in relation to horizons and when reconstructing judicial method in relation to principles and to techniques for

---

53. *See* POSNER, *supra* note 12 at 148–50.

54. Brown v. Board of Education of Topeka, Kansas, 347 U.S. 483 (1954).

55. *See* Donnelly, *Book Review, supra* note 9, referring to Frank, *supra* note 9 at 165–85, 170–71, 175–79, and Hutcheson, *supra* note 10, and LLEWELLYN, THE COMMON LAW TRADITION, *supra* note 28 at 121, n. 154.

crossing horizons. Understanding insight and its role in method is the function of the next part.

6. Insight

Our philosophically inclined personalist judge introspectively reflecting on his experience of legal decision making would encounter the phenomenon we will call insight. At times when he is in a self-congratulatory mood he might call it "a flash of genius." When in practice he may have labored for several days over a brief searching for the argument that would persuade the court. Late one evening perhaps it all came together, a perception of a pattern in the facts or law around which the desired argument could be shaped. His delight and relief may be expressed by saying: "There it is, I see it." Being widely read he may recall the story about Archimedes, the Greek scientist who resided in the city of Syracuse on the island of Sicily. The Tyrant of Syracuse had asked him to find a test to determine whether a crown was composed of pure gold. While taking a bath Archimedes noticed that the water rose and fell as he moved about. With a flash of insight he saw that he could measure the displacement of water by the crown and compare the displacement by an equal quantity of pure gold. Instantaneously he emerged from the bath and ran naked through the streets of Syracuse exclaiming "Eureka." Our judge, when writing an opinion in a difficult case, may suddenly perceive a pattern or a solution and react in a similar although perhaps a more modest manner. Sometimes the flash of insight may occur on the bench while listening to oral argument.[56] David Granfield describes insight as follows:

> "What is insight? It is a bright idea, a snap judgment, a shrewd guess, a tentative understanding. Insights ground every kind of knowledge. But an insight should not be considered to be like seeing something; it is not literally an intuition. The naïve realist thinks that he looks at his experiences, the data of sense and consciousness, and then judges. But he leaves out an essential step, the insight, which occurs when the intelligence compre-

---

56. *See* Donnelly, *Towards a Personalist Jurisprudence, supra* note 1 at 559 (much of the following passage is adapted from *Towards a Personalist Jurisprudence*).

hends in the data some kind of coherence, when the data begins to make sense, to evidence a possibility, to suggest a meaning. An insight as such is unverified and unproved, it may be wrong but its plausible. It is like love at first sight, perhaps an infatuation but perhaps the beginning of a lifelong commitment."[57]

One can agree with Granfield that the moment of brilliant insight, the sudden perception of a pattern in the data should not be the moment of judgment. In science a process of verification should follow the insight, or scientific breakthrough. A theory may be a series of related insights and concepts. Formulation of the theory would be a further step. In science it should be formulated with a view to its falsifiability. There should be a way to determine if the theory is wrong, perhaps on the basis of future discoveries. Likewise in law we should be hesitant to move immediately from the insight to the judgment. There should be a checking out stage.

Jerome Frank inspired by Gestalt Psychology believed that we think in patterns.[58] Like our philosophically inclined judge he recognized a phenomenon he called a lightening gestalt, the sudden perception of a pattern in the facts or law. The judge's perception, Frank argued, would be influenced by his political, social or cultural background, by his relations with his father or perhaps by the bad cup of coffee he had for breakfast. In any event, a disciplined judge should restrain his perception of a pattern in the facts or law until he had adequately studied the case.

Karl Llewellyn called the same phenomenon "hunching."[59] He associated it with what he called "horse sense," the uncommon common sense of one experienced in horse trading. Such an experienced horse trader, or commercial judge may perceive a pattern based on his experience in horse trading or with particular industries. Llewellyn would further associate that hunching with situation sense, the ability to search out and understand commercial patterns or perhaps the ways in which human beings interrelate in life situations. Like Jerome Frank he would recommend restraining one's perception of legal patterns before attempting to understand the human situation.

---

57. See id., referring to LONERGAN, INSIGHT: A STUDY OF HUMAN UNDERSTANDING, supra note 1 at 3–6.

58. See FRANK, supra note 9 at 170–71.

59. See generally LLEWELLYN, THE COMMON LAW TRADITION, supra note 28.

Duncan Kennedy, in "Freedom and Constraint in Adjudication: A Critical Phenomenology," while examining his stream of consciousness in the course of deciding an imaginary case, reports a phenomenon he calls "breakthrough."[60] As he reports that experience it appears to resemble the gestalt, the hunch, the insight. He too recommends checking out this insight against the caselaw rather than moving immediately to judgment.

Being familiar with his own limited knowledge and understanding, our philosophically inclined personalist judge would recognize that his insights, his sudden creative perceptions, occur within the context of his horizons. Possibly some insights happen while he is consciously crossing horizons or inquiring into foreign horizons. In that event the insight may provide a clue to patterns in the strange horizon. Because his perceptions are affected by his established horizons our judge would establish a disciplined method for crossing horizons and for checking out insights.

A legal principle or a legal theory could be described as a connected series of related concepts and insights.[61] As in scientific method, there ought to be a process for checking out a legal principle or theory. As argued in the last part a personalist judge would find a relation between some principles and our great national ideals. Principles, however, and legal theories are developed within horizons and may themselves establish horizons. One process for checking out principles would be to couple their application on a case by case basis with horizon crossing techniques such as interest analysis and situation sense. As the judge uses that process in the course of settling disputes he will be continually checking out his principles and theories. He will continually cross horizons and reassess his positions. In this manner he will replicate in his own decision making process Holmes' conclusion that the life of the law has not been logic but experience.[62]

As our judge is introspectively examining his experience and discovering the relation between insight, principles, theory and horizons he is consciously reconstructing his decision making method. A further stage in that reconstruction would be the development of a theory and process for the critical examination of judicial decision making

---

60. *See* Kennedy, *supra* note 7 at 518, 525.

61. *See* Donnelly, *Towards a Personalist Jurisprudence, supra* note 1 at 564, referring to TRACY, *supra* note 41 at 67–68, 235.

62. *See* Holmes, Jr., *supra* note 11 at 5.

method. Discussion of that critical examination is the function of the next part.

7. Critique of Method

Reviewing his own experience, our philosophically inclined judge would recognize that the great quarrel over method is not merely an aspect of twentieth century legal history it is one of the principal features of our modern intellectual landscape. Some thinkers favor mathematics or logic, others emphasize scientific method perhaps as more loosely applied in the social sciences. A large number want to resolve all problems by economic analysis. Some are skeptical of all forms of reason.

In law we quarrel about our own explicitly legal methods but also about the methods proposed to us by logic, philosophy, the social sciences and literature. We also encounter the imperialism of some methods, for example, the insistence that law is logic, or that all questions are economic and resolvable by economic analysis.

Our judge would conclude that the proliferation of methods, both legal and non-legal, is a major source of confusion not only in law but in modern intellectual life. Because he recognizes that a method can create a horizon, he would be grateful that he is familiar with several methods and not dominated by one approach to intellectual analysis. He also would recognize that he has acquired, often by hard work, most of the specialized intellectual methods he is acquainted with.

As a young person, particularly in the early years before school, he learned a great deal but he did not use consciously any of the specialized methods. In learning to talk, walk, ride a bike, swim, feed himself, relate to others and become acquainted with the world he made progress by acting, by trying to do things, by interaction with others, by gauging their reaction to his clumsy attempts. This fundamental methodology could be described as common sense method, a means of learning by the self-correcting process of living. In *Persons In Relation*, John Macmurray describes a similar process of learning and relating to the world through action and interaction, through touching and experimenting.[63]

---

63. *See* Donnelly, *Towards a Personalist Jurisprudence, supra* note 1 at 554–55, referring to MACMURRAY, PERSONS IN RELATION, *supra* note 1 at 64–85.

One could argue that all other methods are verified into our common sense. From a common sense perspective specialized methods are valuable to the extent that they serve action, interrelations and curiosity. A successful track record in the field a method is designed to serve would lead one to have confidence in the particular conclusions of the method. From a common sense perspective one could recognize that a method has mixed success leading one to have confidence but not great confidence in its conclusions.

Common sense itself has a mixed record. One who uses only common sense may have difficulty crossing and transcending horizons. In previous ages a person using common sense may have reached conclusions we now recognize as wrong. The classic example is the assertion that the world is flat. One reason for creating more specialized methods is to allow us to cross and transcend horizons. In modern times, an experienced educated person would have some understanding of several specialized methods and would have crossed a number of horizons. When that person uses his common sense he can draw on his wide experience, his knowledge of the capacities of more specialized methods and input from their conclusions. We can speak now of a sophisticated common sense which can utilize other methods and their input to reach common sense conclusions. Such a sophisticated common sense method would have some understanding of the limitations as well as the advantages of more specialized methods.

One function of chapter 5 is to examine briefly whether this account of method would survive epistemological scrutiny. Those who desire absolute certainty in order to trust knowledge and who recognize that being immersed in horizons we have no vantage point to make a judgment with absolute certainty would question it. Contrarywise those impressed with the track records of many specialized methods and who seek sufficient emergent probability to justify action and commitment may find the analysis of method helpful.

One could find this analysis of method particularly useful when discussing judicial decision making. Law is an artificial construct designed to coordinate and provide a framework for human interaction. Judicial decision making addresses that construct and human interaction. As maintained in chapter 2 one can argue that it is best understood as dispute settlement. While a number of disciplines are relevant we best understand human interaction and frameworks for it by using our common sense. Law then as well as other disciplines such as history, theology, and horse trading can be described as a specialized common sense method. The view that more specialized methods inform our modern common sense works well with law and contributes to resolving our methodological puzzles. Law then can be described as a sophisticated, specialized common sense method.

When evaluating any particular judicial decision making method a judge would ask such questions as: (1) whether it has a good fit with his self-understanding as a person related to others through action; (2) whether it fits well with his introspective analysis of his own intellectual process; (3) whether it serves the purported functions of the relevant activities, or what he is attempting to do—here settle disputes within the legal system; (4) whether it comports with his sense and understanding of obligation, and (5) whether it will promote the legitimacy of his decisions.

Before answering those questions our personalist judge would review briefly and summarize the reconstructed method. In chapter 2 we argued that a personalist judge would combine the personalist elements of pragmatic-instrumentalist and Dworkinian method. Using that preliminary reconstruction for method the judge would develop the more particular methods described in chapter 2 for deciding common law cases and those concerned with statutory interpretation. One example would be the use of principled reasoning in conjunction with interest analysis. Because he is committed to respect and concern for persons and the attempt to understand their interests and situations, a personalist judge in conversation with the common law tradition and its current practice will be able to reconstruct method by combining those elements which are related to his commitment. At the end of the twentieth and the beginning of the twenty-first centuries the personalist melding of Dworkian and pragmatic instrumentalist method would provide in his view the best basic outline of judicial decision making method.

In this chapter the personalist judge has reflected introspectively on his own intellectual process and on judicial decision making method. In the course of that reflection he has recognized the importance of understanding and critically analyzing method, the role that horizons play in his understanding and the importance of crossing horizons, the intellectual importance of principles but also their relation to horizons and the serious need to relate principled reasoning to method for crossing horizons, the sudden flash of insight and the manner in which that relates to theory, principles and such techniques for crossing horizons as situation sense. In chapter 2 he began reconstructing judicial method while conversing with the common law tradition. In this chapter while engaged in introspective analysis of his own decision making and intellectual process, he has been able to deepen his understanding of that preliminary reconstruction and to relate it to insight, horizons and the serious need to cross horizons. Principled reasoning he recognizes must be related to insight and to methods for crossing horizons.

When evaluating his emerging method he would recognize that his introspective reflection has provided reasons for believing that his method (1) does fit well with his self-understanding as a person related to others through action, and (2) with his review of his own intellectual process. He continues to recognize himself as a person of limited although growing knowledge and understanding. The role he has established for horizons and horizon crossing methods in his decision making process comports well with his understanding of his limitations. He recognizes his flashes of insight and his inclination to act on them immediately and likewise the dominating psychological or logical power of principle. It is necessary then to relate his principled and other legal reasoning to horizon crossing. He can accomplish that by melding pragmatic instrumentalist and Dworkian method. That reconstructed method will be a disciplined means of relating his action and decision making as a judge to others and their needs.

In chapter 2, it was argued that judicial decisions should have the settlement of disputes as their principal goal. It also was argued that the melding of Dworkinian and pragmatic instrumentalist method would contribute to dispute settlement. Now one can add that deliberate use of horizon crossing method would enhance the likelihood that a judge's decision would relate the needs and circumstances of parties to a dispute and others affected by the decision. That should improve the quality of the judge's decisions as a means for dispute settlement. Our personalist judge's reconstructed method appears to satisfy criteria (3); it serves what he is attempting to do, that is—settle disputes.

The reconstructed method (4) comports with our personalist judge's understanding of obligation and (5) enhances the legitimacy of his decisions because it is specifically designed to enhance understanding of and respect for persons. Like his colleagues on the bench our personalist judge would take his oath of office seriously. Because personalism in law is conversation with and represents a reasonable interpretation of the common law tradition, following its methods would fulfill his sworn obligation to uphold the law. The reconstructed method is precisely designed to allow the judge to reach out to others by crossing horizons while adhering to and developing principles which express our great ideals. Use of the reconstructed method will fulfill in his judicial actions, his commitment and obligation to respect, try to understand and be concerned for each person.

Legitimacy was discussed preliminarily in chapter 2 and that discussion will be developed further in chapter 5. There also will be a further discussion of obligation in chapter 5. When critically examining method our personalist judge should determine whether it will enhance the legitimacy of his decisions. In chapter 2 it was argued that a legitimate decision is one which a judge can reasonably expect will be acceptable at several levels to those governed by it. In chapter 5 the concept of ultimate legitimacy will be developed further. A decision has ultimate legitimacy when it has the capacity of appealing to all persons, in all times. Some great opinions although opposed by some at the time rendered could be described as ultimately legitimate. These would include Lord Mansfield's decision in *Somersett v. Stewart*[64] and Chief Justice Warren's decision in *Brown v. Board of Education of Topeka, Kansas.*[65] The reconstructed personalist method is legitimate because it is designed to produce decisions based on respect and concern for all persons and on an attempt to understand those affected by the decisions. One can expect reasonably that such decisions generally would be acceptable and at times may rise to ultimate legitimacy.

One reason chapter 2 questioned pragmatic-instrumentalist method was the rejection by pragmatists of overarching theory. In the absence of an overarching theory related to respect and concern for each person it is difficult to take our great rights seriously. While one should recognize that the reconstructed personalist method is part of that overarching theory it is necessary to articulate a more fundamental foundation for supporting and understanding the great rights. The theory of the common good described in part eight, the next part, will serve that function. In part nine the theory of the common good must be related to a pluralist society and to the problem of horizons and in part ten to a theory of rights which can be employed in the reconstructed personalist decision making method.

---

64. Somerset v. Stewart, 98 Eng. Rep. 499 (K.B. 1772).
65. Brown v. Board of Education of Topeka, Kansas, 347 U.S. 483 (1954).

8. The Common Good

In the Declaration of Independence Thomas Jefferson explained that on the momentous occasion of the separation of one people from another "a decent respect to the opinions of mankind requires that they should declare the causes which impel them to the separation."[66] Some argue that a similar respect for general opinion requires those embarking on a series of significant public actions to explain the consistent set of policies or principles which serve as reasons for those actions. Publication of consistent reasons supporting actions will increase public confidence in the actors and what they are about. For similar reasons judges publish opinions and support their decisions by consistent principles or policies perhaps related to a comprehensive theory of law. In a theory of law where action is central, as in personalism, the judge's decision making method must be considered as part of the theory, as part of the reasons offered to the public to increase their confidence in his decisions.

Ronald Dworkin requires Judge Hercules to develop a comprehensive theory of law and government which will support his interpretation of the United States Constitution and all his judicial decisions.[67] He desires that theory not merely to increase public confidence in Hercules' decisions but in addition because Dworkin's neo-Kantian interpretation of law as Integrity requires such consistency. In partial agreement with Dworkin it has been argued in this and previous chapters that legal pragmatists are not able to take the great rights seriously because they reject an overarching theory which would ground those rights in respect and concern for each person. Dworkin would ground his theory in political friendship or in equal respect or concern for each person.

John Macmurray offers a theory which could explain political friendship and relate it to respect and concern for each person. Ultimately and perhaps with some amendments one could develop Macmurray's theory to explain the great rights and to provide a foundation for interpreting the United States Constitution and for justifying judicial decisions concerning the great rights.

According to Macmurray the personalist ideal "is a universal community of persons in which each cares for all the others" because the

---

66. The Declaration of Independence (U.S. 1776).

67. *See* DWORKIN, TAKING RIGHTS SERIOUSLY, *supra* note 36 at 82–130, *and* DWORKIN, LAW'S EMPIRE, *supra* note 8 at 225–75.

"self-realization of any individual person is only fully achieved if he is positively motivated towards every other person with whom he is in relation."[68] When one is in direct contact or relation with another it is possible to treat him or her as a person entitled to respect and concern. Contrarywise one could treat that person as an object, as something to be exploited for one's own purposes. One can ignore "his freedom and intentionality as another actor.... In slavery, for example, the master regards the slave not as a free, intentional actor, but as an object who possesses certain personal characteristics which render him useful. While the master perceives the slave as both subject and object, the objective aspects dominate the subjective."[69]

When one is indirectly related to others through society it is more difficult to emphasize the personal rather than the objective aspects of the relation. For the purposes of political friendship it is necessary to recognize that others, indeed all others, are persons who act freely and intentionally. By discussing indirect relations Macmurray finds it possible to offer an outline of a personalist theory of political obligation and justice which could be described as a theory of political friendship. On a previous occasion, I explained:

> "The political obligation 'is a derivative and indirect moral obligation.' Justice is a restraint which one person accepts on his own power and action for the sake of preserving the freedom and interests of others. Justice is ultimately for the sake of friendship, for preserving the ideal of a universal community, and the ideal for each individual of positive motivation towards each person he is related to directly or indirectly. Law, in turn, arises when there is a claim of injustice. Courts of law make the adjustments, including changes of custom necessary to reestablish justice. Justice is 'the minimum of morality which can be demanded as necessary to the cooperation of free agents.' Without it we cannot cooperate in society and maintenance of the ideal becomes impossible."[70]

One can build upon Macmurray's theory that justice consists of the necessary restraint to assure that persons related indirectly through so-

---

68. *See* Donnelly, *Towards a Personalist Jurisprudence, supra* note 1 at 585, referring to MACMURRAY, PERSONS IN RELATION, *supra* note 1 at 159.

69. *See id.* at 584–85, referring to MACMURRAY, PERSONS IN RELATION, *supra* note 1 at 29–31, 34–35.

70. *See id.* at 585–86, referring to MACMURRAY, PERSONS IN RELATION, *supra* note 1 at 190–91, 196, 201–05.

ciety are recognized as persons who act freely and intentionally. One can perceive society as a common action of persons acting together. Activities contrary to the common good of those acting together would be those which tend to seriously interfere with the common action or those that tend to prevent any person from participating in that common action.[71]

John Rawls, in a *Theory of Justice*, describes what he calls the primary social goods. The primary social goods are those necessary to pursuing any rational plan in life. In Rawls' theory parties under a veil of ignorance in an original contracting position vote for or agree upon fundamental and more specific principles of justice while basing their vote on a strict rational analysis of which principles will tend to increase their shares of the primary social goods and guard against disastrous losses of those goods. Since parties vote under a veil of ignorance which conceals from them their own concerns, their own projects and advantages and disadvantages they must vote for principles of justice which will protect each person.[72]

The vision of society as persons acting together, a common action, offers a more dynamic model than Rawls' original position. It draws on Macmurray's insight that persons understand themselves more fully as persons when in relation to each other. When acting together persons can perceive each other as acting intentionally and in cooperation. In a large society where persons are indirectly related, one can perceive the civilizing benefits of many persons acting justly and in cooperation which enhances the fullness of each as a person.

Nevertheless one can recognize some resemblance between the model of society as a common action and Rawls' original position and derive insights from Rawls. Rawls proposes a thin theory of the good as a basis for determining the right, the principles of justice.[73] One can develop a similar thin theory in the model of society as a common action. Since each person is entitled under the basic insights and commitments of personalism to participate in the common action, the primary social goods could be defined as those necessary or seriously helpful for participation in the common action of any society and this society. A judge

---

71. *See id.* at 587, referring to WOJTYLA, *supra* note 1 at 280–91.

72. *See* RAWLS, *supra* note 49 at 12–16, 60–65, 90–95, 118, 136–42, 142–61.

73. *See id.* at 396–99, 433–39, 447; *see also* Donnelly, *Towards a Personalist Jurisprudence, supra* note 1 at 587–88 (for a discussion of the same).

concerned for the common good could promote the common action by appropriate policy decisions. A personalist judge concerned for each and every person would preserve and advance the participation of each in the common action by supporting principles and policies designed for that purpose.

As in Rawls the thin theory of the good, the primary social goods, can serve as a foundation of a theory of rights. That theory ultimately would be supported by the personalist respect and concern for each person and would be an explanation of what it means to have respect and concern for persons in a political structure regulating indirect relations. A fundamental right would be the right to participate in society. One participates in the common action politically, socially and economically. "Primary rights would protect against deprivation of the personal, economic, and political goods necessary to basic participation in any society's and in this particular society's, common action."[74]

Our philosophically inclined personalist judge would perceive a number of advantages in the theory of society as a common action through which persons are indirectly related and the corresponding theory of the common good. As a comprehensive theory it provides a basis for relating individual rights and the good of society, for relating what Dworkin would call principle and policy as reasons for decisions. The primary right is the right to participate in society. The primary social goods, then, are those necessary or important for participation in this or any society. From that beginning one can develop a theory of the great or major rights as protections in the indirect relations of society for the primary social goods. Similarly, the common goods, those which facilitate interrelation, and the common good, our common action in society which indirectly relates us all, provide a basis for policy decisions. Ultimately both rights related reasons for decisions and policy reasons are grounded in the commitment of the personalist judge to respect and concern for each person and all persons.

The proposed theory of the common good, our personalist judge would note, not only provides a comprehensive framework for all decisions, but also as a theory of action and participation, provides the flexibility and dynamism necessary to relate to multiple persons over time and in many horizons. He would recognize that the proposed theory has good fit with his basic understanding that he is related to others

---

74. *See* Donnelly, *Towards a Personalist Jurisprudence, supra* note 1 at 589.

through action, including the action of his judicial decisions. Since the theory builds on Macmurray's thought it is consistent with the personalist judge's commitment to respect and concern for each person and all persons.

As one elaborates a personalist theory of rights one should continue to recognize one's horizons. Since we have limited vision, knowledge and understanding our recognition and development of the primary rights may be inadequate to fully afford respect and concern to all persons. A judge using the principles which reflect and support the primary rights to justify his decisions should employ horizon crossing when applying and developing those principles. In a pluralist society one must develop a theory of conversation which will enhance our understanding of the primary rights. The next segment, part nine, of this chapter will describe such a theory. The following segment, part ten, will offer a preliminary elaboration of a personalist theory of rights. Chapter 4 on "Constitutional Interpretation," and chapter 6 will develop that theory further.

9. Horizons and Conversation in a Pluralist Society

Using the terminology of this chapter one could describe a pluralist society as one composed of multiple horizons. Since a fully worked out theory creates a horizon with vision blocking and vision enhancing characteristics, a personalist judge constructing such a theory would confront a paradox. Without an overarching theory he would find it difficult to take rights seriously. The overarching theory itself, however, would serve as an obstacle to respecting and understanding his fellows in the multiple horizons of a complex pluralist society.

Horizons, however, may be crossed. A solution proposed in this chapter to the problem presented by horizons is to include regular use of horizon crossing techniques in a judge's decision making method. When developing the principles or policies grounded in the personalist theory of the common good, our philosophically inclined personalist judge should employ such horizon crossing methods as interest analysis. A principle, for example, could indicate that it is important to protect a significant interest. Rather than deducing a result in a case from that principle, the judge should seek out the other relevant interests affected by his decision and balance the competing interests.

As our personalist judge crosses horizons using interest analysis or other methods he may recognize primary social goods other than those included in his initial list. Rawls would recognize such primary social goods as liberty and a modicum of wealth as necessary to pursue any rational plan in life.[75] John Finnis in *Natural Law and Natural Rights* offers a list of basic goods necessary for human flourishing including life, knowledge, play, aesthetic experience, friendship, practical reasonableness and religion.[76] Although there is some overlap Finnis' list does not resemble that of Rawls. Yet one can recognize that a total deprivation of some of Finnis' goods would constitute a serious violation of human rights. In the pre-Civil War South, for example, it was a crime to teach an African American to read.[77] That deprivation of knowledge which continued in some ways after the war strikes us as a serious crime against humanity. As one's experience expands through the crossing of horizons one's list of the primary social goods may expand. The personalist overarching theory should provide for further development of the list of primary goods necessary or important for participation in any society or one's own society.

Argument between judges in an appellate court or in litigation, as reasons for a decision are presented to a court, may expand a listener's vision. Argument, particularly argument regularly employed as in our adversary system, can be a horizon crossing method. James Boyd White, in *Heracles' Bow*, describes society as constituted by the on-going argument about what society should be.[78] Exchange of thought is an important aspect of human relations. Conversation, itself, can be considered as an action relating human persons. Argument as an important activity in the well-known profession which we practice can be a means for relating persons and for relating those in one horizon to those in another. The great dispute settlement system which our courts provide, then, could be described as an on-going activity which relates through argument the multiple horizons in our pluralist society. Legal argument is one aspect of the on-going argument about what society should be which constitutes society.

---

75. *See id.* at 587–88, referring to RAWLS, *supra* note 49 at 62, 92.

76. *See id.* at 590, referring to JOHN FINNIS, NATURAL LAW AND NATURAL RIGHTS 59–99 (1980).

77. *See generally* RICHARD BARDOLPH, THE CIVIL RIGHTS RECORD: BLACK AMERICANS AND THE LAW, 1849–1970 (1970).

78. *See* JAMES BOYD WHITE, HERACLES' BOW: ESSAYS ON THE RHETORIC AND POETICS OF THE LAW 28, 32–35, 37 (1985).

Ronald Dworkin, in "Hard Cases," a chapter of *Taking Rights Seriously*, offers a theory for deciding such cases which could be described as a theory of argument and conversation.[79] When interpreting a provision of the United States Constitution, Judge Hercules should offer a theory or conceptualization of that provision, of that great contested moral concept. His theory should explain the concept, the clear instances on which there is general agreement, the solution to the hard case before the court and the holdings in other cases which Hercules has decided or will decide under that constitutional provision.[80] Judge X will have a different interpretation or theory of the provision, as will Judge Y and Z. Nevertheless each judge could employ Ronald Dworkin's proposed method of interpretation. In that event each judge's theory should explain the contested concept in the constitutional provision, and the clear instances on which there is general agreement as well as the cases the judge has decided or wants to decide. Although the theories differ, they will converge at least to the extent that they explain the constitutional provision and the clear instances to which it applies. Majority or dissenting judges may find that their competing theories overlap or converge sufficiently to allow them to concur in each other's opinions. As they cooperate on joint opinions they may find that they are borrowing ideas or arguments from each other and incorporating them into their own theories of the constitutional provision.

Bernard Lonergan offers a theory of argument and conversation in his discussion of positions and counter positions.[81] One advancing a position while arguing against a counter position may find a valuable insight in the counter position. One should extract that insight from the counter position and its fundamental theory and analyze the relation between that insight and one's own fundamental theory. H. L. A. Hart, in his multiple conversations with legal philosophers, engaged in a similar practice. For example, his great clarifying concept, the open texture of law, probably was designed to capture and incorporate in his analytical system the American Pragmatist insight that law develops and changes or as Llewellyn would say is constantly in flux.[82] Hart's rule

---

79. *See* Dworkin, Taking Rights Seriously, *supra* note 1 at 81–130.

80. *See id.* at 105–07.

81. *See* Lonergan, Insight: A Study of Human Understanding, *supra* note 1 at 387–90; and Tracy, *supra* note 41 at 151–55.

82. *See* Hart, The Concept of Law, *supra* note 15 at 124–35; cf. Llewellyn, Jurisprudence, *supra* note 29 at 42 ("[F]erment is abroad in the law...").

of recognition could be fruitfully compared as well as contrasted with Hans Kelsen's grandnorm.[83]

A judge committed to respect and concern for others should use argument and conversation as just described as a means for crossing and transcending horizons. Argument and conversation through the legal process is a means for relating the multiple horizons in our pluralist society. In the course of argument, conversation and horizon crossing a personalist judge will develop his theory of the common good further. For example, he will discover primary social goods which are important to persons in other horizons and which are significant means for their participation in the on-going action of society.

John Rawls proposed a thin theory of the good partly because of the distaste in liberal theory for a full theory of the good.[84] In the absence of horizon crossing a full theory of the good could create a horizon and become an instrument of oppression. In a pluralist society, that is, one composed of multiple horizons, a judge who attempts to impose a full theory of the good on foreign horizons could be perceived as acting oppressively. Likewise, Dworkin's Judge Hercules with his comprehensive consistent theory could be perceived as an oppressor particularly because his decision making method does not provide for horizon crossing.

Unlike Dworkin's theory, the personalist theory of the common good is dynamic, action oriented and capable of continual development because it provides for crossing horizons and adding to the list of primary social goods. The personalist theory of the common good when combined with personalist decision making method has the capacity to engage in conversation with the multiple horizons in our pluralist society. Because our personalist judge would be aware of the dangers of a static theory he is capable of taking seriously the rights of others with whom he is as yet unacquainted in his yet unexplored horizons.

In the context of that action oriented theory legal argument can be perceived as a means of conversation across horizons. Litigation and legal argument as part of litigation is a means for crossing and transcending horizons. The assertion of rights in the course of legal argument may be a means of hammering on the door of foreign horizons to

---

83. *See* HART, THE CONCEPT OF LAW, *supra* note 15 at 94–95; and HANS KELSEN, PURE THEORY OF LAW 8–10, 193–95 (Max Knight trans., 2nd ed. 1967).
84. *See* RAWLS, *supra* note 49.

call attention to one's client and his fundamental interests. It is a way of asserting that one's client is a person whose fundamental interests should be recognized by the law. Our pluralist judge may respond to that litigation by crossing horizons with the help of counsel and by perceiving new primary social goods and establishing new rights.

In the next segment, part ten, then, a preliminary sketch of a theory of rights can be offered. That theory will be related to personalist decision making method, to horizon crossing, conversation between horizons in a pluralist society and to the continually developing personalist theory of the common good with its growing list of primary social goods.

10. Rights

Under the personalist theory of the common good rights are grounded in the primary social goods. One may arrive at a theory or list of the primary social goods in a variety of ways. John Rawls defines the primary social goods as those necessary to pursue any rational plan in life.[85] A judge committed to respect and concern for each person may consider protecting the pursuit of rational plans fundamental. To respect a person, at a minimum, means to respect his or her right to live as a human person, to act in some rational ways, to pursue some rational plans. It is apparent, however, that some primary goods, for example, knowledge, which appear on John Finnis' list but not on that of Rawls are important for minimum human flourishing.[86] Personalist theory offers a broader definition of the primary social goods, that is, those necessary or seriously significant for participation in this or any society. Under personalist theory one has a fundamental right to participate in society. While an individual may decline the invitation to participate, he or she nevertheless has a right to the primary social goods which make that participation possible.

Respect, then, for each person's right to participate in "the intersubjectivity or political friendship of the common action, the life of the community" becomes the basis for the primary rights.[87] Primary rights are those which "would protect against deprivation of the personal,

---

85. See RAWLS, *supra* note 49 at 62.
86. See RAWLS, *supra* note 49.
87. See Samuel J.M. Donnelly, *Book Review* 36 AMER. J. OF JURIS. 247 (1991) (reviewing Granfield, *supra* note 32.)

economic, and political goods necessary to basic participation in any society's, and in this particular society's common action."[88]

With that clue one can distinguish between strong rights and weak rights. Strong rights which include those just described as primary rights are those more closely related to protection of the primary social goods. Weak rights are less closely or less directly connected to the goal of assuring a person's share of those goods. One has a weak right if it counts in the reasoning process which leads to a judge's decision. That would include the assertion that one has a right based on precedent. Precedent based rights have weight in the reasoning process and will prevail over some but not all competing considerations.

In contrast strong rights often will prevail in the judicial reasoning process. Speaking generally strong rights are those which outweigh weaker rights. Included as strong rights are those referred to in earlier chapters as major rights or the great rights. These now can be defined as those closely related to protection of the primary social goods. The great rights often are those found in the United States Constitution. Constitutional rights often will outweigh competing rights or policies. Major rights, however, may be found elsewhere. For example, tort law by an action in negligence or by strict liability in tort protects one's right not to be injured by another's fault or by the productive activities of society. That is a strong right closely related to the primary social goods.

This distinction between strong and weak rights can be related to an analysis of Ronald Dworkin's understanding of principles and policies. Principles according to Dworkin are political reasons for decisions based on individual rights. Policies are reasons for decisions based on group goals.[89] In personalist theory principles as Dworkin describes them would be reasons for decisions related closely to the primary social goods. A judge, however, should recognize that some policies relate directly to the goal of protecting or advancing everyone's share of the primary social goods. Contrary to Dworkin in a personalist judge's decision making process some strong policies will prevail over some weaker rights.[90] Of course, in normal legal discourse principles have a variety of meanings. Principles have been defined earlier in this work as policy themes running through a series of cases. Those policies could be

---

88. *See* Donnelly, *Towards a Personalist Jurisprudence, supra* note 1 at 589.
89. *See* DWORKIN, TAKING RIGHTS SERIOUSLY *supra* note 36 at 82–84.
90. *See* DWORKIN, LAW'S EMPIRE *supra* note 8 at 151–55.

ones directly related to the primary social goods. In normal legal discourse a policy also may be a reason based on individual right, a reason Dworkin would define as a principle. Principles running through a series of cases may reflect the great ideals of society. Those ideals may be great rights directly related to protecting each person's primary social goods. They also may be great goals which society pursues for the sake of assuring and enhancing everyone's share of the primary goods. Strong policies designed to pursue those great goals may prevail in the reasoning process over weaker rights.

Dworkin and H. L. A. Hart have made us all aware of the role of rights in legal reasoning. In "Definition and Theory in Jurisprudence" Hart described a right as a conclusion drawn in a system of rules.[91] That conclusion could be drawn by a variety of actors in the legal system. Paraphrasing Hart modestly, a judge could draw a conclusion in his ruling. But continuing to paraphrase Hart an advocate also could draw a conclusion while asserting a client's right by way of a claim or a criticism of a lower court's ruling. Dworkin develops this analysis of legal language usages by describing rights as reasons for drawing conclusions. In the reasoning process rights as reasons may trump competing policy reasons.[92]

Inspired by Dworkin and Hart and their analysis of rights in the legal reasoning process we may reflect more broadly on that reasoning process and may discern other usages of the language of rights. Means-goal reasoning is a typical form of legal reasoning. Rights could be understood as great goals to be pursued by society.[93] In *Brown v. Board of Education of Topeka, Kansas*,[94] Chief Justice Warren understood equal protection and perhaps equality as constitutional goals to be pursued by adequate means. He described the separate but equal doctrine as a failed and inadequate means for pursuing that goal. He offered desegregation as a more adequate means for pursing the goal of equal protection. It is possible then to understand rights as great goals to be pursued. One also may describe rights as means to goals. For example, the right to desegregation is a means in pursuit of the great goal rights of equal protection and equality.

---

91. *See* H.L.A. Hart, *Definition and Theory in Jurisprudence*, 70 LAW Q. REV. 37, 49 (1954)

92. *See* DWORKIN, TAKING RIGHTS SERIOUSLY, *supra* note 36 at 81–130,*and* DONNELLY, THE LANGUAGE AND USES OF RIGHTS, *supra* note 39 at 17–22.

93. *See* DONNELLY, THE LANGUAGE AND USES OF RIGHTS, *supra* note 39 at 24–33.

94. Brown v. Board of Education of Topeka, Kansas, 347 U.S. 483(1954).

In personalist theory means-goal reasoning is an appropriate traditional method of legal reasoning. The great goals closely reflect the primary social goods and are means themselves for assuring everyone's share or each person's share of those goods. Following Robert Summers means-goal reasoning may be grounded in a comprehensive overarching theory of rights and law.[95] A personalist judge then may perceive some rights as goals and some means as rights designed to achieve important goals. In litigation, cases establishing rights may be perceived as resources or means for achieving further goals or objectives. A law reform litigator may perceive his victories as means towards an ultimate law reform goal. Thurgood Marshall when he served as counsel to the NAACP would be an example of such a law reform litigator. Describing rights from the point of view of the younger Thurgood Marshall is an expansion and application of the form of language and reasoning analysis introduced to us by H. L. A. Hart and Ronald Dworkin.[96] That form of analysis will be developed and described further in chapter 6. That form of analysis will be employed occasionally in chapter 4, "Constitutional Interpretation."

The Crits, members of the Critical Legal Studies movement, often assert that rights are grounded in the establishment ideology of current and past society. A Crit engaged in law reform, whether he is a judge or a litigating attorney, first would strive to deconstruct existing rights and then would use rights either existing or newly constructed to achieve his or her ideological goals.[97] A personalist commentary would begin by noting that the Crits appropriately have perceived the problem of horizons. From a personalist perspective the Crits make use of deconstruction as a means for crossing horizons or for hammering on the door of a foreign horizon. All worked out theories including the personalist create horizons and could be described as ideologies. Personalist method, however, provides means for crossing and transcending horizons. Ultimately a personalist judge seeks to make decisions which reflect respect and concern for each person. Some Crits as judges would make decisions to advance their own ideologies which may or may not express respect and concern for each person.[98] Like the pragmatists in law, then,

---

95. *See* ROBERT SAMUEL SUMMERS, INSTRUMENTALISM AND AMERICAN LEGAL THEORY 60–80 (1982).

96. *See* DONNELLY, THE LANGUAGE AND USES OF RIGHTS, *supra* note 39 at 24–33, 35–38.

97. *See id.* at 38–43; *and see generally* Unger, *supra* note 39; Mark Tushnet, *An Essay on Rights,*62 TEXAS L. REV. 1363 (1984); Kennedy, *supra* note 7.

98. *See* Kennedy, *supra* note 7 at 521–22.

most Crits are unable to take rights seriously because they do not ground rights in an overarching theory whose goal is respect and concern for all persons. Most Crits do not purport to take rights seriously.[99]

Chapter 4, "Constitutional Interpretation," will offer a personalist theory and method for interpreting the United States Constitution. In constructing that theory the insights offered in this chapter and chapter 2 will be employed. Traditionally, judges interpreting our constitution use common law rather than civil law method. The personalist conversation with the common law tradition and the more philosophical reflection on personalist method found in this chapter are steps in constructing a method for constitutional interpretation.

The personalist theory of rights, just sketched, will be relevant in developing a theory of constitutional rights. Since constitutional rights are strong examples of legal or institutional rights one must ask what methods are appropriate when interpreting or applying such rights. Dworkin's criteria for a good interpretation, namely, institutional fit and higher moral appeal, are relevant tests.[100]

When interpreting the Constitution a personalist judge would offer a theory of the Constitution based on his background theory of persons acting together in society and his commitment to respect, have concern for, and attempt to understand each person. That theory should be a theory of our Constitution, that is, it should have good institutional fit. A theory of the great Constitutional rights would be grounded in that personalist interpretation. The important Constitutional rights then would be understood as protecting each person's share of the primary social goods, those goods necessary or seriously significant for participation in our society or in any society. The expanded analysis of the language and uses of rights just described will be relevant in chapter 4. That description and analysis will be developed further in chapter 6.

11. Conclusion

This chapter was designed to present a theory of personalism in law. The theory presented is an interpretation of law and offers a series of re-

---

99. *See generally* Tushnet, *supra* note 97.

100. *See* DWORKIN, TAKING RIGHTS SERIOUSLY, *supra* note 36 at 86–88, 106–07, 118.

lated insights and concepts. Because personalism in law is a theory in which the judge's action is central, a critique of method, particularly the judge's decision making method becomes important. A personalist judge should relate his acceptance and critique of method to his self-understanding as a person related to others through action. He also may assess method by asking whether it is well adapted to his purpose in acting, here to settle disputes within the common law tradition.

To make that assessment he should locate and analyze the principal elements of his method. Part of that task was performed in chapter 2, the conversation with the common law tradition. In this chapter partly through an introspective analysis our personalist judge was able to reflect on important aspects of his general intellectual method as related to law. That reflection would include his self-recognition as one who acts in relation to others and who therefore wants to critically examine his decision making method. It also would include his recognition of his horizons and his ability to cross horizons. As a judge committed to respect and concern for others he then would recognize an obligation to cross horizons and to include horizon crossing methods in his decision making method.

As in chapter 2 his choice between competing methods and elements of competing methods will be supported by his commitment to respect and concern for each person. His critical analysis of method now would include an assessment of whether a proposed method has provisions for horizon crossing. All other aspects of common law method or general intellectual method as related to law should then be joined with horizon crossing including sudden flashes of insight, the role of principle and the function of overarching theory.

Overarching theory is important not merely to consistency in action and to public confidence in that action but also as a means for relating strong rights to an interpretation of law grounded in respect and concern for each person. Arguably pragmatic-instrumentalism is unable to take strong rights seriously because it rejects overarching theory. Personalist theory constructed in part from John Macmurray's insights is an interpretation of what it means in the indirect relations of a complex society to have regard for each and all persons, and to take their strong rights seriously.

In a pluralist society, that is, one composed of multiple horizons, one should engage in conversation across horizons concerning fundamental theory. The personalist theory proposed here is not the only way to construct an appropriate overarching theory. Those engaged in conversation with personalist theory may find some helpful suggestions or insights which could be incorporated in competing theories. An important suggestion borrowed from John Rawls is that rights or principles of justice should be designed to advance or protect each person's share of the primary social goods. One should not adhere to a narrow or static list of the primary social goods. While engaged in argument, conversation or horizon crossing one may become aware of the importance of additional primary social goods. That awareness may change one's vision and understanding of persons in other horizons. Ultimately it may lead to reassessment of one's overarching theory and interpretation of law.

In chapter 4 the personalist decision making method will serve as a base for constructing a method for constitutional interpretation and for settling great constitutional disputes. Overarching theory as described in this chapter and related to rights will become a foundation for interpreting our Constitution and developing a theory of the great constitutional rights. Constitutional interpretation, however, should be conducted in conversation with others in our complex pluralist society. When settling disputes concerning the great constitutional rights a judge should include methods for horizon crossing in his decision making method.

The conversation, then, should continue with a discussion of constitutional rights and constitutional interpretation.

CHAPTER IV

Constitutional Interpretation

1. Introduction

When addressing constitutional interpretation the great quarrel over method becomes acrimonious. Our Supreme Court, some would complain, is a countermajoritarian institution whose life tenured members are not elected. The practice of judicial review, then, however one relates it to *Marbury v. Madison*,[1] is a deviant procedure in a majoritarian democracy.

This chapter, in significant part, discusses the intellectual method of a judge interpreting the United States Constitution. Constitutional method in our tradition employs aspects of common law methodology and resembles statutory interpretation in some respects. In contrast, for example, to courts interpreting European Civil Codes, the United States Supreme Court when interpreting our Constitution employs the common law doctrine of precedent and develops constitutional law from case to case by analogy and distinction and with reference to relevant principles. Personalist method as described in chapters 2 and 3 provides a foundation, then, for constructing a theory for constitutional interpretation.

Arguably our Supreme Court is at the apex of a great dispute settlement institution. Our Constitution in Article III Section 2, appropriately under personalist theory, charges our federal courts with deciding cases and controversies, including constitutional questions.[2] When re-

---

1. Marbury v. Madison, 5 U.S. 137 (1803).
2. *See* U.S.C.A. CONST. Art. III § 2. ("[T]he Judicial Power shall extend to all Cases, in Law and Equity, arising under this Constitution, the Laws of the United States, and Treaties made, or which shall be made, under their Authority;...—to Controversies to which the United States shall be a Party;—to Controversies between two or more States;—between a State and Citizens of another State;—between Citizens of different States;...and between a State, or

viewing the Court's history and recognizing that in this provision our highest law created an institution and means for establishing, changing, talking about, fighting about, reconciling and struggling with human relations, some thinkers inquire and others worry about the relation between politics and law.[3] Typically, thinkers prescribing methods for constitutional interpretation propose theories of restraint. Conservative thinkers, as described in chapter 1, "want to preserve in amber the founding generation's supposed interpretation of the drafters' deliberately written general provisions."[4] More liberal thinkers such as John Hart Ely also offer theories of restraint. Ronald Dworkin, while rejecting the pragmatic instrumentalism typical of Warren Court decisions, believes that his more restrained and principled method would support many of the Court's conclusions.

Inspired perhaps by Cass Sunstein, a central concept in the method offered by the chapter is a deliberating society with the Supreme Court at the apex of a great dispute settlement institution which relates segments of our pluralist society through rational argument. While it would be naive to deny that law is part of the political process and is related to politics, it offers an alternate means, rational discussion and argument, for addressing the great issues.

The concept of a deliberating society as described in this chapter differs considerably, then, from that described by Cass Sunstein. Sunstein perceives that a principal function of our Supreme Court is to promote majoritarian deliberation in the larger society. For that purpose he would advocate minimalist decision making by the Court. Without denying that function, the theory offered in this chapter describes the Supreme Court as a principal vehicle for rational deliberation and conversation in our pluralist society. Sunstein is correct that "in a deliberative democracy, a premium is also placed on the exchange of reasons by people with different information and diverse perspectives."[5] However, our Supreme Court and our great legal dispute settlement institution

---

the Citizens thereof, and foreign States, Citizens or Subjects.") *See* also, Samuel J.M. Donnelly, "Towards a Personalist Jurisprudence: Basic Insights and Concepts," 28 LOY.L.A.L. REV. 547–50 (1995).

3. *See* SAMUEL J.M. DONNELLY, THE LANGUAGE AND USES OF RIGHTS: A BIOPSY OF AMERICAN JURISPRUDENCE IN THE TWENTIETH CENTURY, 81 (1994).

4. *See* Chapter I text at Notes 20–21.

5. CASS SUNSTEIN, ONE CASE AT A TIME, 24, 25 (1999).

provide perhaps the best opportunity in our society for that rational exchange and discussion. There will be a further discussion in chapter 5, in the segment on justification, of the differences between personalism and Sunstein's theory. In personalism deliberation concerning our great principles and ideals has a larger role in justifying decisions than portrayed in Sunstein's theory.

In some respects the method presented here resembles that developed by Ronald Dworkin. However, because it has less emphasis on theoretical consistency and more on means-end reasoning, balancing interests, and understanding opposing positions and the concrete circumstances of those appearing before the Court, it may resemble more closely the methods employed by Justice William Brennan. See, for example, his opinion for the Court in *New York Times v. Sullivan*[6] and his understanding that the post Civil War Constitution presents a sparkling vision of concern for the human dignity of each person.[7]

Central concepts in this chapter's discussion of constitutional interpretation include then the Court as the center of a great dispute settlement institution in a deliberating society. In the personalist understanding, the Court is engaged in action and participates in the on-going common action of the society established by the founding generation. The drafters and their generation engaged in a great action. Their task and their principal intention was to establish a government. The Constitution, itself, can be perceived as part of that great action; indeed, it is a continuing part of the on-going action of society. The great American insight and ideal enunciated in the Declaration of Independence but hammered out over two centuries is that each person is worthwhile and entitled equally to government protection for our lives, liberties and property.[8] One can offer a theory of our Constitution as an

---

6. New York Times v. Sullivan, 376 U.S. 254 (1964).

7. William J. Brennan, Jr., *The Constitution of the United States: Contemporary Ratification*, in INTERPRETING THE CONSTITUTION: THE DEBATE OVER ORIGINAL INTENT 23, 28–29 (Jack N. Rakove ed., 1990).

8. *See* U.S.C.A. CONST. Amend. XIV. The Due Process Clause of the Fourteenth Amendment to the United States Constitution provides "nor shall any State deprive any person of life, liberty or property without the due process of law." This statement is applied to the states through the Due Process Clause of the Fourteenth Amendment. Additionally, the key phrase, "life, liberty and property" appears in an early draft of the Declaration of Independence. Thomas Jefferson later revised this statement to read: "We hold these truths to be self-evident, that all men are created equal, that they are endowed by their

on-going action designed to promote that ideal.[9] In constructing a method, then, for deliberating regarding that ideal and the other great moral standards found in our Constitution, it would be appropriate to draw on Dworkinian idealism as well as the pragmatic reasoning of *Brown v. Board of Education of Topeka, Kansas*[10] and *New York Times v. Sullivan.* Arguably *Brown* and *N.Y. Times* used means-end reasoning to promote our constitutional standards. *Brown*, in particular, perceived constitutional interpretation as an on-going struggle to achieve our national ideals by discovery of appropriate means.

In contrast, those who make restraint a principal structural feature of their recommended decision making method not only distort the process of constitutional interpretation but also are counterproductive. By refusing to deliberate or by placing restrictions on deliberation, one may transform the decision making process into one which is more overtly political. For example, one could contend that the conservative theories of constitutional interpretation for political reasons refuse to consider well-reasoned understandings of constitutional provisions. Some liberal insistence on narrow principled reasoning also can be used to advance political positions while refusing to discuss competing reasons or consider competing interests.

A personalist judge engaged in deliberation on the great constitutional standards should recognize his horizons and as part of his method should provide for crossing horizons to understand the many relevant interests in our pluralist society. Contrary to Dworkin, he should be prepared to weigh and reconcile interests, to compromise and seek convergence with competing views.

American constitutional law and theory is the on-going product of our historic struggles.[11] Personalist theory argues that respect for the human dignity of each person is a core American insight which emerged over two centuries. First announced in the Declaration of Independence as an echo of Lockean thought, fought over in our Civil War whose insights were embodied in the Fourteenth Amendment and then distorted in the late nineteenth century, our respect for the life and liberty of each person was revitalized by the core twentieth century decision, *Brown v.*

Creator with certain unalienable Rights, that among these are Life, Liberty and the pursuit of Happiness."

9. *Id.*

10. Brown v. Board of Education of Topeka, Kansas, 347 U.S. 483 (1954).

11. Mark Hancock, my research assistant in 1998, contributed this thought.

Board of Education of Topeka, Kansas and the struggles which followed this landmark case. A personalist theory of constitutional interpretation must be constructed in conversation with our history and our historic and contemporary quarrels including the great quarrel over method which became particularly intense following *Brown*.

As a prelude to that conversation, the next several parts of chapter 4 will offer a brief overview of a personalist theory of constitutional interpretation. Much of that discussion should appear familiar since it is an adaptation of the personalist theory developed in chapters 2 and 3. In part six, our conversation with history begins with the dark period from 1880 to 1937 which has scarred and deeply influenced our understanding of constitutional interpretation. Some have described that era in neutral terms as the period of legal classicism. *Brown* in some respects can be understood not only as a rejection of *Plessy v. Ferguson*[12] but also of legal classicism. Part seven, "Deciding *Brown*", will discuss the pragmatic-instrumentalist style of Chief Justice Warren's opinion in that case. Personalist theory as explained in previous chapters would accept much of pragmatic-instrumentalist decision making method and would attempt to relate that method to Dworkinian idealism. The method and theory gradually developed by Justice William Brennan would serve as a model.

As described in previous chapters, principle serves an important but not dominating role in personalist method. While in the late twentieth and early twenty-first century we have accepted a principled interpretation of *Brown*, Chief Justice Warren's opinion does not employ or appeal to principled reasoning. From hindsight, Dworkin and others have attempted to supply that principled foundation for *Brown*. While personalist thought would seek a principled basis for great constitutional decisions, arguably we are able to articulate those principles only after a period of struggle. Horizons and the need to cross horizons at moments of historic crisis also must be accounted for both in assessing the past and in developing an appropriate method for constitutional interpretation.

Brown was followed by a firestorm of popular and academic criticism. The great quarrel over method in the late twentieth century is the intellectual descendant of that period of criticism. Current discussion of constitutional interpretation must account for that great quarrel and

---

12. Plessy v. Ferguson, 163 U.S. 537 (1896).

the competing methods. In part eight entitled appropriately, "The Great Quarrel Over Method", subpart A will discuss conservative theories of restraint which arguably constitute a refusal to deliberate. In subpart B some liberal theories which also refuse to deliberate will be analyzed. One constructing and explaining a personalist theory of constitutional interpretation would benefit by the contrast with competing theories. At the very least, one can learn from bad examples. At times, however, conversation with opposing theories can provide valuable insights. Other liberal theories, including those of Professors Ackerman[13] and Wellington[14] as discussed in subpart C, provide such insights.

Following that necessary conversation with competing theories, personalist method for constitutional interpretation, including the role for principles can be presented in a more developed form in part nine, "Principles, Pluralism and Conversation" and then can be illustrated by the examples presented in part ten, "Unenumerated Rights—Substantive Due Process" and part eleven, "Interpreting the Eighth Amendment."

2. Interpreting a Written Document

On a national scale when our Constitution was first adopted it was unique because it was a written document. There were written state constitutions. However, the founding generation particularly those members of it who gathered in Philadelphia to draft the Constitution had more on their agenda than writing a memorable piece of prose. Hamilton, Madison and Washington wanted to reorganize the then existing Confederacy to form a newly established national government. They were engaged in an ongoing enterprise, the establishment and conduct of a new government. The written Constitution, however unique, was part of and a tool in that enterprise. Arguably, constitutional interpretation, the interpretation of that written document, is

---

13. *See* Bruce Ackerman, *A Generation of Betrayal?* Vol. LXV, 4 FORDHAM L. REV. 1519–1536 (1997). *See* also Bruce Ackerman, *The Storrs Lectures: Discovering the Constitution,* 93 YALE L.J. 1013 (1984); Bruce Ackerman *Constitutional Politics/Constitutional Law,* 99 YALE L.J. 453 (1989). Ackerman is the Sterling Professor of Law & Political Science, Yale University.

14. *See* HARRY H. WELLINGTON, INTERPRETING THE CONSTITUTION: THE SUPREME COURT AND THE PROCESS OF ADJUDICATION. 43–74 (1990).

part of the great common action initiated by the founding generation, namely, the governance of America.

A famous play, for example, Shakespeare's Hamlet, is, in some respects, a document analogous to our Constitution. Hamlet is a memorable writing, a great work of literature. When writing it, however, Shakespeare had more on his agenda than creating a beautiful work which would be read for generations. Immediately the play was designed to be produced by a company of actors for a specified audience. As an experienced playwriter and actor, Shakespeare would imagine adaptation of the play to various audiences and to the needs of production. If a modern director were to converse with Shakespeare about the appropriate interpretation of Hamlet, one reasonably could expect the exchange of certain classic statements and practical advice. Like many authors Shakespeare might inquire: "What does the play mean to you?" He probably would advise the director to produce and interpret the play in a manner designed to appeal to and meet the needs of his audience.

Like a play, a constitution is a document designed for practical purposes. In the late eighteenth century it was part of a successful effort to establish a new government. While it is a blueprint for the continuing operation of that government, it should be construed as a means for the continued year in and year out successful governance of America. The founders set forth a series of practical purposes and goals in their preamble: "to form a more perfect Union, establish Justice, insure domestic Tranquility, provide for the common defense, promote the general Welfare and secure the Blessings of Liberty to ourselves and our Posterity."[15] The continued operation of our government including the Supreme Court tasks of dispute settlement and constitutional interpretation could be perceived as a great common action in pursuit of those goals.

The original Constitution, which consisted primarily of practical arrangements for the structure and conduct of government, may be interpreted in service of such goals as forming a more perfect Union, establishing domestic Tranquility and promoting the general welfare. In addition, one may need a theory of the structure, a theory of federalism, for example. Beyond adding further practical arrangements, the

---

15. U.S. Const. Preamble states ([W]e the People of the United States, in Order to form a more perfect Union, establish Justice, insure domestic Tranquility, provide for the common defense, promote the general Welfare and secure the Blessings of Liberty to ourselves and our Posterity, do ordain and establish this Constitution for the United States of America.).

Bill of Rights and subsequent amendments contain restrictions on government power and moral claims against government action. These provisions may be interpreted as serving the goals of establishing Justice and securing the Blessings of Liberty. To do so one may need a theory of justice. Personalism offers such a theory of justice as described in the last Chapter.

3. Method

Construction and critical examination of intellectual and decision making method is central to personalist theory. The personalist judge, now a member of the United States Supreme Court, in conversation with methods in current use, constructs a method which satisfies his commitments to have respect and concern for and to attempt to understand each person. Having crossed multiple horizons before reaching the Supreme Court, our personalist judge recognizes his horizons and the need for horizon crossing methods. Because of his basic commitment to persons, he will accept the role of principle as described by Ronald Dworkin when interpreting our Constitution. The moral claims found in the Bill of Rights and the Fourteenth Amendment offer reasons for decisions based on respect and concern for each person. In the reasoning process, however, those claims must be balanced against competing claims and interests. Ultimately, those claims and the need to balance them will be understood in relation to a comprehensive theory of our Constitution. That theory must explain liberty, the pursuit of justice and federalism. Our personalist judge will be inclined to perceive liberty, justice and federalism as goals to be pursued by his decisions and holdings. The great moral claims found in the Bill of Rights and subsequent amendments often may be perceived as means in the pursuit of those goals.

Following Dworkin a comprehensive theory of our Constitution and a theory of a particular provision should have good institutional fit and should make the most that now can be made of our Constitution.[16] A personalist judge should strive to make the most that can be made of our Constitution for this generation and for the future. He would be

---

16. *See* RONALD DWORKIN, TAKING RIGHTS SERIOUSLY (1977). *See* also RONALD DWORKIN, LAW'S EMPIRE (1986).

aware of the analogy between interpreting the Constitution and producing a famous play.

Constructing a method for interpreting our Constitution, however, requires more than a simple summary of personalist decision making technique. For example, relating a deliberating society to Ronald Dworkin's discussion of great contested moral concepts would provide a more developed framework for constitutional interpretation.[17] After that other pieces of the structure including a theory of constitutional rights must be added to the framework.[18]

4. A Deliberating Society

As evidenced by an examination of The Federalist Papers,[19] the founding generation admired the virtue of deliberation. Deliberation could be described as the restraint of precipitous action in favor of reasoned decision and decision making. Hamilton, writing as Publius, relates the virtue of deliberation and the independence of the judiciary in the following passage:

> "The independence of the judges is equally requisite to guard the Constitution and the rights of individuals from the effects of those ill humors which the arts of designing men, or the influence of particular conjunctures, sometimes disseminate among the people themselves, and which, though they speedily give place to better information, and more deliberate reflection, have a tendency, in the meantime, to occasion dangerous innovations in government, and serious oppressions of the minor party in the community."[20]

---

17. *See id.*, referring to, DWORKIN, TAKING RIGHTS SERIOUSLY, *supra* note 16 at 116–17 (1977).

18. *See* CASS R. SUNSTEIN, LEGAL REASONING AND POLITICAL CONFLICT, 194–96, 241 (1996). *See* also Samuel J.M. Donnelly, *Towards A Personalist Jurisprudence: Basic Insights and Concepts*, 28 LOY.L.A.L. REV. 547, 612–15 (1995). Donnelly states that deliberation requires flexibility, conversation, balancing of interests, and the restraint necessary to allow that thought and exchange of views take place. Sunstein further defined "deliberation" as one of the great moral concepts.

19. THE FEDERALIST PAPERS (James Madison)

20. THE FEDERALIST No. 78, at 440 (Alexander Hamilton) (Isaac Kramnick ed., 1987).

The separation of powers and the related independence of the judiciary was designed as Hamilton reports and we know to protect against tyranny. What is interesting is that the founders believed that the separation of powers would promote deliberation because "it is the reason, alone, of the public, that ought to control and regulate the government."[21] Reason and a deliberating society in which reasoned arguments prevail over passion, was an ideal for the founding generation.[22] The separation of powers was designed to cool passions and partisan pursuit of narrow interests and allow reasoned argument to prevail.

Restraining executive and legislative tendencies to tyranny was, however, a purpose of the separation of powers and the independent judiciary. Hamilton explained: "In a monarchy it (the independent judiciary) is an excellent barrier to the despotism of the prince, in a republic it is a no less excellent barrier to the encroachments and oppressions of the representative body."[23] He adds: "there is no liberty if the power of judging be not separated from the legislative and executive power."[24] He contends that: "The complete independence of the courts of justice is peculiarly essential in a limited Constitution,"[25] that is, one in which there are exceptions to legislative authority. When Hamilton wrote portions of the Federalist Papers, he did not contemplate a Bill of Rights. With that addition, however, his argument appears yet stronger. "Limitations of this kind can be preserved in practice no other way than through the medium of courts of justice, whose duty it must be to declare all acts contrary to the manifest tenor of the Constitution void."[26] He added: "Without this, all the reservations of particular rights or privileges would amount to nothing."[27]

The separation of powers and the related independence of the judiciary were designed in Hamilton's view both to restrain tyranny and to promote deliberation. Arguably these goals are related to each other. A temporarily dominant and passionate faction may propose measures to

21. THE FEDERALIST No. 49, at 315 (James Madison) (Isaac Kramnick ed., 1987).

22. *See* SUNSTEIN *supra* note 18.

23. THE FEDERALIST No. 78, at 437 (Alexander Hamilton) (Isaac Kramnick ed., 1987).

24. *Id.*

25. THE FEDERALIST No. 78, at 438 (Alexander Hamilton) (Isaac Kramnick ed., 1987).

26. *Id.*

27. *Id.*

oppress a minority or those out of power. Slowing down the political process while encouraging deliberation may cool passions, allow reason to prevail and protect the minority.

Deliberation, the restraint of precipitous action in favor of reasoned discussion and decision making, is linked to the defense of minorities and civil liberties. Once a Bill of Rights has been added to the Constitution, among other reasons for the purpose of affording minorities that protection, the importance of deliberation becomes greater. As Ronald Dworkin argued, the deliberately general language of many provisions of the Bill of Rights and the Fourteenth Amendment set before us a series of great moral standards whose meaning and extent are by their nature contested.[28] In determining the meaning of the great contested moral concepts the justices of the Supreme Court, to follow the ideals of the founding generation, must engage in reasoned deliberation.

Justice Antonin Scalia, when interpreting the great standards of the Bill of Rights and the Fourteenth Amendment, would seek the plain meaning of these provisions as they would have been understood by the ordinary politically active person of the time.[29] The problem with this originalism is that the politically active people of the time would have recognized the intentionally chosen generality of the language. Ronald Dworkin argues that the drafters of these great standards chose to use a well recognized form of moral discourse.[30] A parent, he notes, engages in that form of discourse when he or she puts the standard of fairness before the children. Later when a dispute arises the parent may say "I thought I told you to act fairly." On hearing the objection, "what we did was fair," the parent must determine whether he or she wants adherence to a particular theory of fairness or the general standard.[31] It appears that the drafters of the Bill of Rights and the Fourteenth Amendment have put general standards before us which may be given a number of different interpretations. The Supreme Court, then, from time to time

28. *See* RONALD DWORKIN, TAKING RIGHTS SERIOUSLY, *supra* note 16 at 132–37 (1977).

29. *See* A. SCALIA, A MATTER OF INTERPRETATION: FEDERAL COURTS AND THE LAW 37–40 (1997) [hereinafter A MATTER OF INTERPRETATION]; A. Scalia, *Originalism: The Lesser Evil*, 57 U.CIN.L.REV. 849, 862–65 (1989).

30. *See* RONALD DWORKIN, TAKING RIGHTS SERIOUSLY, *supra* note 16 at 134 (1977).

31. *See* RONALD DWORKIN, TAKING RIGHTS SERIOUSLY, *supra* note 16 at 134 (1977).

must deliberate on the meaning of the great moral standards in the Constitution. The drafters' use of general language setting forth great moral standards seems to call for such continuing and maturing deliberation. That appears to be one of their intentions and one which would have been recognized by a politically active person at the time of the drafting. One problem with originalism and the related notion of original intent is that it overlooks this basic intention of the drafters.[32]

Later, it will be argued that Scalia's originalism-textualism as well as other conservative and some liberal theories of constitutional interpretation violate the ideals of the founding generation by refusing to deliberate. Majoritarianism, a conservative theory of constitutional interpretation popular in the Burger Court, not only refuses to deliberate but appears to lack good institutional fit with the history and structure of our Constitution. The view that the Supreme Court, when a constitutional concept is general or unclear, should choose an interpretation which reflects the will of the majority is based on a simplistic understanding of democratic theory. Ronald Dworkin offers a more profound understanding which has better institutional fit with the existence of the Bill of Rights and the Fourteenth Amendment. Along with separation of powers, the Bill of Rights appears designed to protect the rights of those in the minority or out of power. As Ronald Dworkin argues, choosing the interpretation preferred by the majority, when there is a clash between majority and minority interests, is to make the majority the judge in its own case.[33] The only way to afford minorities the protection of the great moral standards placed in the constitution for that purpose is for judges to debate, deliberate and stand by the meaning they perceive in the constitutional protections.

One could mistakenly argue for majoritarian interpretation on an understanding of democratic theory. In a democracy, one could say, decisions should be made in accordance with the wishes of the majority. That argument would seem out of accord with the desires of the founding generation to restrain the power of the legislative branch in order to protect those in the minority and out of power and out of accord with the design including separation of powers and the Bill of Rights, which they included in our Constitution. In other words, majoritarian demo-

---

32. *See* Ronald Dworkin's comment, A MATTER OF INTERPRETATION 115, 119–27.

33. *See* RONALD DWORKIN, TAKING RIGHTS SERIOUSLY, *supra* note 16 at 142–44.

cratic theory does not have good institutional fit with the history and structure of the Constitution.

An alternate understanding of democratic theory seems to have better institutional fit. This theory, while recognizing an important role for majority rule, would emphasize the worthwhileness of and the need to protect each person in our country. Majority rule then must be restrained in order to protect each person including those out of power or in the minority. This version of democratic theory has good institutional fit with the checks and balances, the separation of powers and the Bill of Rights which the founding generation built into our Constitution.

This second version of democratic theory also makes more morally of our Constitution than majoritarianism. Rather than promoting liberty by the inadequate although useful means of majority rule, it seeks to protect the rights of each person. Ronald Dworkin would ground a theory similar to that briefly sketched here in an understanding of political friendship[34] or in the fundamental principle, afford all persons equal respect and concern.[35] One could argue that such a theory as this appeals to ultimate legitimacy in as much as it rests on a principle capable of appealing to all persons.

The theory of democracy just offered draws on the thought of Ronald Dworkin and is the beginning of a comprehensive theory of our Constitution. Dworkin would ground such a theory in political friendship or the principle, afford all persons equal respect and concern. Dworkin would use that foundation to develop theories of each of the general provisions of our Constitution, particularly those found in the Bill of Rights and the Fourteenth Amendment. He would describe these general provisions as great contested moral concepts and would recognize that competing theories or conceptualizations could be offered to justify or explain those concepts.[36] A judge would choose between competing theories by the criteria of good institutional fit and higher moral appeal. A theory which does not have the virtue of fit should be discarded. One can argue for a theory on the ground that it has good or better institutional fit than competing theories. When choosing between theories, each of which have good institutional fit, a judge should

---

34. *See* RONALD DWORKIN, LAW'S EMPIRE, *supra* note 16 at 198–99.

35. *See* RONALD DWORKIN, TAKING RIGHTS SERIOUSLY, *supra* note 16 at 132–37.

36. *Id.*

accept the one which makes the most, including the most morally, that now can be made of our Constitution.[37] Arguably fit with an appropriate comprehensive theory would support an argument that the conceptualization of a particular constitutional concept has both good institutional fit and higher moral appeal.

Applying Dworkin, but moving beyond his thought, one could address federalism and the meaning of other practical arrangements found in our Constitution. Here, despite Dworkin's preference for analytical and deductive reasoning, it would seem that means-end reasoning makes the most sense. Dworkin would ground a comprehensive theory of our Constitution in political friendship. Arguably federalism, separation of powers and other practical arrangements in the Constitution are means for promoting or pursuing political friendship. An understanding of federalism, necessary for the interpretation of the commerce clause, for example, should have good institutional fit with the structure including the historic structure of our country and its Constitution. As Dworkin argues, there also should be fit with the evolving case law.[38] Nevertheless, the better interpretation will be one which promotes the general welfare and the well being of the country, not only economically but in terms of political friendship. On that basis the appropriate understanding of federalism and other practical arrangements will change from age to age depending on the condition of our country.

Personalist method would be inspired by Dworkin's idealism. Our personalist judge, now a justice of the United States Supreme Court, would accept Dworkin's foundation, political friendship and afford all persons equal respect and concern, as the beginning of a comprehensive theory of our Constitution. His method for developing that theory and the theories or conceptualizations of particular provisions would differ. Likewise, in applying particular provisions, the personalist judge would often use means-end reasoning as the method of choice.

Justice William Brennan offers a theory that is somewhat similar to that of Dworkin as a general interpretation of our Constitution. He argues that after the Bill of Rights and the post-Civil War amendments,

---

37. *See* RONALD DWORKIN, TAKING RIGHTS SERIOUSLY, *supra* note 16 at 116–17. *See* also RONALD DWORKIN, LAW'S EMPIRE, *supra* note 16 at 230–31.

38. *See* RONALD DWORKIN, LAW'S EMPIRE, *supra* note 16 at 147. Dworkin argues "that the right balance is secured by judges always respecting past explicit decisions of political institutions but not enforcing decisions by default."

our Constitution offers "a sparkling vision of the supremacy of the human dignity of every individual."[39] While the Brennan and Dworkin theories of the Constitution resemble each other, their respective methods of arriving at and developing their theories differ. Justice Hercules, according to Dworkin, when first appointed to the bench should frame a general theory which will consistently govern all his decisions.[40] He may remake this theory from time to time and discard some decisions under a theory of mistakes.[41] What he may not do is to incrementally create or develop his understanding of the Constitution. That would be contrary to Dworkin's virtue of Integrity with its strong emphasis on consistency.[42] In contrast, Brennan's understanding that our Constitution offers a sparkling vision of each person's human dignity represents his mature thought. Probably his understanding of human dignity as an important constitutional value began a sharp but incremental development while he was writing his concurring and dissenting opinions in such capital punishment cases as *Furman v. Georgia*[43] and *Gregg v. Georgia*[44] and continued its more general development in his concurring opinion in *Rhodes v. Chapman*,[45] an Eighth Amendment prison overcrowding case, and ultimately blossomed into a full theory in his mature old age.[46]

A personalist judge, practicing the founding generation's virtue of deliberation, would develop his comprehensive theory gradually and in re-

---

39. *See* William J. Brennan, Jr., *The Constitution of the United States: Contemporary Ratification,* in INTERPRETING THE CONSTITUTION: THE DEBATE OVER ORIGINAL INTENT 23, 28–29 (Jack N. Rakove ed., 1990). *See also* William J. Brennan, Jr., *The Constitution of the United States: Contemporary Ratification,* 27 S.TEX.L.REV. 433,439 (1986) and William J. Brennan, Jr., *Speech at the Text and Teaching Symposium,* Georgetown University (Oct. 12, 1985), in THE GREAT DEBATE: INTERPRETING OUR WRITTEN CONSTITUTION 11, 14 (Paul G. Cassell ed., 1986).

40. *See* DWORKIN, TAKING RIGHTS SERIOUSLY, *supra* note 16 at 118–23.

41. *Id.*

42. *See* DWORKIN, LAW'S EMPIRE, *supra* note 16 at 134–35.

43. *See* Furman v. Georgia, 408 U.S. 238 (1972) (Brennan, J., concurring).

44. *See* Gregg v. Georgia, 438 U.S. 153 (1976) (Brennan, J., dissenting).

45. *See* Rhodes v. Chapman, 452 U.S. 337 (1981) (Brennan, J., concurring).

46. *See* William J. Brennan, Jr., *The Constitution of the United States: Contemporary Ratification,* in INTERPRETING THE CONSTITUTION: THE DEBATE OVER ORIGINAL INTENT 23, 28–29 (Jack N. Rakove ed., 1990). Brennan offers his theory that the post-Civil War Constitution offers a "sparkling vision" concerned with the protection of each person's human dignity.

sponse to his experience of decision making. Often he would deliberate concerning the appropriate means for achieving constitutional goals.

The founding generation admired deliberation which would include reasoned reflection on the great contested constitutional concepts. Arguably, reasoned reflection would lead to the perception of great themes in or the development of a comprehensive theory for the Constitution. Ronald Dworkin has made a major contribution towards reasoned reflection on our Constitution. However, the use of means-end reasoning also constitutes reflection on the appropriate means for pursing the great constitutional goals. The personalist adaptation of Dworkin's method for constitutional interpretation will be illustrated and developed further in the next part.

5. Rights Theory and Constitutional Interpretation

The theory of rights outlined in the last chapter would be relevant in developing a comprehensive theory of our Constitution and conceptualizations of the great contested moral concepts found in the Bill of Rights and the Fourteenth Amendment.

The personalist theory of rights starts with a recognition of the value of each person and the importance of personal relations in which each participant is treated as a person. In the great common action of our society, most people are related indirectly. Law and its protection of rights imposes restraints on action to ensure that members of our society who are related indirectly are treated as persons. In personalist rights theory each person has a right to participate in the common action of society. Rights are designed to protect the primary social goods, those goods necessary or important to participate in any society or this society. Arguably, our Constitution protects a set of the primary social goods and establishes arrangements which will promote participation in our government and society.

When deciding cases while interpreting constitutional provisions a judge, however, should not simply apply personalist rights theory. His interpretation should have good institutional fit as well as higher moral appeal. Some goods necessary to participation in society are not protected by our Constitution. The political process, rather than the judicial system, would have the responsibility for enhancing and protecting those goods.

A personalist judge should recognize his own limited knowledge and understanding and hence his modest grasp of the primary social goods and their role in the lives of various members of our society. Horizon crossing, conversation across the multiple horizons in our pluralist society, and compromise should be regular aspects of his decision making. In particular cases, a personalist judge typically would use means-end reasoning and would construct appropriate means to promote constitutional goals and to enhance the protected primary social goods.

Justice William Brennan's opinion for the Court in *New York Times v. Sullivan*[47] would be a good model for a personalist judge. In *New York Times v. Sullivan,* Brennan modified the common law of libel by holding that a public official suing a newspaper for libel must show malice in addition to the elements of the common law action. He defined malice as the knowing or reckless disregard of truth. This holding balanced the interest of Commissioner Sullivan and other public officials in their reputations against the freedom of the press of The New York Times and the black ministers who published an advertisement which Commissioner Sullivan alleged libeled him. The advertisement which contained some mistaken statements criticized police activities suppressing Rev. Martin Luther King and his supporters.

Brennan in *New York Times*, offered a theory of the First Amendment related to the democratic structure of our society. Adopting a position first offered by James Madison in the Virginia and Kentucky resolutions, he recognized that in a society where the people are sovereign, they are entitled to criticize their public servants.[48] Under democratic theory, he argued, vigorous and robust debate is the appropriate means for the pursuit of truth.[49] The sovereign people need that truth and the debate which sorts it out to make appropriate decisions concerning their government.

While Brennan offered a theory of the First Amendment which is related to a more general theory of the democratic structure of our government, his development and application of his theory employs the pragmatic instrumentalist method typical of the Warren Court. For example, Brennan uses means-end reasoning: vigorous and robust dis-

---

47. N.Y. Times v. Sullivan, 376 U.S. 254, 84 S.Ct. 710 (1964) [hereinafter New York Times].
48. *See id.* at 275.
49. *See id.* at 276.

cussion is a means in the pursuit of truth which in turn serves a sovereign people engaged in self-government. Further, he balances interests, the officials' interest in reputation against the critics' interest in freedom of the press. His rule adding the element of malice to the common law action is a means for accommodating the competing interests.[50]

While Brennan does not refer to a comprehensive theory of our Constitution, he does draw on democratic theory and emphasizes freedom of the press as a means for participation in government. In his opinion he relates constitutional theory to means-end reasoning.

From a personalist perspective, one readily could transform Brennan's discussion of democratic theory into a reflection on a vision of the entire Constitution as designed to promote respect and concern for each person and to support their participation in society. Ultimately, Brennan in his old age was able to articulate a similar vision.[51] A personalist reader of *New York Times* would be impressed particularly by the carefully constructed holding which balanced the interest in reputation against freedom of speech. A concern for settling disputes with respect for competing interests is an important aspect of personalist method. One could contrast the more absolutist position expressed by Justice Black in his concurring opinion in *New York Times v. Sullivan*.[52] Arguably, Brennan made some effort to cross horizons while deciding *New York Times*. His opinion reveals an understanding of the Southern effort

---

50. *See* New York Times, *supra* note 47 at 279–80; *See* also ANTHONY LEWIS, MAKE NO LAW: THE SULLIVAN CASE AND THE FIRST AMENDMENT 144–45 (1991) [hereinafter MAKE NO LAW]. In New York Times, Brennan modified the common law of libel by holding that a public official suing a newspaper for libel must show malice in addition to the elements of the common law action. He defined malice as the knowing or reckless disregard of truth. This holding balanced the interest of Commissioner Sullivan and other public officials in their reputations against the freedom of the press of the New York Times and the black ministers who published an advertisement which Commissioner Sullivan alleged libeled him. The advertisement which contained some mistaken statements criticized police activities suppressing Rev. Martin Luther King and his supporters. Adopting a position first offered by James Madison in the Virginia and Kentucky resolutions, he recognized that in a society where the people are sovereign they are entitled to criticize their public servants. *See* New York Times at 258–59; 273–82 and MAKE NO LAW at 144–45.

51. *See* Brennan, *supra* note 7.

52. *See* New York Times, *supra* note 47 (Black, J. concurring).

to use state libel laws to eliminate support by the Northern press for the desegregation campaign of Rev. Martin Luther King and his associates.[53]

First Amendment theory has continued to develop since *New York Times v. Sullivan.* Professor Steven Heyman's article, *Righting The Balance: An Inquiry Into the Foundations and Limits of Freedom of Expression,*[54] offers a recent theory of First Amendment freedom of speech and press, which with some modest changes, would be compatible with personalist theory.

Justice Brennan's concurring opinion in *Rhodes v. Chapman,*[55] a prison overcrowding case, would offer a second model for a personalist judge developing his method for deciding constitutional cases. Justice Powell, who wrote the majority opinion in *Rhodes,* held that prison conditions "must not involve the wanton and unnecessary infliction of pain, nor may they be grossly disproportionate to the severity of the crime."[56] However, "conditions that cannot be said to be cruel and unusual under contemporary standards are not unconstitutional"[57] violations of the Eighth and Fourteenth Amendments. The prison in question was modern, well conducted but overcrowded. Powell held that double celling, in response to the overcrowding, did not by itself amount to cruel and unusual punishment. Justice Brennan who contrasted the relatively good conditions at this prison with reports from lower court cases of outrageous conditions at other prisons agreed.[58] In *Rhodes,* the Supreme Court, while setting limits, gave its blessing to lower courts reviewing prison conditions.

In his concurring opinion Justice Brennan interpreted the Eighth Amendment in a different manner than Powell and gave more specific guidance to District Court judges. Following his capital punishment opinions, Brennan grounded his interpretation of the Eighth Amendment in respect for the human dignity of each person. "The task of the courts in cases challenging prison conditions" he explained, "is to 'determine whether a challenged punishment comports with human dig-

---

53. *See* New York Times, *supra* note 47 at 258–59.

54. *See* Professor Steven J. Heyman, *Righting The Balance: An Inquiry Into The Foundations And Limits Of Freedom Of Expression,* 78 B.U. L. Rev. 1275, 1278–80 (1998).

55. Rhodes v. Chapman, 452 U.S. 337, 361 (1981).

56. *Id.*

57. *Id.*

58. *Id.*

nity.'"[59] Given that standard, however, he was more concerned with the method for assessing the conditions in a particular prison. The District Court judge, he explained, must not limit his review but must look at the impact of the totality of conditions on the human dignity of the inmates. For example, he instructed the lower courts as follows:

> "In determining when prison conditions pass beyond legitimate punishment and become cruel and unusual, the 'touchstone is the effect upon the imprisoned'.... The court must examine the effect upon inmates of the condition of the physical plant (lighting, heat, plumbing, ventilation, living space, noise levels, recreation space); sanitation (control of vermin and insects, food preparation, medical facilities, lavatories and showers, clean places for eating, sleeping, and working); safety (protection from violent, deranged, or diseased inmates, fire protection, emergency evacuation); inmate needs and services (clothing, nutrition, bedding, medical, dental and mental health care, visitation time, exercise and recreation, educational and rehabilitative programming); and staffing (trained and adequate guards and other staff, avoidance of placing inmates in positions of authority over other inmates).... When 'the cumulative impact of the conditions of incarceration threatens the physical, mental, and emotional health and well-being of the inmates and/or creates a probability of recidivism and future incarceration,' the court must conclude that the conditions violate the Constitution."[60]

What Brennan is strongly recommending to District Court judges is both a close detailed analysis of the prison in question and an attempt to understand the totality of conditions at the prison and their impact on the inmates. A personalist judge would recognize that Brennan is asking the District Court judges to form a gestalt of the prison conditions and to acquire a sense of the situation.[61] He is directing trial judges to use these devices to cross horizons and to attempt to understand the foreign horizon of the prison.

As in *New York Times* Brennan offers a theory of the relevant constitutional provision. The Eighth Amendment's prohibition of cruel and unusual punishment is designed to protect the human dignity of each person. In *Rhodes*, however, the theory of the Eighth Amendment is re-

---

59. *Id.*
60. *Id.* at 354.
61. *See* J. FRANK, COURTS ON TRIAL 165–85 (1950).

lated directly to his developing comprehensive theory that the post-Civil War Constitution presents "a sparkling vision of the supremacy of the human dignity of every individual."[62] The intellectual move from this general standard to the related concrete use of situation sense to understand the totality of prison conditions and their impact on the human dignity of the inmates is remarkable.

Brennan's reasoning process in *Rhodes* offers both an abstract understanding of the Eighth Amendment and related directions for a concrete detailed investigation of the prison. In traditional terms, his decision is principled only because his interpretation of the Eighth Amendment is consistent with his interpretation of the same provision in his capital punishment decisions. Arguably, his emphasis on human dignity is a traditional principle, that is a policy theme running through a series of cases. In Dworkian terms, however, both Brennan's interpretation of the Eighth Amendment and his concrete directions to judges are principles because they are reasons for decisions based on individual rights.[63] The right to human dignity is an abstract right which in the reasoning process supports a concrete right to decent living conditions and the directions to the trial judge to examine those conditions.[64]

Brennan's reasoning process in *Rhodes* and *New York Times* both resembles and differs from that of Dworkin. Like Dworkin, Brennan uses rights in the reasoning process. Like Dworkin he offers a theory of the relevant constitutional provision. In contrast to Dworkin, however, he will cross horizons, balance interests and develop a gestalt of the relevant situation. Those steps could be described as part of Brennan's reasoning process, part of the movement from an abstract understanding of the constitutional provision to a decision concerning the concrete rights in this situation. As in *New York Times*, Brennan often uses means-end reasoning in that process and crafts particular holdings as a means for balancing interests, securing the constitutional goal and serving a more general understanding of the Constitution as designed to protect each person.

Both *New York Times* and *Rhodes* could be understood as protecting primary social goods. Freedom of the press is an important means for

---

62. *See* Brennan, *supra* note 7.
63. *See* RONALD DWORKIN'S, TAKING RIGHTS SERIOUSLY, *supra* note 16 at 194–95.
64. *Id.*

participation in our society. The Southern attempt to limit that freedom was precisely designed to exclude people from full participation in society. The Eighth Amendment's prohibition of cruel and unusual punishment, as Brennan interprets it, is designed to protect the minimal primary goods necessary to living with some human dignity.

A personalist judge, learning from Brennan as well as Dworkin, would move from his abstract background theory of rights to a vision of our Constitution and an interpretation of its particular provisions.[65] Those interpretations could be described as abstract institutional rights. They also could be described as constitutional goals to be balanced against competing goals derived from the abstract background theory of rights and supported by the comprehensive vision of our Constitution. To serve those competing goals a judge should balance interests, craft holdings which provide concrete means for resolving disputes in a manner which serves those competing goals, and cross horizons so that he has a greater understanding of the relevant interests and their relation to his theory of rights and his vision of the Constitution. As argued in previous chapters, the personalist decision making method should be considered part of the theory of rights and the comprehensive theory of our Constitution. In personalist theory, method is important and is a significant way of understanding the role of the Supreme Court in relating persons and horizons in our pluralist society.

In developing his method a personalist judge should engage in conversation with competing methods. Having outlined a personalist method for constitutional interpretation, we should now begin that conversation. In the next part, the conversation will be with an earlier tradition, which set the stage for twentieth century quarrels over methods for interpreting our Constitution. Karl Llewellyn called the period from roughly 1880 to 1920 or 1930 the time of the strict style of judicial decision making.[66] My colleague, Professor William Wiecek, a distinguished legal historian, describes the period from 1886 to 1937 as *The Lost World of Classical Legal Thought*.[67] Legal classicism, as he describes it, came to an end with Franklin Roosevelt's appointments to the United States Supreme Court. From 1937 to the 1954 decision in *Brown*

---

65. *Id.*

66. KARL LLEWELLYN, THE COMMON LAW TRADITION, 465–66 (1960).

67. *See* WILLIAM WIECEK, THE LOST WORLD OF CLASSICAL LEGAL THOUGHT (1998) [hereinafter cited as WIECEK].

v. Board of Education of Topeka, Kansas[68] was a short 17 years and many of the most distinguished Roosevelt appointees were still on the Court. After setting the stage with a brief review of legal classicism and its demise, discussion will center on *Brown* and the decision making method illustrated by Chief Justice Warren's opinion. I have described *Brown* as the triumph or high point of pragmatic instrumentalist method. Perhaps it could be understood better in contrast to or as a response to legal classicism. The acrimonious modern quarrel over methods for interpreting our Constitution followed *Brown* and produced a great proliferation of proposed methods for constitutional interpretation. Following the discussion of *Brown*, I will address this great quarrel over method. After this multilayered conversation with tradition, discussion will return to the further development of personalist method.

6. Conversing with Tradition: Legal Classicism

From time to time, American law seems to be organized around paradigms in the Kuhnian sense. Thomas Kuhn describes a scientific paradigm as a research consensus.[69] A legal paradigm could be defined as a decision making consensus.[70] The central concepts, principles and exemplary cases govern the questions which courts will ask and the arguments they will find acceptable. Legal paradigms, of course, establish horizons as discussed in the earlier chapters.

As my colleague William Wiecek describes the period between 1886 to 1937 in his book, *The Lost World of Classical Legal Thought*, American constitutional law appears to be dominated by a paradigm which he calls legal classicism.[71] Wiecek argues that the dominance of this paradigm among lawyers, judges and others has not been replicated since.

Legal classicism developed and perhaps distorted concepts from the earlier period of constitutional review following *Marbury v. Madison*.[72]

---

68. Brown v. Board of Education, 347 U.S. 483 (1954).

69. *See* THOMAS KUHN, THE STRUCTURE OF SCIENTIFIC REVOLUTIONS 2nd ed (Chicago: University of Chicago Press, 1970) at 144, 148.

70. *See* Samuel J.M. Donnelly, *Principles, Persons and Horizons: A Friendly Analysis of What Dworkin Has Overlooked*, 26 ST. LOUIS L. REV. 217, 265–75 (1982).

71. *See* WIECEK *supra* note 67.

72. *Id.* at 31–32, 100–01, 225.

Among these would be the power of the Supreme Court to declare federal and state legislation unconstitutional, the concept of individual liberty, and a Lockean understanding of the need to protect property. Our Constitution in Article I, Section 10 directs the states not to pass any "Law impairing the Obligation of Contracts."[73] Inspired by the Fourteenth Amendment protection of liberty, legal classicism transformed the prohibition on impairing the obligation of contracts into a protected liberty of contract, which it employed to restrict state police power and to strike down state social legislation. Activities of labor unions were perceived as conspiracies in restraint of trade and were prohibited through use of the labor injunction.[74]

Legal classicism saw itself as protecting and promoting individual liberty against unions and against federal and state regulation. A commitment to an abstract understanding of the equality of all persons, joined with freedom of contract and an individualist view of liberty, provided a basis for opposing both social legislation and labor union conspiracies in restraint of trade.[75] No one should interfere with the bargaining between individuals even if some are rich and others are without resources.

The Supreme Court, during the period of legal classicism, saw itself as enforcing the rule of law.[76] Typically law was common law and not legislation. Wiecek's description of the thought of James C. Carter, known in my youth as "Old Dutch Carter,"[77] is revealing:

> "James C. Carter, doyen of the turn-of-the-century bar, provided a jurisprudential summary of this outlook in *Law: Its Origins, Growth, and Function,* a book that culminated the historical tradition in American law. Society's customs were the dominant

---

73. U.S.C.A. CONST. Art. I § 10 states "[N]o State shall enter into any Treaty, Alliance, or Confederation; grant Letters of Marque and Reprisal; coin Money; emit Bills of Credit; make any Thing but gold and silver Coin a Tender in Payment of Debts; pass any Bill of Attainder, ex post facto Law, or Law impairing the Obligation of Contracts, or grant any Title of Nobility".

74. *See* WIECEK *supra* note 67. While Wiecek summarizes some of the characteristics of legal classicism, this list is by no means all-inclusive.

75. *Id.*

76. *Id.*

77. As I was preparing to join the law firm of Carter, Ledyerd and Milburn, founded by James C. Carter, as a young associate, Arthur Sutherland, historian at Harvard Law School, congratulated me upon joining "Old Dutch Carter's" law firm.

source of law, particularly private law. Law was, he wrote elsewhere, 'the mere jural form of the habits, usages and thoughts of a people.' Legislation could only supplement and confirm that custom. Thus judges find the rules of law in custom....

Written law—that is, legislation or constitutional amendment—should not try to modify or direct custom. Carter chose two examples to demonstrate why: antitrust and black suffrage. He regarded both as failures, mischievous attempts by legislators to thwart objectives that the relevant groups in society, investment capitalists and white supremacists respectively, were determined to achieve. Enfranchisement of the freed men was, to Carter, 'tyranny' in its attempt to force or disappoint custom, in this case, oppression of the freed people. The liberty promoted by law sought 'to leave each man to work out in freedom his own happiness or misery, to stand or fall by the consequences of his own conduct.'"[78]

"Old Dutch Carter," it should be noted, endowed at Harvard the distinguished Carter Chair of Jurisprudence, which during the mid-twentieth century, was held by Professor Lon Fuller. Ironically, the current occupant of the Carter chair is Professor Duncan Kennedy.

The legal science promoted by Harvard's Dean Christopher Columbus Langdell supported legal classicism. Both shared an abstract, principled understanding of law. Natural law principles, as used by the law earlier in the nineteenth century, were transformed by the scientism of Langdell and legal classicism into principles discovered by legal science.[79]

Wiecek emphasizes, however, that constitutional legal classicism must be distinguished from Langdellian formalism. While both paradigms shared characteristics and supported each other, legal classicism was a separate paradigm which developed independently. Formalism was an important but not necessarily the dominant characteristic of the Supreme Court's legal classicism.[80]

Legal classicism, as Wiecek reports, developed against a background of perceived problems and a resulting political consensus. Looking back, we perceive the late nineteenth century as a period of industrial progress, the "Golden Age" of wealth and its influence on politics. In

---

78. *See* WIECEK *supra* note 67 at 99.
79. *Id.* at 102–04.
80. *Id* at 234–38.

contrast, the establishment of the time perceived itself as surrounded by problems and as confronted by serious instability. Among these were Reconstruction in the South, a large number of freed slaves, the advent of mass immigration, labor unrest, and the new threat of communism and socialism. Surprisingly, given our impression of industrial progress, Wiecek reports that the late nineteenth century economically was a time of almost constant depression.[81]

Against that background, legal classicism can be perceived as a consensus for imposing social stability. Formalism in that context, although part of the ideology of legal classicism, could be perceived as supported by policy considerations.

When interpreting legal concepts, formalists typically will understand their plain meaning as extending as far as logically possible or as referring only to the minimal logical content of the concept. H. L. A. Hart described formalism as the vice of juristic theory which denies or disguises the presence of choice. Hart offered his understanding of the open texture of law in part as a refutation of legal formalism.[82] During the period of legal classicism, the Supreme Court when interpreting the due process clause of the Fourteenth Amendment, used both tactics of formalism. On racial issues, the Supreme Court interpreted the Fourteenth Amendment narrowly. When striking down social legislation the Supreme Court interpreted broadly the concept of liberty in the due process clause.

Wiecek describes *Plessy v. Ferguson*[83] briefly and dismisses it as a formalist decision.[84] On rereading, however, the majority opinion appears to be a long policy argument for a narrow formalist interpretation of the Fourteenth Amendment. Mr. Justice Brown, who wrote the majority opinion, appears to draw on the policy consensus, which Wiecek attributes to legal classicism and the views held and reported by James Carter. For example, Justice Brown argues for a narrow interpretation of the Fourteenth Amendment as follows:

> "The object of the amendment was undoubtedly to enforce the absolute equality of the two races before the law, but, in the nature of things, it could not have been intended to abolish distinctions based upon color, or to enforce social, as distinguished

---

81. *Id.* at 107–08.
82. *See* H.L.A. Hart, THE CONCEPT OF LAW 132–38, 249–50 (1961).
83. *See* Plessy *supra* note 12.
84. *See* WIECEK *supra* note 67 at 151.

from political, equality, or a commingling of the two races upon terms unsatisfactory to either. Laws permitting, and even requiring their separation, in places where they are liable to be brought into contact, do not necessarily imply the inferiority of either race to the other, and have been generally, if not universally, recognized as within the competency of the state legislatures in the exercise of their police power. The most common instance of this is connected with the establishment of separate schools for white and colored children, which have been held to be a valid exercise of the legislative power even by courts of states where the political rights of the colored race have been longest and most earnestly enforced."[85]

In contrast, the Supreme Court in *Lochner v. New York*[86] gave a broad interpretation to the liberty of contract protected by the due process clause of the Fourteenth Amendment while declaring the New York statute regulating the hours of bakers unconstitutional. Mr. Justice Peckham, who wrote the majority opinion, explained:

"The statute necessarily interferes with the right of contract between the employer and employees, concerning the number of hours in which the latter may labor in the bakery of the employer. The general right to make a contract in relation to his business is part of the liberty of the individual protected by the 14th Amendment of the Federal Constitution....

The question whether this act is valid as a labor law, pure and simple, may be dismissed in a few words. There is no reasonable ground for interfering with the liberty of person or the right of free contract, by determining the hours of labor, in the occupation of a baker. There is no contention that bakers as a class are not equal in intelligence and capacity to men in other trades or manual occupations, or that they are not equal in intelligence and capacity to men in other trades or manual occupations, or that they are not able to assert their rights and care for themselves without the protecting arm of the state, interfering with their independence of judgment and of action."[87]

Wiecek describes substantive due process as a doctrine that developed gradually during the period of legal classicism. *Lochner* was a high point in its acceptance and application by the Supreme Court. He ar-

---

85. *See* Plessy *supra* note 12 at 1140.
86. Lochner v. New York, 198 U.S. 45 (1905).
87. *See* Lochner *supra* note 86 at 53 and 57.

gues that the "antebellum tradition of higher law remained adrift after the Civil War, lacking a textual anchor."[88] Just before the war in *Dred Scott v. Sandford*,[89] Chief Justice Taney had anchored a doctrine of property rights in the due process clause of the Fifth Amendment.[90] After the war particular justices began to find a theory of substantive rights in the due process clause of the Fourteenth Amendment. Wiecek describes substantive due process as "the enduring core of legal classicism."[91] *Lochner*, he describes as "the capstone of substantive due process and liberty of contract, providing a platform from which the Court would later cantilever extensions of those doctrines into the 1930s."[92]

Under the substantive due process understanding, a statute restricting property rights or liberty, including liberty of contract must do more than provide a fair process, it also must be reasonable. A state regulatory statute which violates legal classicism's theory of liberty of contract would be considered unreasonable.

Wiecek asks "just what was it about Justice Peckham's opinion in *Lochner* that was so wretched?"[93] He offers a number of possibilities: "Substantive due process itself? A misconception of liberty, or of contract? Bad sociology? Outdated economics? Judicial hubris? Indifference to fact and/or reality? Mishandling the ends-means equation?"[94] Following Holmes and James Bradley Thayer,[95] subsequent thinkers have found

---

88. *See* Wiecek *supra* note 67 at 124.

89. Dred Scott v. Sandford, 60 U.S. 393 (1856).

90. U.S.C.A. Const. Amend. V. ("[N]o person shall...be deprived of life, liberty, or property, without due process of law").

91. *See* Wiecek *supra* note 67 at 125.

92. *Id.* at 152.

93. *Id.*

94. *Id.*

95. *See* James B. Thayer, *The Origin and Scope of the American Doctrine of Constitutional Law*, 7 Harv.L.Rev. 129, 147–48, 150 (1893). Thayer's Doctrine holds that under the American system, legislatures are the primary judges of the constitutionality of the laws they make, and courts should review challenges to those laws under a clear error test, rather than de novo. *See* also, James B. Thayer, Preliminary Treatise On Evidence At Common Law 183–262 (Boston, Little, Brown 1898); *See* also, James B. Thayer, Cases On Constitutional Law 672 (Cambridge, Charles B. Sever 1895) (making the connection explicit in relation to Chicago, Mil. & St. P. Ry. v. Minnesota, 134 U.S. 418 (1889), the Supreme Court's first major step away from the hands-off attitude it had taken toward state rate regulation in Munn v. Illinois, 94 U.S. 114 (1876), and the Granger Cases).

the mistake in a lack of sufficient deference to legislative decisions at least on economic questions. Some simply would oppose distorting the due process clause to require anything other than a fair procedure.

Under the inspiration of personalist thought, one could recognize in legal classicism and its doctrines concerning property rights, liberty of contract and substantive due process, an overly abstract and individualist theory of liberty unrelated to an understanding of people and to other constitutional goals. Its theory of liberty and justice was flawed but so was its method. Most explicitly the method failed to incorporate horizon crossing at a time when the paradigm and the Court's vision established narrow horizons. A fuller understanding of persons would have ranked economic liberty and property rights lower in the constitutional hierarchy. An effort to cross horizons may have recognized that while contracting persons are all equal before the law, the law could regulate contracts for the sake of moderating the oppression resulting from unequal bargaining power.

In the late twentieth century, questions concerning the role of substantive due process remain. Perhaps we now recognize that many of these questions should have been addressed more appropriately under the Ninth Amendment's protection[96] of unenumerated rights. The problem of unenumerated rights will not go away and traditionally has been addressed under the due process clause of the Fourteenth Amendment. It will be discussed subsequently. The narrow reading of the Fourteenth Amendment in racial discrimination cases was reversed by the Warren Court.

The era of legal classicism came to an end with Franklin Roosevelt's appointments to the United States Supreme Court and the famous footnote four to Justice Stone's opinion in *Carolene Products*.[97] The demise had been prepared not only by the advent of the New Deal, but by the preceding Progressive Movement in politics and by the pragmatic instrumentalist thinkers in law. The new Roosevelt appointees represented a variety of views. Justice William Douglas was a legal realist. Justice Felix Frankfurter, influenced by Holmes, Brandeis and Pound, was a leading expert on administrative law and an advocate of the deferential view. Wiecek quotes Frankfurter's reflections on the era of legal classicism:

---

96. U.S.C.A. CONST. Amend. IX states ("[T]he enumeration in the Constitution, of certain rights, shall not be construed to deny or disparage others retained by the people.")

97. Carolene Products Co. v. United States, 323 U.S. 18 (1944).

"The coming of the machine age tended to despoil human personality. It turned men and women into 'hands.' The industrial history of the early Nineteenth Century demonstrated the helplessness of the individual employee to achieve human dignity in a society so largely affected by technological advances.... .Adam Smith was treated as though his generalization had been imparted by him on Sinai and not a thinker who addressed himself to the elimination of restrictions, which had become fetters upon initiative and enterprise in his day. Basic human rights expressed by the constitutional conception of liberty were equated with theories of laissez-faire. The result was that economic views of confined validity were treated by lawyers and judges as though the Framers had enshrined them in the Constitution. This misapplication of the notions of classic economists and resulting disregard of the perduring reach of the Constitution led to Mr. Justice Holmes' famous protest in the Lochner case."[98]

7. Deciding *Brown*

From the end of legal classicism in 1937 to the 1954 decision in *Brown v. Board of Education of Topeka, Kansas*[99] was a short but eventful 17 years. Many of the most distinguished Roosevelt appointees were still on the Court. These were, in the order of appointment, Hugo Black, Stanley Reed, Felix Frankfurter, William Douglas and Robert Jackson. Aside from their judicial support for New Deal legislation, there were large and renown differences between the most famous, Black, Douglas and Frankfurter. Both Douglas and Frankfurter were strongly influenced by the pragmatic-instrumentalist thought which had contributed to the demise of legal classicism. William Douglas was a legal realist. Felix Frankfurter was influenced by Pound and Holmes. The remaining members of the Court were three Truman appointees, Harold Burton, Tom Clark and Sherman Minton and Chief Justice Earl Warren who was appointed by President Eisenhower.

The period between 1937 and 1954 was a tumultuous time including the end of the Great Depression, the Second World War, the Holocaust, the Korean War and the beginning of the Cold War confrontation with Russia. Arguably these experiences changed our national outlook and

---

98. *See* WIECEK *supra* note 67 at 246 (quoting American Federation of Labor v. American Sash and Door Co., 335 U.S. 538, 543–44, 549–50 (1949)).
99. Brown v. Board of Education of Topeka, Kansas, 347 U.S. 483 (1954).

understanding. On racial questions, the experience of Americans in the armed forces, Truman's desegregation of the military and the shock of the Holocaust prepared our national culture for a changed position on race. Legally the demise of legal classicism and the advance of pragmatic instrumentalist thought was helpful. The great law reform campaign conducted by lawyers for the NAACP beginning in 1929 had established a series of useful precedent.

Nevertheless legal classicism and its support of racial segregation through a narrow interpretation of the Fourteenth Amendment was a living memory. *Plessy v. Ferguson*[100] was binding precedent and the South and other areas of our country remained segregated. Many were determined to maintain that separation.

Arguably, *Brown* is understood better if we recognize not only the post-World War 2 enlightenment and change of horizons in America but also the lingering impact of legal classicism and the cultural acceptance of segregation in large segments of our country. When one reads Chief Justice Warren's opinion in *Brown*, one should recognize not only the pragmatic instrumentalist style of the opinion but also a serious effort to refute basic assumptions of the previously entrenched paradigm of legal classicism.

A major thrust of Warren's argument was that law changes and should change with important developments in knowledge and substantially altered conditions in society. Because of the vast differences in the development and the societal importance of education in the mid-twentieth century, in contrast to its modest status during the post-Civil War period and at the time of *Plessy v. Ferguson*, neither the divided opinions at the time of its passage on the applicability of the Fourteenth Amendment to segregated education nor the supposedly binding precedent in *Plessy* should serve as obstacles to change in that law.[101]

To a modern reader it may seem that Warren is refuting an original intent understanding of the Fourteenth Amendment. More likely he is arguing that law should change as society changes in an effort to rebut a formalist understanding that law, particularly constitutional law, should not undergo fundamental change and that important precedent, such as *Plessy*, are eternally binding. Warren argues:

"In approaching this problem, we cannot turn the clock back to 1868 when the Amendment was adopted, or even to 1896

---

100. *See* Plessy *supra* note 12.
101. *See* Brown *supra* note 99 at 492–93.

when Plessy v. Ferguson was written. We must consider public education in the light of its full development and its present place in American life throughout the Nation. Only in this way can it be determined if segregation in public schools deprives these plaintiffs of the equal protection of the laws."[102]

Warren also assesses the impact of segregated education in light of modern psychological knowledge on the children excluded from white schools. He concludes that: "Segregation with the sanction of law...has a tendency to (retard) the educational and mental development of Negro children and to deprive them of some of the benefits they would receive in a racial(ly) integrated school system."[103] Again, he argues that social change, here change in society's knowledge, should be followed by legal change:

"Whatever may have been the extent of psychological knowledge at the time of Plessy v. Ferguson, this finding is amply supported by modern authority. Any language in Plessy v. Ferguson contrary to this finding is rejected."[104]

Warren's argument that changing society should be followed by changes in law reflects pragmatic-instrumentalist method. Roscoe Pound argued for an experimenting society.[105] Karl Llewellyn claimed that society is constantly in flux and that law typically changes less rapidly in an inadequate effort to relate to society.[106]

Warren's opinion in *Brown* employs other pragmatic-instrumentalist decision making techniques including impact and interest analysis and means-end reasoning. Having examined the vast changes in education since the Civil War and since *Plessy* and our modern psychological knowledge, he examines the impact of racially segregated schools on those excluded:

"Segregation of white and colored children in public schools has a detrimental effect upon the colored children. The impact is greater when it has the sanction of law; for the policy of separat-

102. *See* Brown *supra* note 99 at 492–93.

103. *See* Brown *supra* note 99 at 494.

104. *See* Brown *supra* note 99 at 494–95.

105. *See* generally, Samuel J.M. Donnelly, *Book Review*, 3 HOFSTRA L. REV. 899, 915 (1975) (reviewing WILLIAM TWINING, KARL LLEWELLYN AND THE REALIST MOVEMENT (1973) AND DAVID WIGDOR, ROSCOE POUND: PHILOSOPHER OF LAW (1973)) [hereinafter Donnelly, HOFSTRA BOOK REVIEW].

106. *See id. See* also Karl N. Llewellyn, *Some Realism About Realism — Responding to Dean Pound*, 44 HARV. L. REV. 1222, 1251–56 (1931).

ing the races is usually interpreted as denoting the inferiority of the negro group. A sense of inferiority affects the motivation of a child to learn."[107]

In essence, Warren finds that the *Plessy* separate but equal doctrine is an inadequate means for achieving the constitutional goal of equal protection. In the pragmatic-instrumentalist tradition, he offers social science knowledge in support of that conclusion. He then establishes a new means, desegregated education, to serve the end decreed by the equal protection clause of the Fourteenth Amendment. *Brown* could be described as a high point in the use of pragmatic-instrumentalist reasoning.

In the pragmatic-instrumentalist tradition, one would have great difficulty in finding in *Brown* any extended discussion of principle or deliberation on the concept of equality or equal protection. Warren, in *Brown*, simply does not offer principled or conceptual analysis as arguments in support of his position.

From hindsight, others have provided a principled framework for *Brown*. Justice William Brennan, writing an essay in 1974 for the Harvard Law Review issue dedicated to the memory of Earl Warren,[108] commented:

> "This thread of concern for human dignity also runs through more famous decisions. He wrote *Miranda v. Arizona* as a step toward enforcing a constitutional framework of criminal justice consistent with human dignity and democratic equality by mandating enlightened and civilized treatment by law enforcement officers of criminal suspects. He wrote *Brown v. Board of Education*, which held that segregated education threatened impairment of the human dignity of black school children and was therefore unconstitutional: 'To separate them from others of similar age and qualifications solely because of their race generates a feeling of inferiority as to their status in a way unlikely ever to be undone.'"[109]

Brennan's comments could be described as an appropriate interpretation of *Brown*. But however pleasing that interpretation may be to personalist readers, it offers an understanding of the case on a higher level of generality than Warren uses. The words "human dignity" which became very important to Brennan's thought do not appear in Warren's opinion.

---

107. Brown v. Board of Education, 347 U.S. 483, 494 (1954).
108. *See* William J. Brennan, Jr., *Chief Justice Warren*, 88 Harv. L. Rev. 1–5 (1974).
109. *Id.* at 3.

In *Law's Empire*, Ronald Dworkin explains how Justice Hercules would decide *Brown*.[110] Hercules, Dworkin notes, has a way with statutes and the Constitution could be perceived as a special type of statute.[111] Because our "Constitution is foundational of other law, so Hercules' interpretation of the document as a whole, and of its abstract clauses, must be foundational as well. It must fit and justify the most basic arrangements of political power in the community, which means it must be a justification drawn from the most philosophical reaches of political theory."[112] Hercules, as an abstract imaginary judge, is free to decide constitutional questions on principle because he is not constrained by the need to compromise to obtain the votes of other justices or to make his decision acceptable to the community. Rather, "he is free to concentrate on the issues of principle that, according to law as integrity, constitute the constitutional law he administers."[113]

In *Brown*, Hercules would start with an "abstract egalitarian idea."[114] Our Constitution, Dworkin explains, insists "that each jurisdiction accept the abstract egalitarian principle that people must be treated as equals, and therefore that each respect *some* plausible conception of equality in each of its decisions about property and other matters of policy."[115] Dworkin describes that as the rationality requirement of the Fourteenth Amendment. Beyond that, however, as Hercules perceives the Constitution, certain individual rights will trump any "collective justification."[116] "The crucial interpretative question," Dworkin explains, "is then what rights these are."[117] Addressing the *Plessy* approval of separate but equal schools, Hercules notes that our Constitution "mandates some individual right not to be the victim of official, state-imposed racial discrimination"[118] and constructs three theories of that right, that is, suspect classifications, banned categories, and banned sources.[119]

Dworkin rejects suspect classification as an acceptable interpretation of equal protection. Suspect classification, as he perceives it, is an appli-

---

110. *See* LAW'S EMPIRE, *supra* note 16 at 379–92.
111. *Id.*
112. *Id.* at 380.
113. *Id.*
114. *See* LAW'S EMPIRE, *supra* note 16 at 381.
115. *Id.* at 382.
116. *Id.*
117. *Id.*
118. *Id.*
119. *Id.* at 382–87.

cation of the rationality requirement. "Race and similar grounds of distinction are special, on this account, only because history suggests that some groups are more likely than others to be denied the consideration due to them."[120] When strictly scrutinizing racial categories in legislation, overriding state interests may show that this classification, despite its discriminatory impact, nevertheless may be rational. Using suspect classifications, one could justify segregated schools "by showing that integration would provide an inferior educational environment."[121] Dworkin's analysis, of course, attacks *Plessy v. Ferguson.* One should recognize, however, that the form of reasoning employed by Chief Justice Warren in *Brown* is also under attack in Dworkin's analysis of suspect classification.

Dworkin would prefer either banned categories or banned sources. Justice Hercules could decide *Brown* under a theory that our "Constitution does recognize a distinct right against discrimination as a trump over any state's conception of the general interest."[122] Racial categories, among others, may not be used to establish different treatment for individuals. Racially segregated schools under this theory are simply impermissible. Banned sources differs from the banned categories theory just outlined. While the use of racial categories in the constitutional reasoning process occasionally may be acceptable, "certain sources or types of preference [those that are rooted in prejudice or the desire to dominate]"[123] will not be allowed to count in the reasoning process. Racial segregation is impermissible because its roots historically are in slavery, a sense of white superiority and a desire to dominate. However, legislation designed to correct imbalances from the past and establish racial equality may be permissible. When deciding *Brown,* Hercules could choose either the banned categories or the banned sources theory of equal protection or refrain from choosing between the two. When deciding *Regents of the Univ. of California v. Bakke,*[124] however, Hercules

---

120. *Id.* at 383.
121. *Id.*
122. *See* LAW'S EMPIRE, *supra* note 16 at 383–84.
123. *Id.* at 384.
124. Regents of the Univ. of California v. Bakke, 438 U.S. 265 (1978) (Held: The University's special admissions program favoring disadvantaged minority student applicants was illegal, however, the court found that race could be considered as one factor in accepting applications since the University was unable to show that Bakke, a white applicant, was not going to be admitted had it not been for the special admissions program).

would choose the banned sources theory of equal protection. Under that theory he would allow admissions to public institutions to be guided by affirmative action.[125]

While Chief Justice Warren in his opinion in *Brown* does not offer a principled interpretation of the equal protection clause of our Constitution, from hindsight, his holding is supportable by great principles. Indeed, the result in *Brown* could be supported by ultimate legitimacy, that is, by reasons that have the possibility of being acceptable to all persons at all times because they are based on respect and concern for each person.

A personalist thinker would agree with Justice Brennan's grounding of *Brown* in respect for the human dignity of each person and would be impressed by Dworkin's analysis. He would find particularly intriguing the banned sources theory of equal protection. He would note, however, that the analysis of both Brennan and Dworkin were offered some years after the decision in *Brown*. We can now accept and justify *Brown* on the basis of strong principles.

While *Brown* in the late twentieth century is widely accepted and often perceived to be supported by deep ethical and constitutional principles, in the mid and late 1950s, a firestorm of criticism followed the decision. One might remember, for example, the "Impeach Earl Warren" bumper stickers. Whether *Brown* in 1954 could have been decided by the Court or accepted by the country on the basis of high principles is a difficult question. One should remember that the Court had only recently crossed the horizon of legal classicism and that segregation was entrenched in many parts of our country. While the experience of the Second World War and the Holocaust among others had made possible a change in the national psychology that development was recent and had made only moderate progress. In the common law tradition, principles often are stated from hindsight and after a series of developments. Given the limited nature of human knowledge and understanding that may be a phenomenon recognizable in cultural psychology as well as law.

A personalist looking back on *Brown* could offer an interpretation of the difficulties of deciding it on the basis of high principle. The country's narrow but changing cultural horizons were reenforced by *Plessy v. Ferguson* and the lingering inheritance of legal classicism. The Court's immediate task, perhaps for itself as well as the country, was to deconstruct previous horizons and to focus attention on the impact of *Plessy* on those denied an adequate education by segregated schools, even

---

125. *See* LAW'S EMPIRE, *supra* note 16 at 393–97.

those with equal facilities. The Court, then, appropriately argued that society had changed since *Plessy* and properly called attention to social science studies of segregation. Impact and interest analysis in personalist thought is a means for crossing horizons and a proper basis for assessing horizon bound law. A court charged with resolving great national disputes should inquire whether extant laws appropriately respect all interests and serve as an adequate means for achieving the constitutional goals. The Court should construct new means for serving those goals more adequately.

While a personalist thinker would prefer to ground means-goal reasoning, such as that used by Chief Justice Warren in *Brown*, in a principled analysis of the great contested constitutional concepts such as equal protection, he would recognize the difficult challenge which impacted although changing horizons present to perceiving and explaining that principled analysis. Our country may now perceive and accept the principles supporting *Brown* because of *Brown* and the experiences which followed it.

In personalist thought, a Court presented with a great national dispute, as the Warren court was in *Brown*, should seek to understand the competing interests and the impact of the law on them. The Court must seek to resolve the dispute in accordance with the text of the Constitution and our great ideals but may be handicapped by its own and the country's limited horizons and vision. Personalist theory accepts such limitations and recognizes that we may be able to justify great decisions by great principles only from hindsight. Personalist theory offers a method of decision making useable in limited horizons to reach out to people and to understand their situations and problems. That method is part of a personalist interpretation of our Constitution and of the Supreme Court as a great dispute settlement institution. The method itself is grounded in political friendship and in an interpretation of our Constitution as designed to promote the human dignity of each person.

Dworkin's theory is able to abstract from the human circumstances in which our great principles are actually understood and formulated because Hercules is an imaginary judge and an analytical giant. While Dworkin implies that the legal pragmatist method employed by Chief Justice Warren in explaining his decision in *Brown* is morally and intellectually bankrupt,[126] we should recognize that the method is responsible in part for some of the great moral breakthroughs in the history of

---

126. *See* LAW'S EMPIRE, *supra* note 16 at 220–21.

the Court. Personalist thought would accept and modify those methods for developing constitutional law while resolving the great disputes.

While as Bruce Ackerman[127] and Harry Wellington[128] would argue, *Brown* has now received popular ratification the firestorm which followed it included academic criticism. Herbert Wechsler attacked *Brown* because it was not and could not be based on neutral principles,[129] a notion which probably is nonsense. Learned Hand, whom Dworkin, his former clerk, respectfully describes as a judge whose only religion was skepticism in morals, argued for deference to majority will.[130] In his Holmes lecture, he argued that these great questions should be settled legislatively through the democratic process rather than by the Court.[131] As a moral skeptic, he perceived that majority will was the only means for society to resolve the great moral questions.

In the late twentieth century that initial criticism of *Brown* was followed, to use our terminology, by the great quarrel over method. That quarrel may have started with the conservative desire for strict construction of our Constitution. In the last half century, however, there has been a great proliferation of methods for constitutional interpretation, both conservative and liberal. In the next part it will be argued that many of the conservative theories constitute a refusal to deliberate.

---

127. *See* Ackerman, *supra* note 13 at 1525.

128. *See* WELLINGTON, *supra* note 14 at 114.

129. *See* H. Wechsler, *Toward Neutral Principles of Constitutional Law*, 73 HARV. L. REV. 1 (1959). [hereinafter cited as Wechsler].

130. *See* TAKING RIGHTS SERIOUSLY, *supra* note 16 at 140.

131. *See* LEARNED HAND, THE CONTRIBUTION OF AN INDEPENDENT JUDICIARY TO CIVILIZATION, IN THE SPIRIT OF LIBERTY 103, 109 3d ed. (Irving Dilliard ed., 1960). "But the judge must always remember that he should go no further than he is sure the government would have gone.... If he is in doubt, he must stop, for he cannot tell that the conflicting interests in the society for which he speaks would have come to a just result, even though he is sure that he knows what the just result should be. He is not to substitute even his juster will for theirs; otherwise it would not be the common will which prevails, and to that extent the people would not govern." *See* also Jerome A. Barron, *Learned Hand: A Judge Who Preferred The People To The Courts*, 63 GEO. WASH. L. REV. 613, 624 (1995).

8. The Great Quarrel over Method

a. Conservative Theories

In "Constitutional Cases," chapter 5 of *Taking Rights Seriously*,[132] Ronald Dworkin analyzes and attacks what he describes as the jurisprudence of Richard Nixon. Nixon wanted Supreme Court justices who would strictly construe the provisions of our Constitution. Dworkin argues that strict construction is an ambiguous notion because it confuses two questions, namely, (i) what sort of decision "is required by strict, that is to say faithful adherence to the text of the Constitution"[133] and (ii) which decision best applies a strict or minimalist understanding of the moral rights which individuals may claim against society. A proper reading of our Constitution's text may support a broad understanding of the claims that we, as persons living here, have against American society and government. Strict construction, that is a faithful reading of the Constitution, then, should support that broad understanding of rights. Strict constructionists, however, will oppose that supposedly correct broad interpretation because it supports results at odds with their political philosophy.[134]

Developing Dworkin's analysis of strict construction, one could recognize in that method both a proposed restraint on judicial activism and a political result, that is, a narrow interpretation of constitutional rights. Arguably, a number of proposed conservative theories of judicial restraint have problems of ambiguity which resemble those of strict construction. These theories of apparent judicial restraint produce a conservatively desirable political result, that is, a narrow understanding of constitutional rights.

Justice Antonin Scalia proposes an originalist-textualist interpretation of our Constitution. Put simply, Justice Scalia wants to understand the constitutional text as it would have been understood by a politically active person at the time when it was adopted. In his Tanner lecture at Princeton, published with the title, *A Matter of Interpretation*,[135] Justice Scalia argues that textualism should not be confused with strict construction which he rejects. Reading a text appropriately, he explains, re-

---

132. *See* TAKING RIGHTS SERIOUSLY, *supra* note 16.
133. *Id.* at 133.
134. *Id.* at 135.
135. *See* A MATTER OF INTERPRETATION, *supra* note 29.

quires that one understand its language in context.[136] Scalia, as explained in an earlier chapter, rejects the use of legislative history. He would not try to discern the intent of the drafters of our Constitution. He would read *The Federalist Papers* written by Hamilton and Madison, who were drafters, and by John Jay, who was not in Philadelphia, at the crucial time. However, his reading would be for the purpose of understanding our Constitution's text as it would have been understood at the time, rather than to discern the intent of the drafters.[137]

Justice Scalia would recognize that our Constitution contains some general language which in some provisions expresses principles and values. The values at the core of constitutional principles, however, should be the values held at the time those constitutional provisions were adopted.[138]

As Justice Scalia explains originalism-textualism in *A Matter of Interpretation*, his method appears more sophisticated than a crude strict construction. Like strict construction, however, arguably it is a method for apparent restraint which produces political results which are desirable from a conservative perspective. That conclusion could be illustrated by examining the exchange over capital punishment between Justice Scalia and Professor Dworkin, whose comments are published in *A Matter of Interpretation*.[139] In the text of his speech, Justice Scalia explains: "No fewer than three of the Justices with whom I have served have maintained that the death penalty is unconstitutional, <u>even though its use is explicitly contemplated in the Constitution</u>."[140] By that, of course, he means that a person charged with a capital crime is guaranteed indictment by a grand jury under the Fifth Amendment[141] and that the due process clauses of the Fifth and Fourteenth Amendments prohibit the taking of life without the due process of law.[142] Reading the

---

136. *Id.* at 23–25.

137. *Id.* at 38.

138. *Id.* at 37–40.

139. *See* A MATTER OF INTERPRETATION, *supra* note 29 at 115–27 (Dworkin's comment to Justice Scalia).

140. *Id.* at 46.

141. U.S.C.A. CONST. Amend. V ("[N]o person shall be held to answer for a capital, or otherwise infamous crime, unless on a presentment or indictment of a Grand Jury...").

142. U.S.C.A. CONST. Amend. V ("[N]o person...shall be deprived of life, liberty, or property, without due process of law."); U.S.C.A. CONST. Amend. XIV § 1 ("[N]or shall any State deprive any person of life, liberty or property, without due process of law.").

Eighth Amendment prohibition of "cruel and unusual punishment" in the context of the Fifth Amendment, one can argue that the drafters did not intend (?) and the eighteenth century readers did not understand that capital punishment would be prohibited as "cruel and unusual." Contrarywise, one could imagine a progressive eighteenth century reader, perhaps Dr. Benjamin Rush, remarking: "Well perhaps it is not cruel now because arguably it is necessary, but it will be cruel once the Walnut Street Jail which we are establishing evolves into the American Prison System."

Scalia's contention is that the eighteenth century readers of the Bill of Rights, because they practiced capital punishment and contemplated continuing that practice for some time as witnessed by the provisions of the Fifth Amendment, could not have believed that the death penalty was cruel. In interpreting the "cruel and unusual punishment" clause of the Eighth Amendment, Scalia contends that judges should confine their understanding of "cruel" to its eighteenth century meaning as illustrated by their practice of capital punishment. He does not discuss the fact that the practice of capital punishment was changing in the late eighteenth century.

Ronald Dworkin urges Justice Scalia to examine "whether capital punishment is in fact cruel" rather than whether eighteenth century readers would have considered it cruel.[143] He also suggests that Scalia look to the "semantic intention" of the eighteenth century drafters.[144] Clearly those drafters meant to write general language and a reader from the time would recognize that. Usually lawyers employ general language when they anticipate future disputes or unexpected problems. Often they expect the meaning of their general language to be debated and further interpreted in the future. "Cruel...punishment" is a moral concept.[145] Politically active citizens of the eighteenth century were accustomed to debating moral concepts and their meaning. Intelligent and active citizens of the time would recognize that the "cruel and unusual" punishment provision of the Eighth Amendment[146] contains general language and a moral concept whose meaning could be de-

---

143. *See* A MATTER OF INTERPRETATION, *supra* note 29 at 120–21.

144. *Id.*; *See* also LAW'S EMPIRE, *supra* note 16.

145. U.S.C.A. CONST. Amend. VIII ("[N]or cruel and unusual punishments...").

146. *Id.*

bated. The drafters meant to write exactly that sort of language. That was their "semantic intention."

Scalia's insistence on interpreting the "cruel and unusual" punishment clause, based on a modest understanding of eighteenth century practice, rather than discussing the meaning of the moral concept, cruel, constitutes a refusal to deliberate. Arguably, the founding generation admired the virtue of deliberation and recognized that the Eighth Amendment and other provisions of the Bill of Rights contained general language and moral concepts whose interpretation required deliberation. As an admirer of such original understanding of constitutional language, Scalia should but refuses to practice the virtue of deliberation.

Justice Scalia is offering a theory of judicial restraint: judges interpreting general language and moral concepts in our Constitution should confine their understanding of those concepts and language to the values, practices and interpretation at the time the provisions were adopted. He avoids moral reflection, a maturing understanding of moral concepts, and possible broader interpretation of constitutional rights. His theory of restraint produces a conservatively desirable political result resembling the result of strict construction, that is, a narrow view of the moral claims which we have against our government.

A crude understanding of original intent, which would be rejected by Scalia, offers the same political advantages. Perhaps unfairly one could label such a view, the Edwin Meese theory. As President Reagan's Attorney General, Meese wanted judges who would interpret our Constitution according to the original intent of the drafters.[147] Put simply and perhaps crudely, that meant that the images of due process, equal protection, or cruel and unusual punishment in the minds of the drafters would prevail over a reasonable reading of the general language which they wrote. If the Congress which offered the Fourteenth Amendment for ratification imagined segregated schools, as evidenced, of course, by their practice in the District of Columbia, and by some

---

147. *See* John Stick, *He Doth Protest Too Much: Moderating Meese's Theory of Constitutional Interpretation*, 61 TUL. L. REV. 1079, 1090 (1987). (asserting that the Supreme Court's interpretation of the Constitution and federal statutes is "supreme". "One can define the constitution as only the words ratified in 1788 along with all amendments, or one can include our broader political traditions: Supreme Court decisions, the Declaration of Independence, and the Gettysburg Address, as well as longstanding institutional accommodations between the executive branch and Congress.") *See id.* at 1079–80.

statements in the debates,[148] then judges in subsequent generations, in *Plessy* and *Brown* should not find that segregated schools were a denial of equal protection. Again a theory of restrained judicial decisions produced a result politically popular among some conservatives.

Original intent, as explained by Judge Robert Bork, is very different and much more sophisticated. Perhaps as the Meese theory matured under the Bork influence it began to acquire some of that sophistication. At times Judge Bork's description of original intent resembles Ronald Dworkin's discussion of his own method. For example, in "*The Tempting of America*,"[149] Judge Bork explains:

> "Judges must never refuse to apply old values to new circumstances, whether those circumstances spring from changes in technology or changes in the impact of traditional common law actions. *Sullivan* was an instance of the Supreme Court doing precisely that, as *Brown v. Board of Education* was more generally an example of the Court applying an old principle according to a new understanding of a social situation. It is not that a court may apply an old principle in new ways because its or the society's views on race have changed, but, as already explained, because it became evident over time that the racial separation the ratifiers of the fourteenth amendment assumed was completely inconsistent with the equal protection of the laws they mandated. The important thing, the ultimate consideration, is the constitutional freedom that is given into the judge's keeping. A judge who refuses to see new threats to an established constitutional value, and hence provides a crabbed interpretation that robs a provision of its full, fair, and reasonable meaning, fails in his judicial duty. That duty, it is worth repeating, is to ensure that the powers and freedoms the founders specified are made effective in today's altered world. The evolution of doctrine to accomplish that end contravenes no postulate of judicial restraint."[150]

Judge Bork in this passage seems closer to Dworkin than to Justice Scalia who opposes the evolution of doctrine.[151] Indeed, Bork is more eloquent than Dworkin. One should note, however, Judge Bork's emphasis on "established constitutional values" and "freedoms the

---

148. *See* Brown *supra* note 68.
149. *See* ROBERT BORK, THE TEMPTING OF AMERICA: THE POLITICAL SEDUCTION OF THE LAW (1990).
150. *Id.* at 169.
151. *See* A MATTER OF INTERPRETATION, *supra* note 29 at 44–47.

founders specified."[152] Those values and freedoms should be developed and protected against new threats in a principled manner. Judge Bork simply opposes the recognition of new unenumerated rights, whether by development of the due process clause or under the Ninth Amendment.[153] In his opinion, the Ninth Amendment was designed to protect rights enumerated in existing state constitutions although not found in the federal constitution or the Bill of Rights.[154] Some provisions of our Constitution, such as the equal protection clause, according to Judge Bork, should be interpreted narrowly.[155] He argues that the principal thrust of the equal protection clause in the view of the Congress which offered it for ratification was to attack racial discrimination. Respecting that value, he argues, we should develop the equal protection clause in a principled manner when questions of racial equality are at stake but should refrain from doing so when other issues are presented. On questions other than racial equality, Bork would apply only the rationality requirement of the equal protection clause. That clause, for example, should not apply to issues of sexual discrimination because opposition to sexual discrimination was not a value held by the generation which adopted the Fourteenth Amendment.[156]

The difficult question of the appropriate level of generality for understanding a constitutional principle or provision is presented by Judge Bork's conclusion that the equal protection clause should be interpreted primarily and to a large extent exclusively as concerned with racial equality. Judge Bork recognizes that choosing the appropriate level of generality is most difficult when interpreting the equal protection clause or "when dealing with the broadly stated provisions of the Bill of Rights."[157] He argues: "In dealing with such provisions, a judge should state the principle at the level of generality that the text and historical evidence warrant."[158] In other words, the post Civil War generation's concern with racial discrimination should prevail over the generality of the language they chose to ratify in the equal protection clause. As Ronald Dworkin suggests, that form of interpretation allows an ar-

---

152. *See* TEMPTING OF AMERICA, *supra* note 149 at 184.
153. *Id.*
154. *Id.*
155. *Id.*
156. *See* TEMPTING OF AMERICA, *supra* note 149 at 184.
157. *Id.* at 149.
158. *Id.*

bitrary understanding of the adopting generation's opinion to prevail over the language they chose to adopt.[159] That narrow interpretation of general moral concepts, such as equal protection, when adamantly adhered to could be described as a refusal to deliberate.

Judge Bork's opposition to *Shelley v. Kraemer*[160] which he would now accept as an established although mistaken precedent which should not be reversed was one ground for the attack made on his nomination to the United States Supreme Court.[161] *Shelley*, one of the precedent developed during the long campaign of the NAACP for desegregation, prohibited the enforcement of racially restrictive covenants in deeds to real property. Since these contracts were private arrangements, the Court had to find the necessary state action in the lower court decisions to enforce the restrictive covenants. Influenced, perhaps excessively, by Herbert Wechsler's theory of neutral principles,[162] Judge Bork continues to criticize *Shelley* because he does not believe that its finding of state action can be supported by a principle that will be neutrally applied.[163] He notes that courts do not and cannot consider all court decisions state actions which, therefore, present constitutional issues reviewable by the Supreme Court. Bork's analysis demonstrates the impractical and probably impossible generality in application which Herbert Wechsler demands of judicial holdings. Applying Wechsler's understanding of neutral principles to criticize *Shelley* reflects legal classicism's view of social custom, property and private rights of contract. It also echoes the views of James Carter and of *Plessy* that social customs separating the races should not be interfered with by judicial interpretation of the Fourteenth Amendment.[164]

Judge Bork does not offer a crude Meese-like understanding of original intent. He recognizes the difficulties of discerning the views of the drafters of the Constitution or of the members of Congress who offered amendments and therefore would not try to perceive the contents of their minds. Rather, like Scalia, he would look to public evidence of

---

159. See A MATTER OF INTERPRETATION, *supra* note 29 at 119–27.

160. Shelley v. Kraemer, 334 U.S. 1 (1948).

161. See TEMPTING OF AMERICA, *supra* note 149 at 184.

162. See Wechsler, *supra* note 129; See also TEMPTING OF AMERICA, *supra* note 149 at 151–53.

163. See TEMPTING OF AMERICA, *supra* note 149 at 184.

164. It should be noted that Bork supports Brown, even though he continues to criticize Shelley.

how they would understand the relevant constitutional language.[165] He would develop the values of the drafters in a principled manner. Nevertheless the arbitrary limits which he places on that principled development constitutes a refusal to deliberate and produces political results which would be admired by some conservative constituencies.

While arguably their theories of restraint by their structure produce conservative political results, it would be unfair to Judge Bork and Justice Scalia to suggest that they developed their methods of interpretation for the purposes of producing conservatively acceptable conclusions.[166] Justice Scalia, for example, is renown for applying his method for interpreting legislation and our Constitution even where his conclusions are contrary to conservative expectations.[167] Probably Scalia's understanding of language contributed to the development of his conservative political views rather than developing as a consequence of his political positions. In his youth, Scalia was good at languages and was a skilled translator of texts.[168]

Majoritarianism, a method by which disputed or open textured concepts in the United States Constitution are interpreted according to some estimate of majority will rests as described earlier in this chapter on one understanding of democratic theory. It was argued earlier that the majoritarian understanding of democratic theory is a less desirable interpretation of democracy and lacks good institutional fit with the structure of our Constitution and our constitutional history. Here, it also should be noted, that it constitutes a refusal to deliberate concerning the great contested moral concepts in our Constitution. For deliberation concerning the meaning of those concepts, majoritarianism substitutes a choice based on majority will thereby avoiding hard mental work and making the majority, as Dworkin explains, the judge in its own case.[169] As a moderate conservative theory, it normally produces moderately conservative status quo results. Its proponents offer it as a theory of deference and restraint but like many theories of restraint its structure produces politically desirable results, here a respect for the status quo.

---

165. *See* TEMPTING OF AMERICA, *supra* note 149 at 184.
166. Critical comment suggested by Michael Donnelly when discussing this passage.
167. *See* A MATTER OF INTERPRETATION, *supra* note 29.
168. Scalia received a traditional classical education including the study of Latin and Greek at St. Francis Xavier High School in New York City.
169. *See* TAKING RIGHTS SERIOUSLY, *supra* note 16.

A modified form of majoritarianism was used in a number of Burger Court opinions to justify the Court's holdings. In some fields, particularly capital punishment, the use of majoritarianism continued in the Rehnquist Court. For example, in *Gregg v. Georgia*,[170] one reason for finding capital punishment constitutional was that after *Furman v. Georgia*,[171] thirty-seven state legislatures had revised their capital punishment statutes in an effort to make them constitutional.[172] The Court perceived this as evidence that capital punishment was not out of accord with the evolving standards of human decency. A similar nose count of state legislatures was used in *Coker v. Georgia*[173] as a reason for finding capital punishment for rape unconstitutional, and in *Sanford v. Kentucky*[174] to uphold capital punishment for juveniles sixteen years of age or older.

One can argue, then, that a number of conservative theories which propose methods for achieving judicial restraint when interpreting our Constitution by their structure, if not their intent, produce conservatively desirable political results. By substituting original intent, an understanding of constitutional principles limited to the primary object, or the popular understanding of the drafting generation or the more sophisticated views of those who were politically active at the time of adoption, or by consulting majority will, or deferring to legislative or executive authorities, judges employing these methods to justify their opinions avoid the hard and controversial work of deliberating on and explaining the meaning of the great moral concepts in the United States Constitution.

Liberal as well as conservative theories at times seek simple formulas, sometimes based on highly sophisticated reasoning, to produce politically desirable interpretations of our Constitution while avoiding the hard work of explaining the meaning of constitutional concepts. The next segment will discuss some examples.

b. Some Liberal Theories

Professor John Hart Ely's ingenuous attempt to justify the work of the Warren Court, while offering a theory of judicial restraint, is an ex-

---

170. Gregg v. Georgia, 428 U.S. 153 (1976).
171. Furman v. Georgia, 408 U.S. 238 (1972).
172. Gregg, 428 U.S. at 153.
173. Coker v Georgia, 433 U.S. 584 (1977).
174. Stanford v. Kentucky, 492 U.S. 361 (1989).

ample of a liberal theory which produces liberally desirable political results while purporting to restrain judicial activism.[175] Professor Ely also
avoids deliberating on the meaning of constitutional concepts. Ely offers a process oriented understanding of our Constitution and charges
judges with securing minority participation in societal decision making. He argues that many of the constitutional provisions are concerned
with participation and process. Judicial intervention is authorized
when process breaks down.[176] Participation in society's ongoing common action by each person is an important personalist value. However,
deliberation on constitutional concepts with personalist values as a potential foundation for understanding those concepts is an important aspect of personalist method. Professor Ely substitutes a simple and artificial formula for that process of deliberation.

Professor Laurence Tribe, one of our most distinguished commentators on the American Constitution, offers a theory that is more elusive
and harder to describe. In his comments published in *A Matter of Interpretation*, Ronald Dworkin argues that Tribe's method of interpretation
resembles the Dworkinian theory in some respects.[177] Professor Tribe,
who also was a commentator, finds both Scalia and Dworkin overly certain in their understanding of constitutional concepts.[178] Tribe, in contrast, appearing to use H. L. A. Hart's analysis of legal concepts,[179] recognizes a core meaning for constitutional concepts but argues that the core
is surrounded by an aspirational penumbra of uncertain dimensions.
Tribe insists on the difficulty of analyzing or ascribing any clear meaning
to that aspirational penumbra. He also finds it difficult to offer any general theory of our Constitution which would provide a basis for analyzing the aspirational penumbra of particular provisions.[180]

Elsewhere Tribe has made clear that unlike some liberal thinkers, he
is not prepared to abandon the Constitution. In his book *On Reading
the Constitution* co-authored with Michael Dorf, Tribe argues that the

---

175. *See* J. Ely, Democracy and Distrust: A Theory of Judicial Review
73–75 (1980).

176. *Id.*

177. *See* A Matter of Interpretation, *supra* note 29 at 123.

178. *Id.* at 68–74 (Laurence H. Tribe's comments to Justice Scalia in A
Matter of Interpretation).

179. *See* H.L.A. Hart, The Concept of Law, *supra* note 82 at 135–36.

180. *See* A Matter of Interpretation, *supra* note 29 at 67–74 (Laurence
H. Tribe's comments to Justice Scalia).

Constitution should channel judicial decisions[181] but is unclear, deliberately I believe, on what channeling means. In that book, however, he offers a theory of judicial restraint, or a method for guiding Supreme Court decisions. An important aspect of that theory and of his understanding of constitutional interpretation is that it is necessary in deciding constitutional cases or to interpret the document itself to refer to values extraneous to the Constitution.[182] Those may be values popular in the current generation or among thinkers that matter. Precedent interpreting constitutional provisions will offer a principled statement of those values as a basis for the decision.[183] In *On Reading the Constitution*, Tribe describes that as classic common law method applied to constitutional interpretation.[184] The reasoned elaboration of the common law as Tribe understands it requires the articulation of and adherence to principle.

In *On Reading the Constitution*, Tribe offers a method for integrating and developing constitutional precedent. Because courts decide cases or controversies and because of the limitations of judicial method, "prior cases will not have spelled out the precise contours of the right designated as fundamental."[185] A court examining previous precedent then must ask: "at what level of generality should the right previously protected, and the right currently claimed, be described?"[186] In determining the level of generality, the Court will make value choices. Tribe explains that the "choice one makes must be justified extra-textually but may and should then be implemented in ways that draw as much guidance as possible from the text itself."[187]

In performing the difficult task of describing the values stated in previous cases at an appropriate level of generality, a judge must consult those previous cases and the practicalities found in the circumstances presented by the cases. Within those dimensions, however, the judge should state the principle extracted from the values expressed in the previous cases at the highest and most abstract level reasonable in the

---

181. *See* Laurence H. Tribe & Michael C. Dorf, On Reading the Constitution 66 (1992).
182. *Id.* at 68–69.
183. *Id.*
184. *Id.* at 20–23, 31, 33.
185. *See* On Reading the Constitution, *supra* note 181 at 73.
186. *Id.*
187. *Id.* at 116.

circumstances.[188] By adhering to that common law, perhaps Langdellian, discipline the judge will avoid importing his private values into the adjudication of constitutional cases.

Later in the chapter, our discussion of unenumerated rights and substantive due process will provide an example of Tribe's argument that judges should interpret previous precedent at the highest and most abstract level that is reasonable. Professor Tribe represented Dr. Quill in *Vacco v. Quill*,[189] a physician-assisted suicide case. He argued that *Cruzan v. Missouri Department of Health*,[190] among other cases, should be read as establishing a constitutional right to die. Chief Justice Rhenquist, who wrote the opinion in both *Vacco* and *Cruzan* replied by insisting that *Cruzan* established only a right in appropriate circumstances to remove life support systems.[191]

At the beginning of this chapter, it was argued that our Supreme Court appropriately uses common law techniques including the principled development of precedent when interpreting our Constitution. Justice Scalia's attack in the main text of *A Matter of Interpretation* on the common law method of interpreting our Constitution[192] could be read as referring primarily to the method offered by Professor Tribe. In commenting on Tribe's method one could start by explaining that it employs an understanding of the common law overly influenced by Langdellian technique. While ancient common law judges employed and referred to principle, the traditional common law was not organized around or controlled by principle. That was a late nineteenth century innovation. Traditional common law was organized around the forms of action and developed by analogy and distinction.

One wonders why Tribe does not use the values extraneous to the Constitution, which he believes are important, to argue for an interpretation of constitutional concepts and for offering a theory of the aspirational penumba of those concepts. Instead he professes a mystical lack of understanding of those aspirational penumbra and substitutes an abstract Langdellian understanding of previous precedent as a way of providing guidance to judges. In other words, he refuses to deliberate concerning the meaning of contested constitutional concepts and offers

---

188. *Id.*
189. Vacco v. Quill, 521 U.S. 793 (1997).
190. Cruzan v. Missouri Department of Health, 497 U.S. 261 (1990).
191. *See* Vacco, *supra* note 189 at 807.
192. *See* A MATTER OF INTERPRETATION, *supra* note 29 at 37–41.

instead a formula for judicial restraint which supports results admired by liberal activists.

In contrast, Dworkin's Judge Hercules would construct and defend an interpretation of the constitutional concepts. He would defend that interpretation on grounds of institutional fit and higher moral appeal. Among several interpretations all of which have good institutional fit, Hercules would choose his interpretation as the one which makes the most that now can be made of the Constitution. Hercules in one of his overly lengthy opinions would argue for the institutional fit of his interpretation and would be prepared to defend his moral theory. That process of reasoned deliberation is what Tribe avoids by alleging a mystical ignorance of the aspirational penumbra of constitutional concepts.

It is apparent that liberals as well as conservatives can refuse to deliberate concerning the great moral concepts in our Constitution. Liberals as well as conservatives can substitute for that deliberation a formula of apparent restraint which through its structure will provide politically desirable results.

c. Other Liberal Theories

For the sake of completeness, we should sample some liberal theories which do not offer a theory of judicial restraint as a noticeable part of a proposed method for constitutional interpretation. Bruce Ackerman, who is Sterling Professor of Law and Political Science at Yale University, offers what could be described as a political scientist's theory of the evolution of constitutional law. He has remarked that "For most judges, the basic unit of the Constitution is The Clause" while "for most law professors, the basic unit is The Theory." In contrast for Ackerman "the basic unit is The Generation."[193] He explains:

> "Constitutional meaning is not primarily created by judges out of texts but emerges in the course of the struggle by ordinary Americans to hammer out fundamental political understandings. This struggle is not fueled by the intellectual curiosity of a juristic elite, but by crucial historical events which provoke popular efforts to modify, sometimes radically, preexisting starting points: the war for independence or the war between the states or the struggle between capital and labor or the struggle against

---

193. *See* Ackerman, *supra* note 13 at 1519.

Naziism and Communism or the struggle for racial equality...."[194]

From time-to-time a generation, or some portion of it, gathers its resources and creates what Ackerman describes as "a constitutional moment."[195] Ackerman's favorite example is the New Deal revision in our understanding of government and constitutional interpretation. The generation's efforts may fail or produce a modest revision rather than a major change in our understanding. Ackerman considers the post Civil War woman's movement, which ultimately led to adoption of the Nineteenth Amendment guaranteeing a woman's right to vote, as an example of a large effort which led to a modest revision easily accommodated by existing society.[196] He does not relate that effort to the late twentieth century women's movement. In contrast, the New Deal changed our entire vision of government.

When a major or important change in our constitutional vision is accepted by the people, Ackerman finds that the change has received popular ratification.[197] An important means, then, as Ackerman perceives it, for changing our Constitution without a formal amendment, is popular ratification of a successful "constitutional moment." Supreme Court Justices who perceive that such a "constitutional moment" is about to happen may appropriately and legitimately change their understanding of our Constitution.[198] The abandonment by the Supreme Court in the late 1930s of legal classicism was such an appropriate and legitimate change of understanding.

A personalist judge could find great insights in Ackerman's analysis which might affect his theory of judicial decision making. Ackerman is describing part of the process by which constitutional legal paradigms rise and fall. Often that change is preceded by a long campaign for reform in the law, such as the woman's movement or the case by case fight led by the NAACP which resulted in *Brown v. Board of Education*.[199] Legal and social horizons often are changed by such generational efforts allowing judges new visions and new perceptions of the meaning of the

---

194. *Id.*
195. *Id.*
196. *Id.* at 1520.
197. *Id.* at 1519–20.
198. *Id.*
199. Brown v. Board of Education, 347 U.S. 483 (1954).

great moral concepts in our Constitution. The change in popular vision, which often accompanies or follows a major constitutional change, could be described as a popular ratification or acceptance of the new position. *Brown,* for example, is now a central and probably unchangeable part of our constitutional law. While originally opposed by many, *Brown* has become part of our national understanding.

A personalist judge should cross horizons, and make a continuing effort to understand new expressions of need and new visions. As he acquires a deeper understanding from that process of crossing horizons he may perceive the great moral concepts in our Constitution differently and may be able to articulate a new interpretation. A principled statement and justification of that new interpretation may require time and experience, as probably happened with our understanding of *Brown.* Nevertheless, a personalist judge, in contrast to Ackerman, will strive to articulate that principled understanding of constitutional concepts.

Ackerman is describing one important aspect of legitimacy, that is, a law which changes in response to society's changing needs and visions. He overlooks, however, the important role which adherence to process, to a written Constitution with its clauses and theories about those clauses, has in our society's understanding. A fuller theory of legitimacy must account for the symbolic role which our written Constitution has in our society's acceptance of law.

Harry Wellington offers a common law method for addressing constitutional issues which in many respects resembles that of Laurence Tribe.[200] Wellington's method, however, emphasizes the humanistic aspects of common law method which would appeal to a personalist judge. He mentions only in passing the sort of artificial principled restraint which is troubling in Tribe's theory. Following Ackerman, Wellington finds a place for popular ratification of constitutional changes.[201] Like Ackerman and Tribe, however, he fails to relate his common law method and popular ratification to deliberation on constitutional concepts.

Wellington distinguishes the dispute settlement and regulatory aspects of the Supreme Court's work and argues that when interpreting our Constitution the regulatory function is the most important.[202] One should, of course, recognize the importance of societal regulation in

---

200. *See* WELLINGTON, *supra* note 14 at 77–158.
201. *See* WELLINGTON, *supra* note 14 at 135.
202. *Id.*

the Supreme Court's work of constitutional interpretation. *Brown* changed basic structures in our society primarily but not exclusively in the South. The holding in *New York Times v. Sullivan*[203] was a carefully crafted regulatory rule designed to balance the interest in reputation of public officials against the interests in freedom of speech and press of their critics. Such regulatory activity, however, takes place in the context and for the sake of dispute settlement. By abandoning segregation *Brown* resolved, in a way that proved satisfactory over time, a great conflict between segments of our society. By establishing a new rule for libel actions, *New York Times* not only resolved the particular dispute but adjusted relations to moderate such disputes in the future.

Unlike legislation, the Supreme Court's regulatory function is exercised only when the parties present a case or controversy. That is a vital difference between legislation and the Supreme Court's work of dispute settlement. In personalist theory, our Supreme Court is at the apex of a great dispute settlement institution, designed not only to deal with particular disputes between individuals but also with the great divisions in our society over deep issues.

In the course of campaigns for law reform, representative groups such as the NAACP may bring litigation before the Court. The representative group is seeking change, new rules, a new regulation of society. When presenting its case, that group may offer a new understanding of constitutional rights. The entire process could be described as a means for hammering on the horizons of society and demanding recognition as persons. That process will be discussed further in chapter 6, which will address the language and uses of rights in society and in the great profession which we practice.

While parties to a case may be seeking regulation or law reform, the Court should hear and resolve a dispute while interpreting perhaps with new understanding the great moral concepts in our Constitution. Rational argument about our national ideals when litigating and deciding a dispute offers an alternate means, an additional societal resource or method, for addressing the great disputes. The existence of the legal process, of law as a great dispute settlement institution with the Supreme Court at its apex, establishes a means for rational discussion and deliberation concerning the great issues in society. Such deliberation is not a-political. Rather, it is part of the political process but a part which emphasizes rational discussion and deliberation as an alternative

---

203. New York Times v. Sullivan, 376 U.S. 254 (1964).

or adjunct to the political struggle in Congress, the state legislatures and the national elections. From time immemorial that rational legal discussion has been part of our political process. Hamilton perceived it as an important aspect of democracy.[204]

9. Principles, Pluralism and Conversation

In some liberal theory a Langdellian style of principled reasoning is perceived as the essence of good lawyering and as an important means for judicial restraint. In conservative method, deferrence to legislative or majority will, or some version of original meaning, often is substituted for principled reasoning as a formula for restraint. In personalist thought, principles are important as a means of organizing our law and for applying the great ideals of our society to the dispute before the court. In personalist constitutional method, a principle always should be related to an appropriate interpretation of a contested moral concept or a clause in our Constitution. In turn, that concept should be understood in relation to an appropriate interpretation or vision of our entire Constitution.

Principles, in personalist thought, are best understood as protecting a particular interest which must be weighed against competing interests in the decision making process. Impact and interest analysis, the location of competing interests and the effort to understand the impact of a proposed decision on them, is an important means for crossing horizons. That and other horizon crossing techniques will relate the abstract reasoning of law to human persons and their needs. As a judge crosses horizons, he may perceive interests with a new vision. That vision may allow a new perception of constitutional provisions and may affect the judge's developing interpretation of the entire Constitution. Arguably, that is what happened as the new vision, made possible by *Brown*, worked its way into our society's understanding.

In personalist thought, then, there is an ongoing relation between deliberation on the great moral concepts in our Constitution, our vision of the entire Constitution, and concern through horizon crossing, interest and impact analysis and an understanding of particular situations for the needs and human dignity of each person in our society.

---

204. THE FEDERALIST NO. 68 (Alexander Hamilton) (Isaac Kramnick ed., 1987).

That concrete concern for human persons is linked through the personalist process of constitutional interpretation to a vision of our Constitution as a means for promoting the human dignity of each person and the right of each to participate in the common action of our society and government.

Deliberation, although an important aspect of a judge's method for decision making and constitutional interpretation, should be perceived as a societal process. On the Supreme Court nine justices with differing views and methods deliberate together often through argument and efforts at persuasion or compromise. The Supreme Court, in personalist understanding, is the apex of a great dispute settlement system, which in turn is a means for rational conversation about great issues across the multiple horizons in our pluralist society. Engaging in that argument and conversation is a means for crossing horizons. As James Boyd White contends, law is an ongoing argument about what society should be that constitutes society.[205] At least it is an important part of the democratic process and an alternate means for addressing the great issues to the raw confrontations of political power, softened, of course, by compromise, of votes in Congress and the national elections.

The Supreme Court's decision making and constitutional interpretation, of course, is part of the political process. Justice Scalia, in *A Matter of Interpretation*, argues against methods which depart from the original understanding of the founding generation on the ground that the public will then perceive the Court's decisions as politically based.[206] The majority in our country, then, will seek the appointment of judges whose constitutional vision reflects majority will. Given the shifting control of our government by different political parties, judicial appointees should over time and from time to time produce a balanced Court or a balance in Supreme Court decisions.

Judges, whose horizons are compatible with the President who appoints them, will enhance our process of deliberation if they do not in-

---

205. *See* Samuel J.M. Donnelly, THE LANGUAGE AND USES OF RIGHTS: A BIOPSY OF AMERICAN JURISPRUDENCE IN THE TWENTIETH CENTURY (1994) (referring to the chapter on "Conversation"). *See also* JAMES BOYD WHITE, HERACLES' BOW: ESSAYS ON THE RHETORIC AND POETICS OF THE LAW (1985).

206. *See* A MATTER OF INTERPRETATION, *supra* note 29, referring to Scalia's argument that if judges are too "free wheeling" with their respective decisions, the public will insist that judges be nominated to the Court who represent their individual points of view.

sist on artificial methods of restraint but rather honestly debate the meaning of the great contested concepts in our Constitution.

In that debate, personalism would offer a different balance between what Ronald Dworkin describes as principle and policy.[207] Both reasons of principle and reasons of policy are related to respect and concern for persons individually and collectively. Some American thought, and perhaps that of Dworkin, affected by our cultural history, tends towards an excessive individualism. In personalist thought, the common good is persons acting together. Proposals, which tend to destroy the common action or exclude an individual, are contrary to the common good. Personalists would view our Constitution, its ongoing interpretation and constitutional government, as a great common action. The clash between individualism and that personalist understanding is part of the ongoing argument about what society should be that constitutes society. That clash will be part of the discussion in the next segment of the chapter.

In the next segment, personalist method in conversation with competing methods should be illustrated and applied to some great constitutional issues. The problem of unenumerated rights presents difficult questions which will not go away and which should be addressed. The discussion in the next part will begin with *Bowers v. Hardwick*[208] and continue with the twin cases of *Vacco v. Quill*[209] and *Washington v. Glucksberg*.[210] Following the discussion of unenumerated rights, the chapter will conclude with the interpretation of a particular constitutional provision, the Eighth Amendment prohibition of cruel and unusual punishment.

10. Unenumerated Rights — Substantive Due Process

The problem of unenumerated rights, as demonstrated by our history, is an enduring one. To avoid the negative implication, the first Congress added the Ninth Amendment to the Bill of Rights stating that:

207. *See* Taking Rights Seriously, *supra* note 16.
208. Bowers v. Hardwick, 478 U.S. 186 (1986).
209. Vacco v. Quill, 521 U.S. 793 (1997).
210. Washington v. Glucksberg, 521 U.S. 702 (1997).

"The enumeration in the Constitution of certain rights shall not be construed to deny or disparage others retained by the people."[211] Legal classicism, with *Lochner v. New York*[212] as its most notorious case, found protection for unenumerated rights in the due process clause of the Fourteenth Amendment. Following the famous footnote four in *Carolene Products*[213] late twentieth century courts, while refraining from interfering with economic policy decisions of state legislatures, have found unenumerated civil liberties in the due process clause. Developing *Griswold v. Connecticut*[214] the right of privacy perceived as a principle running through several of the first ten amendments has been applied through the due process clause to protect a series of previously unenumerated rights. In personalist theory, the discovery of new rights makes sense. As times and horizons change, persons who have been overlooked, inspired by new societal vision, present their problems and disputes to our courts. After deliberation it is appropriate to resolve some of those disputes by the recognition of new rights.

When litigants seek the recognition of unenumerated rights the interpretative problem presented to our Supreme Court is particularly difficult. No specific constitutional clause provides a firm foundation for an interpretation recognizing or rejecting the proposed right. Some then would insist that the Court reject unenumerated rights. Judge Bork wants to brush away the Ninth Amendment while speculating that it was designed to protect only rights enumerated in state constitutions.[215] Justice Scalia argues that the words due process in the Fourteenth Amendment refer only to process and not to substantive rights.[216] Others inspired by *Griswold v. Connecticut* want to run a connecting thread through the Bill of Rights to find a theory or analogy which can serve as a foundation for interpretation. Developing that inspiration, Professor Tribe's mystical understanding of constitutional penumbra and Langdellian approach to principle presents here a particular difficulty of disguising the need to deliberate.[217] In *Bowers v.*

---

211. U.S.C.A. CONST. Amend IX.

212. Lochner v. New York, 193 U.S. 45 (1905).

213. Carolene Products Co. v. United States, 323 U.S. 18 (1944).

214. Griswold v. Connecticut, 381 U.S. 479 (1965).

215. *See* ROBERT BORK, THE TEMPTING OF AMERICA: THE POLITICAL SEDUCTION OF THE LAW (1990) [hereinafter TEMPTING OF AMERICA].

216. *See* A MATTER OF INTERPRETATION, *supra* note 29.

217. *See* ON READING THE CONSTITUTION, *supra* note 181.

Hardwick[218] Justice White, recognizing the potential sweeping power of the Court when addressing unenumerated rights, takes refuge in tradition accepting only those rights implicit in the concept of ordered liberty or deeply rooted in the nation's history and tradition.

Personalist theory offers at least two advantages when addressing questions concerning unenumerated rights. (i) Personalism offers a general theory of our Constitution as designed to protect the human dignity of each person and his or her right to participate in our society and government. That general theory can serve as a foundation for addressing particular unenumerated rights. The abstract institutional right to participate can be understood in view of the abstract background right to protection of one's share of the primary social goods, those goods necessary to participation in this society or any society. (ii) Personalism offers a method which insists on relating interest analysis to that general theory and any developing principles. When addressing any particular proposed right, a personalist judge should ask whether he can perceive its validity under the personalist vision of our Constitution as protecting primary goods necessary to participation in our society or government. He must also ask whether the new right, as articulated by its proponents, needs balancing against competing interests also grounded in the primary social goods.

From a personalist perspective, whether a right can be found in our tradition is relevant but not dispositive. Justice White's warning that the Supreme Court's power is particularly unchecked when addressing unenumerated rights should cause a judge to be hesitant and to engage in deliberation and a conversation with tradition. He should be wary of being controlled by arguments which disguise or deny that need for deliberation, including not only arguments based on original intent or related theories but also arguments developed from a Langdellian principled analysis of previous precedent. Contrarywise, a personalist judge must cross horizons to understand the needs and circumstances of those claiming the new right.

In *Bowers v. Hardwick,* Justice White writing for the five judge majority held constitutional a Georgia statute criminalizing consensual sodomy. After the plaintiff had been arrested for a private homosexual act in his home, he sought declaratory relief in federal court declaring the Georgia statute unconstitutional because it denied him a fundamental right protected by the Ninth Amendment and the Due Process

---

218. Bowers v. Hardwick, 478 U.S. 186 (1986).

Clause of the Fourteenth Amendment. Justice White, contrary to Scalia and Bork, recognized that the due process clause of the Fifth and Fourteenth Amendments "have been interpreted to have substantive content, subsuming rights that to a great extent are immune from federal or state regulation or proscription."[219] Justice White noted that: "Among such cases are those recognizing rights that have little or no textual support in the constitutional language."[220] Those rights should be those "'implicit in the concept of ordering liberty' such that 'neither liberty nor justice would exist if [they] were sacrificed'" or those "'deeply rooted in this Nation's history and tradition.'"[221] Justice White observed that "neither of these formulations would extend a fundamental right to homosexuals to engage in acts of consensual sodomy."[222] He noted the long history of proscriptions of homosexual conduct and concluded that the Court was disinclined to find "new fundamental rights imbedded in the Due Process Clause."[223] He explained that the "Court is most vulnerable and comes nearest to illegitimacy when it deals with judge-made constitutional law having little or no cognizable roots in the language or design of the Constitution."[224]

Justice Blackmun, writing for three of the four dissenting justices, argued that the case was not "about 'a fundamental right to engage in homosexual sodomy'" but "about 'the most comprehensive of rights and the right most valued by civilized men,' namely, 'the right to be let alone,'"[225] particularly in the privacy of one's own home. He found analogies to prior cases recognizing a right to privacy. Justice White found those cases not relevant because they protected family life as opposed to homosexual activity. Justice Blackmun described those cases at a higher level of generality as establishing the right to be left alone, particularly in one's own home.

A personalist judge would be impressed by the arguments for a right of privacy or a right to be let alone. A principle that privacy is a protectable interest appears to run through several of the first ten amendments and is related to each person's human dignity. That

219. *Id.* at 191.
220. *Id.*
221. *Id.* at 191–92.
222. Bowers v. Hardwick, 478 U.S. 186 (1986).
223. *Id.* at 194.
224. *Id.*
225. *Id.* at 199.

analysis provides an appropriate beginning for interpreting our Constitution in *Bowers*. However, a personalist judge would desire a more extensive analysis of constitutional theory. He would enquire whether the right to be let alone is related to fundamental human dignity or to the primary social goods, and whether it requires balancing against competing rights or interests. He would not be deflected from that deliberation and enquiry by a claim that the principle establishing the right of privacy, taken at its highest and most abstract level, simply supports by deduction the right to be let alone while engaged in homosexual activity.

Likewise a personalist judge would be impressed by the argument that the right to engage in homosexual activity is not found in our tradition and is not essential to ordered liberty. He would note, however, that the tradition of ordered liberty is a contested concept requiring interpretation and that recognition that we have not traditionally protected homosexual activity is not dispositive. An absolute reliance on tradition constitutes a refusal to deliberate or cross horizons.

While homosexual activity is not traditionally protected, our horizons have changed partly as a result of *Brown* and the intense conflicts leading to desegregation. Our society is now more concerned with the diverse horizons of those with different lifestyles and with not excluding them from participation in society. Sex is recognized not only as a strong primal drive, which must be restrained and used in responsible ways, but as a means of relating to others and establishing in those relations one's self-identity. To develop and relate appropriately to others one must struggle with one's sexual drives. Those handicapped, for whatever reason, by homosexual inclinations are not relieved of that responsibility and opportunity which in turn is related to moral growth and appropriate relations with society. Traditionally, that struggle and development take place in private and with significant others. A personalist would perceive that struggle for moral growth and appropriate relations as closely related to the primary social goods.

In *Bowers* the activities in question took place in the privacy of the home. Public homosexual or heterosexual activities or abusive actions were not presented to the Court. Any state or private interests in conflict with the right of privacy in this instance would seem to be outweighed by the interest in protecting the primary social good of the struggle for moral growth and appropriate relations with others. A personalist judge, after a fuller analysis and deliberation, would agree with

Justice Blackmun that the Georgia statute in the circumstances presented violates a constitutional right to be let alone.

The twin cases of *Vacco v. Quill*[226] and *Washington v. Glucksberg*[227] present the problem of unenumerated rights in a contrasting context. The cases, which were heard together by the Supreme Court, challenged the laws of the states of Washington and New York prohibiting physician-assisted suicide. The Ninth Circuit and the Second Circuit for differing reasons had found those laws unconstitutional. The Supreme Court reversed the Circuit Courts in both cases by a unanimous vote and found the laws prohibiting physician-assisted suicide constitutional. Chief Justice Rhenquist who wrote for the Court in both cases treated *Glucksberg* as the principal case. Like Justice White in *Bowers*, Rhenquist recognized the continuing significance of substantive due process as a means for addressing unenumerated rights:

> "The Due Process Clause guarantees more than fair process, and the 'liberty' it protects includes more than the absence of physical restraint. The Clause also provides heightened protection against government interference with certain fundamental rights and liberty interests. In a long line of cases, we have held that, in addition to the specific freedoms protected by the Bill of Rights, the 'liberty' specially protected by the Due Process Clause includes the rights to marry, to have children, to direct the education and upbringing of one's children, to marital privacy, to use contraception, to bodily integrity, and to abortion. We have also assumed, and strongly suggested, that the Due Process Clause protects the traditional right to refuse unwanted lifesaving treatment."[228]

Rhenquist, then, examined our tradition to determine whether the narrowly defined right to assistance in committing suicide was "'so rooted in the traditions and conscience of our people as to be ranked as fundamental'... and 'implicit in the concept of ordered liberty,' such that 'neither liberty nor justice would exist if they were sacrificed.'"[229] He then carefully reviewed Anglo-American history beginning roughly with Henry de Bracton and concluded that "we are confronted with a consistent and almost universal tradition that has long rejected the as-

---

226. Vacco v. Quill, 521 U.S. 793 (1997).
227. Washington v. Glucksberg, 521 U.S. 702 (1997).
228. *Id.* at 719–20.
229. *Id.* at 721 (quoting Palko v. Connecticut, 302 U.S. 319, 325–26 (1937)).

serted right, and continues explicitly to reject it today, even for terminally ill, mentally competent adults."[230]

One problem with arguments that a proposed unenumerated right is or is not found in the tradition of ordered liberty is that courts manipulate that history among other means by choosing arbitrary starting points. For example, the Ninth Circuit, which found in *Glucksberg* that there was a fundamental right to physician-assisted suicide,[231] also reviewed history but in contrast to Rhenquist started with the ancient Greeks and Romans who recognized suicide as an honorable practice. In finding our tradition more mixed the Ninth Circuit occasionally cited dubious examples such as the "suicide" of Socrates which most would describe as an execution.

The Ninth Circuit sought to derive its broadly defined right to die from the principle of autonomy which it perceived contrary to Rhenquist as running through *Cruzan v. Director, Missouri Dept. of Health*[232] and *Casey v. Planned Parenthood.*[233] In *Glucksberg*, Rhenquist denied that his opinion in *Cruzan* or the joint opinion in *Casey* recognized the proposed principle. He explained: "That many of the rights and liberties protected by the Due Process Clause sound in personal autonomy does not warrant the sweeping conclusion that any and all important, intimate, and personal decisions are so protected, and *Casey* did not suggest otherwise."[234] Rhenquist noted that his own decision in *Cruzan* had been characterized "as a right to die case," a description he rejected. He explained: "*Cruzan* recognized 'the more specific interest in making decisions about how to confront an imminent death.'"[235]

Having found contrary to the ultimate decision of the Supreme Court that substantive due process protected a broad principle of autonomy, which included a right to die, the Ninth Circuit then balanced that right against competing state interests. The Circuit Court found that in the case of a terminally ill patient, the right to die was not overridden by any compelling state's interests. Among the state interests considered were those of preserving life and preventing suicide. When a

230. *Id.* at 723.

231. *See* Glucksberg *supra*, note 227 at 711.

232. Cruzan v. Missouri Department of Health, 497 U.S. 261 (1990).

233. Planned Parenthood of Southeastern Pennsylvania v. Casey, 505 U.S. 833 (1992).

234. Washington v. Glucksberg, 521 U.S. 702, 727–28 (1997).

235. *Id.* at 722–23.

patient is terminally ill, those interests according to the Court are at their weakest. "While the state has a legitimate interest in preventing suicide in general," the Ninth Circuit explained, "that interest, like the state's interest in preserving life, is substantially diminished in the case of terminally ill, competent adults who wish to die."[236]

While the Ninth Circuit combined principled reasoning with interest analysis in a manner similar to personalist method, by giving little weight to the government interest in protection of life when a person is terminally ill, the Circuit Court established a class of persons, those who are terminally ill, whom the government cannot fully protect. While the Ninth Circuit did recognize a state interest in preventing abuse of the elderly and dying, this removal of an entire class from full government protection remains deeply offensive to a fundamental personalist position, the importance and worthwhileness of each human being.

The Supreme Court and each of its justices was seriously disturbed by the potential for abuse of the elderly. That probably accounts for the unanimous vote against physician-assisted suicide. Justices Stevens and Souter, in their separate opinions, while disagreeing with Rhenquist's formulation of the constitutional issues, voted against physician-assisted suicide in part because they did not perceive means for controlling potential abuse. Justice Stevens concluded that the perceived potential harms "are sufficient to support the State's general policy against assisted suicide...."[237] Justice Souter perceived proposed regulations as insufficient and believed "at least at this moment there are reasons for caution in predicting the effectiveness of the teeth proposed."[238]

The Chief Justice addressed potential abuses when reviewing state interests in protecting the lives of the terminally ill. Rhenquist, because he did not find a fundamental right to make important autonomous decisions nor a right to die, was not required to find a competing and compelling state interest. He reviewed state interests to establish the rationality of the state prohibition. The Chief Justice referred to and relied on the report of the New York Task Force on Life and the Law and its conclusion that "legalizing assisted suicide and euthanasia would pose profound risks to many individuals who are ill and vulnerable...."[239] Rhenquist noted that depression plays a role in suicide deci-

---

236. *Id.*
237. Washington v. Glucksberg, 521 U.S. 702, 749 (1997).
238. *Id.* at 785.
239. *Id.* at 719.

sions and that when depression is treated many who desire physician-assisted suicide withdraw their request. He contrasted his own position with the views of the Ninth Circuit regarding the state's interest in protecting the terminally ill:

"Next, the State has an interest in protecting vulnerable groups — including the poor, the elderly, and disabled persons — from abuse, neglect, and mistakes. The Court of Appeals dismissed the State's concern that disadvantaged persons might be pressured into physician-assisted suicide as 'ludicrous on its face.' We have recognized, however, the real risk of subtle coercion and undue influence in end-of-life situations. Similarly, the New York Task Force warned that [l]egalizing physician-assisted suicide would pose profound risks to many individuals in our society whose autonomy and well-being are already compromised by poverty, lack of access to good medical care, advantage, or membership in a stigmatized social group' ('[A]n insidious bias against the handicapped — again coupled with a cost-saving mentality — makes them especially in need of Washington's statutory protection.') If physician-assisted suicide were permitted, many might resort to it to spare their families the substantial burden of end-of-life health care costs."[240]

In contrast to the Ninth Circuit, the Supreme Court found that the class of the terminally ill might have particular need for the State's protection. The Ninth Circuit believed that in the presence of terminal illness the State's interest in life was low and that the regulations proposed by respondents would be adequate to guard against abuses. By an overconfidence in prospective State regulation, a confidence which the Supreme Court did not share, and by its finding that in the presence of terminal illness the State's interest in protecting life was low, the Ninth Circuit created a class of persons whose lives the state could not seriously protect. The Supreme Court found that persons in this class were particularly exposed to abuse.

A personalist judge would find the Supreme Court's careful review of the interests of the elderly and handicapped and its reliance on the report of The New York Task Force on Life and the Law appropriate. That analysis represents the necessary attempt to cross horizons, to study the situation of those affected by the law and to determine the potential impact of changes on their interests. A personalist judge would not be as

---

240. *Id.* at 731–32.

happy with the Court's reliance on the very open-textured history of ordered liberty. When deliberating it is important to enter into a conversation with tradition. However, tradition and particularly manipulated versions of tradition should not be dispositive. When addressing unenumerated rights a personalist judge would seek to give content to "the tradition of ordered liberty" by referring to the personalist theory of our entire Constitution as designed to protect the human dignity of each person and his or her right to participate in our government and society. Arguably the protection of life, liberty and property by the due process clause of the Fourteenth Amendment guards primary social goods necessary to that participation. When deciding whether there is a fundamental right to physician-assisted suicide, a personalist judge would find it necessary to further develop his theory of the primary social goods. *Glucksberg* presents a potential conflict between life and liberty. One could resolve that conflict superficially by noting that one who chooses physician-assisted suicide is not only giving up his life but also his liberty to participate in the ongoing actions of society. A more profound analysis would enquire whether the interest in life outweighs the interest in liberty.

The traditional formula, life, liberty and property, found in Locke,[241] in slightly altered form in our Declaration of Independence,[242] and in the Constitution's due process clauses, appears to list these interests in an order of priority. Certainly the traditional list is not in alphabetical order. Footnote four to *Carolene Products* implies that liberty interests are more important than economic or perhaps property interests. That ranking would appear to coincide with modern liberal thought.

A personalist, reflecting on his vision of our constitution, could argue that the right to life and the government's obligation to protect each person's life is prior to the liberty interests and the exercise of the great liberties protected by the due process clause of the Fourteenth Amendment. Government is obliged to protect each person's liberty and to refrain from arbitrary interference with the great liberties because each person is worthwhile. Recognition of the worthwhileness of each person is found in the words and structure of the Fourteenth Amendment and in a fair retelling of our history. Justice Brennan has described a sparkling vision presented by our Constitution at the heart

---

241. *See* John Locke, Two Treaties of Government, 348–49, 368–69 (Peter Laslett ed., Cambridge Univ. Press 1960).

242. Thomas Jefferson, et. al., The Declaration of Independence (1776).

of which is a recognition of the human dignity of each person.[243] That ideal of respect and concern for each person is the glory of American democracy, of our Constitution and our history. We cannot have that respect and concern for each person, however, unless we are prepared to protect his or her life, to afford governmental protection to each person's life and to avoid arbitrary governmental taking of that life.

To arbitrarily take a person's life or to exclude that person's life from protection by the government has as great, and indeed greater, impact on his dignity, on our respect for his fundamental worthwhileness, as a similar disregard for his or her liberty. One can have life without liberty but not liberty without life. Protection of life is yet more fundamental to our vision of respect and concern for each person than protection of liberty.

Traditionally one's liberty is limited by others' fundamental interests and integrity. As the old saying puts it: "Your liberty ends at my nose." Normally we would agree that one person's liberty would not justify the taking of another person's life. To pose an extreme example: one person's concept of the meaning of the universe would not justify the human sacrifice of another to his bloodthirsty god.

The importance of the protection of life then is more fundamental than and prior to the importance of protecting liberty and a fortiori property. One can exclude a person from our society more easily by refusing to protect his life or by allowing arbitrary government interference with his life than by denying his liberty in similar ways. Our historic regret at excluding groups of persons from our society should extend to exclusion of their lives from government protection.

A general theory of our Constitution then should recognize that the protection of life is prior to the protection of liberty which in turn is prior to the protection of property. A government makes a greater error by arbitrarily interfering with life than with liberty or property. The protection of life is a more important governmental goal than the protection of liberty which, however, is very important and more so than the protection of property. Personal liberties are more important than economic liberties.

Ronald Dworkin's distinction between principles and policies and his argument that principles as arguments based on individual rights should trump goals as reasons based on group advantage provides a

---

243. *See* Brennan, *supra* note 7.

basis for attacking the position just outlined.[244] The national goal of protecting the lives of the elderly against stingy medical administrators or greedy heirs in his view should not prevail over the liberty interest of the person who desires physician-assisted suicide.[245] Personalist theory as indicated earlier rejects Dworkin's distinction between principles and policies. Strong rights will trump weaker rights and many competing policies. However, some national goals as illustrated by the problem of protecting the elderly, are grounded in our national ideals and the fundamental principle that each person's right to participate in society and his or her share of the primary social goods should be protected. Goals grounded in ideals should compete in the reasoning process with assertions of individual right and the process of deliberation should not be terminated by a formula as simple as that proposed by Dworkin.

Professor Tribe represented Dr. Quill in *Vacco v Quill*. In his brief he argued quoting *Casey* that "the Constitution protects from government intrusion an individual's right to make certain profound, life-shaping decisions" which "involve the most intimate and personal choices a person may make in a lifetime, choices central to personal dignity or autonomy."[246] He did not offer that argument on the basis of a general vision of our Constitution but rather as a principled theory of the Court's decisions including *Casey* and *Cruzan*. He argued: "Indeed if Casey and this Court's other holdings construing 'the substantive sphere of liberty which the Fourteenth Amendment protects'... are to be understood as principled decisions, the Court must recognize the protected nature of this profoundly personal dimension of liberty."[247] This argument employs Tribe's questionable tactic of arbitrarily stating the principles underlying previous cases on the highest and most abstract level of generality reasonably tolerable. An advocate, who describes his understanding of previous cases as principled, avoids the burden of arguing for his position on any other basis than authority. As noted earlier, Chief Justice Rhenquist rejected Tribe's proposed principled description of precious precedent.

Tribe also offered a principled argument grounded in equal protection, which was accepted by the Second Circuit but rejected by the Supreme Court in *Vacco v. Quill*. New York, he argued, allowed those

---

244. *See* TAKING RIGHTS SERIOUSLY, *supra* note 16 at 232–33.
245. *Id.*
246. Vacco v. Quill, 1996 WL 708912, *19 (1996).
247. *Id.*

terminally ill to remove life support and to employ other procedures including a process he termed "terminal sedation." He contended that there is no difference in principle between these medical procedures and physician-assisted suicide. New York, therefore, denies equal protection to terminally ill patients suffering intolerable pain who cannot or will not employ the allowed procedures.[248]

In *Vacco*, Chief Justice Rhenquist writing for the unanimous Court, which reversed the Second Circuit, again lowered the level of generality: "*Everyone*, regardless of physical condition, is entitled, if competent, to refuse unwanted lifesaving medical treatment, *no one* is permitted to assist a suicide. Generally speaking laws that apply evenhandedly to all 'unquestionably comply' with the Equal Protection Clause."[249]

Rhenquist found the distinction between the permitted and prohibited medical procedures traditional and rational. He explained that a patient who refuses continued medical treatment, for example by requesting removal of life support, "dies from an underlying fatal disease or pathology; but if a patient ingests lethal medication prescribed by a physician, he is killed by that medication."[250]

Tribe had attempted to avoid Rhenquist's distinctions by moving to a higher level of generality. By imposing that artificial generality, Tribe would deprive New York of the opportunity to advance its interest in protecting each person's life, an interest grounded in our deepest national ideal, while struggling to accommodate competing interests. Under the theory in this chapter, the ultimate problem with Tribe's logic is that while creating a superficially apparent denial of equal protection by manipulating levels of generality he would have violated a more fundamental principle of equality under which all persons including the terminally ill as equally worthwhile are equally entitled to protection of their lives. That protection is precisely protection against abuse, pressure, and battery, which amount to assaults on their lives. Those attacks must be distinguished from aggressive attempts to relieve pain and from sound decisions to abandon no longer useful medical treatment. Relief of pain would include the use of medication even if it shortens life. The Supreme Court in *Glucksberg* agreed that control of pain required, per-

---

248. Vacco, 1996 WL 708912 at *44, 49.
249. Vacco v. Quill, 521 U.S. 793, 800 (1997).
250. *Id.* at 801.

haps constitutionally, further exploration but that the law of Washington and New York did not prevent serious pain control.[251]

Ronald Dworkin, John Rawls, and Robert Nozick joined by other professors filed an amicus brief in the physician-assisted suicide cases. It was described in the New York Review of Books as the philosopher's brief.[252] Dworkin and his companions supported Tribe's argument that a principle runs through *Cruzan, Casey* and other Supreme Court decisions that protects the individual liberty interest in autonomy when making certain important personal decisions. The philosophers, however, in contrast to Tribe, supported that abstract statement of principle by a vision of our Constitution and of a free society. They argued: "In a free society, individuals must be allowed to make those decisions for themselves, out of their own faith, conscience and convictions. This Court has insisted in a variety of contexts and circumstances, that this great freedom is among those protected by the Due Process Clause as essential to a community of 'ordered liberty.'"[253]

While a personalist vision of our Constitution would accept the importance of that principle of autonomy, a personalist judge would argue under this vision that protection of each person's life and the lives of all the elderly is prior to assurance of individual autonomy. Although the personalist vision differs from that presented by Dworkin and his colleagues, the method for constitutional interpretation employed in the philosophers' brief is superior to that used by Tribe. It is more appropriate to develop a principle on the foundation of one's interpretation of the entire Constitution than simply to assert that it is the highest and most appropriate abstract interpretation of previous cases.

Ronald Dworkin has developed his argument for assisted suicide and for autonomy at greater length in his book, *Life's Dominion: An Argument About Abortion, Euthanasia, and Individual Freedom*,[254] which is

---

251. *Id.* at 791.

252. Ronald Dworkin et, al., *Assisted Suicide: The Philosophers Brief*, THE NEW YORK REV. OF BOOKS, March 27, 1997, at 41–47. *See* also Amicus Curiae Brief in Support of Respondent, Washington v. Glucksberg, 521 U.S. 702 (1997). *See* also Amicus Curiae Brief in Support of Respondent, Vacco v. Quill, 521 U.S. 793 (1997).

253. *Id.*

254. *See* RONALD DWORKIN, LIFE'S DOMINION: AN ARGUMENT ABOUT ABORTION, EUTHANASIA AND INDIVIDUAL FREEDOM (1993) [hereinafter DWORKIN, LIFE'S DOMINION]. *See* also Compassion in Dying v. Washington, 79

cited by the Ninth Circuit.[255] In his book, Dworkin argues for a broader right to die[256] than advocated by the respondents in *Glucksberg* and *Vacco*. In those cases the respondents, who were the original plaintiffs sought constitutional permission for physicians to prescribe for patients, who sought their assistance in obtaining medication which would result in death. Dworkin would support those who want with medical assistance an early peaceful death for themselves or their relatives. Their wishes, he would argue, do not reject the sanctity of life but represent one view of the sacredness of life, a view which requires us to shape our lives into an integral whole. "A competent person making a living will providing for his treatment if he becomes demented is making exactly the kind of judgment that autonomy, on the integrity view, most respects: a judgment about the overall shape of the kind of life he wants to have led."[257] A competent person's right to autonomy requires that his past decisions about how he is to be treated if he becomes demented be respected "even if they contradict the desires he has at the later point."[258] So, for example, we must respect and follow the wishes of a formerly competent person who fearing Alzheimer's disease directs that if he incurs that illness he be put to death.[259]

We must respect the decision regarding the integral shape of his life of the fully autonomous person even if the Alzheimer's patient later rejects those directions. We must do so because adult citizens have a right to autonomy, a right to lead their lives out of a distinctive sense of their own character, a sense of what is important to or for them. We respect autonomy because in a democracy we cherish each person's dignity and hence refuse to deny freedom of conscience. Dworkin would insist that liberty as so understood has a priority over life, the liberty of the fully competent adult over the life of the Alzheimer's patient who is unwilling to die.

One should note that the principle of autonomy as described by Dworkin divides a person's life into parts. His theory ascribes greater dignity to the fully competent adult than to the person at other stages of

---

F.3d 790, 836 n. 132 (Here, the Ninth Circuit established a class of terminally ill whom it excluded from government protection).

255. *See* Glucksberg *supra*, note 234.
256. *See* DWORKIN, LIFE'S DOMINION, *supra* note 254 at 179–243.
257. *Id.* at 226.
258. *Id.* at 228.
259. *Id.* at 226.

his or her life. Dworkin has created a class of those such as Alzheimer's patients, who do not have a right to autonomy and whose lives are subjected to the decisions of the fully autonomous. This is contrary to our deep national insight that each person is worthwhile and entitled to government protection of his life as well as his liberty and property. Contrary to Brennan's argument that we may not discard the life of anyone, Dworkin would allow the autonomous person to direct the disposal of those who lack full autonomy.

In the personalist vision, autonomy is an important liberty interest that is part but only part of our tradition of ordered liberty. Protection of liberty is a broader concept than protection of autonomy. The founding generation primarily was concerned with overtly oppressive intrusions on the traditional liberties of free Englishmen. Freedom of religion and conscience was important. However, it is a more serious invasion of conscience to direct a person to do something contrary to his belief, than to restrain him from an act he believes is necessary or permitted. For example, it is more serious to direct a person contrary to his conscience to worship Jupiter, or to pay taxes to an established church, or to recite a state composed prayer at the beginning of school than it is to prevent him from sacrificing a cock. Activities in accordance with one's conscience or understanding of life are subject to regulation to protect the public order. Everyone's life, liberty and property, everyone's share of the primary social goods is advanced and secured by appropriate public regulation.

Life in personalist thought is more fundamental than liberty or property. Dworkin's argument for autonomy would place the class of elderly and terminally ill at risk for the sake of protecting the autonomy of some. While he and Professor Tribe are concerned for those who are suffering unbearably, it is apparent that they are more seriously concerned with the principle of autonomy. Focusing on that principle will distract us from the complex difficulties of addressing appropriate care for the elderly, the terminally ill and those in severe pain and finding the appropriate balance in their circumstances between autonomy and beneficence.

We have not solved those serious complex problems. For example, some physicians are unwilling to prescribe for the terminally ill pain control drugs which will shorten life. The Supreme Court found that the laws of Washington and New York would allow such prescription.[260]

---

260. *See* Glucksberg *supra*, note 234 at 791.

While we have a long way to go, the temptation to find a shortcut by killing people should be avoided.

Dworkin would argue that only a religious foundation can serve as a basis for denying a person the right to end his life. Dworkin here may be confusing contrasting ethical visions with conflicting religious thought. It would seem simple prudence to maintain the traditional prohibition against A killing B even by providing life ending drugs. Lifting that prohibition for the class of elderly or terminally ill exposes the class to abuse.

While Dworkin's vision differs from personalist thought, his method here is appropriate. Rather than disguising different visions or horizons behind artificial abstract principles, it is appropriate when debating what unenumerated rights should be protected to articulate from the perspective of those conflicting horizons differing visions of our Constitution. Rational argument, then, through our great legal dispute settlement system will serve as a means for relating persons in the different horizons of our pluralist society. The argument about what society should be, as James Boyd White explains, will constitute society.[261]

It should be noted that Dworkin also has addressed the issue of physician assisted suicide in chapter 14, "Sex, Death and the Courts" of *Sovereign Virtue: The Theory and Practice of Equality*. His argument there appears to more closely resemble the Tribe position. In *Sovereign Virtue*, Dworkin contends that society should seek an equality of resources and that liberty is one of those resources and hence an aspect of equality.[262]

The dispute over unenumerated rights presents an opportunity to discuss in one context methods for constitutional interpretation. In the next part we will examine the interpretation of a particular clause, the Eighth Amendment's prohibition of cruel and unusual punishment.[263]

---

261. *See* SAMUEL J.M. DONNELLY, THE LANGUAGE AND USES OF RIGHTS: A BIOPSY OF AMERICAN JURISPRUDENCE IN THE TWENTIETH CENTURY (1994), referring to JAMES BOYD WHITE, HERACLES' BOW: ESSAYS ON THE RHETORIC AND POETICS OF THE LAW (1985).

262. *See* RONALD DWORKIN, SOVEREIGN VIRTUE, THE THEORY AND PRACTICE OF EQUALITY (Harvard University Press, Cambridge, Mass; London, England 2000). *See* particularly, Chapter 14, "Sex, Death and the Courts," at 453 et seq.

263. U.S.C.A. CONST. Amend. VIII ("[E]xcessive bail shall not be required, nor excessive fines imposed, nor cruel and unusual punishments inflicted.").

11. Interpreting the Eighth Amendment

During the late twentieth century, three justices of the United States Supreme Court, Justices Brennan, Marshall and Blackmun, took distinct but significant positions in opposition to capital punishment. A personalist judge, when presented with a challenge to the constitutionality of the death penalty under the Eighth and Fourteenth Amendments,[264] would meld aspects of their positions.

In *Furman v. Georgia*, Justice Brennan argued: "In comparison to all other punishments today...the deliberate extinguishment of human life by the State is uniquely degrading to human dignity."[265] In *Gregg v. Georgia*, he explained in dissent: "The fatal constitutional infirmity in the punishment of death is that it treats members of the human race as nonhumans, as objects to be toyed with and discarded. [It is] thus inconsistent with the fundamental premise...that even the vilest criminal remains a human being possessed of common human dignity."[266]

Justice Brennan's position on capital punishment resembles his comprehensive vision of the Constitution. His argument that protection of each person's human dignity is at the heart of the Eighth Amendment's prohibition of cruel and unusual punishment is an intellectual ancestor of his interpretation of the post-Civil War Constitution as presenting a sparkling vision of the human dignity of each person.[267]

Justice Marshall, dissenting in *Gregg v. Georgia*, argued that capital punishment serves no legitimate penological purpose. Retribution, in his view, is not a legitimate goal for criminal punishment because it has no direct relation to prevention or reduction of crime. An important crime prevention goal of criminal punishment is general deterrence. A large portion of Marshall's dissent argues that there is no generally ac-

---

264. U.S.C.A. CONST. Amend. VIII supra & XIV (stating..."[n]or shall any State deprive any person of life, liberty, or property, without due process of law; nor deny to any person within its jurisdiction the equal protection of the laws").

265. Furman v. Georgia, 408 U.S. 238, 290 (1972).

266. Gregg v. Georgia, 428 U.S. 227, 230 (1976).

267. *See* William J. Brennan, Jr., *The Constitution of the United States: Contemporary Ratification*, in INTERPRETING THE CONSTITUTION: THE DEBATE OVER ORIGINAL INTENT 23, 28–29 (Jack N. Rakove ed., 1990). Brennan offers his theory that the post-Civil War Constitution offers a "sparkling vision" concerned with the protection of each person's human dignity.

cepted empirical evidence that capital punishment has a greater marginal deterrent impact on murder than life imprisonment. He concludes that in the absence of a legitimate penological goal, capital punishment is excessive and hence cruel and contrary to human dignity.[268]

Personalist theory shares Brennan's sparkling vision of our Constitution as designed to protect each person's human dignity. Constitutional rights, personalist theory would add, are designed to protect each person's share of the primary social goods. Both a murder and an execution completely deprive their victims of primary social goods, of any further opportunity to participate in society. Marshall would allow capital punishment if it served the crime control goal of general deterrence. Arguably, if there were serious and generally acceptable evidence that capital punishment produced a significantly greater marginal deterrence of murder than life imprisonment, then it would not be an unconstitutional cruel and unusual punishment. Rather, the death penalty would serve the legitimate penological and constitutional goal of protecting life. Contrary to our current information, if the death penalty discouraged murder more effectively than life imprisonment, then imposing it would be consistent with the priority for life. However, as Marshall argued, and the plurality in Gregg recognized, there is no serious statistical showing that capital punishment has a greater marginal deterrent effect than life imprisonment.[269] In the modern era, with our wealth of statistics concerning capital punishment and the murder rate, statistical proof is the only serious form of evidence that capital punishment has the required deterrent effect. In the absence of that evidence, imposition of the death penalty is contrary to the priority for life. Because life imprisonment is as effective in deterring murder, execution is an unnecessary, excessive and hence cruel punishment. As Brennan explains, it is contrary to human dignity. While balancing competing interests in the manner of Marshall, personalist thought like Brennan would interpret the Eighth Amendment prohibition of cruel and unusual punishment as designed to protect the human dignity of each person.

Early in his Supreme Court career, Justice Blackmun supported the plurality position in Gregg v. Georgia and in accordance with that posi-

---

268. See Gregg supra note 266 at 231. See also, Sarat and Vidmar, *Public Opinion, The Death Penalty and the Eighth Amendment: Testing the Marshall Hypothesis*, 1976 WIS.L.REV. 171.

269. See Gregg supra note 266 at 234.

tion voted to find capital punishment constitutional in some cases and unconstitutional in others. By 1986, however, about the time of *Mc-Cleskey v. Kemp*,[270] a case in which he dissented, Justice Blackmun began to vote regularly against the death penalty.[271] By 1994, in *Callins v. Collins*[272] he finally concluded that capital punishment was unconstitutional in all cases because it cannot be fairly administered. He explained:

> "From this day forward, I no longer shall tinker with the machinery of death. For more than 20 years I have endeavored—indeed I have struggled—along with a majority of this Court to develop procedural and substantive rules that would lend more than the mere appearance of fairness to the death penalty endeavor. Rather than continue to coddle the Court's delusion that the desired level of fairness has been achieved and the need for regulation eviscerated, I feel morally and intellectually obligated to concede that the death penalty experiment has failed."[273]

While Justice Blackmun's concern for fairness does not appear at first to emphasize the priority for life, there is some relation. The plurality position in *Gregg*, which Blackman supported, required a high degree of fairness in capital punishment cases because the death penalty was uniquely severe.[274] Because Blackmun continued to adhere to that position, he ultimately concluded the death penalty was unconstitutional.

Personalist thought would agree that a uniquely severe penalty must be administered with a uniquely high regard for fairness. Respect for the human dignity of the accused, who is threatened with loss of his life, loss of all opportunity to participate in society, demands the utmost fairness. Like Justice Brennan, a personalist judge would engage in conversation and argument with those who support the death penalty concerning the fairness of their decisions. Through that dialogue, Brennan and Marshall were able to attract Justices Blackmun and Stevens and at times White and O'Connor to their position.[275]

---

270. McCleskey v. Kemp, 478 U.S. 1019 (1986).

271. *See* Samuel J.M. Donnelly, *Capital Punishment: A Critique of the Political and Philosophical Thought Supporting the Justices' Positions*, 24 St. Mary's Law Journal 1, 102–03 (1992).

272. Callins v. Collins, 510 U.S. 1141 (1994).

273. *Id.* to Callins, 114 S.Ct.1127, 1129 (1994).

274. *See* Gregg *supra* note 266 at 187. Stewart, J. concurring. ("[W]hen a defendant's life is at stake, the Court has been particularly sensitive to insure that every safeguard is observed.").

275. *See* Donnelly, *supra* note 271 at 23–27.

While the great classic positions of Brennan, Marshall and Blackmun differ from each other, they illustrate together not merely the flaws in the administration and theory of capital punishment but also an important aspect of constitutional decision making. Inevitably, the justices arrive at their respective understandings of the Constitution differently and on the basis of their own developing experiences. An important aspect of that experience, as happened between Justices Brennan and Blackmun, is conversation with each other, exchange of thought and ultimate convergence on conclusions. The conversation and convergence between these justices illustrates, then, the process of deliberation.

In contrast, Justice Scalia's originalism, which was described above as a refusal to deliberate, can be illustrated by arguments in his opinions in support of capital punishment. In his Tanner lecture, published as *A Matter of Interpretation*,[276] Justice Scalia now describes his method as textualism as well as originalism. He wants to read the text of the Constitution in context and in a sophisticated way but as it would have been understood by a politically active person of the time when it was adopted. In his concurring opinion in *Callins v. Collins,* Justice Scalia argues in reply to Justice Blackmun that the Fifth Amendment provisions regarding due process for one accused of a capital crime "clearly permits the death penalty to be imposed, and establishes beyond doubt that the death penalty is not one of the 'cruel and unusual punishments' prohibited by the Eighth Amendment."[277]

Cruel and unusual punishment is an ancient concept found in the British Bill of Rights and before adoption of our federal constitution in the Bill of Rights of many of our original thirteen states.[278] In the 1790s, when the Eighth Amendment was adopted, politically sophisticated persons would have recognized that it represented a growing and evolving tradition. At that time, the excessive use of capital punishment was under challenge and arguably would have been considered cruel. The overuse of capital punishment was under attack in Europe, in England and particularly in the United States at the very moment that the Fifth and Eighth Amendments were written. In Philadelphia, shortly after

---

276. *See* ANTONIN SCALIA, A MATTER OF INTERPRETATION: FEDERAL COURTS AND THE LAW, 45–47 (1997). Scalia discusses reading the Constitution in context and in a sophisticated way.

277. Callins v. Collins, *supra* note 272.

278. *See* Case of Titus Oates, 10 HOW.ST.TR. 1079, 1316 (K.B. 1685) reprinted in 5 PHILIP B. KURLAND & RALPH LERNER, THE FOUNDERS' CONSTITUTION 368 (1987).

the Bill of Rights[279] was offered to the States for ratification, the Walnut Street Jail, the first beginning of our modern prison system, was established to provide a substitute for capital punishment.[280] A politically active citizen of Philadelphia, at that time, could read the Fifth and Eighth Amendments together and contemplate the possibility that capital punishment over time would become cruel and unusual.

In *Harmelin v. Michigan*,[281] Justice Scalia, writing for the Court, argues that to be unconstitutional a punishment must be both cruel *and* unusual, italicizing the word "and" to emphasize his point.[282] Understanding the *and* here as conjunctive, allows Scalia to argue that theoretical understandings of cruelty are an inappropriate basis for declaring a punishment unconstitutional. The focus shifts to the customary practices both at the time of the Constitution and since.

However, it is not clear that the words, cruel and unusual, were meant to be understood conjunctively. One could object both to cruel punishments and unusual punishments just as one could instruct one's child not to throw sticks and stones. Indeed, at the time the Eighth Amendment was offered to the states, the Delaware Declaration of Rights and Fundamental Rules read: "That excessive Bail ought not to be required, nor excessive Fines imposed nor cruel or unusual punishment inflicted."[283] Indeed, a Declaration of the British Parliament around 1786 read "nor" in a manner similar to the Delaware "or": "That excessive bail ought not to be required, nor excessive fines imposed, nor cruel nor unusual punishment inflicted."[284]

---

279. U.S. Const. Amends I–X.

280. *See* Michael Sherman & Gordon Hawkins, Imprisonment in America: Choosing the Future 50–51 (1981); *See also* Norval Morris, The Future of Imprisonment 5, 13–15, 29 (1974).

281. Harmelin v. Michigan, 501 U.S. 957 (1991) (Justice Scalia does not propose "a blind incorporation" of an originalist interpretation of the British Declaration of Rights into the U.S. Constitution. Rather, the Justice argues a normal originalist view that we should interpret it by examining "what its meaning was to Americans who adopted the Eighth Amendment." Justice Scalia argues that "unusual" should mean "not regularly or customarily employed." 501 U.S. at 976.

282. *Id.* at 984.

283. *See* Delaware Declaration of Rights and Fundamental Rules § 16 (1776) reprinted in 5 Philip B. Kurland & Ralph Lerner, The Founders' Constitution 373 (1987).

284. *See* Case of Titus Oates, 10 How.St.Tr. 1079, 1316 (K.B. 1685) reprinted in 5 Philip B. Kurland & Ralph Lerner, The Founders' Constitution 368 (1987).

One can choose between competing interpretations of the text both of which are plausible and indeed between different interpretations of our tradition by asking which is in accord with the highest moral interpretation of our constitution and hence makes the most that can be made of the Eighth Amendment. Recognizing that the prohibition of cruel punishment, closely tied as it is to the protection of human dignity, is supported by a comprehensive understanding of our Constitution, as designed and developed to protect the life, liberty and property, the human dignity, of each person, one can choose that interpretation. That interpretation also has good institutional fit.

Justice Scalia objects also to the equation of "cruel…punishment" with excessiveness.[285] He notes that that clause of the Eighth Amendment does not mention excessiveness. The note of excessiveness, however, appears throughout the Eighth Amendment. The provision begins by prohibiting excessive bail and excessive fines. Normally, when one finds broader language at the end of a statutory series, a proper interpretation includes the earlier notes in the broader language. The usual interpretation of cruel which includes excessive punishments is in accord, then, with a correct grammatical reading of the Eighth Amendment.

A personalist interpretation of the Eighth Amendment can begin with a carefully grammatical reading of the text and an examination of our tradition. An appropriate interpretation of a particular constitutional provision must have good institutional fit. When alternate interpretations all have good fit, a judge can ask which is most in accord with a vision of our Constitution as designed to protect the human dignity of each person and which makes the most that now can be made of our Constitution.

Scalia rejects that sort of deliberation. In *Thompson v. Oklahoma,*[286] he made clear that drawing on philosophical thought to understand what might be a cruel or an excessive punishment is inappropriate.[287] It is clear that Justice Scalia rejects the virtue of deliberation. One should note that his position also rejects the priority for life.

The plurality opinion in *Gregg v. Georgia*[288] written by Justice Stewart, uses majoritarian arguments but does not reject deliberation. On

---

285. *Id.*
286. Thompson v. Oklahoma, 487 U.S. 815 (1988).
287. *Id.* at 859.
288. *See* Gregg, *supra* note 266.

the basis of the plurality arguments in *Gregg*, the Supreme Court has both upheld the constitutionality of capital punishment and rejected it in particular cases. In *Coker v. Georgia*,[289] for example, the Court while using majoritarian arguments found capital punishment for rape unconstitutional. In *Thompson v. Oklahoma*,[290] again with the help of a rather crude nose count, the Supreme Court found capital punishment for fifteen year olds unconstitutional.

One reason majoritarianism, in the earlier capital punishment cases, did not completely eliminate deliberation was that it was used in conjunction with other concepts. In *Gregg*, Justice Stewart combined with majoritarianism a concept of fairness and a seat of the pants understanding of retribution and general deterrence as legitimate goals of criminal punishment.[291] Capital punishment, then, in the plurality view was constitutional because (one) a majority of state legislatures favored it; (two) it could be administered fairly; and (three) in the view of those legislatures it served the legitimate goals of retribution and general deterrence. In *Coker*, Justice White, writing for the plurality, found capital punishment for rape unconstitutional because it was supported by only a small minority of states, because taking a life was not appropriate retribution for rape and hence was not a fair punishment.[292] Justice Stewart, in *Gregg*, related majoritarianism, fairness and his estimate of retribution and general deterrence to the language of the Eighth Amendment. Capital punishment was not cruel or excessive because it served the legitimate goals of retribution and general deterrence in the views of the state legislatures. It was not unusual because it was in accord with the evolving standards of human decency as demonstrated by the support of the state legislatures.

Nevertheless, the plurality position in *Gregg* is heavily influenced by majoritarianism, which makes the majority the judge in its own case. Inevitably, it will clash with fairness. Ultimately, the Court will have to choose between majority will and fairness. In the view of Justice Black-

---

289. *See* Coker, *supra* note 173.

290. *See* Thompson, *supra* note 286.

291. *See* Gregg v. Georgia, 428 U.S. 153 at 184–86 (Stewart, J., plurality opinion). Here, Stewart recognized that statistical evidence would not support a conclusion that capital punishment had a greater marginal impact on deterring murder than life imprisonment, nevertheless, Stewart believed in its deterrent value. *See id.* at 179–80.

292. *See* Coker, *supra* note 173 at 584.

mun, the current administration of capital punishment is irretrievably unfair. There is a deep contradiction, then, a conflict between fairness and majoritarianism in the Court's basic theory supporting capital punishment.

Personalism, following Dworkin, would reject majoritarianism. It is based on an understanding of democratic theory that does not have good institutional fit with our Constitution. A different understanding of democratic theory, in which constitutional rights serve as a check on majority will, has better institutional fit; it also affords respect and concern to each person. In personalist theory, then, it has a higher moral appeal than majoritarianism.

That better understanding of democratic theory, however, requires judges to deliberate on the meaning of particular constitutional provisions, such as the prohibition of cruel and unusual punishment. In personalist method, that deliberation begins with a careful analysis of the text and our history. When great contested concepts such as "cruel... punishments" are found in the text, a judge should offer a theory of those concepts. In constructing that theory and examining the text, the judge should choose between theories and understandings of the text which have good institutional fit. A personalist judge would choose an interpretation which has both good institutional fit and higher moral appeal. In personalist thought, the appropriate interpretation would be consistent with an understanding of our constitution as designed to protect the human dignity of each person.

Interest balancing is important. When interpreting the Eighth Amendment a personalist judge would combine the views of Brennan and Marshall. Under its abstract background theory, a personalist understanding of our Constitution would perceive it as designed to promote and protect each person's share of the primary social goods. The interest in life of potential victims must be balanced against the interests of those accused.

12. Conclusion

A personalist judge recognizes his horizons, his own limited but growing knowledge and understanding. When appointed to the United States Supreme Court, he or she is a person of great experience who has crossed many horizons. In conversation with our history and with competing theories, he will construct a theory of our Constitution and a method for interpretation which will be in accord with his commitment to afford all persons deep respect and concern and to try to understand persons, their needs and their horizons. This chapter on "Constitutional Interpretation" has offered an example of such a personalist theory and method and the process by which they are constructed. A personalist theory emerges in the course of a conversation with our history and with competing methods. When deciding a constitutional case, a personalist judge would begin with a careful examination of the text and its history. He would examine any proposed or developing principle for institutional fit and would compare it with his comprehensive theory of our Constitution. As generally in personalist theory, a principle would be construed as protecting an interest which must be balanced against competing interests. Interests related under personalist background theory to primary social goods are more significant. Variations on personalist method in more complex circumstances have been discussed. Among these are the problem of determining whether to recognize proposed unenumerated rights.

The account in this chapter of constitutional method presents a number of disputable points and hard questions which should be addressed. That is the subject of the next chapter.

Among the questions addressed is how a judge of limited, although growing knowledge and understanding, can justify his decisions to his many constituents in the complex and multiple horizons of our pluralist society. The personalist method for constitutional interpretation is supported by an abstract background theory of human rights. That theory was described in chapter 3. A further hard question is whether one can offer an acceptable foundation for a theory of human rights, at least as found in our constitutional history. An important contention in chapter 5 is that Personalist theory is legitimate and has fewer legitimacy costs than competing theories. Chapter 5, then, should further develop the theory of legitimacy.

CHAPTER V

Justification, Legitimacy and Moral Judgment

1. Introduction

This is not a book about human rights or moral judgment. Rather its purpose is to demonstrate that one can construct a personalist jurisprudence and method of judicial decision making while remaining in conversation with our common law tradition and our current methods for adjudication. Nevertheless, both on constitutional and common law issues, personalism offers positions grounded in strong adherence to human rights and takes a non-skeptical stance on moral judgment. A theory of rights was offered in chapter 3 and applied to constitutional decision making in chapter 4. In this chapter we should discuss briefly a personalist account of the foundations for human rights and moral judgment. A series of related topics also should be discussed including justification for judicial decisions, a personalist understanding of the common good (see also chapter 3), a more epistemological account of intellectual and legal method and the relation of each of these topics to the legitimacy of judicial decisions.

In our pluralist society multiple thinkers offer strong and perceptive but differing positions on these topics. A personalist who recognizes his growing but limited knowledge and understanding should enter into conversation with and learn from those thinkers. Differences should be accounted for and an explanation should be offered for personalist choices. The fundamental personalist choice is in the commitment to afford all persons equal respect and concern and to attempt to understand others. That position itself should be justified but in turn it provides support for other positions.

A twenty-first century lawyer recognizes human rights ideology as part of her milieu. That ideology developed during the seventeenth and eighteenth centuries and flourished during the last half of the twentieth century. Because personalist thinkers are committed to respect and concern for each person, personalist theory would support the ideology of human rights. A series of questions remain, however, including whether human rights are absolute. A discussion of human rights will contribute to a fuller understanding of personalist theory.

Richard Posner's skepticism about legal reasoning offers a challenge to any explanation of judicial decision making method. The proliferation of multiple strong intellectual methods and the puzzle that poses for those reflecting on law may account in part for Posner's skepticism. A personalist account of legal method must encounter and discuss legal skepticism and the confusion presented by the multiplicity of strong intellectual methods.

Because this chapter is short the discussion of these topics will be summary and necessarily inadequate. A sketch of potential personalist positions on these larger questions, however, may provide background for a more comprehensive understanding of personalist theory. Because the purpose of this work is to construct and argue for the legitimacy of a personalist interpretation of American law and judicial decision making methods, one should recognize that there is no obligation to defend intellectual or moral judgment, human rights or international human rights law. Rather it is necessary to show that the personalist interpretation including its non-skeptical position on moral judgment and legal reasoning and a human rights foundation for constitutional law is legitimate and will enhance the legitimacy of judicial decisions.

Discussions of legitimacy are closely related to the question of whether judicial decisions can and should be justified. Richard Posner argues that a judge should offer an explanation rather than justification for his decision because in our pluralist society it is not possible to justify a decision.[1] Both Ronald Dworkin and Cass Sunstein offer positions on justification which are closely related to their understanding of legitimacy.[2] One could divide a discussion of legitimacy into two parts. In one part discussion would center on the foundations in one's own theory for the legitimacy of a judicial decision. That appears to be the primary focus of Dworkin's analysis.[3] In the other part one would inquire

---

1. See generally RICHARD A. POSNER, THE PROBLEMS OF JURISPRUDENCE at 124–57 (1990).
2. See RONALD DWORKIN, LAW'S EMPIRE at 190–95 (1986).
3. See generally id.

why a judicial decision would appear legitimate or acceptable to those who do not share one's own theory. Inevitably the discussions overlap as they do in this chapter. Dworkin appears to overlook issues concerning the acceptability of a decision to those who do not share his understanding of legitimacy.

The discussion in this chapter and the argument for the legitimacy of personalist method will begin, then, with an analysis of the justification for judicial decisions. The argument will conclude in the last two parts of the chapter with an analysis of legitimacy and then of questions concerning the authority of judicial decisions and the relationship of that authority to legitimacy and the use of force. As a prelude to that discussion the intervening parts will discuss the foundation for human rights, the personalist theory of the common good and its relation to an understanding of human rights, intellectual method and moral judgment.

While this chapter offers a personalist account of moral judgment, intellectual method and human rights as a foundation for a personalist interpretation of American law and judicial method, other foundations are possible. The personalist interpretation of our law potentially could be supported by some pragmatists particularly those who recognize the importance of relating law to persons, by some adherents of natural law, by Aristotelian or related Thomist thought, by neo-Kantian analysis, by some religious thought and by those who more generally are attracted by human rights ideology or who are committed to American ideals. Under John Rawls' Theory of Justice, the contracting parties at the third stage choosing principles for just adjudication should consider a personalist interpretation of American law and personalist method for judicial decision making.[4]

2. Justification

Ronald Dworkin argues that a judge should offer principled justification for his decisions. He should base that justification on the principles, which provide the best explanation for the existing legal authority including case law, constitutions, and the established ways of working with the law. The principles which best justify existing authority should

---

4. See JOHN RAWLS, A THEORY OF JUSTICE at 195–201 (1971).

have good institutional fit and should make the most, including the most morally that now be made of that law.[5]

Cass Sunstein described Dworkin's account as requiring "judges to develop high-level theories" which do not "favor theoretical modesty."[6] "In Dworkin's hands," he explains, "the relevant theories are large and abstract; they sound just like political philosophy or moral theory."[7] Sunstein contends, however, that "this is not how real lawyers proceed."[8] Most significantly he argues that Dworkin's method prevents "people who disagree on large principles from reaching consensus on particular outcomes."[9]

In contrast Sunstein offers a minimalist approach to legal justification. Typically a minimalist judge should prefer narrow decisions that "are no broader than necessary to support the outcome."[10] In justifying her decisions a minimalist judge should offer shallow rather than deep arguments. According to Sunstein, "minimalists generally try to avoid issues of basic principle."[11] He explains:

> "They want to allow people who disagree on the deepest issues to converge. In this way they attempt to reach incompletely theorized agreements. Such agreements come in two forms: agreements on concrete particulars amid disagreements or uncertainty about the basis for those concrete particulars, and agreements about abstractions amid disagreements or uncertainty about the particular meaning of those abstractions. Both forms are important to constitutional law."[12]

Sunstein prefers incompletely theorized agreements because setting aside disagreements over basic principles will promote convergence between differing positions and potential consensus. Lowering the discussion's level of generality can avoid the sharp dispute over basic principles in our pluralist society.[13]

---

5. *See* Dworkin, Law's Empire, *supra* note 2 at 243, 44.

6. Cass R. Sunstein, Legal Reasoning and Political Conflict 49 (1996).

7. Sunstein, Legal Reasoning and Political Conflict, *supra* note 6 at 49.

8. *Id.* at 49.

9. *Id.*

10. Cass R. Sunstein, One Case At A Time: Judicial Minimalism on the Supreme Court 11 (1999).

11. Sunstein, One Case At A Time, *supra* note 10, at 11.

12. *Id.* at 11–12 (emphasis in original).

13. *See generally* Sunstein, One Case At A Time, *supra* note 10.

A personalist would recognize the deep wisdom of Sunstein's insight into dispute settlement. A personalist judge recognizing his own limited knowledge and understanding often would decide cases narrowly and would seek convergence through modest justification. He would develop his deep theory of law gradually.

Ronald Dworkin, however, offers an understanding of conversation and convergence between justices interpreting the United States Constitution that should be compared to Sunstein's insight. Each justice should present a theory or conceptualization of the relevant contested constitutional concept. That theory should explain the concept, the clear instances of the concept, and the cases the justice wants to decide under that provision.[14] Since Justice A and Justice B are explaining the same concept and the same clear instances their theories of the constitutional provision necessarily will overlap and often will show considerable convergence.[15] In capital punishment cases as discussed in chapter 4, there is a remarkable convergence between Justices Brennan, Marshall and Blackmun from different and well-articulated theoretical positions. A tactic often employed by Justice Brennan was to offer arguments from a differing theoretical position, for example, from Blackmun's concern for fairness, while maintaining his own fundamental position that the Eighth Amendment protects the human dignity of each person.[16]

While a personalist judge often would offer incompletely theorized arguments to support his holdings, he also would follow the example of Justice Brennan as he gradually developed a comprehensive theory of our Constitution and law and a method for deciding cases compatible with that theory. Arguably signaling from time to time his basic theory would give the legal community greater confidence in his decisions among other reasons because they would be more predictable. To the extent that basic theories of constitutional provisions reflect our great national ideals, holdings supported by those theories would have a greater appeal to legitimacy.

Dworkin's highly theoretical method for constitutional interpretation is challengeable and has been criticized in previous chapters be-

---

14. See RONALD DWORKIN, TAKING RIGHTS SERIOUSLY 93, 106–07 (1977).
15. See generally id.
16. See McClesky v. Kemp, 481 U.S. 279, 321 (1987) (Brennan, J., dissenting).

cause it incurs legitimacy costs. Dworkin's consistent use of high theory prevents his ideal judge, Hercules, from struggling with the competing interests and circumstances of the parties to the case. Personalist method requires a judge to engage in that struggle and to reveal his struggle in his opinion. Legitimacy would be enhanced by recognition that the judge has considered the interests of the parties and the concrete circumstances of the case.

In contrast Sunstein's method incurs legitimacy costs because a judge using it would not give guidance to the bar by revealing his deeper positions and would be handicapped in appealing to our great national ideals.[17] Personalist method avoids both sets of legitimacy costs.

Sunstein's minimalism is related to his understanding of democracy as a deliberating society. In *Democracy and the Problem of Free Speech*, Sunstein is eloquent when he describes a deliberative democracy. For example, he argues that a "large point" of our system "is to ensure discussion and debate among people who are genuinely different in their perspectives and position, in the interest of creating a process through which reflection will encourage the emergence of general truths."[18] He explains further:

> "A distinctive feature of American republicanism is extraordinary hospitality toward disagreement and heterogeneity, rather than fear of it. The framers believed that a diversity of opinion would be a creative and productive force. The prominent antifederalist Brutus, an eloquent opponent of the proposed Constitution, insisted: "In a republic, the manners, sentiments, and interests of the people should be similar...." Speaking for the Federalists, Alexander Hamilton responded that in a heterogeneous republic, discussion will be improved. Indeed, "the jarring of parties.... will promote deliberation." The American Federalists did not believe that heterogeneity would be an obstacle to political discussion and debate. On the contrary, they thought that it was indispensable to it. If people already agree, what will they talk about? Why would they want to talk at all?"[19]

Judicial minimalism, narrow and silent about deeper positions, is designed, according to Sunstein, to promote that discussion in society.

---

17. Cass R. Sunstein, Democracy and the Problem of Free Speech 241 (1993).

18. Sunstein, Democracy and the Problem of Free Speech, *supra* note 17, at 241.

19. *Id* at 241–42.

Sunstein's understanding of minimalism rests to some extent on a majoritarian theory of democracy and bears a family relationship to the thought of John Hart Ely.[20] His notion of deliberating democracy, then, while inspiring, is very different from the deliberating society described in chapter 4. Our judicial dispute settlement system with the United States Supreme Court at its apex, under that chapter's personalist theory, is a principal means for settling great disputes in our society by rational deliberation and for reflecting on our great national ideals. America often legalizes its great disputes and arguably that is an important means for rational deliberation in our society. Our legal system and thought provide a great resource for rational discussion and deliberation to our country. Sunstein by and large would abandon that resource.

Sunstein, of course, is influenced by Pragmatism's distaste for large theories.[21] Richard Posner's rejection of justification in *The Problems of Jurisprudence*, is a much harsher articulation of that pragmatist distaste. Posner does not believe that the great decisions can be justified by rational argument in our pluralist society.[22] In that homogenous society envisioned by the anti-federalist, Brutus, where many assumptions are shared in a common culture, it may be possible to offer a justification based on shared premises. In our more complex society Posner would offer an explanation rather than a justification because of the paucity of shared premises. Posner's skepticism extends to the whole range of legal reasoning. He argues against any "confident sense in the law's autonomy and objectivity."[23] According to Posner "there is no such thing" as an autonomous and objective "legal reasoning."[24] Since the courts are "[u]nable to base decision in the difficult cases on either logic or science"[25] he contends that "judges are compelled to fall back on the grab bag of informal methods of reasoning that I call 'practical reasoning.'"[26] He concedes that "[t]hese methods often succeed"[27] but regrets that "they sometimes fail"[28] and argues that "they owe less than one might

---

20. *See generally* SUNSTEIN, DEMOCRACY AND THE PROBLEM OF FREE SPEECH, *supra* note 17.

21. *See generally id.*

22. *See generally* POSNER, THE PROBLEMS OF JURISPRUDENCE, *supra* note 1.

23. POSNER, THE PROBLEMS OF JURISPRUDENCE, *supra* note 1, at 458.

24. *Id.* at 459.

25. *Id.* at 455.

26. *Id.*

27. *Id.*

28. *Id.*

think to legal training and experience."[29] "In particular, reasoning by analogy has been oversold as a method of reasoning at once cogent and distinctively legal."[30]

Posner at times would find inspiration for a decision in an analogy. He perceives traditional common law reasoning by analogy and distinction simply "as a stimulus to thinking."[31] That, of course, is not sufficient because "the law seeks a logic of justification rather than merely or primarily a logic of discovery."[32] However, "a precedent's analogical significance means simply that the precedent contains information relevant to the decision of the present case."[33]

As an erudite student of methodology, Posner would prefer scientific method. However, he recognizes that the methods and attitude of science are not "at home" in the law.[34] A justification "akin to scientific verification" by demonstrating "that a decision is correct", that is, that, in fact, it produces the best results for the future, "often is impossible."[35] That is, because there is not sufficient feedback in law and no established means for feedback, the law cannot imitate the methods of the sciences or the social sciences. Roscoe Pound's experimenting society has failed because we have not followed his recommendations and probably are unable to do so.

In *The Problematics of Moral and Legal Theory*, Posner argues for a new professionalism in law which would include a greater role for the social sciences and the building of a body of knowledge which would enable the courts to support their decisions in a more professional manner. Posner offers that new professionalism as a substitute for the use of moral theory in law.[36]

Justification on the basis of great principles or ideals is not available because there are no "moral reals,"[37] "no overarching concepts of justice that our legal system can seize upon to give direction to the enter-

---

29. *Id.*
30. *Id.*
31. *Id.*
32. *Id.*
33. *Id.* at 456.
34. *Id.*
35. *Id.* at 459.
36. RICHARD A. POSNER, THE PROBLEMATICS OF MORAL AND LEGAL THEORY, at 185–227 (1999).
37. *Id.* at 460.

prise."[38] In addition the consensus which prevailed during the 1950s has been lost. We have a pluralist society which does not have an agreement on shared premises. Justification similar to that argued for by Dworkin on the basis of the best interpretation of law will not suffice because "there is no longer a useful sense in which law is interpretive."[39] Posner argues that the "essence of interpretive decision making is considering the consequences of alternative decisions."[40]

Posner, then, while opposing nihilism in law and morals, would perceive himself as a skeptic in both. However, as a good post Rorty neopragmatist, Posner is prepared to soldier forward to decide cases as best he can in the hope of producing the best results for the future. Although he is pessimistic about it, he would prefer that lawyers receive greater training in the social sciences, particularly economics. Though he now considers wealth maximization as a secondary rather than a primary goal of law, he believes that training would enhance our ability to make decisions with the best consequences and to design institutions which would improve our future.[41] Posner's opposition to moral theory does not constitute a rejection of moral intuition. In *The Problematics of Moral and Legal Theory* he supports moral intuition at times against the competing conclusions of moral theory.[42]

While granting that Posner is a shrewd and experienced observer of law and a good analyst of legal, scientific, and social science methodology, one nevertheless can argue that he has a deeply mistaken understanding of law. When Ronald Dworkin in Law's Empire attacks the legal pragmatist, he probably comes closest to describing Richard Posner.[43] The legal pragmatist, Dworkin contends, believes that legal decisions should produce the best result for the future.[44] Arguably Posner's skepticism about legal reasoning is related in part to this misinterpretation. Plainly legal reasoning will lead to holdings which produce the best result for the future only if the judge is both fortunate and wise.

Personalist theory, as offered here, proposes dispute settlement as the principal function of our court system. By appropriately settling

---

38. *Id.*

39. *Id.* at 460.

40. *Id.* at 460.

41. *See generally* POSNER, PROBLEMS OF JURISPRUDENCE, *supra* note 1.

42. See POSNER, THE PROBLEMATICS OF MORAL AND LEGAL THEORY, *supra* note 36 at 142–43.

43. *See* DWORKIN, LAW'S EMPIRE, *supra* note 2 at 151–75.

44. *Id.*

disputes, parties are encouraged to present their arguments in court and to abide by the result rather than using private violence or other action in the streets. By providing a public forum, our court system suppresses private violence and advances the rule of law. The English-speaking countries of the world are renown for their success in establishing the rule of law in part with the help of an independent judiciary. Despite the use of arbitration and other means of alternate dispute settlement our American society is very litigious. People in large numbers bring their disputes to court. However critical one may be of particular aspects of our law, we should recognize that our courts continue to maintain the rule of law successfully and thereby perform their basic function.

Over the ages, our courts have developed the common law and have created and recreated decision making methods as part of what we could describe as the common law tradition. A similar development of method has established a growing tradition for deciding constitutional cases. In previous chapters, it has been argued that our courts following those traditions have established a means for rational argument about small and great disputes in our society. Argument and deliberation about great public disputes take place in our courts and with use of our tradition of legal argument. That is a great resource for society, for maintaining the peace and preserving the rule of law.

Arguably, our courts make their greatest contributions to the future of our society by successfully maintaining our great public dispute settlement institution and by cultivating our legal culture with its constitutional and common law traditions and transmitting that culture to the next generation. In that context, we can assess more appropriately the traditional tools for legal reasoning.[45]

In the common law tradition, it is customary for a judge to offer a written opinion in support of his decision. In his opinion, he will argue for his holding on the basis of precedent. He will analogize or distinguish previous precedent and perhaps explain the principles or policies supporting those analogies and distinctions. By arguing that their decisions are consistent with previous law, judges are not only supporting the legitimacy of their holdings but also are maintaining across the United States a common legal language and culture. An attorney edu-

---

45. *See* James Boyd White, Heracles' Bow: Essays on the Rhetoric and Poetics of the Law (1985).

cated at Harvard, Georgetown or Syracuse can practice law before courts in California or Oregon.

As described in previous chapters, a personalist judge in his opinion would do more than fulfill the minimum requirements for legitimacy by offering good legal arguments for his holding. Out of respect for his fellow lawyers and judges and to preserve the common law tradition he would offer such good legal arguments. Beyond that, however, his opinion should reveal his analysis of the problems and the concrete circumstances of the parties. On appropriate occasions, he should argue that his holding is in accord with our great principles and ideals. When sensible he should portray his effort to cross horizons.

These additional aspects of personalist and other methods would enhance the legitimacy of decisions. A personalist judge would ground his interpretation and development of common law method in his commitment to respect, have concern for and attempt to understand each person. A method grounded in that commitment and developed under those guidelines should enhance the legitimacy of decisions because those decisions and that method should have the potential of appearing reasonable to each person.

Personalist theory describes a pluralist society as one composed of multiple horizons. Both Sunstein and Posner, are troubled by the disagreement on basic principles in our pluralist society.[46] Posner also rejoices in that disagreement which he believes will enhance our ability to find new and better paths for the future.[47] The personalist response to fundamental disagreement between persons in different horizons is two fold. First, a judge with personalist commitments should develop horizon crossing methods as part of his decision making process and when making decisions should strive to cross horizons. In his opinion, he should reveal those methods and should report the effort. The openly acknowledged struggle to cross horizons should enhance the legitimacy

---

46. *See generally* POSNER, PROBLEMS OF JURISPRUDENCE, *supra* note 1; SUNSTEIN, ONE CASE AT A TIME, *supra* note 10. See also, Posner, The Problematics of Moral and Legal Theory *supra* note 36 at 60–63 where Posner argues that disagreements over basic principles and moral theory cannot be settled methodologically or empirically as in scientific method. Posner's preference for scientific reasoning apparently rests on his discomfort with disagreement on basic moral issues. Relating to one's fellow humans, however, requires sorting out such disagreements.

47. *See* POSNER, PROBLEMS OF JURISPRUDENCE, *supra* note 1 at 458.

of his decision in a pluralist society. It also should enhance the quality of dispute settlement. Second, a personalist judge would ground his method, his principles and his decision in his commitment to respect, have concern for and attempt to understand each person. That foundation should enhance the legitimacy of his method and his decision in our pluralist society. Decisions using that method and so grounded should have a greater capacity for appearing reasonable to each person.

Nevertheless, lawyers and other persons will disagree, often vigorously, with judicial decisions and the principles on which they are based. James Boyd White describes law as the on-going argument about what society should be that constitutes society.[48] Personalist theory, as offered here, portrays our court system with its common law and constitutional law traditions, our great dispute settlement institution, as a principal means for carrying forward that on-going dialogue about what society should be. Arguably personalist method will enhance that exchange of thought and respect for all persons including the participants in the argument. In that context Posner is correct, a judicial opinion should offer arguments which appear reasonable and not a Dworkian rigidly demonstrated justification for the decision.[49] Arguably, however, personalist method and its legitimacy is the justification for the decision.

Skepticism, particularly of the pragmatic variety, is an important participant in our national dialogue and has important contributions to make to our understanding of law and legal reasoning. Nevertheless, legal skepticism incurs legitimacy costs. Open skepticism or a concealed slight of hand, as Dworkin argues, treats legal rights as if they exist thereby eroding public confidence in decisions.[50] Personalism in contrast recognizes some legal rights including those based solely on precedent as weak rights which must be weighed against competing principles and policies. Likewise, skepticism about our great national ideals erodes public confidence in our great decisions. Personalism recognizing that our great ideals are disputed concepts would participate in the on-going national argument and deliberation about those ideals and would contribute the theory that our ideals are grounded in respect and concern for each person as well as for the common good. Arguably that participation in the national dialogue and that theory will enhance the

---

48. *See generally* WHITE, *supra* note 45.
49. *See generally* POSNER, PROBLEMS OF JURISPRUDENCE, *supra* note 1.
50. *See* DWORKIN, LAW'S EMPIRE, *supra* note 2, at 154–55.

legitimacy of judicial decisions and of our court system, our national dispute settlement institution.

Posner could argue that the personalist position as just described resembles the various neo-traditionalist theories which he comments on and rejects in chapter 14 of *The Problems of Jurisprudence*.[51] The neo-traditionalists in various ways want to preserve the autonomy of legal reasoning.[52] The personalist theory as offered here describes law as a specialized and sophisticated common sense method. Like Posner, a personalist judge would draw on the insights of economics and the social sciences as well as philosophy. A personalist educator would want new lawyers trained in those disciplines. While recognizing Posner's insights into our failure to function as an experimenting society, personalists would prefer to continue the pursuit of that ideal. Nevertheless, law as a specialized discipline using a common sense method has its own functions and goals as described above. The argument for law as a sophisticated, specialized common sense method will be developed further in part five of this chapter. In that part, the intellectual problems presented by the proliferation of powerful methods in our society, problems which also trouble Posner, must be addressed.

Personalist overarching theory is grounded in respect and concern for each person and a desire to understand human beings. That commitment grounds the personalist theory of human rights described in chapter 3 and applied to constitutional interpretation in chapter 4. The basic personalist principles, as so grounded, support the personalist vision of our Constitution and the personalist methods for constitutional interpretation and common law decision making. Posner's skepticism concerning overarching theory and principles present a challenge to personalist foundations.[53] His moral and legal skepticism about our great principles and ideals resembles in some respect a variety of qualified positions regarding our growing tradition of human rights.[54] In the next two segments of this chapter, parts three and four, arguments against the personalist position on human rights and the common good will be assessed and the personalist position will be developed in dialogue with those arguments.

---

51. *See* POSNER, PROBLEMS OF JURISPRUDENCE, *supra* note 1 at 423–53.
52. *See id* at 434.
53. *See generally id.*
54. *See generally id.*

3. Human Rights

The modern understanding of human rights can be described as an ideology which developed in Europe and America during the seventeenth and eighteenth centuries. John Locke, for example, was an early contributor to rights theory.[55] His thought had great influence on our founding generation before, during and after the American Revolution.

As a novel development in European history, theories of natural rights were influenced by prior religious and philosophical thought, including the tradition of natural law, but were not derived from that prior thought. For that reason, some adherents of the natural law tradition argued and continue to argue that human rights are not grounded in natural law. More skeptical thinkers such as Jeremy Bentham, the founder of modern utilitarianism, found the arguments for natural rights implausible. Bentham described rights as nonsense and natural rights as nonsense on stilts.[56]

Nevertheless, with the help of American constitutional theory, the traumatic events of the Second World War and the establishment of the United Nations, the ideology of human rights has prospered. Today it could be described as one of the more successful of the competing ideologies to emerge from the twentieth century.

During the twentieth century, international law became a principal political vehicle for the discussion and advance of human rights. Important documents are the Universal Declaration of Human Rights adopted by the United Nations General Assembly in 1948, the International Covenant on Civil and Political Rights and the International Covenant on Economic, Social and Cultural Rights. Nevertheless, American constitutional law and theory remains an important means for the development of thought concerning human rights.

Personalism, as described in earlier chapters, offers a theory of human rights and applies that theory to constitutional interpretation. One should recognize that in this book there is no obligation to defend human rights ideology generally or international human rights law. Rather, it is necessary to show that a human rights foundation for con-

---

55. *See generally* JOHN LOCKE, TWO TREATISES OF GOVERNMENT (Peter Laslett, ed., 1960).

56. Jeremy Bentham, *Anarchical Fallacies* (1843), quoted in THE OXFORD DICTIONARY OF POLITICAL QUOTATIONS, 37 (Anthony Jay, ed., 1996).

stitutional interpretation is legitimate and will enhance the legitimacy of judicial decisions. Nevertheless, we should recognize the controversies that arise when human rights are discussed. In the world arena some argue that the ideology of human rights is western in origin, culturally based, and should not be imposed on differing cultures. From a similar perspective, others argue that economic rights should be considered prior to civil and political rights particularly in underdeveloped third world countries.

Some perceptive utilitarian thinkers such as H.L.A. Hart have set aside Jeremy Bentham's skeptical opposition to human rights and have offered a utilitarian analysis of rights.[57] Employing a version of rule utilitarianism their argument is that human rights normally serve the greater good of the greater number or the greater average utility.[58] By protecting against unreasonable invasions of privacy or personality, for example, the courts would promote a greater feeling of security and hence stability in society. Nevertheless, one should recognize a certain utilitarian opposition to human rights on the grounds that an individualist understanding of rights against the state does not serve the common good, particularly when defined as the greater good of the greater number. Jeremy Bentham's skepticism about rights continues to be an important position. It has, for example, influenced Richard Posner.

Michael Perry recently in *The Idea of Human Rights* has provided an impressive analysis of some basic issues concerning human rights. He starts with the question of whether "the idea of human rights is ineliminably religious"[59] and concludes that there is, "finally, no intelligible secular version of the idea of human rights."[60] He rejects "the relativist challenge to the idea of human rights—to the idea that (because every human being is sacred) there are things that ought not to be done to any human being and things that ought to be done for every human being,"[61] but recognizes that we have "deep differences about the human good", that we have a pluralist understanding of the human good and human flourishing.[62] The question of whether human rights are universal, he argues, is often confused with the question of whether human

---

57. *See* H.L.A. HART, PUNISHMENT AND RESPONSIBILITY 54–89 (1968).
58. *See generally id.*
59. MICHAEL PERRY, THE IDEA OF HUMAN RIGHTS 35 (1998).
60. *Id.* at 35.
61. *Id.* at 70.
62. *Id.* at 70.

rights are absolute. While human rights are universal, Perry is not prepared to concede that they are absolute. Nevertheless, he argues, it
makes good sense to treat international human rights as "non-derogable."[63] "Whether or not any human rights are, as moral rights, unconditional,"[64] he claims that "some human rights should be established by
law, as unconditional rights."[65]

I want to disagree with Perry's conclusion that the idea of human
rights is in the final analysis, religious. Perry's defense of a religious understanding of human rights is eloquent and persuades me that religious conviction is the strongest support for an ideology of human
rights and for the basic idea of human rights that there are certain
things that we should never do to any human being and likewise that
there are things we should do for every human being. Perry recognizes
that a variety of thinkers would accept and support the basic idea of
human rights on non-religious grounds.

Perry reviews at length two alternate strategies for supporting the
basic idea of human rights from a non-religious perspective. One which
has a neo-Kantian flavor he describes as the "definitional strategy,"[66] and
the other which offers prudential reasons based on self-interest he calls
the "self-regarding strategy."[67] He finds both inadequate because ultimately they do not provide sufficient reasons to support adoption of
the moral perspective or for maintaining human rights regardless of
competing prudential reasons.[68]

Those supporting the definitional strategy, according to Perry, argue
that to look at things morally is to look at the things impartially. One
finds echoes here of the Kantian categorical imperative. If one's position does not apply universally then it is not a morally obligatory position. From the moral point of view, then, there are certain things that
never should be done to any human being. Perry, argues, however, that
in the modern world of what personalism would call multiple horizons,
the moral point of view, itself, is in need of justification.[69] Why should

---

63. *Id.* at 105.
64. *Id.*
65. *Id.*
66. *Id* at 29–32.
67. *Id* at 32–35.
68. *See id* at 35.
69. *See id* at 31–32.

one not support one's family, one's tribe or one's nation in preference to the human rights of all?

Perry considers the self-regarding strategy which offers prudential reasons for supporting the human rights of all as more serious and less easily dismissed.[70] He finds in international law "at least a hint of a self-regarding argument, namely if you want to enjoy the fruits of peace in the world, you must extend your respect and concern to all human beings."[71] One can find that thesis stated in the preamble to the basic international documents on human rights.[72] "The Universal Declaration, the International Covenant on Economic, Social and Cultural Rights and the International Covenant on Civil and Political Rights all state... that 'recognition... of the equal and inalienable rights of all members of the human family is the foundation of freedom, justice and peace in the world' (emphasis added)."[73]

A speech by former U.S. Secretary of State, Warren Christopher, particularly impressed Perry, Christopher argued: "A world of democracies would be a safer world.... States that respect human rights and operate on democratic principles tend to be the world's most peaceful and stable.... Denying human rights not only lays waste to human lives; it creates instability that travels across borders."[74]

While Perry finds the self-regarding strategy persuasive, he argues that it is inadequate.[75] "The self-regarding reasons are, after all, abstract and highly speculative; their applicability to many concrete contexts is either just barely plausible or not plausible at all."[76] In other words, when presented with a conflict between immediate national self interest and the human rights of a Bosnian Serb, the self-regarding reasons for respecting the individual's human rights may not prevail. Perry concludes that "no political argument for our nation taking the human rights of distant peoples seriously will begin to have the power of an argument that appeals at least in part to the conviction that all human beings are sacred."[77] He adds, making a point important to the legitimacy

---

70. PERRY, *supra* note 59, at 33.
71. *Id.*
72. *See* PERRY, *supra* note 59.
73. *Id.* at 33–34 (emphasis added).
74. *Id.* at 34.
75. *Id.*
76. *Id.*
77. *Id.*

of the personalist position, that this, "conviction, after all, is partly constitutive of the American identity."[78]

Perry does not discuss the merits of the self-regarding arguments as the foundation for a choice of a long term national strategy in a difficult and complex world.[79] Arguably, even if one occasionally departs from human rights ideology, promoting human rights as a long term means of securing peace during the twenty-first century makes prudential sense. Likewise it would make sense as a means for keeping the peace within the boundaries of our own complex country with its pluralist society composed of multiple horizons.

Albert Camus, as Perry acknowledges is an outstanding example of an atheist who was committed to the sacredness of his fellow human beings.[80] He notes that atheists, agnostics, and others who do not share Perry's fundamental views may nevertheless support the basic idea of human rights that there are some things which never should be done to any human being and some things which should be done for every human being.[81] However, he argues, "as the example of Camus attests, to be connected to that truth existentially, as Camus certainly was, is not necessarily to affirm it intellectually."[82]

I want to use a Perry concession as a starting point for disagreeing with him. Perry concedes that "if the other really is, in some deep sense, one's sister/brother, then it would be surprising if every non-religious person were existentially disconnected from that truth."[83] Indeed if God, as many religious thinkers perceive, has created each person in his image and likeness and loves each person, then, the deep worth and value of each person should be perceivable to some extent even by those who do not believe in God.

Normally, a person's moral development proceeds through several stages. Recognizing with Lon Fuller the reciprocity of human relations is one insight. The value of what Perry describes as the self regarding strategy is another.[84] Experiencing human love, or great tragedy or witnessing unspeakable evil sometimes will be the occasion for perceiving

---

78. *Id.*
79. *See generally* PERRY, *supra* note 59, at 35.
80. *Id.*
81. *Id.*
82. *Id.*
83. *Id.*
84. *See* PERRY, *supra* note 59 at 32–35.

moral obligation related to the humanity of one's fellow human beings. Once one perceives moral obligation related to the personhood of others, that perception can be extended logically to others perceived as persons and ultimately to all human beings. The ever broadening horizons of the twentieth century, the advent of radio, television and the internet have allowed many to understand human beings across the world as persons to whom they have moral obligations. The Holocaust, the Vietnam War, the ethnic cleansing in Bosnia and Kosovo and other scenes of great human suffering have led many to the position that certain things should never be done to any human being.

That moral insight is articulated and developed by various thinkers and by persons in different horizons. That moral insight can support the neo-Kantian development of what Perry describes as the definitional strategy.[85] Whatever difficulty one has with the categorical imperative, it is a philosophical development of the moral insight that each person should be respected and treated as an end rather than a means. The very success of the ideology of human rights provides a vehicle for those who want to develop their moral insight in more popular terms.

Perry argues that these non-religious strategies are inadequate intellectually because those who hold them cannot offer sufficiently strong prudential reasons for regarding each person as sacred.[86] His preference for prudential reasons is indicated by Perry's comment that the "distinction between 'prudential' and 'moral' is deeply problematic, at least for anyone with an Aristotelian understanding of morality."[87] Ultimately, however, the great saints do not love God or their fellow human beings for prudential reasons. Rather they perceive their devotion as a response to God who has first loved them.

John Rawls offers his Theory of Justice as a middle level theory supportable by those who hold multiple deeper positions.[88] He argues that Kantian thought, various religious thinkers and those who simply adhere to American ideals could support his Theory of Justice. Rawls argues that his readers may find the Theory of Justice a satisfactory way of ordering their considered moral judgments. Likewise those who accept

---

85. *Id* at 29–32.
86. *Id.* at 31.
87. *Id.*
88. *See generally* John Rawls, *Kantian Constructivism in Moral Theory*, 77 J. Phil. 515 (1980); John Rawls, *Justice as Fairness: Political Not Metaphysical*, 14 Phil & Pub. Aff. 233 (1985).

American ideals and participate in American experience may find that Rawlsian theory offers a good way of ordering their thought.[89]

Arguably, human rights ideology is a middle level political position which, like Rawl's theory, may be supported by those who hold a multiplicity of deeper positions. Some who support human rights offer less serious positions than others do. Rorty, for example, while rejecting all foundationalism, nevertheless would promote and popularize "our Eurocentric human rights culture" because it is an attractive position which we hold.[90] Perry rightly finds that Ronald Dworkin does not understand what it means to hold that each human person is sacred.[91] Dworkin argues that a human being has the value of a great work of art. In contrast, those who hold stronger positions would perceive a serious violation of a person's human rights as striking at the moral foundations of their self-understanding or in violation of their world view or the moral order of the universe.

Personalist theory would support the ideology of human rights because personalist thinkers are committed to respect and concern for each person. If this book were a discussion of international rather than American law, it would be appropriate to offer a personalist interpretation of human rights ideology. That interpretation would resemble to some extent the theory of human rights described in chapter 3 and applied to constitutional interpretation in chapter 4. A personalist thinker could accept John Macmurray's position that we understand ourselves as related to other persons through action and that the "self-realization of any individual person is only fully achieved if he is positively motivated towards every other person with whom he is in relation."[92]

As an interpretation of American law, personalism offers a middle level theory which hopefully will appeal perhaps in part to many American lawyers despite their multiple horizons. That interpretation is supportable not only by those impressed with the thought of John Macmurray or other personalist thinkers, but also by religious thinkers, and by adherents of natural law, neo-Kantian or Aristotelian.[93] It also is sup-

---

89. *See generally* Rawls, *Justice as Fairness: Political Not Metaphysical,* 14 Phil & Pub. Aff. 233.

90. *See* PERRY, *supra* note 59 at 35, 37.

91. *See* PERRY, *supra* note 59 at 37.

92. Samuel J.M. Donnelly, *Towards a Personalist Jurisprudence: Basic Insights and Concepts,* 28 LOYOLA L. REV. 547, 585 (1995) (quoting JOHN MACMURRAY, PERSONS IN RELATIONS, 159 (1961)).

93. MACMURRAY, *supra* note 92, at 159.

portable by those who find it an attractive interpretation in American Law of our American ideals and by those who accept the ideology of human rights for whatever reason.

Personalism, as an interpretation of American law grounded in respect and concern for each person, is legitimate in part because the foundation reflects the successful ideology of human rights and hence a position that is acceptable to many persons and thinkers in differing horizons in our society.

Perry has a perceptive discussion of whether human rights are universal which he distinguishes from the question of whether human rights are absolute.[94] The relativist challenge to the universality of human rights contends that even if all human persons are sacred nevertheless "there are no things that ought not to be done...to any human being."[95] That relativist position should be distinguished from claims such as those made by the Nazis that not all members of the species homo are human or entitled to be held sacred.[96]

Given our multiple horizons and the many cultures in our world, the essence of the relativist challenge according to Perry, is the contention that "nothing is good and nothing is bad for every human being."[97] What is good and bad depends on the context or circumstances in which human beings live.[98]

In reply to the relativist challenge, Perry cites a series of outrageous events in the former Yugoslavia.[99] In sum, he argues that some acts are so horrible that regardless of culture no human being should be subjected to such cruelty.[100] For example, in no culture should a mother be raped before her children and then made to witness the death of those children.[101] Not only are some things bad for every human being but some things are good regardless of culture.[102] For example, to provide food to victims of an earthquake is good regardless of culture.[103] Perry

---

94. PERRY, *supra* note 59, at 57.
95. *Id.* at 58.
96. *Id.* at 58.
97. *Id.* at 61.
98. *Id*
99. *Id.* at 62–63.
100. *Id.*
101. *Id.*
102. *Id.*
103. *Id.*

concludes that the "relativist challenge to the idea of human rights is not plausible."[104] He argues that it seems plausible to some because they confuse it with a different and correct contention that there is a pluralism of opinion about the human good.[105]

One should recall that personalist judicial decision making method responds to the multiple horizons in our pluralist society by requiring a judge to cross horizons in an effort to understand the impact of his decision on others. The personalist judge should attempt to locate, access and weigh the conflicting interests of those differing horizons.

The question of whether human rights are universal also should be distinguished, according to Perry, from the question of whether human rights are absolute.[106] Can we say that normally there are things which ought not to be done to any human being but that these acts are permissible in some, perhaps imaginary, circumstances?

Perry notes that no one argues that every human right ought to be absolute.[107] In addition, the exercise of many rights often must be restricted for the protection of competing rights.[108] International law, then, according to Perry, appropriately distinguishes between some rights which are derogable and others which are non-derogable.[109] Perry notes that there are some rights which "Article 4(2) of the ICCPR makes non-derogable: 'the inherent rights to life' (Article 6); the right not to 'be subjected to torture or to cruel, inhuman or degrading treatment or punishment' (Article 7); and the right not to 'be held in slavery... [or] in servitude' (Article 8(1) & Article 8(2))."[110]

Classically, Perry inquires whether "the human right not to be subjected to torture is an absolute right,"[111] and argues that an "affirmative answer is counterintuitive."[112] He imagines a nuclear bomb in a large city and an apprehended terrorist and argues that it would be fanatical to place restrictions on what could be done to extract the requisite in-

---

104. *Id.* at 63.
105. *Id.*
106. *Id.* at 63.
107. *Id.* at 89.
108. *Id.*
109. *Id.*
110. *Id.* at 91–92.
111. *Id.* at 93.
112. *Id.* at 94.

formation.[113] He imagines, for example, "that the terrorist will disclose the location of the bomb only if an innocent person dear to him is tortured."[114] Perry is not prepared to prohibit that torture.[115]

Perry nevertheless argues that some human rights as international legal rights should be protected unconditionally.[116] While morally no human right is absolute, international legal rights, he claims, may be unconditional.[117] In support of that conclusion he offers a series of arguments; (1) the imaginable circumstances under which a seemingly absolute human right morally should be violated are unlikely to exist. (2) Making legal rights conditional rather than non-derogable to provide for imaginable but highly unlikely situations would provide political authorities with too great a loophole for unconscionable violations of human rights. (3) If one of those imaginable but unlikely situations were in fact to occur, we can anticipate that political authorities unmoved by scruples would deal with it appropriately despite international law.[118]

Perry's arguments in favor of some non-derogable international rights also would support treating some American constitutional rights as legally absolute.[119] Again, however, I want to disagree with Perry and use as a starting point for that disagreement his concession that the circumstances are unlikely to occur in which it would be morally permissible to violate a seemingly absolute right.[120] The precise position I want to disagree with is that it would be fanatical to insist that such rights are truly absolute.

My first argument rests on our limited knowledge and understanding. As Posner recognizes we have great difficulty particularly in circumstances of haste and confusion in foreseeing the consequences of our actions and decisions.[121] Not only are the situations in which one could argue that a seemingly absolute right should be violated unlikely to occur, but if such a situation were presented we would have difficulty in knowing what actions would produce the best consequences. As a fanatic, himself, the terrorist who has planted a bomb may resist all ef-

---

113. *Id.*
114. *Id.*
115. *Id.*
116. *Id.* at 106.
117. *Id.*
118. *Id.*
119. *Id.*
120. *See generally* PERRY, *supra* note 59, at 106.
121. POSNER, PROBLEMS OF JURISPRUDENCE, *supra* note 1 at 458–59.

forts to persuade him to reveal its location. He may rejoice, for whatever reason, in seeing his friend tortured. The bomb threat may be a fake, and may be made precisely for the purpose of exposing our willingness to violate our ideals of human rights. In any event the example given on one occasion may encourage others to force similar violations of our ideals for the purpose of tearing down those ideals and the structure of our society. When we speculate about unlikely events which we imagine as possible we are even less able to foresee the consequences of our imagined future actions.

After the destruction of the World Trade Center and the attack on the Pentagon on September 11, 2001 the threat of terrorism is more immediate and real. However, it also is apparent that terrorist attacks may take place in strange and imaginative ways and that the terrorists may seek imaginative means for challenging our economy, democracy and culture. The exact circumstances and the costs and benefits of various responses remain unclear and speculative.

Skeptics and others including utilitarians customarily propose a series of horrible examples to demonstrate that human rights are neither universal nor absolute or to show that individual rights should not prevail over the greater good of the greater number. Those speculative, unlikely to occur or imaginary examples are offered for the purpose of challenging, changing or weakening our national adherence to individual human rights. The imaginary situations are designed for the purpose of establishing a slippery slope. My second argument is that it is not fanatical but rather a sensible way of avoiding mistakes to refuse to start down that slippery slope on the basis of imagined, speculative or unlikely to occur events.

The issue posed is not whether it is fanatical to hold absolutely to certain individual human rights but rather in what circumstances the good of society should prevail over the good of the individual. That issue will be assessed in part four, "The Common Good," which is the next segment of this chapter. Utilitarianism, which prefers the good of society to the good of individuals, should be contrasted there with individualist understandings of human rights. Personalism, as one may anticipate, will seek a path between those extreme positions. A related question that also must be addressed is whether economic rights should be considered the most important or whether John Rawls correctly ranks civil and political rights as lexically prior to fair distribution.

My third argument in reply to Perry is that the commitment to respect and concern for all persons logically requires that some human rights be accepted as finally absolute. This argument will be developed further in part six of this chapter, which will address moral judgment. In brief outline some of us perceive a moral obligation to respect and concern for some others whom we understand to be persons like ourselves. When we logically extend the obligation and that understanding to the whole of humanity on the argument that each one is a person like ourselves the inviolability we seek for ourselves and our inner circle necessarily applies to all others. The next part will consider whether competing obligations to the common good outweigh that logically developed obligation to each individual. That is the key question that Perry should have addressed.

In part four which is the next part we should proceed to discuss, then, the relation between the common good and individual rights.

4. The Common Good

In personalist theory the common good is perceived as a set of on-going complex direct and indirect relations between persons participating in a common action. That human interaction is a good which we share in common. The common good is promoted by constructing and maintaining those relations and the institutions that make them possible. Contrary to the common good are those actions that tend to destroy or impair the common action and those relations and institutions which provide the framework or context for persons acting together. Because participation by each individual in the common action is important under personalist theory and commitments, any action that tends to prevent or eliminate any person's participation in the common action is contrary to the common good. Persons understand themselves best in personalist theory in relation to others. The primary social goods as described in chapter 3 are those important or necessary to participation in this society or any society.[122] One can promote the common good, then, by enhancing our shares of the primary social goods and by building the institutions and relations which will advance the primary social goods. Denying a person the modest minimum social goods necessary to participation in society not only is an attack on her

---

122. *See supra* Chapter 3, Personalist Theory.

fundamental rights but also an action contrary to the common good. Personalist rights theory as described in chapter 3 and applied to constitutional interpretation in chapter 4 uses the primary social goods as a concept for understanding and describing human rights.

Personalist theory as just briefly summarized presents a middle way between theories which emphasize the importance and primacy of society and individualism. One can imagine an extreme individualism which "sees in the individual the supreme and fundamental good."[123] Confronting that individualist extreme, one can pose, on the basis of our experience of totalitarian societies, an "objective totalism" which "relies on the opposite principle and unconditionally subordinates the individual to the community or the society."[124]

In developing our interpretation of American law it would be better to analyze a more modest confrontation. To represent an individualist understanding of legal and human rights one could select Ronald Dworkin rather than, for example, Robert Nozick. Modern utilitarian thought, as found, for example, in the work of H.L.A. Hart would offer a theory which emphasizes the good of society or the greater good of the greater number while providing a theory of rights.

According to Dworkin, a court should justify its decision by arguments of principle, that is, by arguments based on individual assertion of rights. Arguments of principle should trump policy reasons, that is, arguments based on group goals.[125] In contrast, a judge following personalist method should weigh reasons of policy against reasons of principle. Strong policy reasons will outweigh weaker principles. Principles based on our most important national ideals will trump strong policies. Dworkin emphasizes individual rights but does not discuss the common good or any similar concept when presenting his theory of judicial decision making.[126]

Modern utilitarian thought emphasizes the common good described as the greater good of the greater number or the greater average utility but nevertheless can construct a theory of rights. Respecting some rights, under utilitarian theory, normally will promote the greater good of the greater number. Promoting certain rights, for example, will provide most people with a higher level of satisfaction and a greater feeling

---

123. KAROL WOJTYLA, THE ACTING PERSON 273 (1979).
124. *Id.*
125. *See* DWORKIN, TAKING RIGHTS SERIOUSLY, *supra* note 14 at 82–88.
126. DWORKIN, LAW'S EMPIRE, *supra* note 2.

of security. In some circumstances, however, it will be clear that the greater good requires that even the most important individual rights should be set aside.[127]

John Rawls describes an imaginary society in which slavery for twenty-five percent of the members would increase significantly the average utility for all members of society.[128] In those circumstances utilitarian theory would choose a societal structure in which slavery is permitted. Personalist thought and the parties in the Rawlsian original position would reject that structure.

Under personalist theory one has an obligation to promote the common good. Society is composed of individual persons acting together. Since personalists are committed to respect and concern for each person, they logically should be concerned for the good of all persons acting together. One should recall that under personalist theory an individual perceives himself as a person in action and in relation to another. As under Aristotelian and Thomist thought personalism understands persons as essentially social. Humans live more fully in society, in relation to others. Language, itself, for example, is an interpersonal phenomenon. One does not learn language and hence does not think complex thoughts absent a relationship with others. A personalist who is committed to individuals must then be committed to promote and facilitate human relations.

In a complex society persons relate to each other directly and indirectly in a large variety of circumstances and with the aid of a number of institutions. The personalist commitment to promote the common good should require one to build and preserve the institutions which enhance the common good and provide the means for human relations. Our great legal dispute settlement institution which preserves the rule of law and which provides a means for rational discussion and resolution of major national quarrels is one of the institutions which a personalist should preserve and promote. Using that example one should note that many of our institutions are artificial constructions which we have developed in our culture over many centuries. The development and maintenance of such institutions is an important task under personalist theory.

---

127. *See* HART, PUNISHMENT & RESPONSIBILITY, *supra* note 57 at 72–83.
128. RAWLS, *supra* note 4 at 167.

Human relations develop in concrete contexts and circumstances. When disputes arise, one must strive to settle those quarrels with reference to those concrete circumstances and to the relevant artificial institutions. Under personalist decision making method a judge is required to cross horizons and to attempt to understand the parties and their circumstances. That task is facilitated by classic common law reasoning by analogy and distinction. In contrast abstract reasoning whether on the basis of economic theory or highly principled deduction from major premises would seem counterproductive. The personalist commitment to the common good includes encouraging human relations in complex concrete contexts. A personalist judge does that by settling disputes.

Personalist theory, then, requires promotion of human relations in concrete circumstances and through institutions. In judicial decision making that means crossing horizons and the weighing of policies and interests. A Dworkian emphasis on principled reasoning overlooks human relations and the common good. Personalist theory also requires respect and concern for each person and that strong rights closely related to our national ideals and to the primary social goods govern our decisions. A difficult problem is presented when the personalist commitment to the common good appears to be in direct conflict with the personalist commitment to strong individual rights.

An example of that direct conflict was presented in the last part. Assume that a terrorist believed to have planted a nuclear bomb is apprehended. Would one's commitment to the common good require one to torture an innocent person in order to extract the requisite information from the terrorist? Probably utilitarian rights theory would require that our normal understanding of rights be set aside in those circumstances. In personalist theory one has strong commitments both to promote the common good and to protect basic individual rights. Unlike utilitarian thinkers, a personalist cannot resolve that dilemma by counting the numbers; both commitments are strong.

A traditional distinction between direct violations of one's obligations and permitting an action contrary to those obligations may be helpful. A person who chooses to torture another directly violates his obligation to respect that person's fundamental rights. If he fails to discover the nuclear bomb, the tragedy which ensues is an event which he possibly might have prevented but which he did not intend.

While in the presence of a great disaster that distinction may appear artificial, it nevertheless may provide a clue. The common good, here the prevention of the nuclear explosion, may be pursued by multiple means. A personalist has an obligation to find, create and use those other means. A society contemplating a real threat from nuclear terrorists should take serious steps to prevent disasters and to protect the persons threatened by the terrorists. Certain means such as torture of innocent persons are contrary to personalist commitments. Nevertheless other means should be pursued diligently and creatively.

One can argue that focusing on means which violate human rights is a distraction from the planning and dialogue required to develop other means, means which are more likely to succeed in protecting the threatened city. Particularly when such imagined events are pictured in the abstract and long in advance, the appropriate answer is that one should find alternate means. In the current crisis created by the September 11, 2001 terrorist attacks and the suicide bombings in Israel, an important means for encouraging future restraint would be to seek and promote a consensus against killing civilians for religious and nationalist reasons. The torture of innocent persons in the exigency of a particular crises would be counterproductive to the strategy of establishing a moral consensus against terrorist attacks on civilians. Widespread discussion or advocacy of torture before the event would be inconsistent with the effort to produce a moral consensus against the killing of innocent persons.

A second argument is that concentrating on means which violate fundamental human rights is corrupting. Granting permission to use such means in extreme circumstances will encourage governments, armed forces and the police to set aside the development of better means not only to deal with extreme circumstances but to solve more ordinary problems. Difficult circumstances not amounting to a great disaster can prove sufficiently troublesome to persuade some that violations of human rights are appropriate.

The personalist commitment to promote the common good and not to violate individual human rights also is relevant when assessing the argument that in some circumstances economic rights should prevail over civil and political rights. John Rawls makes a strong argument that civil and political rights are lexically prior to the economic right to fair distribution.[129] Contrary to Rawls, representatives from some third world countries would argue that economic development is more im-

---

129. *See generally* Rawls, *supra* note 4, at 42–45

portant in circumstances where people are seriously oppressed by poverty. They would argue that it is appropriate to suppress civil liberties in order to secure economic progress.

Again the temptation to suppress civil liberties presents an easy and corrupting route. The harder but more promising task to which personalists are committed is to both promote economic development and protect civil and political liberties. Both aspects of the task may require the hard and perhaps slow work of developing appropriate institutions. In contrast shortcuts in the long term may prove counterproductive. One suspects although it is difficult to prove empirically that countries which develop democratic institutions also advance their economic well being. Rephrasing Rawls, a personalist would express a commitment both to economic development and to civil and political liberty.[130]

Dialogue and conversation with those who hold opposing views is a personalist tool of choice. A Rawls proposal for third world countries offers a potential starting point for dialogue with those who prefer economic rights. In the second stage of deliberation, the stage at which the principles for a just constitution are considered, Rawls' imaginary veil of ignorance is slightly lifted, sufficiently to reveal the circumstances of one's country.[131] Assuming that country is in a state of poverty, in great need of economic development and divided by tribal warfare, Rawls believes that a constitution would be reasonable if it provided for a ruling party and a president for life.[132] Nevertheless he believes that the parties should choose to have an independent judiciary and a bill of rights.[133] That modification of civil and political liberties in difficult political and economic circumstances also would seem to be an appropriate choice, under personalist theory. One should note that it represents some stages in the development of English political liberty.

One should note another potential arrangement which could be presented in the course of dialogue for the sake of enticing one's third world conversational partner. One could reverse the lexical order of Rawls' first two principles of justice. The principle of equal liberty could be described as lexically subordinate to the principle of fair distribution or to an alternate principle requiring economic development. In that event the principle of equal liberty, now lexically subordinate,

---

130. *See id* at 60.
131. *See id* 195–201.
132. *See id.*
133. *See id* at 60.

would require the protection of liberty in so far as that protection does not violate the principle of fair distribution or the principle of economic development.[134] Neither Rawls nor a personalist thinker would approve the suggestion just made. Nevertheless, in conversation it may prove enticing to some engaging in an exchange of thought. Following this suggestion would provide a protected place for civil and political liberties in a country otherwise dedicated to economic development.

While personalist thinkers would engage in dialogue with those who offer differing understandings of the common good, personalist theory for the reasons outlined requires commitment both to the common good and to the protection of strong individual rights. A personalist should advance both goals and when preserving the common good should not violate strong rights.

In the next two parts of this chapter, part five on method and part six on moral judgment a personalist account of the development of those commitments will be offered. In personalist thought method is important to moral judgment. The account of method, then, should be presented first.

5. Method

One marvelous aspect of our modern civilization is the proliferation of multiple and strong intellectual methods. Of these the scientific method has the greatest prestige. Historically, however, it was preceded by the logical and mathematical methods. Striving to imitate science the various social sciences have developed their own methods. Of these the strongest is the method employed by economics. Our intellectual skills, however, are not confined to those just listed. Universities offer education in a wide range of disciplines. Some non-scientific fields are highly specialized and esoteric. For example, in my youth, for good or ill, I was seriously enamoured of a specialty known as military science and tactics.

While our intellectual power has been enhanced by the great variety of intellectual methods and specialties, the proliferation of methods also is the source of problems. Because each method creates an intellectual horizon, our ability to understand each other and conduct a common discourse has become more limited than in the past. Some practitioners of strong intellectual methods suffer a tendency to imperialism.

---

134. *See id.*

I remember a good colleague who claimed that all reasoning was fundamentally that of political science. Scientists, particularly physicists, are renown for claiming that only their methods provide reliable knowledge. We are also acquainted, however, with thinkers who will reduce all questions to those of logic, mathematics or economics. Typically some bright young people attracted by logic, science or economics seize on their chosen method and seek to universalize it while ignoring competing methods.

The temptation to skepticism becomes greater both because of the multiplicity of methods and the tendency of some to intellectual imperialism. Presented with the conflicting claims of multiple disciplines a person may be puzzled as to what makes sense. One may be skeptical in regard to legal or moral reasoning, for example, because one accepts the claim that only scientific method or in the alternative only logical or economic reasoning is valid. Arguably Richard Posner's skepticism has roots both in the multiplicity of disciplines and in the imperialist claims of science, logic and economics.

Our modern legal culture in a manner similar to our general intellectual life is confused by the multiplicity of relevant disciplines. Posner, for example, finds that the traditional methods of legal reasoning are quite modest when compared to the power of scientific or economic thought. In making a legal decision it is relevant to consider contributions from philosophy, economics, sociology and political science. When attempting to critique or improve legal reasoning one can argue that it should more closely resemble scientific reasoning (a possibility which Posner rejects) or economic reasoning or that it should be more strongly logical and principled. We are confused and perhaps skeptical regarding legal reasoning because of the multiplicity of relevant methods and because of the imperialism of some.

Personalist thought as described in the earlier chapters offers an analysis and critique of method which may be helpful in sorting through the confusion created by the multiplicity of relevant disciplines. When critiquing a method we should ask what its purpose is and how successful the method is in pursuing that purpose. This checking out process is similar to but not the same as verification. For example, it would be difficult to argue that we verify the scientific method by the scientific method. Rather, our common sense understanding recognizes that science has been enormously successful in pursuing its purposes. While we are tempted not to limit the range of successful methods, arguably our common sense recognizes limitations. Normally, for example, one would not use the scientific method to manage a business.

One can recognize a common sense method which could be described as the self correcting process of learning through living. Common sense method chronologically is our first method. When we are young we learn language, how to walk and how to relate to others by the common sense method. Later we learn how to ride a bicycle, to swim and the basic facts about the world by a common sense learning process. We develop a fair range of our knowledge and understanding by a common sense method before we begin serious study, usually in high school, of the more highly specialized methods. Over the history of our world we can recognize similar progress. Much of our basic knowledge accumulated over the ages by common sense methodology. The more specialized methods began to develop in the early Mediterranean civilizations and elsewhere since 5,000 B.C. but did not flourish until the Renaissance and afterwards.

While we have confidence in our common sense because of successful experience we also, particularly in modern times recognize its limitations. We could summarize many of those limitations by saying that common sense reasoning finds it very difficult to transcend horizons. In the past many guided by their common sense believed the earth was flat and refused to recognize that the earth moved around the sun. Recognizing a series of mistakes we have concluded that our common sense has a limited reliability.

We should recognize, however, that in the twenty first century our common sense is more sophisticated than it would have been five hundred or a thousand years ago. We are familiar, now, with the problems and flaws of common sense. In our drive for knowledge, and in part to overcome the defects of common sense we have developed highly specialized methods. Because we have practiced those specialized methods for five hundred or more years we have developed a great store of knowledge which has become part of our common sense. We also have a common sense understanding of intellectual method from experience with the more specialized methods. That knowledge and understanding coupled with the wide experience available to many in modern times provides us with the foundation for a sophisticated common sense, which will serve us well in making many decisions and judgments.

One could offer a modest example of a common sense judgment which we could make with great confidence in the context of our complex modern society. Suppose one were to ask whether the city of London was in existence a half hour ago. A person in New York could answer affirmatively and with confidence. Imagine a person who had visited London and therefore had personal experience of its existence at some point in the past. Assume also that he was a regular educated consumer of media output. He could conclude reasonably that the media would have informed him if a disaster had struck the London he had visited. Because it takes a short period of time for the media to react he would have less confidence in an assertion that London exists at this very minute.

Our modern sophisticated common sense is strong enough to recognize the value and the limitations of the more highly specialized methods. Actually some specialized methods could be described more aptly as specialized common sense methods. These would include history, theology and law. Unlike science or mathematics these disciplines employ the methods of practical reasoning which we develop by the self-correcting process of learning through living.

Law has been described in earlier chapters as a sophisticated specialized common sense method. In the twenty-first century a legal thinker or a judge has available to her input from a wide range of other methods and disciplines. Arguably that input should be more systemically available and lawyers should be better trained in those disciplines and their use. Nevertheless law remains a common sense discipline which will use that input and place limits on it in a common sense manner while employing practical reasoning to address human relations and resolve disputes. Arguably practical common sense reasoning is the appropriate method of choice when working with human relations. Psychology, sociology, economics and statistical studies can inform us about human relations but the art of dealing with human relations is a common sense discipline. Contrary to Posner, then, the law appropriately employs the practical reasoning of common sense properly supplemented by input from more highly specialized disciplines.[135] From successful experience we have confidence in common sense reasoning but we recognize its flaws. Our legal institutions have successfully maintained the rule of law in our society partly by the appropriate settlement of disputes. We know, however, that our legal institutions have made many mistakes and that areas of law are badly in need of reform.

In particular, reasoning by analogy and distinction, the traditional vehicle for legal reasoning, frees judges from an overly rigid under-

---

135. *Compare* RICHARD POSNER, PROBLEMS OF JURISPRUDENCE, *supra* note 1 at 71–124.

standing of legal doctrine to examine the human circumstances in the situation. A judge using his common sense can relate his skill at horizon crossing and his understanding of the situation to the relevant precedent and legal doctrine. He can then settle disputes while maintaining our common legal culture. Using that form of practical reasoning he can settle disputes between those in different horizons while responding to the basic principles of our law by affording deep respect and concern for those persons. In contrast, Posner by his technical concern for what is technically best for the future and Dworkin by his adherence to rigid principle overlook the human relations of those in the situation and fail to afford them deep respect and concern.

Reflecting on the history of human knowledge as well as on our own intellectual development we should recognize that we have a limited but growing knowledge and understanding. Our life experience is one of finding our way while our knowledge grows. Lawyers have two somewhat similar experiences of being thrown, as Martin Heidegger describes it, into a world.[136] Foremost in their consciousness, probably, is the first year law school experiences when in the midst of a strange horizon, they had to find their way. That probably resembles the experience of an infant trying to puzzle out his strange surroundings.

John Macmurray in *Persons in Relation* offers an analysis of the development of a child's skill and knowledge in the context of interpersonal relations.[137] In his chapter on Mother and Child he notes how the infant is taught and demands a relationship with surrounding adults. Macmurray explains:

> "The whole of this aspect of human development, then, falls within and helps to constitute its positive aspect. It falls, that is, within the 'You and I' of the mother-child relation. For the mother plays the child, and the child responds; the child calls for the participation, or at least the attention of the adult, and for the admiration and approval of his success....The reference to the mother is pervasive in all the child's activities. He does not merely learn, as animals do, by instinct helped out by trial and error; he is taught. His acquirement of skills is an education. It is a co-operative process which requires from the start the foresight, judg-

---

136. *See* MARTIN M. HEIDEGGER, IDENTITY & DIFFERENCE 34–35 (Joan Stambaugh trans. 1969); MARTIN M. HEIDEGGER, BEING & TIME, 191–93 (John Macquarne & Edward Robinson trans., 1962).
137. MACMURRAY, *supra* note 92, at 44–63.

ment and action of a mature person to give it an intentional form. Because of this, the child's development has a continuous reference to the distinction between 'right' and 'wrong'. He learns to await the right time for the satisfaction of his desires, that some activities are permitted and others suppressed, that some things may be played with and others not. He learns, in general, to submit his impulses to an order imposed by another will than his; and to subordinate his own desires to those of another person. He learns in a word to submit to reason."[138]

In that process of learning the child begins to understand the value of method. Activities conducted in a certain way may prove more successful. One acquires knowledge by common sense and begins to trust that method. "Insight," a sudden perception of a pattern in the data, is a high point in the learning process. Educators strive to convey a series of insights to their pupils. When an insight is grasped one perceives that one truly understands. Later one will understand that a series of related insights can constitute a theory and that theory can be checked according to the criteria of more advanced methods.

In sum, our experience over a lifetime is one of growing and hence limited knowledge. Nevertheless, our experience, often, is that we do have knowledge and that we do truly understand. That experience, again often, is verified by successful action.

Skeptics want to argue, contrary to our experience, that our knowledge is not merely limited but also not trustworthy. One ground for that argument is that our knowledge does not meet the criteria or is not within the limitations imposed by one or more of the advanced specialized disciplines we have developed. For example, one could argue that our common sense knowledge does not satisfy the criteria of scientific method or that our moral judgments are not capable of being scientifically verified. On the basis of the analysis of method offered above one could argue in reply that criticizing all knowledge on the basis of criteria developed in the advanced disciplines is a methodological mistake, a category mistake in the field of method. Rather we have acquired much of our knowledge by methods we have confidence in because of successful achievement. Arguably, that conclusion corresponds better with our experience that we have limited but growing knowledge, with our experience of successful action, and with our experience that we often truly understand than does the skeptical analysis and conclusion.

---

138. MacMurray, *supra* note 92, at 59.

Sometimes the critique of knowledge simply rests on a mistaken method. Arguably Descartes' methodical doubt is such a mistaken method. Applying that method Descartes is able to doubt everything but his own existence. From that conclusion he moves to the existence of God and then deduces the validity of other knowledge from the existence of God.[139] As a great mathematician Descartes strives to imitate in his philosophy the clarity of mathematical analysis. Arguably we should not conclude with Descartes that it is difficult to have confidence in the existence of the world around us. Rather we should conclude that Descartes has offered us a mistaken method. In a similar manner one could conclude that the various criteria for knowledge offered by skeptics are the product of a mistaken application of method. Much of our knowledge is developed appropriately by a general empirical method or methods which we have confidence in because of successful experience.

6. Moral Judgment

In the *Concept of Law*, H.L.A. Hart distinguishes between having an obligation and being obliged. Hart explained that one did not have a legal obligation because a sovereign had threatened sanctions for breaking his commands. Rather one has a legal obligation because the legal system has been accepted. Hart rejected the notion that law as the command of the sovereign backed by sanctions had authority because it could be analogized to a gunman. One may be obligated or compelled by a gunman to follow his orders but that is not what we mean by having an obligation.[140]

Hart argued that we can recognize an obligation better from an internal point of view than from the perspective of an external observer recording regularities of behavior.[141] When people offer a rule as a reason for their actions we can perceive that internally they have accepted an obligation to obey the rule. From a personalist perspective as we reflect internally on our own experience we can recognize our acceptance of a legal or moral obligation when we offer that obligation as a reason for our conduct.

---

139. *See generally* RENE DESCARTES, DISCOURSE ON METHOD; AND, MEDITATIONS OF FIRST PHILOSOPHY (Donald A. Cress, translator, 1993).
140. *See* H.L.A. HART, CONCEPT OF LAW 20–25 (1961).
141. *See* HART, CONCEPT OF LAW, *supra* note 140 at 82–91.

We can conclude reasonably, then, that a large number of people in our society accept both legal and moral obligations because they offer those obligations as reasons justifying their conduct. In personalist theory one would perceive a moral obligation in the course of action in relation to others. Reflecting on our judgment and our actions we can recognize and articulate an obligation as a reason for our actions and judgments.

In personalist thought one perceives oneself as person and the other as person in the course of action. As John Macmurray explains one who is acting will encounter resistance and will recognize some resistance as intentional. In that experience one perceives the other as one who acts intentionally. In the course of acting together with another on a common project we can perceive the common effort, intelligent relation to a common plan, the desire to cooperate and reciprocal relations. At an early point in our development we recognize the importance of reciprocal relations. From infancy and early childhood our learning, including our understanding of language, and our knowledge of basic facts about the world and human relations have developed in the context of family and with other human beings. Our basic self-understanding, then, is relational. John Macmurray's chapter on "Mother and Child" is an excellent account of our development as persons in the context of interpersonal relations.[142]

With the help of parents, teachers and friends most of us go through a process of moral growth in which we learn rules, reciprocal relations, the prudence of treating others well, ideals, idealism, religion and moral theory. Many of us engage in a moral struggle in an effort to develop our moral ideals and to act in accordance with them. As we participate in common action with our fellows sometimes we can perceive that they too are struggling to act morally and to adhere to their ideals. Sometimes that struggle involves suffering and we can perceive ourselves and others suffering while engaging in moral effort. Suffering is part of the human condition; we can recognize our suffering and understand our fellows as suffering. We can experience and understand the presence of great evil in the world and the suffering which follows from that. While we are young we engage in common action with our family and later with a great variety of people. Ultimately we can understand ourselves and others as engaged in a common struggle with

---

142. MACMURRAY, *supra* note 92, at 44–63.

the human condition. Phrased differently we can perceive ourselves and others as common actors in the human drama.

Applying the analysis of method from the last part, in the course of our moral development we find successful ways of relating to others, moral method which we have confidence in because of successful experience. In the course of developing that moral method we have moral insights, moments of understanding. Among those insights are the perception of others as persons and the perception of moral obligation. Reflecting on our actions and judgments we can articulate that moral obligation. We are obliged to have respect and concern for others because they are persons like ourselves. The respect and concern we desire for ourselves, then logically should be afforded to others. Because we perceive others as persons capable of suffering, engaged in moral struggle and a common effort with ourselves we understand their needs, desires and their dignity as persons.

In the course of the last century we have expanded enormously our experience of others throughout the world as engaged in the human struggle. On television we witness the disasters of earthquakes, floods and war. We see mothers striving to save their children and families suffering from genocide. We have experienced two World Wars, the Holocaust, and the resulting moral growth throughout the world. In the United States we have had the experience of desegregation and the cultural and moral change which followed after that. These experiences have changed and expanded our horizons so that many of us now are able to perceive all human beings as persons to whom we owe a moral obligation of respect and concern. That expansion of horizons has been a process of moral experience and growth. One can articulate it in logical form as a process of induction and deduction. Because we perceive many others as persons like ourselves engaged in moral struggle, in human suffering, with human desires, aspirations and feelings, we are able to generalize and conclude from our experience that all human beings are persons like ourselves. We understand then that each human being is entitled to the respect and concern that we desire for ourselves. When one human being presents a claim we can then deduce from our previous general conclusion that he should receive our deep respect and concern. We can reason further and conclude following Macmurray that it is appropriate to have systems for the protection of rights which in the indirect relations we have with most will allow us to maintain respect and concern for each.

One can offer prudential reasons to support those conclusions. The strongest prudential reason is that if we afford others equal respect and concern and respect their rights then our own rights are more likely to be respected. That prudential reason supports our early perception of the benefits of reciprocal relations with others. In our struggle to maintain peace and the rule of law in our country that prudential reason is a strong support. Arguably it provides an important ground for our long term strategy of maintaining peace in our world. However, it fails to capture the strength of the moral argument that each person is entitled to respect and concern because he or she is a person like ourselves.

Jean-Paul Sartre perceived that strength of that moral argument when applied to those engaged in a common struggle. He offered as an example the French partisans who perceived themselves as comrades under the condemning look at the Nazis. Sartre, however, found it difficult to generalize from that experience to the whole of humanity. He opined, contrary to his own belief, that if God exists, then all human beings might perceive themselves as comrades under the gaze of the Almighty.[143] Again, in my opinion, we must grant that the religious argument provides the strongest support for the human dignity and rights of each person created by God. Nevertheless, contrary to Sartre but using a method analogous to his we can conclude without reference to God that we are brothers and sisters because we are engaged in a common action, the human drama, the common human struggle.

When discussing moral theory, it is customary to contrast Utilitarian method described as teleological with Kantian thought referred to as deontological. Actually Aristotelian, Thomist, and related thought also employ teleological method. In the pursuit of *eudaimonia*, which many translate as happiness, Aristotle argues that the highest good for a person is the fulfillment of his or her function. By using *phronesis* which could be translated roughly as practical reason a person discovers means and intermediate ends which in turn serve as means to the ultimate end of *eudaimonia* or living well.[144]

The personalist theory of law and the personalist theory of human rights as described in this and previous chapters could be described as

---

143. JEAN-PAUL SARTRE, *Existentialism is a Humanism* in EXISTENTIALISM FROM DOSTOEVSKY TO SARTRE 289–96 (Walter Kaufman ed., 1956).

144. *See generally* Aristotle, *Nichomacean Ethics* in READINGS IN ANCIENT GREEK PHILOSOPHY 666 (S. Marc Cohen, Particia Curd, & C.D.C. Reeve, eds., 1995).

teleological because it uses means-end reasoning. One promotes the human good, particularly each person's share of the primary social goods by appropriate means. Those means include the establishment of a theory of rights, the development of law, a legal culture and particularly our court system, our great legal dispute settlement institution. As in Aristotelian and Thomist thought one seeks to promote the human good by means properly chosen with the help of practical reason.

However, personalist theory more closely resembles Kantian deontology when it recognizes the moral obligation to afford each person deep respect and concern. One has that duty to other persons because one recognizes them as persons like oneself. That duty of respect and concern will prevail in some instances despite perceived consequences.

John Rawls argues that one requires at least a thin theory of the good to establish a theory of the right to prevail over competing perceptions of the good.[145] As briefly described here the personalist theory of human rights begins in logical rather than experiential order with the perception that one owes a duty of respect and concern to other persons. On the basis of logic and experience that obligation is extended to all other persons. In fulfilling that obligation one uses practical reason, experience, and means-end reasoning.

In personalist thought and human experience our lives are a process of moral growth and development. Developmental psychologists such as Jean Piaget in his study, *The Moral Judgment of the Child*, likewise have recognized a process of moral growth.[146] Subsequent studies of cognitive development have discovered that children are more advanced in their understanding than Piaget thought. For example, "Piaget probably underestimated the importance of social interaction and language in cognitive development. Much of the new research suggest children are extremely sensitive to social information and are tuned into the social world from an early age."[147] Nevertheless the development of rational moral judgment appears to track the child's general development of rationality.[148] While Piaget's stages of development probably are too broadly stated [certainly Lawrence Kohlberg's are],

---

145. *See* RAWLS, *supra* note 4 at 395–99.

146. JEAN PIAGET, THE MORAL JUDGMENT OF THE CHILD (1965).

147. RUTLEDGE ENCYCLOPEDIA OF PHILOSOPHY, vol. 7, 383 (1996).

148. J.H. FLOWELL, THE DEVELOPMENT PSYCHOLOGY OF JEAN PIAGET 296 (1963).

there seem to be stages in the development of moral judgment as well as other rational activity.[149]

Moral growth and development, then, is part of the human condition. While one should rejoice in that constant although haphazard progress, it presents a difficult problem for moral theory and legal justification. Constantly and inevitably human beings are in different stages of moral development. Horizons are established, then, not only by geography, by one's intellectual and moral theories, and by one's culture but also by one's stage of moral development. Justification of a legal decision by grounding that justification in a higher moral theory becomes more problematical.

A person trapped in an early stage of moral development and inclined to skepticism might, for example, inquire of a personalist by asking, "What experience of moral obligation?" and commenting perhaps accurately, "I do not have that experience." A conscientious personalist who sincerely wants to further his interlocutor's moral development could enter into dialogue and direct him to experiences which might provide occasions for moral insights. That process of dialogue, however, is different than abstract justification of a legal decision.

One could suggest serving food to the poor in a local soup kitchen or watching an appropriate movie such as Schindler's List[150] or Dead Man Walking[151] or reading Camus or Dostoevsky or Michael Ignatieff's, *The Needs of Strangers*.[152] Entering into dialogue and in the course of that conversation engaging in an exchange of experience would be a typical personalist response to a disagreement about ethics.

Justifying a legal decision to a person with a different ethical horizon or at a different stage of moral development, however, is a different task than entering into dialogue with a skeptic. Nevertheless it may require an honest exchange of experience. Justification when the task is presented in this manner requires an explanation of the legitimacy of the decision. Legitimacy as related to justification, then, it the topic for the next part of this chapter.

---

149. *See* Lawrence Kohlberg, Moral Development, More Education, and Kohlberg: Basic Issues in Philosophy, Psychology, Religion, and Education (Sand A Messey, ed.) (1986).

150. Schindler's List (Universal Studios 1993).

151. Dead Man Walking (Gramercy Pictures 1995).

152. Michael Ignatieff, The Needs of Strangers (1985).

7. Legitimacy

Cass Sunstein and Ronald Dworkin both present theories of legitimacy. Both theories are related significantly to their respective theories of justification. Sunstein presents a shorter explanation which we can discuss first. He argues:

> "Legitimacy stems not simply from principled consistency on the part of adjudicators, but from a justifiable exercise of authority, which requires a theory of just institutions. That theory should in turn be founded in democratic considerations suitably constrained by an account of what interests should be immunized from democratic intrusions. Legitimacy is an outcome of well-functioning democratic processes, not of a system of distinction-making undertaken by judges. Even if done exceptionally well, distinction-making by principled judges is too court-centered as a source of legitimacy."[153]

Sunstein offers a theory of legitimacy which will support his argument for judicial minimalism and incompletely theorized justifications for judicial decisions. He explains: "For reasons of both policy and principle, the development of large-scale theories of the right and the good is a democratic task, not a judicial one."[154] Rather courts should promote democratic deliberation in the larger society.

Again Sunstein overlooks the historically vital role of the American courts and our legal culture in democratic deliberation. With some reservations he leans toward a majoritarian interpretation of democracy which itself, as explained in previous chapters, presents problems of legitimacy. Contrary to Sunstein, our courts by appropriate decisions accompanied by reasonable explanations contribute to maintaining the rule of law which in turn provides a major ground for believing that our institutions are just and legitimate.

Ronald Dworkin's more lengthy account of legitimacy is also more adequate. He rejects a variety of attempts to support obligations to others from an individualist perspective and argues that obligation within a political community should be based on association.[155] He explains:

> "We are at last able to consider our hypothesis directly: that the best defense of political legitimacy—the right of a political

---

153. *See* SUNSTEIN, LEGAL REASONING, *supra* note 6, at 53.
154. SUNSTEIN, LEGAL REASONING *supra* note 6, at 53.
155. *See* DWORKIN, LAW'S EMPIRE, *supra* note 2 at 190–216.

community to treat its members as having obligations in virtue of collective community decisions—is to be found not in the hard terrain of contracts or duties of justice or obligations of fair play that might hold among strangers, where philosophers have hoped to find it, but in the more fertile ground of fraternity, community and their attendant obligations. Political association, like family and friendship and other forms of association more local and intimate is in itself pregnant of obligation."[156]

Dworkin offers a theory of legitimacy, then, which appropriately resembles his understanding of political friendship. Personalist thought would agree that political obligation to the community and hence the legitimacy of the community arises from living together, from the association of persons in the community. Both Dworkin and personalist thought would agree that political obligation to the community depends upon the community qualifying under certain standards of reasonableness. There is further agreement that the legitimacy of judicial decisions is related to enhancing the legitimacy and reasonableness of the community and hence the political obligation which citizens have to the community.

I disagree, however, with Dworkin's account of legitimacy on two points. First, Dworkin contends that a "conception of law must explain how what it takes to be law provides a general justification for the exercise of coercive power by the state."[157] According to Dworkin, if the state is justified in using coercion to enforce its citizens' obligations, then it is legitimate. As explained in earlier chapters it is a mistake to make the justified use of force central to legitimacy or to judicial decision making. Rather the settlement of disputes in order to promote the rule of law should be the central focus in understanding and practicing judicial decision making. Enhancing the common action and increasing everyone's share of the primary social goods is central to increasing the legitimacy of our basic institutions. Discussion of the justified use of force should be secondary and should be the object when constructing a theory of self-defense including defense of the community and its common action.

Second, Dworkin contends that his interpretation of law as integrity fits best with a community of principle and hence will best "support the legitimacy of our institutions, and the political obligations they assume,

---

156. *Id.* at 206.
157. *Id.* at 190.

as a matter of fraternity."[158] I agree with Dworkin that a "community of principle... can claim the authority of a genuine associative community and can therefore claim moral legitimacy."[159] Personalist method provides an important role for strong principles closely related to our national ideals. Personalist theory centers on the commitment to afford each person deep respect and concern. However, Dworkin's interpretation of law as integrity with its emphasis on rigid justification of judicial decisions by consistent principles is not a workable means for promoting political friendship. As Cass Sunstein argues, "the idea of integrity... does not provide a convincing theory of legitimacy."[160] "Integrity," he claims, "is neither necessary nor sufficient for legitimacy."[161]

In personalist theory one has an obligation to cooperate in building and maintaining the reasonable institutions of the society in which he finds himself. That is because one has a duty of respect and concern for the persons with whom one inevitably is engaged in interaction. One interacts with others through language, through the circumstances of daily living, through all the ways in which one exists in modern society. One understands himself as a person through that interaction with other persons whom one perceives in the course of actions as persons.

That obligation is present even in non-democratic or pre-democratic societies. On this point compare Rawls, *A Theory of Justice*, regarding the choice of principles for a just constitution in some third world countries.[162] In Anglo-American history as we evolved towards democracy there were a series of non-democratic or pre-democratic governments. Of course, it is reasonable to move those societies toward democracy. Also, in appropriate circumstances there is a right to revolution.

A society is legitimate to the extent that it strives to advance and protect everyone's and each one's share of the primary social goods. The judicial system is legitimate because by reasonable settlement of disputes it advances and maintains the rule of law. A judge enhances the legitimacy of society and the judicial system by employing a decision making method which strives to afford respect and concern to each person, which uses means for crossing horizons, and which weighs and balances the relevant competing interests.

---

158. *Id.* at 215.
159. *Id.* at 214.
160. SUNSTEIN, LEGAL REASONING, *supra* note 6, at 53.
161. *Id.*
162. *See* RAWLS, *supra* note 4 at 197.

When explaining a judicial decision a judge should reveal his method, portray his struggle to cross-horizons and to consider the relevant interests. That explanation will be legitimate because it shows respect and concern for the person affected by his decision. His opinion also should show respect for the legal culture and relevant ideals of his society. By showing respect and concern in this manner, a judge advances the rule of law by encouraging persons to bring their disputes to court. That will enhance the legitimacy of his society, and will support the obligation of participants in society to cooperate in the maintenance of its institutions. In personalist theory following and revealing an appropriate method is justification for the decision.

There remains the question of how one justifies a judicial decision to a person with a different ethical horizon or at a different stage of moral development and why that decision is legitimate. Consideration of that question would include discussion of the moral skeptic and the person, or group, who challenges the legitimacy of a decision which denies his right to oppress others. As an example of the latter one could remember those who questioned the legitimacy of *Brown v. Board of Education of Topeka, Kansas*[163] with the then popular bumper stickers, "Impeach Earl Warren," as a vivid reminder.

Considering first those in other moral horizons one should recall that personalist method requires a judge to cross horizons, to locate and weigh competing interests and to reveal that process in his opinion. Also a judge should enter into dialogue with those from other horizons who understand the law differently in an effort to establish not only conversation but convergence. Again a model was provided by Justice Brennan in his capital punishment opinions. Brennan would argue for his conclusions not only from his own perspective but also from that of others with the result that his colleagues often joined in supporting his proposed holding. Dialogue and conversation may lead to convergence. Arguably that personalist style explanation of judicial decisions is superior when addressing those in differing moral horizons to rigid Dworkian principled justification.

A more serious difficulty is presented by those who wish to oppress others. Personalist thought requires respect for those with differing opinions, for their moral growth and for their present stage of moral development. Respect for competing opinions, however, rests on the

---

163. Brown v. Board of Education of Topeka, Kansas, 347 U.S. 483 (1954).

duty to have respect and concern for each person. A personalist judge, then, is not required to respect the desire of some to oppress others.

Nevertheless, in an imperfect and pluralist society those who desire to oppress others may have sufficient power to maintain and promote their position. Appropriate dialogue, compromise and convergence, then, may become necessary means for promoting personalist ideals. That always is a delicate process because one does not want to cooperate in the oppression of others.

In a democratic although imperfect society that opportunity for dialogue, compromise and convergence is present. An important means for that rational deliberation about our great ideals is our court system and our legal culture. The political process also offers many occasions for debate, deliberation, compromise and convergence. The great mistake is to refuse to deliberate. Arguably that is the mistake the Confederate States made historically when they left the union on the election of Abraham Lincoln. Lincoln was arguing for restriction of slavery in the territories but had not yet accumulated the political power to accomplish it. The Confederate States left because deliberating on the restriction was offensive to them.

Personalism is a legitimate interpretation of American law because it uses methods within the traditions of the common law and constitutional adjudication. Personalist decisions offer the potential of being acceptable to each person because they rest on respect and concern for and an attempt to understand the interests and circumstances of each person. Personalist method, also, requires dialogue, compromise and convergence with those who hold different positions. The personalist interpretation of American law is legitimate among other reasons because it proposes to continue the process of national deliberations on our great ideals.

Because the personalist theory of legitimacy is grounded ultimately in respect and concern for each person and all persons it offers a more fundamental foundation for the legitimacy of society and law than Jürgen Habermas in *Between Facts and Norms*.[164] Habermas would ground rights and the legitimacy of law in the circumstances necessary for com-

---

164. *See* JÜRGEN HABERMAS, BETWEEN FACTS AND NORMS: CONTRIBUTIONS TO A DISCOURSE THEORY OF LAW AND DEMOCRACY (William Relig trans., 1996). *See also Exploring Habermas on Law and Democracy*, Fifth Annual Legal Theory Symposium, 76 DEN. UNIV.L. REV. 927 (1999).

munication and discourse in a democratic society. Nevertheless, I want to offer the possibility that the personalist interpretation of American law and the personalist method for judicial decision making sufficiently overlap Habermas to meet his test for legitimacy. Despite Cass Sunstein's adaptation of Habermas' theory, *Between Facts and Norms* may support a strong role for courts in conducting rational dialogue and protecting the rights necessary to participation in democratic discourse.

8. Authority, Legitimacy and the Use of Force

A reasonable objection to the understanding of our legal system as a great dispute settlement process is that those who seek a court's assistance are not asking for arbitration or mediation but an authoritative decision according to law. After considering and offering a theory of legitimacy it is possible to reply to that objection.

That reply would begin by explaining that a government has moral and legal authority because it is the accepted government and because it conforms to the requirements of legitimacy. Those requirements include striving, among other means by establishing appropriate institutions, to promote and protect everyone's and each person's share of the primary social goods. To the extent a government does not perform that task it loses legitimacy and may cease to be acceptable. A judicial system shares in that task by offering a process of dispute settlement which promotes the rule of law, that is, which encourages persons to bring their disputes to court and abide by the result.

A court has authority and renders authoritative decisions because it has legitimacy and because it shares the authority of a legitimate government. For that reason a court has a claim to respect and obedience for its decisions. In personalist thought an individual has a duty to support and obey court decisions because the judicial system is an appropriate and accepted means for conducting many of the multiple human relations in our society. For that reason a court has authority and can be asked to render authoritative decisions.

Our government appropriately has a monopoly on the use of force in our society. Court decisions properly are backed not only by the authority but also by the power of government. Those who seek the assistance of courts may be seeking the application of force. Nevertheless, it was argued earlier that it is a mistake to focus on that use of force rather than on the legal and moral authority of the court. The duty to obey the court is derived from that legal and moral authority rather than from the government's power to use force. That authority exists and is preserved because it is an appropriate means for advancing human relations.

It is better to account for the government's proper use of force under a self-defense theory, a theory of the government's right and duty to defend itself, its institutions and the persons within its jurisdiction. For example, those who refuse to follow authoritative court orders pose a challenge to the continued effectiveness of the courts as a means of furthering human relations and therefore can be threatened with or subjected to force in order to defend the continuing authority of the court.

Criminal law presents the most serious challenge to that analysis. However, one can argue that a criminal court decision is an authoritative disposition of a dispute between the government and the accused concerning the appropriate use of government force to defend the law and the persons in its jurisdiction.

Government and the courts are not legitimate because their decisions are backed by force. They are legitimate because they are accepted as an appropriate means for advancing human relations. Judicial decisions advance that legitimacy better by affording all and each person deep respect and concern and by seeking to reconcile the competing interests relevant to the case before the court.

Arguably Sunstein's method for justification suffers legitimacy costs because it only makes restricted appeals to the ideals of our society.[165] Dworkin's method of justification by rigid principles has legitimacy costs because his ideal judge, Hercules, can not address the real interests and circumstances of the persons who appear before his court.[166] Personalist method does not incur those legitimacy costs.

One could argue, perhaps, that because personalist method does not employ rigid principled justification the decisions of a personalist judge are not authoritative decisions according to law. That argument must rest on an interpretation of American law that lacks good institutional fit and higher moral appeal. Historically American courts have not jus-

---

165. *See generally* SUNSTEIN, LEGAL REASONING, *supra* note 6; SUNSTEIN, ONE CASE AT A TIME, *supra* note 10; SUNSTEIN, DEMOCRACY AND THE PROBLEM OF FREE SPEECH, *supra* note 17.

166. *See generally* DWORKIN, LAW'S EMPIRE, *supra* note 2.

tified their decisions by rigorous principled analysis. That form of justification prevents a court from affording respect and concern for real persons and their interests. Personalism offers an interpretation of American law which has better institutional fit and which continually struggles to afford respect and concern to real persons and their interests as perceived in the multiple horizons of our pluralist society. A personalist judge would render an authoritative decision according to law because it would rest on an appropriate and legitimate interpretation of American law.

A legal skeptic, such as Judge Posner, might contend at this point in the argument, with the use of his pungent phrase, that interpretation "butters no parsnips." Posner, of course, would perceive a discussion of interpretation as relevant only if it could be demonstrated that one interpretation would produce better consequences for the future.[167] One should not overlook, of course, that Posner, himself, with his legal skepticism and his Pragmatist Manifesto, offers an interpretation of American law.[168]

What Posner overlooks is that understanding a phenomenon such as American law or the United States Constitution requires an honest exchange of human experience. Gadamer when he discusses interpretation speaks of a merging of present and past horizons.[169] Statements about law and its interpretation always are made within a horizon even when one attempts to cross horizons in the process. In justifying a legal decision one offers an interpretation of law. In justifying that interpretation one necessarily offers an explanation based on one's growing experience including the attempt to cross horizons. It is that honest exchange of experience that continues the great argument about what society should be that constitutes our society and that contributes to and enhances the legitimacy and authority of judicial decisions.

The next chapter, chapter 6, will offer a vision of and further interpretation of American law as a means for conducting that on-going argument about what society should be and for relating persons in the multiple horizons of our pluralist society.

---

167. *See generally* POSNER, PROBLEMS OF JURISPRUDENCE, *supra* note 1 at 457.

168. *See id.* at 454–70.

169. *See generally* HANS-GEORG GADAMER, TRUTH AND METHOD 306–07 (Joel Weinsheimer & Donald G. Marshall, trans., 1975).

CHAPTER VI

The Language and Uses of Rights: Relating the Multiple Players in the Game of Law across Horizons

1. Introduction

An artist who paints a portrait could be said to offer an interpretation of his subject. Since this book describes a personalist interpretation of American law, metaphorically one could say that it is painting the law's portrait. Most of the book has interpreted American law and legal method from the point of view of a deciding judge. The painting, then, appears more like a portrait of Lord Mansfield, John Marshall, Earl Warren or William Brennan than a picture of the multiple activities which take place every day in American legal circles. This chapter is designed to retouch that painting or rather to create a sidebar, like a wing on a triptych, to make the whole portrait seem more like a picture of multiple legal activities. Rather than a Gainsborough portrait of a great judge the picture sketched in this chapter should resemble more closely a classic Breughel painting of the activities of a multiplicity of villagers.

One can paint a portrait as interpretation of a scene or a person. Also, however, one can interpret a painting. Dworkin has argued that we should take an interpretive stance towards law. What does it mean to interpret? This chapter not only should offer an illustration of interpretation but should begin in the next part with a discussion of interpretation itself.

247

Arguably we engage in interpretation on a daily basis as we attempt to understand each other's language. Since each of us understands and uses language in a slightly different horizon, interpreting what another means resembles in some respects the attempt to translate a foreign language. H.L.A. Hart has provided some important tools for understanding legal language, particularly the language of rights.[1] Central to this chapter is a further development of Hart's tools to elucidate the multiple different uses of the language of rights. Rights and the language of rights, it will be argued, are important tools in "the game of life," "significant means by which persons establish, change, talk about, fight about, reconcile, and struggle with human relations."[2] The discussion of rights, then, will analyze a microcosm of the activities in the world of law.

A law reform litigator arguably uses rights and the language of rights to hammer on foreign horizons demanding that society and the law recognize his clients as persons entitled to respect and concern. An analysis of the many uses of rights by those seeking law reform will illustrate a personalist interpretation of other action in the law than that of the deciding judge.

The great use of rights and the language of rights in personalist theory is to engage in communication and conversation across the multiple horizons in our pluralist society. Rights litigation is a means for carrying forward what James Boyd White calls that on-going argument about what society should be that constitutes society.[3]

After discussing interpretation itself in part two, the next part, the chapter will continue in part three, with a vision or interpretation of American law as an activity engaging multiple players from different points of view. An analysis of the language and uses of rights in part four will provide a microcosm of that activity. Obligation, a topic discussed in the last chapter, provides a foundation for reconciling the different uses of rights. In part five obligation as perceived by persons in many different horizons will be related to the language and uses of rights. The law reform litigator as described in part six uses the language of rights to relate his client's interest to the obligations of those in

---

1. H.L.A. Hart, *Definition & Theory in Jurisprudence* 70 Law Q. Rev. 37 (1954).

2. Samuel J. M. Donnelly, The Language & Uses of Rights; A Biopsy of American Jurisprudence in the Twentieth Century 1 (1994).

3. James Boyd White, Heracles' Bow: Essays on the Rhetoric & Poetics of the Law 28–48 (1985).

foreign horizons thereby establishing the communications across horizons discussed in part seven.

The personalist interpretation of American law will continue, then, in the next part with a discussion of interpretation itself.

2. Interpretation

The art of interpretation, often referred to as hermeneutics, is a high discipline with many specialized branches. Nevertheless it would be inappropriate to describe it as a science. Rather using the analysis of method as developed in earlier chapters it could be classified along with law as a specialized sophisticated common sense method. Commentators on hermeneutics describe it as a process of human understanding and refer to the hermeneutical circle. When interpreting a famous painting, for example, Rembrandt's *The Prodigal Son*, one understands the whole by analyzing the parts, the father and the two sons. Nevertheless one understands the parts better in relation to the whole. An interpreter who sees the painting in his own horizon nevertheless may seek an understanding of Rembrandt's horizon, and the horizons of those who have seen and enjoyed the painting over the years.

For some viewers engaged in interpretation there is an "event," an "experience," a moment of understanding that was not recognizable in their own horizons before the process of interpretation. Applying the analysis of method described in earlier chapters that "event" could be defined as an insight, the perception of a pattern in the data. A series of related insights could be combined to offer a theory or understanding of the painting. One could explain that theory to others and engage in dialogue. If others agree that the theory enlightens their understanding of the painting and that sharing of experience proves fruitful in the interpretation of a series of paintings, then the interpreter has established a method in which he should have confidence.

Interpretation, then, requires a sharing of horizons.[4] All interpretation occurs within a horizon.[5] Nevertheless one seeks to understand the horizon within which the painting was created and often one wants to

---

4. HANS-GEORG GADAMER, TRUTH AND METHOD 306–07 (Joel Weinsheimer & Donald G. Marshall, trans., 1975).

5. GADAMER, *supra* note 4 at 303.

communicate that interpretation to others who may understand it although their horizons are at least slightly different. The insight or series of related insights at times may be recognized as moments of understanding not only by the interpreter but by others. Interpretation is a sharing or communication of human experience.[6]

Interpreting an important legal document such as the United States Constitution likewise requires a sharing of horizons and a communication of human experience. Despite Justice Scalia one never can fully penetrate the horizon of the founding generation. Nevertheless, one can engage in a conversation with their thought particularly as set forth in the constitution. In chapter 4 on "Constitutional Interpretation" it was argued that our Constitution, like a famous play, was designed by the creators to be produced for many audiences over the generations. Those engaged in interpreting the Constitution from generation to generation seek to translate the insights they acquire from the founders and their document to their own society. Interpretation of a great document is a sharing and communication of experience.

Despite Judge Posner one cannot describe interpretation in scientific terms. One does not choose between interpretations on the basis of what is best for the future. Hopefully one's choice will prove satisfactory for the future. But one rather is seeking an understanding in accord with our national ideals as developed over the ages, or in accord with the demands of justice and the insight found in the Constitution regarding those demands or an interpretation consistent with the respect and concern for all found in provisions of our Bill of Rights and post Civil War Amendments.

The art of interpretation as a common sense method using practical reason is employed by most of us day to day in ordinary human relations. We never can understand our fellow human beings completely. Rather we interpret their speech and actions with the aid of prior experience and in the context of our interrelations. In our ordinary relations we share on various levels our experiences with our friends and associates. What Dworkin, Scalia and Posner all overlook in varying ways is that interpretation requires a seeking and sharing of human experience.

In this chapter a personalist interpretation will be offered of non-judicial activity in American law. The use of the language of rights from multiple points of view but particularly in law reform litigation will be

---

6. GADAMER, *supra* note 4 at 303.

analyzed as an important example of that activity. In developing that interpretation the art of interpretation as just described will be employed with the hope that a series of insights, moments of understanding, will be uncovered.

3. Contrasting Visions

In earlier chapters two contrasting visions of law were presented, one, an understanding of law as an activity in which we all engage and the other as a system of rules accepted by the people. Justice Holmes and Judge Posner agree with personalism in understanding law primarily as action.[7] Holmes, helpfully for this chapter, interpreted law as a well-known profession which we practice.

H. L. A. Hart in *The Concept of Law* describes law as a system of rules, a sophisticated combination of primary rules of obligation and secondary rules that describe what to do with primary rules.[8] Hart who is a subtle legal philosopher with great insight captures in his secondary rules some aspects of law as action.[9] Among the secondary rules are rules of change and adjudication.[10] Judges, of course, in the process of adjudicating disputes change and develop the law. One can understand the law as a system of rules including rules which designate judges to adjudicate disputes and authorize them to change and develop the law.

Hart again captures some aspects of the law as action when he describes some rules as power conferring.[11] The secondary rules which tell us what to do with primary rules are power conferring rules. Those rules, for example, may confer on a judge the power to adjudicate and to change and develop the law. However, there are other power conferring rules including those which grant power to private individuals. The law of contracts confers on private parties the power by agreement to establish rules for themselves which will be enforced by a court. Likewise the law of wills empowers individuals to establish rules which will be enforced by a court concerning the distribution of their property. In

---

7. Oliver Wendell Holmes, Jr., *The Path of Law*, 10 HARV. L. REV. 457, 457 (1897); RICHARD POSNER, PROBLEMS OF JURISPRUDENCE 459 (1990).

8. H.L.A HART, THE CONCEPT OF LAW 91–99 (1985).

9. *Id.*

10. *Id.*

11. *Id.* at 28.

a more action oriented understanding Henry Hart and Albert Sacks in their interpretation of the legal process described the use of similar rules as private ordering.[12]

James Boyd White describes law as an inherited legal culture which hopefully we will pass on to the generations which succeed us.[13] Personalism would interpret that legal culture which includes the great profession which we practice as an on-going activity relating multiple persons now and over the ages. As a metaphor, one could imagine a great on-going conversation between many people. As the conversation proceeds new participants arrive, listen, find the context of the discussion and begin to contribute their thoughts. From time to time old participants drop out. In our legal culture Alexander Hamilton and James Madison were early participants. Later on Abraham Lincoln and Oliver Wendell Holmes, Jr., joined the discussion and the on-going inherited legal cultures. We are now engaged in the on-going common action, that culture inherited from the past.

When we pass on that culture to students and new lawyers we do more than convey a system of rules, although we also do that. The new participants are welcomed to and trained in a culture including ways of using rules, making arguments, on-going quarrels about method, ways of arguing for and representing clients, of planning estates and commercial transactions and multiple other aspects of our culture. New lawyers while continuing their training are put to work, sometimes under supervision representing clients.

When people, as H. L. A. Hart argued, accept the law, they do not accept simply a system of rules.[14] Rather they accept an on-going legal culture, an activity in which they may become participants. That activity includes the drafting of wills and contracts, the planning and development of commercial and corporate transactions, and the use of the language of the law to discuss problems, conduct negotiations and make arguments, in court or outside. Legal language provides the framework and tools for conducting many of our transactions and private relations. It is very difficult, for example, to understand or conduct the buying and selling of goods without referral to legal language.

Language in personalist thought is action and by its structure is inescapably interpersonal. Legal language, then, not only is designed and

---

12. H. Hart & A. Sacks, Legal Process 208 (1994).
13. White, Heracles' Bow, *supra* note 3 at 223–29.
14. Hart, Concept of Law, *supra* note 8 at 211–15.

employed to relate persons, it is interpersonal in its origin and structure. One could illustrate that by offering a personalist interpretation of the law of wills or of commercial transactions. Because Karl Llewellyn, a legal pragmatist concerned with the relation of law and human beings, was the principal drafter of the Uniform Commercial Code, a personalist analysis of commercial transactions could prove enlightening. More consistent with the developing themes of the book, however, would be an analysis of the language and uses of rights.

H. L. A. Hart in "Definition and Theory in Jurisprudence" offers an elucidation of rights as language usage which will provide helpful tools for that analysis. Hart contends that we should not try to define abstract legal terms such as state, a corporation or a right. Rather we should place that term in a sentence and examine how that sentence is appropriately used.[15] Rather than defining a right, then, we should ask how the sentence, A has a right to paid 10 £ by B, is used in the game of law. Hart argues that that sentence implies the existence of a legal system and some official, probably a judge, who will use that sentence to draw a conclusion within a system of rules.[16]

Hart, however, also contends that the statement, A has a right to be paid 10 £ by B, can be used meaningfully in other contexts than a judge's ruling. An attorney, for example, could use that statement in the course of an argument to a judge contending that the judge should conclude that A has a right to be paid 10 £ by B. A law review editor could use that statement while criticizing a judge's decision ignoring A's right. On appeal, the lawyer who lost in the trial court could criticize the trial judge's decision in a similar manner. As Hart explains, a statement concerning rights can be made by way of ruling, claim, or criticism.[17] These are meaningful statements because they are arguments that a conclusion concerning that right should be drawn within the system of rules. The system of rules is a hard reference point for the statement.

Note that Hart explains that the language of rights can be used from different points of view and for different purposes. A judge uses the statement about rights to make a ruling. An appellate attorney with a different point of view and a different task than the judge uses the same language to make an argument, a claim or a criticism. Hart's analysis of

---

15. Hart, *Definition & Theory in Jurisprudence, supra* note 1 at 41.
16. *Id.* at 49.
17. *Id.* at 43.

the language of rights in terms of its usage from different points of view provides a valuable tool for understanding the many different classic statements about rights made as American jurisprudence evolved during the past twentieth century.

A personalist would argue that understanding language in terms of usage by persons in different contexts necessarily relates persons in action through language usage. The structure of Hart's analysis, contrary to Hart, then, implies that understanding law as action is primary while interpreting law as a system of rules is to perceive a secondary aspect of that activity.

In the next part, Hart's analysis of the language of rights in view of its usage from different points of view will be used to examine a series of classic but different statements about rights and to illustrate the manner in which statements concerning rights are used by many players in our legal culture to relate persons in our society.

4. The Language and Uses of Rights

a. Rights as Remedies, the Predictive View of Law

As American law began to emerge from the dark period of Langdellian formalism, first Holmes, and then the Legal Realists who developed some of his insights argued that law is a prediction of what courts will in fact do. Rights, then, could be understood as Karl Llewellyn argued as prophecies that courts would provide remedies.[18] As a prediction a statement about rights is made from the point of view of a practicing attorney forecasting a result in court. An attorney counseling a client could be advising litigation or suggesting that it should be avoided. However, he also may be giving planning advice concerning the drafting of a will or the development of a corporate structure. Holmes when he first offered the predictive understanding for law was placing action by the courts squarely in the center of his portrait of law. His predictive theory is consistent with an interpretation of law as action, as a great profession which we practice, rather than as a system of rules. Despite the Scandinavian Legal Realists, however, a judge does not make the

---

18. Karl N. Llewellyn, *A Realistic Jurisprudence—The Next Step*, 30 Colum. L. Rev. 431, 462–63.

prediction. Predictions are made by private attorneys for the sake of advising clients.

b. Rights as Conclusions in a Legal System

A clue to understanding the most important works of H. L. A. Hart is to perceive him in conversation with Holmes and his followers, the pragmatic instrumentalists including Roscoe Pound and the Legal Realists. "Definition and Theory in Jurisprudence" arguably was written to demonstrate that the predictive theory of law, the definition of law as predictions of what courts will in fact do, is not the best or the only appropriate interpretation of law.

Rights and rules are not simply related to the power of the courts, and are not used by lawyers primarily to predict results in court. Lawyers also make arguments to courts, statements of claims and criticism. In addition they argue with each other. Those are meaningful activities in law, appropriate uses of the language of law or the language of rights.

To illustrate that, H. L. A. Hart imagines a game of cricket in which a fan disagrees with an umpire's ruling.[19] Hart argues that the fan's statement of criticism while not an official ruling is a meaningful use of rules because like the ruling it is used to draw a conclusion within a system of rules here by way of argument or criticism. While Hart is arguing that law is a system of rules his argument and his illustration necessarily shows the relations between human activity, the many players in the game of law, and rules, and the manner in which the rules, the language of law, is used in the course of action, here the game of cricket or law, to relate persons.

c. Rights as Reasons; Rights as Trumps

Hart's understanding of legal rights and rules in terms of their usage by multiple players in the game of law opens many doors. When he added in *The Concept of Law* that legal rules necessarily are and ought to be open textured he opened those doors wider.[20] Now a judge making a

---

19. Hart, *Definition & Theory in Jurisprudence, supra* note 1 at 42.
20. HART, CONCEPT OF LAW *supra* note 8 at 120–32.

ruling or a lawyer making an argument is drawing a conclusion within an open textured system of rules. As Ronald Dworkin appropriately perceived, then, the judge who rules or the lawyer who argues must offer reasons for drawing that conclusion.

In *Law's Empire*, Ronald Dworkin ultimately rejects Hart's understanding of legal rules as open textured and labels that description of law as a semantic sting. Hart, Dworkin contends, offers open texture, with rules having a clear core meaning and a shadowy or penumbral surrounding area in which a judge specifies the rule's meaning, as a description of language. Rather, Dworkin argues, it is an interpretation pretending to be a description of language, hence a semantic sting.[21] Legal concepts, according to Dworkin, often are contested concepts but an interpretation of the concept should apply to the entire concept and all instances under the concept without distinguishing between clear core cases and cases in the penumbral area.

Whether legal rules are open textured as Dworkin may have perceived when he wrote *Taking Rights Seriously* or contain contested concepts which must be interpreted, a judge making a ruling or a lawyer making an argument should offer reasons for his conclusion. Dworkin, then, has added the legal reasoning process to the many usages of the language of rights and rules.

Rights, then, are not merely conclusions drawn within a system of rules but reasons for those conclusions. Dworkin recognizes that rights compete in the judge's reasoning process with other reasons for drawing conclusions. Dworkin argues, however, that principles as reasons for a decision based on an individual's assertion of right should trump competing reasons particularly policies which he describes as reasons for decisions based on group goals.[22] Dworkin, then, has added two additional uses of rights and the language of rights. In the legal reasoning process rights are not merely used to draw conclusions, they serve as reasons which can trump competing reasons. Rights are reasons and rights are trumps.

Dworkin's ideal Judge Hercules uses rights as reasons and rights as trumps when arriving at and justifying a holding in a case. However, in view of Hart's analysis, a lawyer arguing a case or a law review editor criticizing a decision can also use rights as reasons and rights as trumps.

---

21. Ronald Dworkin, Law's Empire 45–46 (1996).
22. Ronald Dworkin, Taking Rights Seriously 85 (1977).

One can argue to a court or in an article that a conclusion should be drawn by a court because a proposed right supports that conclusion and trumps competing reasons.

Again a judge is engaged in action relating to other persons when he decides a case and offers reasons for his holding. An attorney arguing the case and offering rights as reasons is related to the judge, to his clients, and to their opponents by the use of language. He too is engaged in action relating persons.

d. Rights as Goals; Rights as Means

In *Brown v. Board of Education of Topeka, Kansas*, Chief Justice Warren treated the Fourteenth Amendment guarantee of equal protection of the law as a goal to be achieved by appropriate means.[23] He found that the separate but equal doctrine was an inadequate means for reaching the goal of equal protection and substituted desegregation of the schools as a better means for serving that goal.[24] A right can be understood, then, as a goal, the goal of equal protection, for example. A right also may be understood as a means, for example, the right to desegregation as established by Warren's holding, as a means for achieving equal protection.

In earlier chapters it was argued that the pragmatic instrumentalist means-goal reasoning was an appropriate method for judicial decision making. In chapter 4 constitutional rights were understood as means for protecting each person's share of the primary social goods and hence his or her right to participate in the common action of society. Rights as goals, and rights as means can be used, then, in a judicial reasoning process grounded in respect and concern for each person. Rights in this understanding can be perceived easily as tools for establishing and changing human relations. They also are tools in the reasoning process. Rights as goals, and rights as means are reasons for conclusions that can be weighed and balanced against competing reasons including respect for competing interests. One can argue that a goal right should trump a competing interest.

Again a judge using means-goal reasoning to decide cases and offer reasons for his holding is engaged in action relating to other persons.

---

23. Brown v. Board of Education of Topeka, Kansas, 347 U.S. 483 (1954).
24. *Id.*

An attorney arguing to the court can urge rights as goals and rights as means as reasons to persuade a judge to reach a holding favorable to his client. In the legal reasoning process, rights as goals and rights as means can be used from multiple points of view to engage in the on-going argument about what society should be that constitutes society.

e. Rights as Resources

Some goal rights are difficult to achieve. For example under Article 25 of the Universal Declaration of Human Rights everyone "has the right to a standard of living adequate for the health and well being of himself and of his family."[25] Like the right to economic development this right to social security requires an allocation of resources which may not be available. However, one can argue that society should pursue diligently the rights to economic development and an adequate standard of living. At the time of *Brown v. Board of Education* the rights of students attending segregated schools to desegregation and to equal protection were goals which would not be achieved automatically upon announcement of that case's decision. Great effort over a number of years was required to effectuate the Court's holding in *Brown*.

The NAACP under the direction of Thurgood Marshall and others conducted a long law reform campaign which began in 1929 and led to their victory in *Brown*. From the point of view of Thurgood Marshall and other law reform attorneys the rights to desegregation and equal protection were goals to be pursued. One chosen means for pursuing those goals was the careful management of litigation to produce a series of preliminary decisions whose holdings could be used as precedent in a culminating case like *Brown*.

As Stuart Scheingold argues, then, in *The Politics of Rights*, rights may be used as resources in a law reform campaign.[26] Previous decisions, for example, may be used as precedent and hence as resources in arguing for further development of law. Rights also, however, are political resources. When a law reformer has effectively established a preliminary right, a stepping stone in his law reform campaign, then the campaign and the pursuit of further change in law acquires legitimacy

---

25. *Universal Declaration of Human Rights*, Dec. 10, 1948, G.A. Res. 217 A (III), U.N. Doc.A/810, at 71 (1948).
26. STUART SCHEINGOLD, THE POLITICS OF RIGHTS 83–84 (1974).

power. A claim of right coupled with legitimacy power may be used to rally one's adherents and to attack opponents. The legitimacy power accompanying a claim of right may produce a cultural change, a transcending or crossing of horizons. *Brown v. Board of Education* became a resource, a source of legitimacy power, in the further campaign for desegregation of public and private facilities and in the continuing pursuit of equal protection.

f. Anti-Rights Rhetoric and the Use of Rights

Members of the Critical Legal Studies Movement (Crits) as dedicated deconstructionalists have attacked regularly the rhetoric of rights as designed to protect the interests, property and social outlook of the dominant classes in our society.[27] Morton Horvitz, an important legal historian as well as a founding member of the Critical Legal Studies Movement argues that the "history of rights for 150 years of our constitutional history has basically been the doctrine of the wealthy and powerful. It is only in the last 50 years that this has changed."[28] Mark Tushnet contends that the "use of rights in contemporary discourse impedes advances by progressive social forces, which I call the party of humanity."[29] Rights talk as embedded in an establishment ideology, according to the Crits, prevents the reshaping of society and genuine discussion about what society should be.

Nevertheless, the Crits employ both the rhetoric of rights and anti-rights rhetoric in a manner similar to other users of the language of rights. As Stuart Scheingold maintains a law reformer will use rights as political resources to rally his supporters and attack his opponents.[30] Duncan Kennedy, another founder of the Critical Legal Studies Movement, in his remarkable article, "Freedom and Constraint in Adjudication: A Critical Phenomenology," uses rights rhetoric with its legitimacy power to advance his political agenda.[31] Roberto Unger, again a founder of the movement, would use rights as a means of constructing his ideal

27. DONNELLY, THE LANGUAGE AND USES OF RIGHTS *supra* note 2 at 38.
28. *Id.* at 39.
29. Tushnet, *An Essay in Rights*, 62 TEX. L. REV. 1363, 1364 (1984).
30. SCHEINGOLD, *supra* note 26.
31. Duncan Kennedy, *Freedom and Constraint in Adjudication: A Critical Phenomenology* 36 J. LEGAL EDUC. 518 (1986).

society around his ideology.[32] In that society Unger would provide for destabilization rights so that society can be changed periodically.[33]

As deconstructionalists the Crits would use anti-rights rhetoric to tear down establishment horizons, to destabilize society. Where an oppressive society has an impacted field of law supporting dominant interests, that is a praiseworthy endeavor. Like the law reformers use of rights it is a means of hammering on foreign horizons seeking recognition for the humanity of those who are oppressed.

g. Analyzing Horizons and Points of View: Understanding the Various Uses of Rights

Every statement about rights is made within a horizon and from a point of view. While we regularly cross and transcend horizons in our pluralist society we always find ourselves thinking and acting within a horizon. That may be the new horizon we have acquired by studying and understanding a specialized method or by learning a foreign language and visiting the country of its origin. As Gadamer suggests there may be a fusion of horizons.[34] Nevertheless we should recognize that horizons affect our understanding and our statements including interpretations of and uses of the language of rights. When interpreting or attempting to understand an argument or a statement about rights, it would be helpful to discuss or try to analyze the speaker's horizon and his purpose for using the language of rights.

It also is helpful to recognize the point of view of the one making the statement about rights. For example, a prosecutor's point of view and hence his statement about rights is very different than that of a defense attorney or a judge. The various classic statements about rights just reviewed are all made within a horizon and from a point of view.

When offering their predictive understanding of law, and contending that one has a right when one can predict that a court will afford a remedy, Holmes and the Legal Realists were developing a vision of law designed to destabilize late nineteenth and early twentieth century formalism. Nevertheless when understood from the point of view of a

---

32. Roberto Unger, *The Critical Legal Studies Movement* 96 HARV. L. REV. 563 (1983).

33. *Id.*

34. GADAMER, *supra* note 4 at 306–07.

practicing attorney advising a client about potential litigation, it is an enlightening understanding of the functioning of rights in that setting. Understanding the usage of rights in the day to day activities of the law is a helpful way of interpreting those activities and rights as means for relating persons. Holmes' predictive view of law struck many practicing attorneys as a candid and enlightening statement about the great profession which they practiced.

The predictive view of law, however, when it becomes central to one's interpretation of our profession, itself creates a horizon which enhances and confines vision. H. L. A. Hart sought to transcend that horizon by his analysis of the many uses of the language of rights. His analysis provides a foundation for understanding the many different points of view from which the language of rights is used. Hart, of course, wanted to emphasize the importance of language and of rules as language because he was endeavoring with the help of Wittgensteinian language analysis to develop and support a more enlightened theory of legal positivism.

While Ronald Dworkin shares Hart's interest in language analysis and his understanding of law as rules, language and, Dworkin would add, principles, he does not support Hart's legal positivism. Like Holmes, and indeed many Americans, Dworkin examines law from the point of view of a deciding judge. Examining the reasoning process, he would recommend to his ideal judge Hercules, he discovers that rights are used in that process not merely as reasons for conclusions but also as particularly powerful reasons which will trump other reasons. He is able, then, to tie rights as used in reasoning to his judge's vision and interpretation of law, a vision that grounds law in respect and concern for each person.

Robert Summers recognizes that pragmatic means-goal reasoning can be related in a manner similar to Dworkin's principled reasoning to the great ideals and visions of our society.[35] Summers' discovery provides a basis for analyzing a judge's reasoning process in a manner similar to but different from Dworkin. His thought provides a foundation for understanding the relation between a judge's ideals and reasoning and the persons affected by his decision without being trapped by Dworkin's rigid analysis and application of principles. Most pragmatic

---

35. ROBERT SUMMERS, INSTRUMENTALISM AND AMERICAN LEGAL THEORY 60–66 (1982).

instrumentalists, of course, would have difficulty with relating means-goal reasoning to overarching theory. Nevertheless that use of ideals or overarching theory provides a basis for re-interpreting *Brown v. Board of Education* as grounded in the most fundamental ideals of American society, an interpretation which best represents our current acceptance and understanding of that decision.

Despite their importance, judges are not the only players in the game of law. The power of Holmes' predictive understanding of law comes not only from putting the judge as a most important actor at the center of his portrait of law but also from providing a candid and persuasive interpretation of the practicing lawyer's job. When advising clients a practicing lawyer is to predict what courts will in fact do. Hart provides an alternate interpretation of that task: the practicing lawyer using the language of rules and rights is to make arguments by way of claim or criticism.[36] Legal pragmatism offers a further interpretation, those arguments are to include a discussion of policies, of goals and means for attaining those goals. Robert Summers transforms that pragmatic reasoning and makes it possible to relate rights as means and goals to our great ideals, to take rights seriously when using that pragmatic method for reasoning and arguing.[37]

A law reformer, such as Thurgood Marshall is likely to confront persons, often hostile, whose horizons make it difficult for them to understand the arguments he is making. A law reformer makes statements about rights from the point of view of one arguing to a court or to society that existing law and existing circumstances should change. Within his own horizon he perceives his clients' interests and problems. His task is to bring those in other horizons to an understanding of those interests and problems which will persuade them to change the law. Statements about rights, then, from his point of view are tools for penetrating foreign horizons, appealing to more fundamental commitments of persons in those horizons, and for persuading them to transcend their horizons to recognize the personhood and rights of his clients. Because law reform requires endurance and persistence over time, the reform litigator may perceive rights as goals to be pursued. From his point of view rights also may be perceived as means for the establishment of fur-

---

36. Hart, *Definition & Theory of Jurisprudence* 70 L. QUART. REV., *supra* note 1 at 46–49

37. SUMMERS, *supra* note 35.

ther rights, and to advance the interests of his clients including their fundamental interest and right to participate in society.

The Crits have a point of view similar to law reformers. Like law reformers they are seeking change, perhaps fundamental structural change in society and law. Because they confront horizons organized as they perceive around establishment ideologies and interests, a basic task is to deconstruct those horizons. Deconstruction, then, and anti-rights rhetoric is a tool of law reform and a means of breaking through foreign horizons. It is a means for conducting that on-going argument about what society should be that constitutes society.

Dworkin, of course, has a vision of what society should be, a society of principle and deliberation about principle grounded in political friendship. In dialogue with Dworkin personalism also offers a vision of society and law grounded in an interpretation of political friendship which differs from that of Dworkin. Part of the on-going argument including the discussion with the Crits would be about those differing visions of society. From a personalist perspective the Crits have contributed valuable tools and important insights into oppression.

Point of view analysis, that is, analyzing statements about rights from the point of view of the speaker, is helpful, then, in understanding how the multiple players in the game of law use the language of rights. Point of view analysis also helps us to relate statements about rights to the speaker's horizons and to observe when that language is being used to hammer on, penetrate or transcend the horizons of the hearers of the statements about rights.

Recognizing that every statement about rights is made from a point of view and within a horizon has helped, then, in analyzing and interpreting many of the classic statements about rights made during the preceding twentieth century. In the next part, the understanding of obligation as presented earlier in chapter 5 will be used as a tool for further interpreting those classic statements about rights.

5. Obligation

Anglo-American jurisprudence during the past century as explained in earlier chapters can be understood as a grand conversation.[38] H. L. A.

---

38. *See generally* DONNELLY, *supra* note 2 at chapter 2.

Hart who has engaged in conversation with many of the leading thinkers can be perceived as the host of that party who encouraged the guests to intermingle. The analysis just offered of the language of rights provides a slice of life, a microcosm, not only of activity in law but also of that grand conversation. H. L. A. Hart's analysis of language usage in "Definition and Theory in Jurisprudence" provides a means for interpreting the classic statements made about rights during the twentieth century as usage of the language of rights from the points of view of the many players in the game of law.

In the *Concept of Law*, Hart contributes the analysis of obligation which was discussed in chapter 5.[39] Understanding obligation will provide a further means of analyzing and reconciling the classic statements about rights. Hart argued that we can best understand obligation from an internal point of view.[40] Persons can be perceived as recognizing an obligation to rules or, we could add, commitments when they offer those as reasons justifying their actions.[41] A personalist would have an obligation to support the legal system because he is committed to respect and concern for each person and has a derivative commitment to support and develop the means for advancing human relations. Those commitments will provide a foundation for a theory of rights. Other thinkers and participants in our society, of course, would perceive and explain their obligations differently. Like rights, obligations are understood within horizons, indeed within the multiple horizons of our pluralist society.

One can use the concept of obligation, particularly obligation as perceived differently in the context of different horizons, to analyze further the manner in which we use the language of rights. In an earlier book, *The Language and Uses of Rights: A Biopsy of American Jurisprudence in the Twentieth Century*, I offered a helpful formula: X has a right if Y has an obligation.[42] The formula provides a framework for discussing the relation between obligations as perceived within different horizons and statements or arguments about rights.

The formula resembles and may be inspired by Wesley Hohfeld's *Fundamental Legal Conceptions*, particularly his first set of jural correla-

---

39. HART, THE CONCEPT OF LAW *supra* note 8 at 79–89.
40. *Id.* at 86–88.
41. *Id.*
42. DONNELLY, THE LANGUAGE AND USES OF RIGHTS *supra* note 1, at 97.

tives which establish that Y has a duty where X has a right.[43] The formula and its use, however, differs from Hohfeld's analysis in significant ways. Hohfeld's formula most aptly describes the legal relations between private parties so that if X has a right under a contract with Y, then Y has a duty to fulfill his contractual obligation to X. The formula proposed here and in my previous book best applies to the relation between a judge and a litigant: X, the litigant, has a right, if Y, the judge has an obligation. In some instances, the judge, X, may perceive his obligation as the basis for drawing a conclusion within a set of open textured rules. However, the formula is abstract and may be applied to many different circumstances and sets of persons. It can be used, for example, to analyze the relation between obligations as perceived within different horizons and the classic statements about rights discussed earlier in this chapter.

For example, one could analyze the predictive view of rights using the formula, X has a right if Y has an obligation. The judge whose decisions are being predicted might be Dworkin's ideal judge, Hercules, or a personalist whose method to some extent resembles that of Justice Brennan, or a legal pragmatist such as Judge Posner. Judges, then, perceive their obligations within different legal, moral and intellectual horizons. If a lawyer advising a client on the potential results of litigation knows the court, as Llewellyn recommended, and knows or can guess the judge's perception of his obligation then he can make a related prediction regarding rights. In the alternative he can base his prediction on regularities of behavior including the decision of previous cases.

If Dworkin's Judge Hercules is about to decide his case, then a litigant's counsel can predict that his client has a right which will trump competing policy considerations provided that right corresponds with a principle which under Hercules' theory provides the best explanation for existing law.[44] If Judge Posner will decide the case then a litigant's counsel should not base his prediction on overarching theory or principles. As a conscientious but pragmatic judge, Posner in routine cases would use ordinary legal reasoning.[45] Posner can be said to accept the legal system. A litigant, then, usually will have the normal set of legal rights. In some cases Posner would depart from routine analysis to pro-

---

43. WESLEY HOHFELD, FUNDAMENTAL LEGAL CONCEPTIONS (1919)

44. Stephen Guest, Ronald Dworkin, *in* JURISTS: PROFILES IN LEGAL THEORY 240–42 (William Twining & Neil MacCormick eds., 1991).

45. See POSNER, PROBLEMS OF JURISPRUDENCE, *supra* note 7 at 83–84.

vide the result he would perceive as best for the future. In contrast to Posner, a judge who is a deep moral and legal skeptic may not perceive any obligation to arrive at any particular decision. Unless one can predict his decision from regularities of behavior one may have to conclude that the judge is unable to take rights seriously and that X does not have a right because Y does not recognize any obligation.

Duncan Kennedy, in "Freedom and Constraint in Adjudication: A Critical Phenomenology," discusses the manner in which he as an imagined United States District Court Judge, would arrive at a decision.[46] While he would strive to justify his decision by good legal arguments he would reach his conclusion and make those arguments to advance his political agenda.[47] In Judge Kennedy's court a litigant has a right if it is in accord with Duncan Kennedy's political ideology and agenda.[48] An attorney familiar with Kennedy's views could predict when his client has a right. A litigant (X) before the imaginary Judge Kennedy (Y) has a right if Judge Kennedy under his ideology perceives an obligation to recognize that right.

An attorney about to appear before a personalist judge can advise his client that the judge will allow strong legal rights to trump most competing considerations and that the judge will inquire into and balance the interests of the competing parties. The attorney would be better able to predict a personalist judge's decision because that judge from time to time would reveal his commitments and method in his opinions. Again X has a right because the judge, Y, has an obligation to afford him deep respect and concern which includes weighing his interests and advancing his right to participate in society.

The formula, X has a right if Y has an obligation can be used to describe the task of an attorney arguing before a court. To represent his client the attorney must argue that the right his client claims is supported by an analysis of law in accord with the judge's perception of his obligation. If the client's claim is not reasonably supportable by the judge's normal interpretation of law, an interpretation supported by the judge's perception of obligation, then the attorney must persuade the judge to cross or transcend horizons. Hopefully, then, the judge may perceive his obligation and his interpretation of law differently because the change of horizons, perhaps modest, has changed his perception.

---

46. Kennedy, *supra* note 31.
47. *Id.*
48. *Id.*

Changing point of view from that of the practicing attorney arguing a case or predicting a decision to the perspective of a deciding judge, one can continue to apply the formula: X has a right if Y has an obligation. A judge should interpret the law in accordance with his understanding of why he has accepted the law. While judges often do not articulate their fundamental understanding, nevertheless, their perception of the law will reflect that understanding. A judge will and should recognize X's right if it is supported by the judge's interpretation of law and his corresponding understanding of his obligation to support that law.

From the judge's point of view his obligation as related to his interpretation of law will determine when a right should be accepted as a reason for a decision, should trump competing considerations or should be the conclusion of his reasoning process. Rights then are conclusions, reasons or trumps if the judge within his horizon perceives an obligation to respect or recognize that right.

Obligation, then, is a hard reference point which allows us to understand the multiple ways in which we use the language of rights. When the concept of obligation is used analytically in conjunction with point of view and horizon analysis it provides a means for interpreting and reconciling the apparently conflicting classic statements about rights made during the course of the last century.

6. The Task of the Law Reform Litigator

Over the course of Anglo-American legal development, law reform litigation has a long and honorable history. It is not just a recent phenomenon. A great example is the career of Granville Sharp whose work in London during the mid-eighteenth century led to the 1773 decision of King's Bench in *Somersett v. Stewart* which in effect abolished slavery in England and became a continuing source of legitimacy power for the abolition movement both in England and the United States.[49] Granville Sharp also participated in the effort subsequent to *Somersett* to abolish the slave trade.

Sharp had obtained a writ of habeas corpus on prior occasions from Lord Mansfield who was then Chief Justice of King's Bench.[50] Although

---

49. Somersett v. Stewart, 20 How. St. Tr. 1 (1772).
50. *Id.*

Sharp was not a lawyer he had prepared and circulated a brief in the Inns of Court concerning the status of slavery in England and had attracted representation. On the return of the writ in previous cases, Lord Mansfield had persuaded the parties to settle the case without a decision regarding the legality of slavery in England. As part of the settlement the former black slave would be freed.

In *Somersett* Mansfield strove for a similar settlement and in that effort postponed the case from time to time over the course of a year. Nevertheless Stewart, the master, and probably those who were supporting his position, refused a settlement and demanded a decision according to law.[51] Using our common sense to understand that foreign horizon we could guess that those involved with slavery and the slave trade including the British West Indies Company were tired of Granville Sharp's harassment. Probably angered by the refusal to settle, Lord Mansfield at the end of the year uttered his famous dictum which could be paraphrased as follows: If you want a decision according to law you shall have a decision according to law; let justice be done though the heavens may fall.[52] In his opinion supporting the Court's decision to free Somersett, Mansfield found no legal basis for slavery in England. There was no relevant legislation. He distinguished prior contrary cases by pointing out that habeas corpus had not been sought in those cases and that therefore "the person" of the slave had not been at stake. Mansfield concluded that slavery was too obnoxious to be established on the basis of custom without positive law. As a result of the decision in *Somersett* and its precedential value about 16,000 slaves held in England were freed. *Somersett*, however, did not abolish the slave trade. England was then the leading slave trading country.

Somersett became a resource in the subsequent campaign for abolition of slavery in the United States.[53] As an English decision prior to 1776 it was an important precedent for the new states after the revolution. Theoretically its holding should prevail in the absence of contrary legislation. Dred Scott urged arguments derived from *Somersett* in his case before our Supreme Court.[54]

In England, *Somersett* was a source of legitimacy power in the subsequent effort to abolish the slave trade. About 1780 Lord Wilberforce,

---

51. *Id.*
52. *Id.*
53. Scott v. Sanford, 60 US 393 (1856).
54. *Id.*

who was then a young member of parliament, but became England's Foreign Minister during the wars with Napoleon began filing annually a bill to eliminate the slave trade.[55] In the early nineteenth century effective 1806 he finally succeeded in having his bill passed. Granville Sharp had some influence on young Wilberforce.

Law reform is for the long-winded and persistent. From the point of view of the law reformer, a right such as the right to abolition of slavery is a goal to be pursued by a variety of means including litigation and legislation. An important decision such as *Somersett* can be a means towards further goals. By conferring legitimacy power on the campaign for reform it becomes a political resource. The right not to be a slave in England although important for its own sake, is a means for persuading Parliament to abolish the slave trade and a precedent for eliminating slavery in the American states. From the point of view of the law reformer rights are means and rights are goals.

The great task of the law reformer is to persuade those in different horizons to recognize the personhood and suffering of those he is representing. To perform that task the law reformer himself may need a sense of outrage at oppression and a critical analysis of law and its impact as perceived within his clients' horizon. Somehow he must persuade judges, legislators and society to cross into his clients' horizons sufficiently to understand their problems, needs and rights. A classic means for doing that is to narrate, to tell the clients' story perhaps quietly but in dramatic terms. Basically one crosses horizons, including physical horizons, by going there perhaps by automobile, or by reading a travelogue or a story. By effectively telling his clients' story, a law reform attorney can take the court or society into their horizon. Skillful appellate attorneys are able to tell that story not merely in the statement of facts but also through legal arguments.

One also can attack, tear down, or deconstruct existing social and legal horizons. A campaign of deconstruction may remove the barriers to vision created by society's existing horizons. Again that deconstruction has the purpose of allowing society to perceive the circumstances, needs and rights of the oppressed.

Hopefully, once the obstacles to vision are removed either by persuading judges or society to cross horizons, or by deconstructing existing horizons, the relevant decision makers will recognize the clients'

---

55. J. STEVEN WATSON, THE REIGN OF GEORGE III; 1760–1815 301 (1960).

personhood, the manner in which their participation in society is threatened, and an obligation to protect the right necessary to produce change. Recognizing others as suffering can give us an insight into their personhood, and can help us to perceive an obligation to assist them. One's previous perceptions of obligations, however, can create impacted horizons and effective barriers to vision. A law reformer may recognize that his task includes not only an appeal to existing perceptions of obligation but an effort to change a judge's or society's understanding of their obligations. The change in American culture from widespread opposition during the 1950s to *Brown v. Board of Education* to the present general and often principled acceptance of that decision is an example of a gradual change in society's perception of obligation.

From the point of view of a law reformer, then, rights are goals and means for achieving those goals, means for appealing to the obligations existing or newly perceived of those in differing but perhaps changing horizons. We can analyze, then, and interpret a law reformer's task and his or her use of the language of rights with the help of point of view and horizon analysis joined with a theory of obligation as related to rights and as perceived within the multiple horizons of our pluralist society.

7. Conversation: Communication across Horizons

The great use of rights and the language of rights is to carry on across the multiple horizons in our society that conversation about what society should be that constitutes society.[56] The portrait and interpretation of the law reformer just offered is an example of how that conversation can be conducted across horizons. The law reformer is a principal participant in the game of law and in that conversation. However, he is not the only participant.

In chapters 4 and 5 judges, particularly justices of the United States Supreme Court, were also described as principal participants in that conversation. Our court system, our great legal dispute settlement institution, and our legal culture provide important means for carrying forward that conversation.

---

56. Donnelly, The Language and Uses of Rights, *supra* note 2 at34–35.

Rights can be understood as entitlements from the point of view of a personalist judge or of Dworkin's Judge Hercules who has a strong obligation to recognize certain rights.[57] In this chapter, however, rights were described as tools, as usage of language in the game of law. As such they are used across horizons to "establish, change, talk about, fight about, reconcile and struggle with human relations."[58] The great use of the language of rights, however, in our legal culture is to converse, to deliberate collectively about the relations between persons in our society and about our great national ideals.[59]

One can analyze the various uses of the language of rights, including conversation, in terms of point of view, horizons, and obligations. At its best, however, that conversation requires a seeking out and sharing of human experience, perhaps across horizons. The personalist judge should use horizon crossing techniques to seek out experience as part of his decision making method. A law reform attorney by narration and otherwise should attempt to convey the experience of needs, problems, oppression in his clients' horizon to those in different horizons.

James Boyd White, in *Heracles' Bow*, contrasts the use of clever arguments by the crafty Odysseus with persuasion by an honest exchange of human experience.[60] Since the 1950's our society has been brought to a general and principled acceptance of *Brown v. Board of Education* not by clever legal arguments but by a change of perception related to our on-going exchange of human experience. Breaking down the barriers to vision found in impacted horizons, however, also may require clever and astute legal argument.

Earlier it was argued that the interpretation of great legal documents such as the United States Constitution requires that same seeking out and exchange of human experience. All the horizons relevant to law reform may be pertinent when developing the Constitution. Beyond that, however, one must engage in conversation with the document and with the horizons of the founding generation and of those who have interpreted the document over the ages. Conversation across horizons by an honest seeking out and exchange of human experience is a fundamental and often overlooked aspect of law.

---

57. DWORKIN, LAW'S EMPIRE, *supra* note 21 at 176–224.
58. DONNELLY, THE LANGUAGE AND USES OF RIGHTS, *supra* note 2 at 45.
59. *Id.*
60. WHITE, HERACLES' BOW, *supra* note 3 at 19–22.

8. Conclusion

In this chapter, then, by analyzing the multiple uses of the language of rights as found in a series of classic statements an effort was made to portray twentieth century jurisprudence as a grand conversation, an exchange of wisdom and insight among many great thinkers. By concentrating on a slice of life, a portion of that conversation, one can gain insight into that exchange of thought. Arguably, the contributions of H. L. A. Hart make it possible to construe twentieth century jurisprudence as a conversation. Hart's analysis of the usage of rights from different points of view and his concept of obligation when coupled with the personalist concept, horizons, were important tools for understanding the classic statements about rights and reconciling them.

That analysis allowed the portrayal of the use of rights and the language of rights in our great profession as important means for relating persons. Rights, as Dworkin contends, can be used in the reasoning process of judges. Private attorneys, however, including law reformers can use rights as arguments for a conclusion favorable to their clients. Law reformers, particularly, address those arguments to society as well as to courts. The law reformer's use of rights offers a microcosm of participation by private attorneys in that great argument about what society should be that constitutes society. One can interpret a law reformer's work as a means for enabling his clients to participate in the common action of society.

The analysis offered in this chapter of a microcosm of law, the language and uses of rights, and the work of the law reformer, illustrates the multiple players in the game of law, our legal culture, engaged in a common action, a great argument or conversation which relates persons in our society. Private attorneys including law reformers as well as judges are important participants in our legal culture and the common action of society. The analysis offered in this chapter, then, contributes to portraying the law not as a Gainsborough painting revealing a great judge but a Breughel which shows many persons interacting.

CHAPTER VII

The Personalist Agenda

1. Introduction

H.L.A Hart once claimed that Americans are all mad.[1] We have been driven mad, he argued, by the power of our Supreme Court. Following Oliver Wendell Holmes, Jr., then, we tend to develop our legal thought around the work of judges. With Holmes a number of thinkers perceive law primarily as action, an activity, a great profession which we practice rather than as a system of language and rules. Holmes' confrontation with Langdellian legal formalism and its understanding of law as system and language, rules and principles was an important beginning for what David Granfield calls a piecemeal recovery of a role for the person in law. As argued in previous chapters the jurisprudence of the last century could be understood as a step by step recapture of persons as central to the law.

In the early years of the twenty-first century, then, arguably the next logical step for American legal thought is to construct a jurisprudence and an understanding of judicial decision making method centered on the human person. This book is a contribution to that task. Its purpose is to construct a personalist method for deciding common law cases and interpreting the United States Constitution, a personalist interpretation of American law, and to argue for the legitimacy of that method and that interpretation.

Ronald Dworkin argues effectively that we should take an interpretive stance towards law. In *Law's Empire* he describes three interpretations of law, conventionalism, legal pragmatism and law as integrity.[2] A

---

1. H.L.A. Hart, *American Jurisprudence Through English Eyes: The Nightmare and the Noble Dream*, 11 GA. L. REV. 969, 969–70 (1977).
2. RONALD DWORKIN, LAW'S EMPIRE, 45–86 (1986).

fourth interpretation would be a personalist interpretation, a version of which is offered in this book. The theory of personalism in law as offered here and the personalist decision making method were constructed in part by gathering personalist insights from many twentieth century philosophers of law. Important sources of inspiration, however, were the tradition of European personalism, and in particular the thought of John Macmurray as found in *The Person As Agent*[3] and *Persons In Relation*.[4] The personalist decision making method constructed and described here like that of Dworkin rests on a commitment to afford all persons and each person deep respect and concern. Unlike Dworkin's ideal Judge Hercules, however, a personalist judge would recognize his own limited but growing knowledge and understanding, his horizons, and his need to cross horizons in order to afford others appropriate respect and concern.

However, a personalist interpretation of American law can be developed from different foundations. Margaret Jane Radin from a background of pragmatism and feminism as applied to law, has offered a number of personalist insights.[5] Alan Gewirth, in a different context than this book has offered an important theory of personalism in law.[6]

Personalist theory was described in chapter 3 and a potential foundation for that theory was offered and discussed briefly in chapter 5. However, the personalist interpretation of American law and personalist method as offered here can be supported by a variety of other deeper positions including those held by a number of religious thinkers, by some adherents of natural law, by neo-Kantian thought, and by those who accept and want to implement American ideals. John Rawls, likewise, offers his theory of justice as a middle level position supportable by a number of deeper stances.

Assuming, then, that for whatever reason, one finds personalist insights into American law attractive, how would one further develop a personalist understanding of law and contribute to the on-going conversation about our law? One could begin a further creative development of personalist thought as suggested by part two of this chapter by entering into a conversation with personalist thought and with the the-

---

3. John MacMurray, The Self As Agent (1999).
4. John MacMurray, Persons in Relation (1999).
5. Margaret J. Radin, *The Pragmatist and the Feminist*, in Pragmatism in Law and Society 127 (Michael Brint & William Weaver, eds., 1991).
6. *See* Alan Gewirth, Reason and Morality (1978).

ory offered in this book. From that beginning one could develop, improve and perhaps offer a better personalist or other interpretation of American law. Using personalist insights one could continue the conversation with American law as it develops and changes during the twenty-first century. The great quarrel over method undoubtedly will continue and new methods for judicial decision making will be constructed and offered. Personalist thought can continually construct and reconstruct decision making method in conversation with the developing traditions of the common law and constitutional interpretation.

Much of this book has imagined a common law judge advancing in his career and growing in wisdom and understanding. The private practice of law, however, is the backbone of our legal culture. During the last half of the twentieth century there were a series of creative contributions to the art of practicing law. Among these would be Robert Keeton's development of trial practice courses and A. James Casner's study of estate planning. A question which requires exploring is whether personalist theory can contribute insights to understanding the work of the practicing attorney. Part three will examine briefly and preliminarily whether that task should be part of the personalist agenda for the twenty-first century.

In chapter 6, the last chapter, an analysis of the language and uses of rights was offered from the perspective of a law reformer partly for the purpose of portraying law as an activity engaging many actors. Among these would be the private attorney in his role as law reform litigator. Since personalism is concerned with the impact of law on the interests of persons in many horizons and with the rights of each person to participate in our society, law reform is a continual aspect of the personalist agenda. In this chapter, part four will address the personalist concern for understanding and removing oppressive structures in society.

When conducting law reform or serving as a judge a personalist lawyer will encounter horizons, his or her own and those of others. A method for horizon crossing of serious importance in law reform is empirical research. Part five of this chapter will address preliminarily the personalist perspective and a role for social science in understanding law. During the twenty-first century social science can be important in promoting law reform and in furthering our understanding of the relation between persons, law and society.

For those concerned with the development of personalist theory the critical analysis and rethinking of particular fields of law offers a rich opportunity. Part six of this chapter offers a brief overview and part seven an illustration, "Rethinking Criminal Justice." Beyond offering a new theory one may want to contribute to actual reform of the institutions and law in a particular field. Critical analysis on the basis of a new theory may be helpful in reform. Social science can contribute to the development of theory and empirical studies are useful in understanding and demonstrating the oppressive impact of current law and institutions. Nevertheless, the reform of law even in well-structured long-term campaigns takes place case by case, institution by institution and person by person.

The discussion in part seven of the reform of criminal justice illustrates that process and offers a brief overview of a personalist theory of criminal justice. Developing that theory and participating in the reform of criminal justice should be on the personalist agenda for the twenty-first century. As argued in part two personalism can be understood as a perennial philosophy of law continually engaged in reinterpreting American legal tradition, recreating methods and rethinking and re-forming particular fields.

2. Conversation; Continued Development of Theory

a. Have a Conversation with This Book

Classically, when we read literature or works of philosophy from the past, we should enter into a conversation with the author's thought. Stages in that conversation would include examining the author's horizon, asking how he would have perceived the questions important to him in that horizon and how the insights we perceive as valuable were developed in the context of that horizon and the author's theory. Undoubtedly the author in the context of his horizon will have overlooked issues, problems, and insights. When reading we seek moments of understanding and insight but we also should ask what the author has overlooked.

H. L. A. Hart who entered into conversation with many of the legal philosophers of the twentieth century benefited from their insights. For example, his concept of rules as open textured, fairly apparently, was designed to capture in analytical theory the insight of the pragmatic instrumentalists that law is full of leeways and continually changes and develops. Hart's rule of recognition probably was inspired by Hans Kelsen's concept of the grundnorm.

Following Hart's example when reading a legal philosopher one can gather insights which can be transferred into one's own theory, horizon or developing understanding. Within the new theory or perhaps in relation to a new set of commitments or basic principles those insights can be transformed or further developed.

In the same manner one should enter into a conversation with this book, and with the proposed personalist interpretation of law and method for deciding cases. A reader whose law school training introduced him to the mainstream of American legal method in the pragmatic instrumentalist tradition should find much that is familiar but perhaps some new insights or new questions to be asked. He or she can take those insights back into his or her own developing thought and understanding of legal method. Those insights then provide an occasion for creative development.

As the twenty-first century advances, hopefully, our knowledge and understanding of law and the human person will continue to grow. Some readers may come to this book with or may acquire later a deeper understanding of the relation between law and persons. Perhaps agreeing with the basic outline of personalist theory such a reader could develop the personalist interpretation of law further or provide it with better foundations in non-legal thought. In the course of that creative development new insights and new ways of understanding how persons and law relate may emerge.

b. Method; Construction and Reconstruction

The method for judicial decision making offered in the earlier chapters was developed in conversation with many thinkers about law in the twentieth century. As argued above twentieth century jurisprudence can be perceived as a series of partial recoveries of a role for the person in law. Through conversation one can extract those insights from various legal philosophies and methodologies and then relate them to the commitment of a personalist judge to afford all persons and each person deep respect and concern and to his recognition of his horizons, his own limited but growing knowledge and understanding.

The pragmatic instrumentalists beginning with Holmes and continuing through Richard Posner, Margaret Jane Radin, and Cass Sunstein are responsible for recognizing many of our insights into the person in law and for incorporating those insights into legal method. The work of

Roscoe Pound, Karl Llewellyn and Jerome Frank was a high moment for recovery of a role for the person in law. Ronald Dworkin's idealism provides a foundation for relating our national ideals to judicial decision making method and to an interpretation of law. The personalist method of deciding common law and constitutional law cases was developed by combining insights from Dworkin and the pragmatic instrumentalist tradition and by relating those insights to the commitments of a personalist judge and to personalist concepts such as horizons, insights and critique of method.

The great quarrel over method as described in earlier chapters continues vigorously in the first years of the twenty-first century. New methods, some hopefully representing a further recovery of a role for the person, will develop and will be opposed by other methods offering apparently conflicting insights. This on-going argument about what law should be is an important, creative and vigorous part of our legal culture. Those inspired by personalist insights should join that discussion vigorously but with an inclination to converse as well as argue. New insights can be captured from new creative contributions to the quarrel over method. New methods can be molded, combined and related to personalist commitments and insights. In the common law tradition method continually evolves and should be continually criticized and improved. Personalist method as developed in this book offers a potential model for continued construction and reconstruction of method.

c. The Personalist Interpretation of American Law: A Perennial Philosophy of Law

The personalist interpretation of American law, then, may offer a perennial philosophy of law, a continual source for creative and critical thought contributing to the on-going conversation about our law. One reason why continued creative development of personalist thought is possible is because the limited but growing nature of our knowledge and understanding is recognized. A second reason is the continued need in personalist thought to strive to understand persons in multiple horizons in order to afford them appropriate respect and concern. As persons and their needs change, the personalist understanding of law should change and develop in response.

During the twenty-first century, then, as the great quarrel over method continues and as society changes the personalist interpretation of American law and its understanding of decision making method also should develop creatively. Those inspired by personalist thought should be continually striving to cross horizons while engaging in conversation with new methods and with our changing society and law.

d. The Personalist Scholar

In earlier chapters a personalist interpretation of American law was developed from the point of view of a judge committed to respect and concern for each person and all persons. Because he recognizes his limited knowledge and understanding that judge develops his method and interpretation of law over time and strives to cross horizons.

A scholar developing personalist insights also should recognize his or her limited knowledge and understanding. Horizon crossing and conversation with the rich thought of American legal theory would seem appropriate. As a young faculty member a new professor has an experience similar to that of a new judge. He or she is thrown into a delightful and somewhat strange new world. In some respects that world is narrower than that of the judge. The new professor's efforts will be devoted to a small portion of the law, the subject he or she will teach. Contacts with students, in depth research, opportunities for public service and law reform, however, offer opportunities for crossing and transcending those narrow horizons. Like the judge, a new faculty member, with personalist commitments, who undertakes to cross horizons and engage in conversations with multiple thinkers in our pluralist society will grow intellectually and morally over time. Much of the rest of the chapter is relevant to that process at least to the extent that one engages in public service and law reform. A faculty member may undertake reform in particular fields. The discussion and illustration in part seven, "Rethinking Criminal Justice" is then relevant.

At the moment a number of new faculty have been engaged during law school and otherwise in the Critical Legal Studies movement, in Feminist Jurisprudence, or in Critical Race Theory. With the help of those movements personalist insights into law have been multiplying during the late twentieth and early twenty-first century. Bringing those new insights to personalist development of law would be an important contribution. Indeed one could engage as a personalist thinker in critical legal studies, feminist jurisprudence, or critical race theory.

An important personalist criteria for assessing proposals for reform in particular fields and the development of new ideological positions would be the impact on persons and their interests. To the extent that new theories and ideologies create impacted horizons, understanding and hence respecting persons is hindered. To the extent that one is continually engaged in conversation, crossing horizons, and inquiring into the impact of proposed theories and reforms on the interests of affected humans, respect and concern for persons is advanced.

3. The Role of the Practicing Attorney

At the Harvard Law School during the second half of the twentieth century there were a number of courses which made creative contributions to the practice of law. Beginning with A. James Casner's course in Estate Planning several professors developed the planning approach to law. Business Planning was another important development from that perspective. Robert Keeton's creation of trial practice courses has contributed seriously to the development of the trial bar. Alternative dispute settlement and the study of negotiation has made a similar contribution. See, for example, Fisher and Ury, *Getting to Yes.*[7] As good lawyers, personalist thinkers, of course, can make their own contributions to that valuable and creative study of the practice of law. A question worth discussing, however, is whether personalist theory, as such, can contribute to understanding the practice of law.

Along with Holmes and others, as noted earlier, personalist theory would understand law as an activity, a great profession which we practice. Abandoning the positivist and Langdellian interpretation of law as primarily a system of rules should encourage a scholar to study our activity, how we practice our profession. Developing method for an activity concerned with representing persons in their relations with others should appeal to a personalist thinker.

Point of view analysis, understanding statements about law, arguments, rights and the task of the lawyer from the point of view of the speaker or doer is helpful in analyzing the various law jobs. For example, the planning point of view is distinctly different than the point of view of the judge or a litigating attorney. A mistake practicing lawyers may be particularly prone to making is to perceive the planning job from a litigating point of view. At times in the heat of combat, a litigating attorney may offer the arguments he or she has available even if the

---

7. ROGER FISHER & WILLIAM URY, GETTING TO YES (1983).

weight of precedent is against that argument. To rely on such an argument from the planning perspective would be a mistake. The planner more conservatively wants to guard against a range of competing arguments which may appeal to a future judge. A planning attorney from time to time will advise his client to take carefully calculated risks but will want to hone his plan to minimize those risks.

Horizons may be a helpful concept when analyzing negotiation as well as litigation. In the last chapter the task of the law reformer as litigating attorney was explained, in part, as one of penetrating foreign horizons. In negotiation, one may encounter an impacted horizon, perhaps that of one's client, which may make it difficult to negotiate. Horizons can be created by existing ways of doing business or by a position which one holds firmly and which may be associated with one's self image. The Fisher and Ury recommendation that in the course of negotiation one should focus on interests rather than positions may prove, then, a helpful means of moving parties beyond their horizons.

In "The Path of the Law," Holmes gave a concluding peroration addressing his audience of law students as prospective practicing attorneys and encouraging them, for their own sakes, to pay attention to theory.[8] Of course, the theory he had just creatively explained to them was a theory of law as action rather than as logic and rules. Happiness he argued "cannot be won simply by being counsel for great corporations."[9] He added:

> "An intellect great enough to win the prize needs other food besides success. The remoter and more general aspects of the law are those which give it universal interest. It is through them that you not only become a great master in your calling, but connect your subject with the universe and catch an echo of the infinite, a glimpse of its unfathomable process, a hint of the universal law."[10]

In his book, *The Inner Experience of Law, A Jurisprudence of Subjectivity*, David Granfield, likewise addressing students as well as other participants in law, has a remarkably parallel passage:

> "Judges, lawyers, professors, and even law students develop a characteristic mentality. Law transforms them for better or worse. If it remains merely a job, a prestigious way of making a living, a sophisticated dialectical skill, or a springboard to a posi-

---

8. Oliver Wendell Holmes, Jr., *The Path of Law*, 10 HARV. L. REV. 457, 478 (1897).

9. *Id.*

10. *Id.*

tion of power and influence, it splits their life into uncoordinated personal and professional compartments. The result is that one may become worldly wise without being truly wise; for true wisdom keeps asking relevant questions and keeps trying to verify and unify insights and to integrate all of life's experiences."[11]

Both Holmes and Granfield recommend an integration between the practice of law and one's personal growth. Personalist theory would argue that one more fully understands oneself as a person in relation to others. One grows in wisdom and understanding, as well as skill, person by person, as one wrestles one at a time with many persons' problems, and as one experiences their cooperation in a common action, or penetrates their horizons and overcomes their refusal to cooperate, and as one understands their moral struggle and perhaps their suffering. Resolving one person's problems or establishing or re-establishing one set of human relations, in some respects and in some views, is akin to rescuing the whole of humanity. As one understands human beings and one's profession, person by person, one captures what Holmes calls "an echo of the infinite." That, of course, is the great personalist insight into the practice of law and a clue to a fuller development of a personalist theory of legal practice.

The glory of American law is that each person, particularly each accused criminal defendant, is entitled to be represented by counsel devoted to his interests. As Justice Brennan explained, in our legal culture and under our national ideals "even the vilest criminal remains a human being possessed of common human dignity."[12] The personalist theory of the common good offers a basis for commenting on the regular objections to representation of criminal defendants.

In personalist theory, as described in earlier chapters, society is perceived as persons acting together. Contrary to the common good are any actions that tend to destroy or frustrate the common action or to prevent any person from participating in society. A personalist would perceive an obligation to cooperate in the common action and in developing its institutions. Our legal system, which is one of those institutions, appropriately under personalist theory, provides representation for those accused of crime. That representation is a proper recognition of the accused's human dignity and his fundamental right to participate

---

11. David Granfield, The Inner Experience of Law, A Jurisprudence of Subjectivity 274 (1988).

12. Gregg v. Georgia, 428 U.S. 227 (1976).

in society. Counsel for the defense is fulfilling the personalist obligation to afford each person deep respect and concern. However, the defense counsel also is serving the common good by performing a role provided for him in our legal justice system. By providing for defense counsel our legal system serves the common good by protecting the participation in our society of all persons including the accused.

Personalist theory, and several concepts used in constructing that theory can contribute to analyzing the work and role of the private attorney. While personalist theory as developed in this book concentrates on the work of the judge, the role of the private attorney as one who relates persons to each other and to the common action is significant in personalist theory. As the preliminary analysis in this part indicates further development in personalist theory of an analysis of private practice belongs on the personalist agenda for the twenty-first century.

4. Law Reform

While law reform in some legal circles is a currently respected and popular activity, it has deep roots in the common law. Historically reforms in the law have not always been successful. A classic set of reforms in real property mortgage law by their failure provide an enduring symbol of potential frustration.

Originally a mortgage, a dead pledge, was a deed to real property subject to a defeasance clause which declared the deed null, void and of no effect if the bond or note secured by the deed was paid on the law day. If payment was not made in accordance with the bond, the deed established a fee simple absolute. However, the ancient courts of equity would prevent that forfeiture of property by providing a right of redemption.

To avoid destroying the usefulness of mortgages as security for loans, the courts of equity then had to balance the interests of debtor and creditor by recognizing the creditor's petition to forever foreclose the right of redemption. The debtor would be allowed a short period of time to exercise the right of redemption which would then be foreclosed. Ultimately to avoid a windfall the sheriff's sale was invented. That sale was designed to protect the debtor in circumstances where the property was worth considerably more than the debt. After paying the debt the surplus would go to the debtor. Normally, however, there is no surplus. Property is rarely sold for more than the amount of the debt. Rather the debtor often loses his property and becomes liable in addition for the deficiency. Historically, one of the most significant efforts at debtor protection became a means for oppressing debtors.

Law regularly becomes a means for oppressing persons. In addition to the obvious influence of our evil inclinations, that oppression develops because of our limited knowledge and understanding. Horizons are created by current legal practice joined with the interests of those who benefit from present law. Horizons, then, prevent us from perceiving the oppression which often is obvious to those in different horizons. In most fields of law there are practices badly in need of reform. In some fields the law is pervasively oppressive. Arguably criminal law despite our reforms in constitutional criminal procedure is one of those fields. Rethinking criminal law from a personalist perspective will be a topic for discussion later in this chapter.

Law reform, then, should be high on the agenda of an attorney who accepts the personalist commitment to afford each person deep respect and concern. However, because of horizons, our limited knowledge and understanding, an attorney often will stumble haphazardly across the opportunity for law reform. Then as part of the law reform the reformer will need to overcome horizons, his or her own, as well as those of society.

Chapter 6 offered a personalist analysis of the use of rights during a long-term law reform campaign. Notoriously, even modest efforts at reform require the reformer to be long winded and enduring. However, a personalist insight into private practice noted in the previous part of this chapter also is relevant here. One relates to clients and grows in wisdom, knowledge and understanding case by case, person by person. Today, many attorneys are engaged in significant although at times modest and short term efforts at law reform. Historically we also have the great long-term campaigns. However, often law reform is effectuated by being present, by representing clients on a regular basis. Capital defenders, case by case, are currently restricting and perhaps reversing the practice of capital punishment. A legal services attorney who specializes in the protection of consumer debtors begins to reform local collection practices simply by being available to represent clients. An activist attorney who devotes ten percent of his practice to representing prisoners in the local jail will become a shield against beatings and other abusive practices. Over time his successful suits may result in a change of jail administration. One shows respect and concern for the oppressed by representing them and seeking to understand their problems. One way to cross into a foreign horizon is simply to go there. Under Macmurray's analysis of interpersonal relations, then, the attorney should perceive himself or herself and the other more fully as persons.

Normally law reform requires a team effort. As Stuart Scheingold explains in *The Politics of Rights* and as many of us know from the practice of law reform, the team may include political activists, social workers, friendly public officials, members of the client community and others attracted to the cause.[13] Law reform, as a team effort, may pursue many routes including for example, academic empirical studies, legislation and litigation. One can manage the team effort, probably haphazardly, so that those various routes are linked and lead from one to the other.

A personalist analysis of law reform should recognize that the team effort, including the coordination of those pursuing many routes to the desired goal, is an example of persons acting together. In the course of the common action one may recognize the intentional participation of others in the common effort, their moral struggle, suffering and joy at overcoming oppression. In the common action one not only understands others more fully as persons but also as friends.

An academic engaged in law reform can integrate that activity with her research, writing and teaching. At times research, particularly empirical research or teaching a seminar related to law reform may lead to recognition of the oppressive practice. That discovery, then, can be related to one's public service activities, perhaps on a legal services board, or as counsel for a legislative committee. After a successful coordination of research, legislation and litigation one can feed that back into further teaching and writing. Students, then, may participate at least vicariously, in the common action and perceive the practice of law as an important means for participating in the great common action of society. Law reform, then, should be high on the academic personalist agenda for the twenty-first century.

Among the personalist tools for analyzing the theory and practice of law reform are concepts such as acting together, horizons, the use of rights and the language of rights as means for hammering on foreign horizons (see chapter 6) and a new concept added in this part which could be called presence. One respects the other and relates to him as a person simply by showing up regularly and agreeing to represent him.

---

13. Stuart Scheingold, The Politics of Rights: Lawyers, Public Policy and Political Change 36 (1974).

Regular presence also can be a means for reforming oppressive practices and a way for the attorney, herself, to cross horizons.

Listening, as well as presence, is an important means for crossing horizons and showing respect for the other. Oppression and loneliness in the face of oppressive practices can be remedied in part simply by having someone pay attention. Careful listening rather than imposing one's own horizon, agenda or problem solving abilities not only shows respect and concern for the person but also may lead to understanding including perhaps the perception that law reform is needed.

Attorneys, at times, fail to listen because they bring to the encounter their horizon as attorneys, or as middle class white persons or as long-term political activists with certain views. For example, an interview in jail between defense counsel and accused may be limited because of the lawyer's perception of his role, his concern for fees or his perception that criminal defendants are often bad people who are probably guilty. Likewise, however, a liberal activist as defense counsel may bring his own horizon to a similar interview. Learning to listen is a skill important from a personalist perspective.

An encounter may be less effective or may fail because one erects barriers to understanding and conversation. While those barriers are related to one's horizon they are actively built in response to a challenge from a foreign horizon which is perceived as placing one's self image at issue. Deliberately cultivating a discipline of listening is a way to avoid erecting barriers.

Faced with the multiple horizons in our pluralist society, some and perhaps all of us may respond by erecting barriers to conversation which strengthen the boundaries of our horizon and fortify our self image. An attorney encountering oppression may need to overcome that response in his own mind. Crossing horizons to respond to oppression may be particularly difficult when others by their efforts at law reform are challenging one's self image. On a national scale, then, to continue conversation in the common action of society may require deliberate and disciplined listening. That listening may be particularly important when those who perceive themselves as oppressed are engaged in organized action to respond to oppression.

One could offer Critical Race Theory as a current example of an organized response to oppression which may challenge the self image of some lawyers.

Critical Race Theory could be described as a movement designed to challenge deep seated racism in the American society by examining the relation between law, the construction and maintenance of social domination, and mainstream America's constructed understanding of racism.

The movement began relatively recently during the 1980s partly in response to the difficulties traditional civil rights lawyers encountered during the 1970s. Professor Derrick Bell who taught at the Harvard Law School during the early 1980s influenced the initial development of Critical Race Theory as did the Critical Legal Studies movement which was then flourishing. When Professor Bell left Harvard and was not replaced by an African-American professor there was a student protest accompanied by a boycott and the creation of an alternative course to replace Bell's teaching on race and the law. Bell's book, *Race and Racism in American Law*[14] "used racial politics rather than the formal structure of legal doctrine as the organizing concept for scholarly study."[15] His course on the same topic "taught legal doctrine from a race conscious viewpoint."[16]

The Critical Legal Studies National Conference in 1987 also was an important moment in the development of Critical Race Theory. The Critical Legal Studies Movement was attractive to black scholars and influential in the creation of Critical Race Theory because of its energy and because it was an ideological movement from the left offering a political and philosophical analysis and deconstruction of law. In 1987, however, the creators of Critical Race Theory discovered their differences with the predominantly white lawyers in the Critical Legal Studies Movement.

One difference was with the Critical Legal Studies Movement's attack on rights. While Critical Race Theorists were prepared to oppose traditional civil rights discourse they recognized the benefits and significance of the civil rights movement. Their position on rights could be summarized as follows:

> "Crits of color agreed to varying degrees with some dimensions of the critique—for instance, that rights discourse was indeterminate. Yet we sharply differed with critics over the normative implications of this observation. To the emerging race crits, rights discourse held a social and transformative value in the con-

---

14. DERRICK BELL, RACE, RACISM, AND AMERICAN LAW (1980).
15. KIMBERLE CRENSHAW ET AL., CRITICAL RACE THEORY, THE KEY WRITINGS THAT FORMED THE MOVEMENT XX (1995).
16. *Id.*

text of racial subordination that transcended the narrower question of whether reliance on rights could alone bring about any determinant results. Race crits realized that the very notion of a subordinate people exercising rights was an important dimension of Black empowerment during the civil rights movement, significant not simply because of the occasional legal victories that were garnered but because of the transformative dimension of African-Americans re-imaging themselves as full rights-bearing citizens within the American political imagination."[17]

The Critical Race Theory movement wants to understand how white supremacy was created in America and maintained. From the Critical Legal Studies Movement its theorists learned how law is the product of social power and in turn produces social power. That insight was a clue to the relation between law and racial power. The goal of the Critical Race Theory movement is to understand that relation and change it.

From that perspective one can argue that the understanding of equal protection in the main stream of American law is racist. The reforms in race relations during the mid-twentieth century served to legitimize American meritocracy. So long as racism is narrowly defined as constituting isolated irrational acts one can exclude fundamental attacks on American institutions and the distribution of power in our society as the product of historic racism. A color-blind interpretation of equal protection is a means, one could argue, for preserving traditional arrangements whose roots are in racist society. The Critical Race Theory movement can be explained as follows as a response to that color-blind but racist understanding of American law:

"The task of Critical Race Theory is to remind its readers how deeply issues of racial ideology and power continue to matter in American life. Questioning regnant visions of racial meaning and racial power, critical race theorists seek to fashion a set of tools for thinking about race that avoids the traps of racial thinking. Critical Race Theory understands that racial power is produced by and experienced within numerous vectors of social life, Critical Theory recognizes, too, that political interventions which overlook the multiple ways in which people of color are situated (and resituated) as communities, sub-communities and individuals will do little to promote effective resistance to, and counter-mobilization against, today's newly empowered right."[18]

---

17. Crenshaw et al., *supra* note 15 at xxiii–xxiv.
18. Crenshaw et al., *supra* note 15 at xxxii.

Critical Race Theory, then, is part of and has benefitted from the gradual recovery of a role for the person in American law. Personalist concepts may be helpful in developing insights from Critical Race Theory and vice versa. During the twenty-first century possibly a scholar could develop and use both personalist and critical race theory. As a major reform movement directed at pervasive oppression in American society Critical Race Theory, or at least conversation with and learning from it, must be on the agenda for personalism during the twenty-first century. Listening and learning should be the beginning of that conversation.

5. Social Science and Law

Empirical studies are and have been important in reforming the law. Perhaps the most dramatic instance is Gunnar Myrdal's *An American Dilemma*,[19] a study of segregation, which was cited by the Court in *Brown v. Board of Education*[20] and was otherwise significant in developing our attention to that most serious oppression. However, small studies also can be seriously helpful. Simply recording and publishing in local newspapers the facts about overcrowding in a jail can be the foundation for change. In my experience, a modestly more disciplined study of imprisonment for debt became a catalyst for law reform.[21] That study was modeled on the work of David Caplovitz, *Consumers in Trouble, A Study of Debtors in Default*[22] which itself became an important instrument in the reform of debt collection and civil procedure.[23]

In earlier chapters impact and interest analysis was described as an important part of judicial decision making method. A judge using his experience, his sophisticated common sense, and his skill at issue spotting should locate the relevant interests and assess the impact of his proposed holding on those interests. The availability of pertinent empirical studies would allow a judge to be more accurate and sophisticated when doing an impact and interest analysis. Legislators reviewing

---

19. GUNNAR MYRDAL ET AL., AN AMERICAN DILEMMA (1964).

20. Brown v. Board of Education, 347 U.S. 483 (1954).

21. Richard M. Alderman, *Imprisonment for Debt: Default Judgments, the Contempt Power, and the Effectiveness of Notice Provisions in the State of New York*, 24 SYR. L. REV. 1217, 1224 (1973).

22. DAVID CAPLOVITZ, CONSUMERS IN TROUBLE, A STUDY OF DEBTORS IN DEFAULT (1974).

23. *See also* DAVID CAPLOVITZ, THE POOR PAY MORE (1965).

an area of law sometimes rely on or will commission empirical studies. In criminal justice, statistics should be particularly helpful. The Bureau of Justice Statistics are voluminous and very helpful.[24]

Roscoe Pound proposed an experimenting society. When a court announces an important holding or a legislature enacts a statute reforming an area of law, a prediction should be made of the impact of that change on relevant interests. Subsequently social scientists should conduct empirical studies to determine what the actual impact was. Informed by those studies legislatures can reassess and again revise the law. Courts from time to time can reconsider their holdings.

As Richard Posner has explained the proposal for an experimenting society has failed and is likely to continue to fail. We simply do not have the necessary empirical studies and it is not reasonable to expect that we will have that information. An increasing number of important and helpful studies will accumulate and from time to time will have a significant impact on judicial or legislative decisions. However, judges, legislators, and lawyers are not trained regularly in the use of social science materials. The pressures of time seriously restrict the ability of judges and legislators to consult empirical studies and at least in regard to legislators one could add the pressures of politics.

Posner recommends that lawyers receive more serious and systematic training in the social sciences. Likewise, the legal academy could more regularly welcome social scientists who wish to understand the arcane ways of the law. Ultimately, social science analysis and studies should be made routinely and regularly available to courts and legislatures.

For personalist theory the experimenting society remains an ideal. A personalist judge or legislator, however, because of his commitment to respect and concern for each person should seek to understand the impact of his decisions on the persons affected by them. Serious use of social science studies and analysis is one of the best means for assessing the effect of judicial and legislative decisions. Social scientists also can assist us in locating, understanding and eliminating oppression. Working towards a more systematic legal use of social science should be high on the personalist agenda for the twenty-first century.

Richard Lempert and Joseph Sanders in their book, *An Invitation to Law and Social Science*, make a fascinating proposal for a new discipline

---

24. The Bureau of Justice Statistics, U.S. Department of Justice, *Bureau of Justice Statistics.*

whose goal would be to develop "an empirically based understanding of all matters pertaining to law and the legal system that can be so understood."[25] They would name the discipline law and social science, rather than sociology of law, and they imagine educating Ph.D's who could develop that specialized body of knowledge. They explain basic aspects of the new discipline as follows:

> "Law and social science is rooted in and grows out of law— related subfields that have long existed in the various social science disciplines. It differs from the subfields because the question it constantly asks is 'What can this...tell us about how law functions in social life?' Other disciplines address their own central questions."[26]

Lempert and Sanders would use multidisciplinary method in doing law and social science and in studies would treat law as a variable. "In this book," they explain, "we are concerned with the essential characteristics of different laws, the features that shape law and the effects that law has on society."[27] One could imagine a program in law and social science for graduate students pursuing a Ph.D. in sociology, political science or economics and simultaneously for L.L.M. candidates or second and third year law students with some undergraduate background in social science.

The most serious obstacle to establishment of such a program is the division of the university into departments and disciplines and the horizons thereby established. Overcoming horizons is a personalist chore and relating social science to a personalist understanding of law would be a task important to scholars attracted by personalist insights.

The Law and Society Association has contributed strongly to overcoming the horizons which divide law and the social sciences as witnessed by its journal, the Law and Society Review. One way to overcome horizons, as noted above regularly, is simply to go to the foreign horizon. Social scientists can study or conduct studies of law. Lawyers who have studied social science can do social science studies of law, perhaps with the assistance of more advanced scholars in the social sciences. The work of Elizabeth Warren and Jay Westbrook, pursue that

---

25. RICHARD LEMPERT AND JOSEPH SANDERS, AN INVITATION TO LAW AND SOCIAL SCIENCE, DESERT, DISPUTES AND DISTRIBUTION 1 (1986).

26. LEMPERT, *supra* note 25 at 1.

27. LEMPERT, *supra* note 25 at 2.

292 · THE PERSONALIST AGENDA

pattern in *As We Forgive Our Debtors* and other studies important to understanding bankruptcy.[28]

My colleague, Richard Schwartz, is a great worker in the field and often offers insights appealing from a personalist perspective. See, for example, his chapter, "Bureaucracy and the Public, Observations and Reflections from Field Research" in D. Rosenbloom and R.D. Schwartz, *Handbook of Regulation and Administrative Law* and more significantly his chapter, "Law and Normative Order" in Leon Lipson and Stanton Wheeler, *Law and The Social Sciences*.[29] Another approach to understanding law in the lives of persons can be found in P. Ewicks and S. Silbey, *The Common Place of Law: Stories From Everyday Life*.[30]

While from a personalist perspective relating law and social science would be beneficial to the future of law, a critical question arises from that conclusion: Did chapter 5 erroneously follow Ronald Dworkin in criticizing Richard Posner because he would seek in his judicial decisions the best consequences, that is, what is best for the future. In analyzing that question some distinctions should be considered. Legislators as opposed to courts should be concerned with the best consequences and indeed with what is best for the future. Empirical studies, and at times, economics can be helpful in understanding the consequences of legislation.

Sometimes law reformers are concerned with what is best for the future. Law reformers also are concerned with oppression and other current aberrations and will offer empirical studies to courts and legislators for the purpose of challenging existing structures. Perhaps removing oppression would be best for the future. From a personalist perspective eliminating oppression and advancing human rights is a compelling goal even if that in some ways will not produce the best results for the future. Law reformers primarily employ empirical studies to call our attention to injustice.

---

28. TERESA SULLIVAN, ELIZABETH WARREN & JAY LAWRENCE WESTBROOK, AS WE FORGIVE OUR DEBTORS, BANKRUPTCY AND CONSUMER DEBT IN AMERICA (1989).

29. DAVID ROSENBLOOM & RICHARD SCHWARTZ, HANDBOOK OF REGULATION AND ADMINISTRATIVE LAW (1994); LEON LIPSON AND STANTON WHEELER, LAW AND THE SOCIAL SCIENCES 63–107 (1986).

30. PATRICIA EWICKS AND SUSAN SILBEY, THE COMMON PLACE OF LAW: STORIES FROM EVERYDAY LIFE (1998).

A personalist judge as argued in earlier chapters should perceive his role as settling disputes in accord with our national ideals and an appropriate interpretation of law. To settle disputes in a manner which respects persons he should employ impact and interest analysis. His balancing of interests and his holding, hopefully, will produce a rule which will resolve the dispute for some period of time. To do that may require an assessment of future consequences. Those consequences, however, are not the focus of the judge's effort. Rather his object is settlement of the dispute. Like the law reformer, the personalist judge is concerned with justice and the elimination of oppression. Success in that effort may or may not have the best consequences for the future. The judge's contribution to the future is to preserve the rule of law and our judicial system by settling disputes appropriately. Contrary to Dworkin, impact and interest analysis accompanied by empirical studies is important in doing justice for real persons in the multiple horizons of our pluralist society.

6. Personalist Theory and Reform of Particular Legal Fields

During the twenty-first century personalist theory can provide a basis for rethinking particular fields of law. In part seven, "Rethinking Criminal Justice," by way of illustration, a brief overview of a personalist theory of criminal justice will be offered. The personalist understanding of the common good and the role of the primary social goods can serve as a foundation for a theoretical analysis of particular legal fields.

In personalist theory society is a common action of persons acting together. Each individual has a right to participate in society. As described in chapters 3, 4, and 5 the primary social goods are those important or necessary for participation in any society or this society. To deny a person an appropriate share of the primary social goods is contrary to the personalist commitment to afford each person deep respect and concern. That denial also is contrary to the common good. Actions contrary to the common good are those which tend to seriously hinder the common action or prevent any person from participating in society. In chapter 5 there was a discussion of the personalist commitments both to the common good of all persons and to each person. Since both commitments are strong it is not appropriate to allow one to prevail over the other. Rather we must seek proper means for serving both.

In chapters 3, 4, and 5 the personalist theory of the common good became the basis for a theory of human rights which in turn was helpful in developing a theory for constitutional interpretation. In other legal fields, such as criminal justice and bankruptcy, the theory of the common good, likewise, can provide a foundation for theoretical analysis. While the theory of a particular field would have the theory of the common good as a foundation, the theories of human rights or constitutional interpretation would not be directly relevant. For example, a theory of bankruptcy law would not be deduced from the theory of human rights.

To actually reform a field of law, in contrast to developing a new theory, may require law reform litigation or legislation. As a prelude one may have to deconstruct old theories and old horizons. Crossing horizons by empirical studies may be helpful in understanding oppression, in locating the interests which are affected by established law, and in convincing others to recognize those interests and the humanity of those adversely impacted by current law. Social science analysis may be helpful in framing the new theory and arguing for it. A new theory should balance appropriately the common good and the competing interests discovered by empirical studies and other means for crossing horizons.

One can begin the process of reform, however, by preliminarily sketching a personalist theory of the particular field. In part seven a preliminary sketch will be presented of a personalist theory for criminal justice.

In criminal justice, personalist theory provides a basis for critical analysis and rethinking fundamental issues. In contrast, in some other fields, for example, bankruptcy law, personalist theory may provide a basis for choice between competing views and some tools for understanding and conducting the struggle for law reform. That struggle is distinctively relevant in criminal justice.

7. Rethinking Criminal Justice

Traditionally the goals for criminal punishment are divided into the Kantian goal, retribution, and the Utilitarian or crime control goals, deterrence, general and special, rehabilitation and incapacitation. Immanuel Kant, "argued that a criminal should not be punished for his own good or the good of society, but simply because he deserved punishment."[31] In contrast, classic Utilitarian theory would justify punishment because it advances the greater good of the greater number or the greater average utility. Normally, the greater good of society is achieved by controlling crime.

Modern theories of criminal justice, striving for a more sophisticated analysis, tend to combine the goals of criminal punishment. For example, in *The Limits of the Criminal Sanction*, Herbert Packer while offering a Utilitarian theory found a role for retribution or desert as a desirable check on the use of criminal punishment.[32] In his integrated theory Packer proposed two basic principles for the justification of punishment. First, "It is a necessary but not a sufficient condition for punishment that it is designed to prevent the commission of offenses." Second, "It is a necessary but not a sufficient condition of punishment that the person on whom it is imposed is found to have committed an offense under circumstances that permit his conduct to be characterized as blameworthy."[33]

H.L.A. Hart in *Punishment and Responsibility* offered a Utilitarian argument for a similar but slightly different combination of retribution with the crime control goals.[34] Punishment as an institution, Hart contends, should have the purpose of crime control. However, an individual person normally should be punished only if he deserves it. Restricting punishment to those who deserve it, Hart argues, normally serves the greater good because that course encourages a general feeling of security among the law abiding persons in society who are protected against arbitrary punishment. Hart and Packer treat desert as a limitation on punishment rather than a reason for punishing.

Norval Morris who is influenced by Kantian thought would impose punishment because it is deserved. However, he offers a series of principles in *The Future of Imprisonment* to guide decisions to imprison.[35] If a punishment is deserved, then, it may be imposed if a "lesser punishment would depreciate the seriousness of the crime," a principle related to retribution, or if "imprisonment of some who have done what this

---

31. Samuel J.M. Donnelly, *The Goals of Criminal Punishment: A Rawlsian Theory (Ultimately Grounded in Multiple Views Concerned with Human Dignity,* 41 Syr. L. Rev. 741 (1990).
32. Herbert Packer, The Limits of The Criminal Sanction 62 (1968).
33. *Id.*
34. H.L.A. Hart, Punishment and Responsibility 173–83 (1968).
35. Norval Morris, The Future of Imprisonment 59–60 (1974).

criminal did is necessary to achieve socially justified deterrent purposes", a crime control goal.[36]

John Rawls in his *Theory of Justice* at the third stage offers a theory of criminal responsibility.[37] Rawls is strongly influenced by Kantian thought. In that tradition he argues that a person who commits a bad act incurs a responsibility to repair the fabric of society which was impaired by his crime. He repairs society by subjecting himself to incapacitation, rehabilitation or the punishment necessary to deter himself and others from continuing to follow his bad example. If punishment would not repair the fabric of society then it should not be imposed.

My article on "The Goals of Criminal Punishment" was an earlier effort to find a person centered theory of criminal justice by developing Rawls' theory of criminal responsibility.[38] Studying Rawls was a fruitful source of insights. However, it is somewhat unwieldy to construct subordinate principles of criminal justice acceptable to the contracting parties in the Original Position.

A personalist theory of criminal justice would be grounded in the commitment to afford each person deep respect and concern and in the personalist theory of the common good. As Justice Brennan observed: "even the vilest criminal remains a human being possessed of common human dignity."[39] Under the personalist theory of the common good, one should not eliminate anyone from the common action, that is, one should not deprive a person totally of the primary social goods necessary to participate in society. Crime can deprive a person of the primary social goods. The accumulation of criminal activity can inhibit the common action and reduce all of our shares of the primary social goods. Government, then, has a duty to develop and maintain institutions of criminal justice designed to control crime and to protect each person's and all persons' share of the primary social goods.

As in Utilitarian thought, then, the personalist reason for having institutions of criminal justice and for imposing criminal punishment is to control crime. Deterrence, general and special, at least in theory, is a prime goal of criminal punishment. Again at least in theory rehabilitation is appropriate for the purpose of reducing a person's criminal ac-

---

36. MORRIS, *supra* note 35 at 60.
37. JOHN RAWLS, THEORY OF JUSTICE at 241 (1971).
38. Donnelly, *supra* note 31 at 741.
39. *Gregg*, 428 U.S. at 230.

tivity. Some persons need to be incapacitated so they will not continue their criminal careers.

Nevertheless, punishment, in personalist theory should not be imposed on a person unless he deserves it. Developing H.L.A. Hart's analysis but transforming it to conform to personalist theory, imposing punishment for crime control purposes such as general deterrence on those who do not deserve it is an unjustified deprivation of that person's primary social goods and right to participate in society. Unjustified punishment becomes an arbitrary threat to everyone in society, increases their feelings of insecurity, and inhibits the common action, our interaction in society. Punishment without desert, then, in personalist theory would be contrary both to the commitment to respect and concern for each person and to the common good.

Nevertheless, contrary to Kantian theory, punishment should not be imposed on the sole ground that a person deserves it. Rather desert should be a check on punishment imposed to advance the common good by controlling crime. Controlling crime increases everyone's share of the primary social goods. Punishing only because the defendant deserves it, however, is not designed to advance the common good. Punishment without a crime control goal deprives the individual who is convicted of a substantial share of the primary social goods without any advantage for society, without enhancing anyone else's share of the primary social goods. Under personalist theory punishment without a crime control goal, then, is not permissible.

Following Packer, then, personalist theory would agree that there should be an integrated theory of criminal justice. Contrary to Utilitarian theory, however, the new principles for criminal punishment would not be grounded in the greater good of the greater number. Rather the integrated theory would be grounded in the personalist commitment to respect and concern for each person and all persons. The two basic principles of that theory, then, would be:

> "1. Criminal punishment is permitted only if it is demonstrated that it serves the goal of crime control;
>
> 2. Criminal punishment is permitted only if it is demonstrated that the person on whom it is imposed deserves that punishment."[40]

---

40. Donnelly, *supra* note 31 at 770.

Personalist theory, then, offers a set of integrated principles for criminal punishment which relate the crime control goals to the common good and the commitment to respect and concern for each person. Pursuit of the crime control goals is checked by the requirement that punishment is deserved. In the abstract, then, deterrence, general and special, rehabilitation and incapacitation apparently are appropriate goals for criminal punishment.

In personalist theory, however, one should inquire regarding the actual impact on crime control and on the persons whose interests are affected by punishment for the purposes of deterrence, rehabilitation and incapacitation. Social science studies and analysis can be helpful in crossing horizons from abstract theory to an understanding of the impact of criminal punishment. To develop a series of subordinate principles, then, a more particular examination of each of the crime control goals should follow.

General deterrence is a threat made to everyone to discourage them from committing crime. Special deterrence in contrast is a threat made to an individual. As Frederick Zimring and Gordon Hawkins point out in their book, *Deterrence — The Legal Threat of Crime Control*, a threat to be effective must be communicated.[41] As in all failures to communicate, problems may be located on the side of the speaker or that of the hearer of the threat. In our society most people do not know the details of our criminal laws. Rather they have a sense that certain acts are wrong and probably will be punished. Even a new law student must be taught the definition of crimes. Many graduate from law school without any clear knowledge of the sentences related to crimes. One can conclude that our penal codes with their careful definitions and our tightly controlled sentencing guidelines have minimal deterrent impact because they are not effectively communicated. Rather one must seek deterrence from the simple existence of the criminal justice system. In general the criminal justice system generally deters.

The problem of predicting a deterrent impact from crime control measures becomes more complex when one examines the hearer of the threat. Zimring and Hawkins offer a long list of various circumstances in which the threat may or may not be heard. For example, persons with aggressive or non-aggressive personalities would hear and respond to a threat differently.

---

41. FRANKLIN ZIMRING AND GORDON HAWKINS, DETERRENCE — THE LEGAL THREAT OF CRIME CONTROL (1973).

Historically our society has a tendency to escalate sentences arguably for the sake of deterring crime. Given the problems of predicting deterrent impact, however, the use of severe sentences for the purpose of deterrence may not make sense. Probably deterrence is more likely if we improve the communication of the threat, and the consistency and likelihood of the punishment. One should note that whatever the necessity or good sense of plea bargaining, that practice probably destroys the deterrent impact of any detailed provisions in the penal code regarding the definition of crimes or the required sentences. There remains, however, the amorphous general deterrent effect from the existence of a criminal justice system.

Escalation of sentences, then, probably produces at best only modest deterrent impact while significantly depriving a prisoner of primary social goods. In personalist theory the use of increasingly long sentences would be a questionable practice. Rather one might consider a subordinate principle of criminal justice such as:

"3. As the punishment increases in severity, the justification for the punishment for the reasons set forth [above] in 1 and 2 must be more serious and more rigorously demonstrated."[42]

For example, if one argues for long sentences for the crime control purpose of deterrence, that serious deprivation of an individual's primary social goods should be rigorously shown to actually promote deterrence. Otherwise the use of long sentences appears contrary to human dignity.

Rehabilitation, theoretically, is a desirable means for achieving crime control. In Utilitarian thought rehabilitation is a crime control goal because, as Herbert Packer puts it, we reform the criminal "so that he will cease to offend."[43] In personalist thought that benefit to the common good is worthwhile. However, the respect apparently afforded to the individual by making him a better person also is appealing. Nevertheless, that inclination to do good to the individual by changing him may be deeply contrary to human dignity. Herbert Packer similarly points out the anti-human aspects of the behaviorist desire to modify human behavior. Rehabilitation was an important goal for our prison system when it was first established. The quaint notion was that a criminal could be rehabilitated by isolating him in a single cell, compelling si-

42. Donnelly, *supra* note 31 at 790.
43. PACKER, *supra* note 32 at 53.

lence, providing a Bible, and allowing him to mediate on his sins. Rehabilitation, of course, takes time. That goal, then, was an initial reason for long sentences. Herbert Packer explains that the principal problem with rehabilitation is that we do not know how to do it. Norval Morris who wants to rehabilitate the rehabilitative ideal nevertheless describes rehabilitation as a "noble lie" and would not permit a sentence to prison for the sake of rehabilitation.

One, then, could add a further set of principles regarding rehabilitation to the personalist theory of criminal justice:

    "4. Sentencing a person convicted of crime to prison, or determining the length of his sentence for the purpose of rehabilitation, is unjust in the present state of our knowledge and prisons;

    5. Sentencing a person convicted of crime to prison without providing an opportunity and programs for rehabilitation is unjust and contrary to human dignity."[44]

    6. Nevertheless choosing a less severe punishment or an alternative to incarceration for the purpose of rehabilitation is permissible."

The juxtaposition of subordinate principles 4 and 5 addresses a modern dilemma: if we do not know how to rehabilitate then why have costly and unpopular rehabilitation programs in our prisons. Norval Morris comments that a prison without rehabilitation programs would be more difficult to administer humanely. He also urges experimentation to discover better ways to rehabilitate. In personalist theory one should not deprive a person of the primary social goods beyond the necessary requirements for the protection of others. A prisoner should have the opportunity for rehabilitation so that he can rejoin the common action of society. As Norval Morris explains, an opportunity to voluntarily choose rehabilitation may be successful. It is the coercive nature of current rehabilitation which is counter productive. Normally one changes only if one is willing to change.

Incapacitation can provide a convenient substitute rationalization as a justification for long prison terms. If rehabilitation in current understanding is a "noble lie," then, criminals need to be excluded from society for long periods of time to protect others from their propensities to crime. Norval Morris argues, however, that we have only a modest abil-

---

44. Donnelly, *supra* note 31 at 790.

ity to predict future dangerousness. Psychiatrists or criminologists predicting future violent crime will have both false positives and false negatives. In his principles governing decisions to imprison, Morris states that: "Prediction of future criminality is an unjust basis for determining that the convicted criminal should be imprisoned."[45] Michael Sherman and Gordon Hawkins in their book, *Imprisonment in America* disagree modestly with Morris' analysis.[46] Some repetitive criminals, particularly those who are repetitively violent, require incapacitation. The largest benefit to society of incapacitation, according to Sherman and Hawkins, occurs during the first year. They contend, "the first year of a prison sentence prevents far more crimes than the tenth year."[47] Explaining the proper use of society's scarce resource of imprisonment, they argue:

"How long is long enough to maximize the incapacitative gains and yet not exceed the desert limit? We suggest five years, as a maximum. This is controversial: to many on the right there is something very satisfying about the broad option of throwing the key away, and on the left we have seen an acceptance in some quarters for time served as long as thirty years. But we need not repeat the costs in inefficient incapacitation, violations of fairness, and excessive prison populations and budgets. The satisfaction that comes from the option of throwing the key away or even the reality of it in a small number of cases is empty. It makes harder, not easier, the use of prison as it should be used: to limit directly the amount of crime we would otherwise have."[48]

Considering then an appropriate administration of our scarce crime control resources and our difficulties in predicting future dangerousness we can frame an additional subordinate principle of criminal justice. Ultimately the personalist analysis of incapacitation would rest on concern for the common good, that is, the proper use of scarce resources to control crime, and respect and concern for the criminal who may be incarcerated well beyond what he deserves or what is needed to protect society. A principle reflecting these considerations would be:

45. MORRIS, *supra* note 35 at 62–73.

46. MICHAEL SHERMAN AND GORDON HAWKINS, IMPRISONMENT IN AMERICA 106, 107 (1981).

47. SHERMAN AND HAWKINS, *supra* note 46 at 110.

48. *Id.*

"7. Despite statistical predictions of recidivism, a person should be imprisoned for no longer than he deserves for the last crime committed, and normally for no longer than is required minimally for general and special deterrence; a person who has demonstrated an inclination to violent crime may be incarcerated for the minimum period necessary for age and maturity to check his violent propensities provided that period does not exceed the time normally believed to be deserved for the last crime he has committed."[49]

Framing a personalist theory of criminal justice begins with a critical analysis of the goals of criminal punishment using basic personalist theory. One should then examine the functioning of those goals in modern circumstances and with the aid of social science and criminology. From that process one may develop a series of subordinate principles of criminal justice examples of which were just offered. The next step is to use those principles and basic personalist theory to critique the institutions of criminal justice. In the following paragraphs, as examples, a brief analysis will be offered of capital punishment and then of our sentencing practices, using the federal sentencing guidelines as an exemplary target.

Constitutional interpretation as applied to capital punishment was discussed in chapter 4. Here, a critical analysis should be offered of the institution of capital punishment. The goals of rehabilitation and special deterrence are not relevant when discussing the death penalty. Under personalist theory retribution standing alone is not a justifiable purpose for imposing criminal punishment. One cannot totally remove a person from participation in society without an argument that his loss of primary social goods will protect others and their share of those goods. More succinctly the law should not kill one person unless it will protect the lives of others. Retribution or rather desert in the personalist theory of criminal justice is a condition for justified punishment rather that a reason for imposing punishment.

General deterrence and incapacitation conceivably could be appropriate goals properly served by the death penalty. As a punishment escalates in severity, under personalist principles, the more rigorous must be the demonstration that it serves appropriate goals of criminal punishment. For example, a statistical demonstration that capital punishment produces a seriously significant deterrent impact would be part of

---

49. Donnelly, *supra note* 31 at 790–91.

such a rigorous showing. However, that demonstration at the moment cannot be offered probably because capital punishment does not have greater marginal deterrent effect than life imprisonment. Given our inability to predict soundly future dangerousness, execution for the purpose of incapacitation would be quite literally overkill. Capital punishment, then, in modern America with our present state of knowledge cannot be justified under personalist theory by any of the goals of criminal punishment.

Sentencing statutes can be understood as plans for the appropriate use of our prisons. Long sentences have been a characteristic American practice since the nineteenth century. Sherman and Hawkins in *Imprisonment in America* offer an explanation.[50] Serving time became a prominent aspect of criminal punishment when the prison was substituted for the physical punishments. Whipping or branding a person, for example, is not a lengthy process. Rehabilitation, however, normally requires time. Sentencing practices that equate time with punishment, then, became part of our penal system with the advent of the modern prison.

Rehabilitation, according to Sherman and Hawkins, was the initial foundation in America for long sentences. Later rehabilitation became a basis for choosing indeterminate rather than fixed sentences. Sentencing a criminal to five to fifteen years rather than a fixed sentence of seven years would allow the parole board, after the minimum sentence of five years was served, to examine the prisoner periodically to determine whether he was sufficiently rehabilitated to be released.

After an initial reluctance to accept the abandonment of physical punishments, according to Sherman and Hawkins, a general enthusiasm developed in America for the new prison system. Even those who favored severe punishments began to recognize the advantages, from their perspective, of imprisonment for long periods of time. Reformers continued to support prisons and long sentences in contrast to physical punishment as a promising means for rehabilitating prisoners.

The current crisis in rehabilitation theory has eliminated the consensus in favor of long sentences and has removed the rehabilitative rationalization for indeterminate sentences. If prisons do not rehabilitate then it does not make sense to have a parole board periodically review a prisoner to determine whether he is sufficiently rehabilitated to release.

---

50. SHERMAN AND HAWKINS, *supra* note 46 at 49–52.

A modern reform in sentencing, adopted by the federal sentencing guidelines, is to eliminate indeterminate sentences and substitute fixed sentences imposed by the court subject to administrative or legislatively adopted sentencing guidelines. A sentencing commission, such as the federal sentencing commission, usually reviews present sentencing practices and restates those practices in uniform terms and in the form of recommended fixed sentences rather than the previously used indeterminate sentences. Judges, then, are required to follow the sentencing guidelines unless they justify departure from those guidelines in a written opinion. A decision to depart from the guidelines can be reviewed in an appellate court.

The federal sentencing guidelines are accompanied by a table indicating appropriate sentencing. Across the top of the table are criminal history categories, I, II, etc. Down the far left column of the table are levels of crime numbered one to more than forty. The intersection of the criminal history categories and the levels of crime are graphically presented by a large number of small boxes, over a hundred, which contain the recommended sentences stated in months for a defendant who falls in the particular intersection or box.[51]

The federal sentencing commission acknowledges that this is a restatement rather than a reconsideration of previous sentencing practices. The argument against reassessing the appropriate goals for punishment and whether the sentencing practices serve those goals is that in the present state of disagreement about those goals reform is possible only in the form of a restatement of past practices. The inevitable result of that process, however, is to continue past mistakes and to preserve unjustifiable past sentencing practices. For example, we will continue to use the long sentences originally supported by the now obsolete vision that prisons rehabilitate.

Under a personalist analysis our practice of imposing long sentences preserved in the federal sentencing guidelines generally is unjustifiable by the goals of criminal punishment. Some long sentences such as those for the higher degrees of homicide are justifiable. While many would support long sentences for reasons of retribution even if those sentences do not serve a crime control goal, that practice is not permissible under the integrated personalist principles of criminal justice. Given the com-

---

51. United States Sentencing Commission, FEDERAL SENTENCING GUIDELINES MANUAL (West 1999).

plexity of the sentencing guidelines normally a lawyer is required to decipher them. Unless, lawyers contrary to the Canons of Ethics are advising criminals concerning proposed crimes, the particular sentences set forth in the guidelines are not sufficiently communicated to serve the purpose of general deterrence. In any event, because the Sentencing Commission decided not to reform plea-bargaining only a general amorphous deterrent effect remains. An obsolete policy of sentencing to long terms for the sake of rehabilitation remains as the historical but not presently relevant basis for the long sentences. One could substitute an incapacitation rationalization but that rests on a confidence that we can predict future dangerousness that is not supportable. Probably short sentences in most instances more effectively relate the goals of incapacitation to our scarce crime control resources.

With the demise of the rehabilitation rationalization, it makes sense to conclude that indeterminate sentencing is obsolete and to substitute fixed sentencing. Sentencing commissions which will develop sentencing guidelines is an effective strategy. However, simply restating past practices preserves the mistakes of the past and the oppression which resulted. Refusing to examine the goals served by our prisons and our sentencing practices is a deliberate choice of mindlessness.

The result of obsolete sentencing practices and the mindlessness of our criminal justice system is that our prison population continually rises, our sentences are the longest in the world and our prisons are overcrowded. In personalist theory a substantial number of persons are deprived of substantial primary social goods and are barred from full participation in society beyond what is required for crime reduction. For reasons tangential to criminal justice large portions of those imprisoned come from minorities in our society. A further impact of our mindlessness in criminal justice is the oppression of minority communities. A personalist objective should be to remove that oppression.

Theoretical analysis, however, is only the beginning of law reform. The reform of capital punishment, prisons and sentencing plainly will be a long process which will proceed case by case, prison by prison, and state by state. Laborers in the field of capital punishment include Anthony Amsterdam, David Baldus, Barry Scheck and Sister Helen Prejan who bring their different resources, skills and methods to the task.

Filling out and further or differently developing this brief theoretical analysis arguably, however, is a contribution to improving our law during the twenty-first century despite the mindlessness of the federal sentencing commission.

8. Conclusion

During the twenty first century there will be a rich array of possibilities for developing personalist insights and theory. As the great quarrel over method continues personalist thinkers can participate in that discussion vigorously while gathering new insights which can contribute to the construction and reconstruction of method. One can develop personalist theory as our understanding of human persons grows and as new insights into method emerge. In a number of particular fields of law personalist theory can contribute to a rethinking of law and critical analysis of institutions. The brief sketch in the last part of rethinking criminal justice provides a potential pattern which is applicable to some but not all fields.

Because personalism perceives law as an activity one also can develop theories of the great profession which we practice and its various phases. Action in removing oppressive structures and in conducting other law reform would be an appropriate response to personalist insights and commitments. Representing persons and growing in one's understanding of life and law case by case and person by person also is an appropriate application of personalist insights.

Concluding Postscript

The culture of American law has roots at least 800 years in the past. The names of great judges echo down the ages, Henri d'Bracton, Fortesque, Coke, Mansfield, Marshall, Story, Holmes, Brandeis, Cardozo, Warren, Brennan. Our methods for judicial decision making have evolved over the generations in multiple layers. Early nineteenth century American judges inherited the common law tradition which had periodically been transformed in previous ages. In the mid and late nineteenth century Langdell, Holmes and others substantially recreated the common law, restructuring it around rules and principles. Langdell and others then favored a decision making style which tended to resemble a closed logical system. In the Supreme Court during the late nineteenth and early twentieth century judicial decision making style suffered through a parallel dark period. The vision of law which emerged from that era was centered on language, rule, and system. Beginning with Holmes' challenge to that understanding of law we have gradually, step by step and in multiple versions, recovered a vision of law in which persons, those who make law and adjudicate cases and those affected by law, are perceived as central to understanding judicial method and legal theory. In the 1930s, 40s and 50s courts and scholars began to recapture what Karl Llewellyn called the grand style of judicial decision making. In the late twentieth century as the great quarrel over method has continued judicial methods have proliferated.

Because our discussions and creation of method are in the common law tradition most have a family resemblance. Our inherited decision making styles build on the contributions from the past beginning with the classic precedent oriented decision making of the common law. Our current methods are influenced strongly by the Langdellian restructuring and by the pragmatic instrumentalist rebellion.

Since Holmes legal theories also have proliferated. Pragmatic instrumentalist thought had a dominant role in the development of American theory during the twentieth century and contributed some high moments in the recovery of a role for the person. In the last quarter of the twentieth century with the advent of critical legal studies, feminist jurisprudence, and critical race theory the growth of our insights concerning the relation between persons and law accelerated. The idealism of Ronald Dworkin represents another high moment in the recovery of a role for the person in law. In the twenty-first century, according to the argument in this book, the next step should be to develop an explicit person centered jurisprudence.

The purpose of this book is to construct a person centered jurisprudence and judicial decision making method and to argue for their legitimacy. Drawing on insights from the European personalist tradition as exemplified by John Macmurray joined with a critical analysis of method the theory and method offered here was constructed from those insights, from the common law tradition and from the contributions by Dworkin, the pragmatic instrumentalists and some post modern thought.

Legitimacy is a contested concept which has multiple layers of meaning. Theories of justification overlap with competing understandings of legitimacy. Lon Fuller offered an important argument when he contended that we should examine the conditions which make acceptance of law possible. The argument in this book is that a judicial method grounded in a deep respect and concern for persons and an effort to understand their circumstances and interests will enhance the acceptability and hence the legitimacy of law. Methods which overlook one aspect or another of the human person suffer legitimacy costs.

Arguably the personalist method and interpretation of law proposed here is legitimate for a series of reasons. Both the judicial decision making method and the interpretation of American law are constructed from and bear a family resemblance to the common law tradition and the major twentieth century theories of our law. Both interpret and apply not only our traditions but American ideals when developing and understanding our law. Because the personalist judicial method is grounded in deep respect and concern for each person and all persons and is committed to the effort to understand persons, their interests and circumstances, those using it normally should make decisions and offer reasons which enhance the acceptability of law. At times the decisions of personalist judges should have ultimate legitimacy, that is, the capacity of appealing to all persons, at all times.

Because personalist judges and thinkers should recognize their own limited knowledge and understanding and should engage in conversation with our changing law and learn from the theories offered from time to time, personalist theory should change and develop creatively during the twenty-first century. For that reason personalism as method and theory has the capacity of continuing to enhance the legitimacy of our law by relating to our changing society and the newly discovered needs and circumstances of persons.

By engaging in a conversation with pragmatism, Dworkian idealism, neo-Kantian thought, natural law theory, critical legal studies, feminism, critical race theory, and yet newer understandings of law, personalist theory offers the possibility for a rich creative development during the twenty-first century. That development could consist of further construction of jurisprudential theory and judicial method or the critical rethinking and reform of particular fields of law. Arguably as specific reforms are proposed or new theories are constructed the critical test should be whether they can be grounded in respect and concern for each person and all persons. Regularly an inquiry should be made into the impact of law, new theories and proposals for reform on the interests of persons in the multiple horizons of our pluralist society.

Ultimately respect and concern for persons and an effort to understand their needs and circumstances is a reasonable, supportable and legitimate choice which can be used to construct and reconstruct an interpretation of law, a method for judicial decision making and a theory of rights. This book is offered as a contribution to that effort.

Index

A Matter of Interpretation (Scalia), 31,
51, 125–126, 153–155, 157,
159–160, 162, 164, 170, 172, 191
A Theory of Justice (Rawls), 8, 87,
100–101, 199, 215, 241, 274, 296
Ackerman, Bruce, 120, 152, 165–167
acting together, 8, 18, 74–77, 101,
111, 171, 221, 223, 234, 282, 285,
293
action, 8–10, 16–20, 71, 74–79,
94–97, 99–104, 106–108, 112,
117–118, 121–123, 130–132, 162,
170–171, 216, 221–224, 232, 234,
236, 240, 248, 251–252, 254–255,
257, 272–273, 281–283, 285–286,
293, 296–297, 300, 306
activity, 3–4, 14, 19, 27–29, 76, 78,
104, 248, 250–252, 254–255, 264,
273, 275, 280, 283, 285, 306
Alderman, Richard, 289
*American Jurisprudence Through Eng-
lish Eyes: The Nightmare and the
Noble Dream* (Hart), 273
American pragmatists, 3, 28, 37, 79
An American Dilemma (Myrdal), 289
An Invitation to Law and Social Science
(Lempert, Sanders), 290–291
Anglo-American jurisprudence, 4, 14,
23, 25, 263
anti-rights rhetoric, 259–260, 263
Aristotle, 236
art of interpretation, 14, 23, 249–251
As We Forgive Our Debtors (Sullivan,
Warren, Westbrook), 292
Austin, John, 3, 62

authority, 241, 244–246
Bell, Derrick, 287
Bentham, Jeremy, 210–211
Between Facts and Norms (Habermas),
23, 243–244
Bill of Rights, 18, 121–122, 124–128,
130, 155–156, 158, 171–172, 176,
191–192, 226, 250
Blackmun, Justice, 174, 176, 188–191,
201
Bork, Judge, 31, 157–160, 172, 174
Bowers v. Hardwick, 171–176
Brennan, William, 6, 9–10, 117, 119,
128–129, 131–136, 147, 150,
180–181, 186, 188–191, 195, 201,
242, 247, 265, 282, 296, 307
Breughel, 247, 272
*Brown v. Board of Education of Topeka,
Kansas*, 10, 31, 78, 90, 98, 109,
118, 137, 144–152, 157, 166, 242,
257–259, 262, 270–271, 289
Bureau of Justice Statistics, 290
Burger Court, 32, 126, 161
Callins v. Collins, 190–191
capital punishment, 129, 135,
154–155, 161, 188–192, 194–195,
201, 242, 284, 302–303, 305
Caplovitz, David, 289
Casner, A. James, 275, 280
common action, 8–9, 17–20, 74,
101–102, 106–108, 117, 121,
130–132, 162, 170–171, 221–222,
234, 236, 240, 252, 257, 272,
282–283, 285–286, 293, 296–297,
300

common good, 8–9, 17–20, 74,
98–103, 106–107, 171, 197, 199,
207–209, 211, 220–225, 227,
282–283, 293–294, 296–299, 301
common law method, 6–7, 11–12, 17,
21–22, 25–27, 32, 34, 40–41,
43–45, 73, 96–97, 111–112, 115,
163–164, 167, 206–207, 209, 249,
273, 275, 278, 307–308
common law tradition, 5–6, 8, 17,
21–23, 25–70, 72, 78–79, 81,
87–88, 90, 92, 96–97, 111–112,
115, 136, 150, 197, 206–207, 278,
307–308
common sense method, 7, 11–12, 73,
94–96, 209, 228–230, 232,
249–250, 289
communication, 75–76, 243–244,
248, 250, 270, 299
competing conceptualizations, 127
consequences, 205, 219–220, 237,
246, 292–293
conservative theories of constitutional
interpretation, 116, 118, 126,
153–161
constitutional interpretation, 4–5,
9–10, 18, 20–22, 26, 32, 70, 74,
88, 103, 110–111, 113, 115–196,
201, 209–211, 216, 222, 250, 275,
294, 302
constitutional rights, 12, 18, 31–32,
38–39, 74, 103, 108, 111, 113,
122–123, 125–126, 130–136,
143–144, 153, 156, 160, 164, 168,
171–172, 174, 189, 192, 195–198,
209–210, 216, 219, 222, 257, 259,
294
construct, 5, 8, 16, 22–23, 51, 59, 70,
95, 112, 131, 151, 165, 195,
197–198, 222, 273, 275, 308–309
Consumers in Trouble, A Study of
Debtors in Default (Caplovitz), 289
contested concept, 105, 169, 175, 201,
256, 308
conversation, 4–5, 8, 14–16, 21, 25,
28, 37, 40, 46, 52, 54, 59, 71–72,
78, 81, 87, 96–97, 103–107,
111–113, 116, 119–120, 122–123,
131, 136–137, 169–171, 173, 180,

190–191, 195–197, 201,
226–227, 238, 242, 248, 250, 252,
255, 263–264, 270–272,
274–280, 286, 289, 309
conversation across horizons, 106,
112, 131, 170, 248, 270–271
cricket, 255
crime control, 189, 294–299, 301,
304–305
criminal justice, 15–16, 19–20, 147,
276, 279, 290, 293–302, 304–306
criminal law, 15, 245, 282, 284, 290,
293–294
criminal punishment, 20, 188, 194,
294–299, 302–304
critical analysis of method, 73, 76, 83,
112, 308
critical legal studies, 4, 15, 33, 35,
82–83, 86, 110, 259–260, 279,
287–288, 308–309
critical phenomenology, 34, 36, 65,
72, 93, 259, 266
critical race theory, 15, 279, 286–289,
308–309
Critical Legal Studies Movement, 4,
15, 33, 35, 82–83, 86, 110,
259–260, 279, 287–288
Critical Race Theory, The Key Writings
That Formed the Movement
(Crenshaw), 287
critique of method, 7, 10, 15–17, 21,
27, 31, 34, 73, 83, 94, 112, 228,
233, 278
crits, 82, 110–111, 259–260, 263,
287–288
crossing horizons, 8–9, 12, 15–17, 60,
72–74, 83, 85–87, 89, 91, 93,
95–98, 103–104, 106–107, 110,
112, 118, 122, 131, 151, 167,
169–170, 224, 241, 259, 271,
279–280, 286, 294, 298
cruel and unusual punishment,
133–134, 136, 155–156, 171,
187–189, 191–192, 195
Cruzan v. Missouri Department of
Health, 164, 177, 182, 184
Dead Man Walking (Prejean), 238
Definition and Theory in Jurisprudence
(Hart), 28, 109, 253, 255, 264

deliberating society, 9–10, 116–117, 123–124, 202–203

deliberation, 9, 58, 64, 116–118, 123–126, 129–130, 147, 156, 160, 162, 165, 167–170, 172–173, 175, 182, 191, 193–195, 202–203, 206, 208, 226, 239, 243, 263

Democracy and the Problem of Free Speech (Sunstein), 202–203, 245

Descartes, Rene, 75, 233

desert, 291, 295, 297, 301–302

destabilization rights, 260

deterrence, 188–189, 194, 294, 296–299, 302, 305

Deterrence—The Legal Threat of Crime Control (Zimring, Hawkins), 298

dispute settlement, 6, 8–10, 12, 17, 25, 27, 45, 49, 51, 53, 57, 60–65, 67–69, 95, 97, 104, 115–117, 121, 151, 167–168, 170, 187, 201, 203, 205–206, 208–209, 223, 237, 244, 270, 280, 293

Dorf, Michael, 162–163

Douglas, William, 143–144

Dworkian idealism, 9–10, 17, 21, 309

Dworkian method, 9, 17, 21, 27, 34, 40, 69, 81, 83, 96–97

Dworkin, Ronald, 4, 6–7, 12–13, 15, 17, 21, 23, 26–27, 30–33, 35–40, 43–46, 49, 51, 54–70, 72–73, 75–77, 80–83, 85–88, 99, 102, 105–106, 108–111, 116–119, 122–123, 125–130, 135–137, 148–155, 157–158, 160, 162, 165, 171, 181–182, 184–187, 195, 198–202, 205, 208, 216, 222, 231, 239–241, 245, 247, 250, 256, 261, 263, 265, 271–274, 278, 292–293, 308

Eighth Amendment, 120, 129, 133–136, 155–156, 171, 187–189, 191–195, 201

Ely, John Hart, 32, 116, 161, 203

empirical research, 275, 285

equal respect and concern, 33, 36, 80, 87–88, 127–128, 197, 235

Ewicks, P., 292

Existentialism is a Humanism (Sartre), 236

experience, 5–6, 11, 23, 29, 32–33, 73, 81, 84–85, 90–95, 104, 145, 150, 167, 191, 195, 204, 216, 222, 229–238, 246, 249–250, 271, 279, 281–282, 289

Federal Sentencing Guidelines Manual, 304

Federal Sentencing Guidelines, 302, 304

Federalist Papers (Hamilton, Madison, Jay), 123–124, 154

feminism, 15, 82, 274, 309

feminist jurisprudence, 33, 279, 308

Finnis, John, 104, 107

First Amendment, 35, 39, 131–133

Fisher, Roger, 280–281

force, 6–7, 17, 27, 42, 50, 60–64, 68, 139, 178–179, 199, 202, 220, 240, 244–245

foreign horizon, 73, 89, 110, 134, 268, 281, 284, 286, 291

formalism, 32, 51, 54, 79, 81, 139–140, 254, 260, 273

Fourteenth Amendment, 18, 69, 117–118, 122, 125–127, 130, 138, 140–143, 145, 147–148, 156–159, 172, 174, 180, 182, 257

Frankfurter, Felix 143–144

Freedom and Constraint in Adjudication: A Critical Phenomenology (Kennedy), 34, 65, 72, 93, 259, 266

Fuller, Lon, 4, 22, 27, 33, 40, 52, 54, 66–67, 139, 214, 308

Fundamental Legal Conceptions (Hohfeld), 264–265

Furman v. Georgia, 129, 161, 188

fusion of horizons, 260

Gadamer, Hans-Georg, 83, 86, 246, 249–250, 260

Gainsborough, 247, 272

gestalt, 73, 90, 92–93, 134–135

Getting to Yes (Fisher, Ury), 280

Gewirth, Alan, 71, 274

Goals of Criminal Punishment (Donnelly), 295–296, 302–304

grand conversation, 4, 14, 25, 37, 263–264, 272

grand style of the common law, 30, 79, 89

Granfield, David, 32–34, 81, 87, 91–92, 107, 273, 281–282
great quarrel over method, 4, 6, 8, 10, 21, 26, 28–34, 78, 80–81, 87, 94, 115, 119–120, 137, 152–153, 275, 278, 306–307
greater average utility, 211, 222, 295
greater good of the greater number, 211, 220, 222, 295, 297
Greenman v. Yuba Power Products, Inc., 40, 46, 48–49
Gregg v. Georgia, 32, 129, 161, 188–190, 193–194, 282, 296
group goals, 20, 38, 44–45, 108, 181, 222, 256
Habermas, Jürgen, 23, 243–244
Hamilton, Alexander 120, 123–124, 154, 169, 202, 252
Handbook of Regulation and Administrative Law (Rosenbloom, Schwartz), 292
Haring, Bernard, 71
Harmelin v. Michigan, 192
Hart, H.L.A. 3–4, 14, 22, 27–28, 40, 51–57, 62, 66, 75, 80, 105, 109–110, 140, 162, 211, 222, 223, 233, 248, 251–253, 255, 261, 264, 272–273, 276, 295, 297
Hart, Henry, 80, 252
Hawkins, Gordon, 192, 298, 301, 303
Heidigger, Martin 5, 83
Henningsen v. Bloomfield Motors, Inc., 40, 46, 48–49
Heracles' Bow (White), 25, 104, 170, 187, 206, 248, 252, 271
hermeneutics, 249
Hohfeld, Wesley, 264–265
Hollenbach, David 20
Holmes, Oliver Wendell, 3–4, 11, 14, 28–31, 33, 41, 43, 60–61, 73–74, 76, 78–79, 87, 93, 142–144, 152, 251–252, 254–255, 260–262, 273, 277, 280–282, 307
horizon crossing method, 9, 73, 87, 97, 103–104, 106–107, 112–113, 143, 275
horizons, 8–9, 12, 14–17, 19, 30–31, 36–38, 41, 44, 58, 60–61, 72–74, 83–91, 93, 95–98, 102–104,

106–107, 110, 112–113, 118–119, 122, 131–132, 134–137, 143, 145, 150–151, 166–170, 172–173, 175, 179, 187, 195–196, 207, 212, 214–218, 224, 229, 231, 235, 238, 241–242, 246–250, 259–260, 262–266, 269–272, 274–275, 277–282, 284–286, 291, 293–294, 298, 309
Horvitz, Morton, 259
human dignity, 10, 20, 69, 117–118, 129, 133–136, 144, 147, 150–151, 169–170, 173–175, 180–181, 188–190, 193, 195, 201, 236, 282, 295–296, 299–300
human experience, 23, 33, 104, 235, 237, 246, 250, 271
human relations, 14, 17, 19, 26, 49, 64, 68, 79, 104, 116, 214, 221, 223–224, 230–231, 234, 244–245, 248, 250, 257, 264, 271, 282
human rights, 12–14, 18–20, 31, 39, 68–69, 135, 144, 189, 196–199, 209–220, 222, 225, 236–237, 248, 257–258, 292, 294
human rights ideology, 197–199, 210–212, 214–217
ideals, 8, 10, 12, 17, 39, 45, 58, 61, 64, 67, 73–74, 81, 87–88, 90, 93, 98, 109, 117–118, 125–126, 151, 168–169, 182, 199, 201–204, 207–209, 215–217, 220, 222, 224, 234, 241–243, 245, 250, 261–262, 271, 274, 278, 282, 293, 308
ideology, 36, 82, 88, 110, 140, 197–199, 210–212, 214–217, 259–260, 266, 288
Ignatieff, Michael, 238
impact and interest analysis, 15, 30, 37, 39, 79, 86, 89, 146, 151, 169, 289, 293
Imprisonment for Debt, 289
Imprisonment in America (Hawkins, Sherman), 192, 301, 303
incapacitation, 294, 296, 298, 300–303, 305
insight, 11, 35, 57, 61, 71, 73, 75, 88, 90–93, 96–97, 101, 105, 112, 117–118, 186, 201, 214–215, 232,

249–251, 270, 272, 276, 282, 284, 288

integrated theory of criminal punishment, 20, 295, 297–298

integrity, 7, 35, 49, 51, 55, 88, 99, 129, 148, 185, 240–241, 273

intellectual method, 10–11, 16, 83, 87, 94, 96, 112, 115, 119, 122, 197–199, 227, 229

interest analysis, 8, 15, 30, 37, 39, 73, 79, 86, 89–90, 93, 96, 103–104, 146, 151, 169, 173, 178, 180, 289, 293

interest balancing, 9, 39, 45, 195, 293

internal point of view, 233, 264

International Covenant on Economic, Social and Cultural Rights, 210, 213

International Covenant on Civil and Political Rights, 210, 213

interpretation, 4–7, 9–14, 16–23, 26, 31–32, 35, 40, 49–52, 54–56, 59, 69–71, 74, 88, 96–97, 99, 103, 105, 110–113, 115–196, 198–199, 201, 205, 207, 209–211, 216–217, 222, 239–241, 243–256, 261–263, 266–267, 270–271, 273–275, 277–280, 288, 293–294, 302, 308–309

interpretation of statutes, 7, 50–65

judicial restraint, 153, 156–157, 161, 163, 165, 169

jurisprudence of subjectivity, 32, 81, 281–282

justification, 6, 11–12, 17–18, 35, 60–61, 66, 75, 117, 148, 167, 197–246, 295, 299–300, 308

Kant, Immanuel, 86–87, 294

Kantian, 212, 215, 236–237, 294–297

Karl Llewellyn and the Legal Realist Movement (Twining), 37, 50, 89

Keeton, Robert, 48, 275, 280

Kennedy, Duncan, 15, 34–36, 46, 65, 67–68, 72, 82, 93, 110, 139, 259, 266

King's Bench, 41–42, 267

Langdell, Christopher Columbus, 28–29, 43–44, 73, 75, 78, 139, 307

Langdellian, 30, 32, 37, 43–44, 47, 64, 81, 139, 164, 169, 172–173, 254, 273, 280, 307

Langdellian legal formalism, 139, 254, 273

language, 3–4, 13–14, 19, 25, 27–29, 40, 51–56, 59, 74, 79, 82–84, 109–111, 116, 125–126, 146, 154–156, 158–160, 168, 170, 174, 187, 193–194, 206, 223, 229, 234, 237, 241, 247–273, 275, 285, 307

language of rights, 3–4, 13–14, 19, 25, 74, 82, 109–111, 116, 168, 170, 187, 247–272, 275, 285

law and economics, 11, 15, 30, 291

law reform, 13, 15, 19, 82, 110, 145, 166, 168, 230, 248, 250, 258, 262–263, 267, 269, 271, 275–276, 279, 283–286, 289, 294, 305–306, 309

law reformer, 13–14, 258–259, 262, 269–270, 272, 275, 281, 284, 293

legal classicism, 119, 136–145, 150, 159, 166, 172

legal culture, 9, 14, 20, 206, 228, 231, 237, 239, 242–243, 252, 254, 270–272, 275, 278, 282

legal process, 80, 168–169, 252

legal realism, 33, 49

legal realists, 29, 33, 79, 82, 254–255, 260

legal rights, 12, 14, 30–31, 35, 37–39, 56, 69–70, 80–81, 99, 106, 108–111, 208, 219, 222, 248, 254–256, 258–259, 265–266, 271, 287–288

legitimacy, 7, 10, 12–13, 17–18, 21–23, 26–27, 36, 62, 65–69, 96–98, 127, 150, 167, 196–246, 258–259, 267–269, 273, 308–309

legitimacy costs, 10, 22–23, 196, 202, 208, 245, 308

legitimacy power, 22, 36, 65, 259, 267–269

legitimate decision, 6, 21–22, 65, 67–68, 98, 199, 242, 308

Lempert, Richard, 290–291

level of generality, 147, 158, 163, 174, 182–183, 200

liberal theories of constitutional interpretation, 126, 161–169
Life's Dominion (Dworkin), 184–185
Llewellyn, Karl, 3–4, 25, 29–31, 33,
37–38, 42–43, 46, 50–51, 59, 73,
78–80, 86, 89–90, 92, 105, 136,
146, 253–254, 265, 278, 307
Lochner v. N.Y., 29, 141–142, 144, 172
Locke, John, 69, 180, 210
logic, 11, 29, 44, 73, 93–94, 183,
203–204, 228, 237, 281
Lonergan, Bernard, 11, 71, 83–85, 92,
105
long sentences, 299–300, 303–305
Macmurray, John, 7–8, 71–72, 74–77,
94, 99–101, 103, 112, 216,
231–232, 234–235, 274, 284, 308
MacPherson v. Buick Motor Co., 40,
46–48
Madison, 120, 123–124, 131–132,
154, 252
majoritarianism, 32, 68, 126–127,
160–161, 194–195
Mansfield, Lord, 98, 247, 267–268,
307
Marshall, John, 247, 307
Marshall, Thurgood, 110, 188–191,
195, 201, 258, 262
McCleskey v. Kemp, 190
means-end reasoning, 9–11, 59,
117–118, 128, 130–132, 135, 146,
237
means-goal reasoning, 39, 109–110,
151, 257, 261–262
Meese, Edwin 156–157
method, 4–13, 15–18, 20–23, 25–29,
31–32, 34–35, 38–41, 43–45,
58–61, 68–73, 76–78, 80–88,
90–91, 93–99, 103–107,
110–113, 115–120, 122–123,
128, 130–134, 136–137, 143,
146, 151–154, 157, 160, 162–165,
167–171, 173, 178, 184, 187, 191,
195–202, 204, 206–209, 218,
222, 224, 227–230, 232–233,
235–236, 241–247, 249–250,
252, 257, 260, 262, 265–266,
271, 273–275, 277–280, 289,
291, 306–309

Method in Theology (Lonergan), 71,
84–85
middle level position, 216, 274
moment of understanding, 249
moral judgment, 12–13, 18, 197–246
Morris, Norval, 192, 295–296,
300–301
Myrdal, Gunner, 289
NAACP, 110, 145, 159, 166, 168, 258
narration, 271
Natural Law and Natural Rights (Finnis), 104
New York Times v. Sullivan, 10,
117–118, 131–133, 168
Nichomacean Ethics (Aristotle), 236
Ninth Amendment, 143, 158, 171–173
Nixon, Richard, 153
no vehicles in the park, 52
Nozick, Robert, 184, 222
obligation, 3, 13, 19, 28, 62, 65–67,
75, 96–98, 100, 112, 138, 180,
198, 210, 215, 221, 223–225,
233–235, 237–242, 248, 251,
263–267, 270–272, 282–283
obliged, 62, 180, 233, 235
On Reading the Constitution (Dorf,
Tribe), 162–163, 172
open texture, 52, 105, 140, 256
originalism, 125–126, 191
overarching theory, 29, 31, 37, 39,
45–46, 49, 69–70, 81, 98–99,
103–104, 110–113, 209, 262, 265
Packer, Herbert, 295, 297, 299–300
paradigms, 41, 46, 49, 137, 139, 166
participate, 5, 19–20, 101–102, 107,
130, 170, 173, 180, 182,
189–190, 208, 216, 234, 257,
263, 266, 272, 275, 282, 285,
293, 296–297, 306
participation, 8, 18, 20, 32, 77,
101–102, 104, 106–108, 111, 130,
132, 136, 162, 173, 175, 180, 208,
221, 231, 244, 270, 272, 283, 285,
293, 302, 305
Perry, Michael, 211–221
person, 3, 5–8, 10–12, 15–16, 18–23,
25, 27, 33–34, 36, 39–40, 45–47,
49, 56, 58, 63–65, 67–78, 80–82,
84, 88, 94–103, 107–113,

117–118, 122, 125–127, 129–130, 132–135, 141–142, 150–151, 153–154, 162, 169–170, 173–174, 178, 180–189, 191, 193, 195, 198, 201, 207–209, 214–217, 219, 221–224, 228–230, 232, 234, 236–238, 241–245, 247, 257, 261, 264, 268, 273–279, 282–286, 289–290, 293, 295–300, 302–303, 306, 308–309

personalism, 4–5, 7, 12, 16, 18, 45–46, 49, 59–60, 69, 71–72, 75–77, 80, 97, 99, 101, 111–112, 117, 122, 171, 173, 195, 197, 208, 210, 212, 216–217, 220, 223, 243, 246, 251–252, 263, 274–276, 289, 306, 309

personalist agenda, 14–15, 273–306

personalist judge, 5–9, 13–17, 19, 25–27, 40, 45, 49, 58–59, 68–70, 72, 74, 77–81, 83, 86–91, 93, 96–98, 102–104, 106, 108, 110–112, 118, 122, 128–131, 133–134, 136, 166–167, 173–175, 179–180, 184, 188, 190, 195–196, 201–202, 205, 207–209, 218, 222, 224, 242–243, 245–246, 265–266, 271, 274–275, 277–279, 290, 293

personalist jurisprudence, 1, 5, 8, 11, 14–16, 21, 23, 33–34, 71–73, 76–77, 81, 83, 91, 93–94, 100–102, 108, 116, 123, 197, 216, 279

personalist principles of criminal justice, 300, 302, 304

personalist theory, 8–9, 13–21, 26, 40–41, 49, 61, 64, 69–113, 115, 118–120, 122, 130, 132–133, 136, 151, 168, 172–173, 175, 180, 182, 189, 195–196, 198–199, 203, 205, 207–209, 216, 221–224, 226–227, 234, 236–237, 241–243, 248, 274–277, 279–280, 282–283, 285, 289–290, 293–294, 296–300, 302–303, 305–306, 309

personalist theory of rights, 9, 13, 18–20, 69–70, 74, 98, 102–105, 107, 110–111, 130, 136, 172,

198–199, 209, 216, 221, 224, 236–237, 248

persons acting together, 8, 18, 74–75, 77, 101, 111, 171, 221, 223, 282, 285, 293

Persons In Relation (Macmurray), 8, 71, 75–77, 94, 100, 231, 274

physician assisted suicide, 187

Piaget, Jean, 237

piecemeal recovery, 4, 15, 23, 33, 72, 81–82, 273

planning, 225, 252, 254, 280–281

Plessy v. Ferguson, 119, 140–141, 145–151, 157, 159

pluralist society, 9, 12–13, 19, 68, 74, 98, 103–104, 106–107, 112–113, 116, 118, 131, 136, 170, 187, 196–198, 200, 203, 205, 207–208, 214, 218, 243, 246, 248, 260, 264, 270, 279, 286, 293, 309

point of view, 5, 13–14, 66, 79–80, 110, 212, 233, 247, 253–254, 258, 260–264, 267, 269–271, 279–280

policy, 38, 42–46, 48–49, 53, 55, 84, 87–88, 102, 108–109, 135, 140, 146, 148, 171–172, 178, 222, 239, 265, 285, 305

policy arguments, 49, 222

policy reasons, 45, 55, 102, 109, 171, 222, 239

political friendship, 33, 36, 39, 65, 80, 82, 88, 99–100, 107, 127–128, 151, 240–241, 263

political resources, 258–259

portrait of law, 14, 247, 254, 262, 270

Posner, Richard, 3–4, 11–12, 15, 23, 28–30, 39, 43, 46, 61, 73–74, 90, 198, 203–205, 207–209, 211, 219, 228, 230–231, 246, 250–251, 265–266, 277, 290, 292

post modern thought, 17, 308

Post Civil War Amendments, 250

Pound, Roscoe, 3–4, 11, 29–31, 33, 37, 42–43, 73, 78–79, 86, 89, 143–144, 146, 204, 255, 278, 290

practicing attorney, 15, 254, 261, 267, 275, 280

pragmatic instrumentalist, 7, 10, 17, 27, 31, 39–40, 43–46, 57, 59, 63–64, 66, 78, 81, 83, 86, 96–97, 131, 137, 143, 145, 257, 277–278, 307

pragmatism, 7, 12, 30, 39, 46, 69, 71, 74–75, 79–80, 82, 203, 262, 273–274, 309

Pragmatism in Law and Society (Brint,Weaver), 71, 274, 309

pragmatist, 3, 8, 31, 39, 69, 71, 80, 105, 151, 203, 205, 246, 253, 265, 274

predictive view of law, 254, 260–261

primary social goods, 8–9, 18–20, 101–102, 104, 106–111, 113, 130–131, 135, 173, 175, 180, 182, 186, 189, 195–196, 221–222, 224, 237, 240–241, 244, 257, 293, 296–297, 299–300, 302, 305

principled justification, 66, 167, 199, 242, 245–246

principled reasoning, 8, 43–44, 73, 89, 96–97, 118–119, 169, 178, 224, 228, 261

principles, 6, 8–10, 12, 16–17, 20, 28–32, 35–38, 41, 43–45, 49, 55, 61–63, 65, 67–70, 72–73, 75–78, 80–82, 85, 87–88, 90, 93, 96, 98–99, 101–103, 108–109, 113, 115, 117, 119–120, 135, 137, 139, 150–152, 154, 159, 161, 169, 173, 181–182, 187, 199–200, 204, 206–209, 213, 222, 226, 231, 241, 245, 256, 261, 265, 273, 277, 295–298, 300–302, 304, 307

profession, 3, 19, 28, 74, 76, 78, 104, 168, 251–252, 254, 261, 272–273, 280, 282, 306

Punishment and Responsibility (Hart), 211, 295

Race and Racism in American Law (Bell), 287

racism, 286–288

Radin, Margaret Jane, 43, 71, 274, 277

rational plan in life, 101, 104, 107

Rawls, John, 8, 15, 87, 101–102, 104, 106–107, 113, 184, 199, 215–216, 220, 223, 225–227, 237, 241, 274, 296

Reason and Morality (Gerwith), 71, 274

reconstruct, 5, 27–28, 34, 59–60, 81, 96, 275, 309

recovery of a role for the person, 8, 15, 23, 27, 33, 72–73, 81–82, 273, 278, 289, 308

reform litigator, 110, 248, 262, 267, 275

refusal to deliberate, 32, 120, 152, 156, 159–160, 175, 191

regulatory function, 57, 62, 167–168

rehabilitation, 294, 296, 298–300, 302–303, 305

Rehnquist Court, 161

restraint, 32, 35, 100, 116, 118, 120, 123, 125, 138, 153–154, 156–157, 160–161, 163, 165, 167, 169, 171, 176, 225

rethinking criminal justice, 276, 279, 293–294, 306

retribution, 188, 194, 294–295, 302, 304

right to die, 164, 177–178, 185

rights, 3–4, 6, 8–9, 12–15, 17–20, 25, 30–33, 35–40, 44–46, 49, 51, 55–56, 58, 60–61, 68–70, 74, 80–82, 85, 87–88, 98–99, 102–113, 116, 118, 120, 122–130, 135–136, 141–144, 148, 152–153, 155–156, 158–160, 164, 168, 170–177, 180–182, 187, 189, 191–192, 195–199, 201, 208–227, 235–237, 243–244, 247–272, 275, 280, 284–285, 287–288, 292, 294, 309

rights as claims, 13, 122

rights as conclusions, 13, 109, 255–257, 261

rights as criticism, 253

rights as goals, 109–110, 122, 136, 181–182, 257–258, 262

rights as ideology, 197, 210, 214, 217, 259

rights as means, 19, 109–110, 112, 122, 168, 176, 210, 214, 257–259, 261–262, 285

rights as predictions, 13

rights as reasons, 38, 45, 109, 181, 255–258, 261

rights as remedies, 13, 254

rights as resources, 110, 258–259
rights as rhetoric, 259
rights as trumps, 255–256
rights discourse, 14, 19, 108, 244, 259
role of the person, 8, 15, 23, 27,
    33–34, 72–73, 81–82, 273,
    277–278, 289, 308
rules, 3, 7, 13, 27–28, 43, 50, 52,
    57–58, 60, 62–63, 75–76, 78–81,
    109, 139, 168, 190, 192, 234,
    251–256, 261–262, 264–265, 273,
    276, 280–281, 307
Sacks, Albert, 80, 252
Sanders, Joseph A., 290–291
Sanford v. Kentucky, 161
Sartre, Jean-Paul, 236
Scalia, Antonin, 31–32, 43, 50–51,
    125–126, 153–157, 159–160, 162,
    164, 170, 172, 174, 191–193, 250
Scandinavian Legal Realists, 254
Scheingold, Stuart, 258–259, 285
Schindler's List, 238
Schwartz, Richard, 292
scientific method, 11, 93–94, 204,
    207, 227–229, 232
Scott v. Sandford, 142, 268
semantic sting, 256
sentencing statutes, 303
sharing of horizons, 249–250, 271
Sharp, Granville, 267–269
Sherman, Michael, 192, 301, 303
Silbey, Susan, 292
situation sense, 30, 37, 39, 79–80, 86,
    89–90, 92–93, 96, 134–135, 231
skeptical challenge to legal reasoning,
    21
slavery, 100, 149, 218, 223, 243,
    267–269
social engineering, 11, 30, 33, 79, 89
social science, 15, 30, 147, 151, 205,
    227, 275–276, 289–292, 294, 298,
    302
society, 8–10, 12–15, 17–20, 32–33,
    36, 39, 49, 58, 64, 67–68, 71,
    74–76, 82, 87, 98, 100–104,
    106–113, 116–118, 123–124,
    130–132, 136, 138–139, 144–146,
    151–153, 157, 162, 166–171, 173,
    175, 179–182, 184, 187, 189–190,

196–198, 200, 202–209, 211, 214,
    217–218, 220–223, 225, 229–230,
    234, 239, 241–246, 248, 250, 254,
    257–264, 266, 269–272, 274–275,
    278–279, 282–286, 288–291,
    293–302, 305, 309
Somersett v. Stewart, 98, 267–269
sovereign virtue, 187
statutory interpretation, 5, 40, 50–51,
    56, 59, 70, 88, 96, 115, 193
Stewart, Justice, 190, 193–194,
    267–268
story, 33, 41, 63, 91, 269
strict construction, 31, 51, 152–154,
    156
strong rights, 8, 12–14, 38–40, 45–46,
    49, 58, 69–70, 108, 111–112, 182,
    197, 224, 227, 266
substantive due process, 10, 120,
    141–143, 164, 171, 176–177
Sullivan, Teresa, 292
Summers, Robert, 39, 110, 261–262
Sunstein, Cass, 9, 21, 116–117,
    123–124, 198, 200–203, 239, 241,
    244–245, 277
Supreme Court, 6, 9–10, 17, 60, 85,
    90, 115–116, 120–122, 125–126,
    128, 133, 136, 138–143, 151, 153,
    156–157, 159, 163–164,
    166–168, 170, 172–173, 176–179,
    182–184, 186, 188–189, 194–195,
    200, 203, 268, 270, 273, 307
Syracuse, 16, 84, 91, 207
system of language and rules, 28, 273
system of rules, 3, 13, 27–28, 75–76,
    78, 80, 109, 251–256, 273, 280
terrorist, 218–220, 224–225
textualism, 51, 153, 191
The Acting Person (Wojtyla), 71, 101,
    222
The Common Law (Holmes), 4, 11,
    73, 93
The Common Place of Law: Stories
    from Everyday Life (Ewicks, Sib-
    ley), 292
The Concept of Law (Hart), 3, 22, 28,
    51–53, 57, 62, 66, 75, 80,
    105–106, 140, 162, 233, 251–252,
    255, 264

The Future of Imprisonment (Morris), 192, 295, 303
The Goals of Criminal Punishment (Donnelly), 295–296, 299, 302
The Idea of Human Rights (Perry), 211–219
The Inner Experience of Law, A Jurisprudence of Subjectivity (Granfield), 32, 81, 281–282
The Language and Uses of Rights (Donnelly), 259, 263, 270–271
The Limits of the Criminal Sanction (Packer), 295
The Moral Judgment of the Child (Piaget), 237
The Needs of Strangers (Ignatieff), 238
The Path of the Law (Holmes), 3, 11, 28, 61, 74, 251, 281
The Politics of Rights (Scheingold), 258, 285
The Poor Pay More (Caplovitz), 289
The Pragmatist and the Feminist (Radin), 71, 274
The Problematics of Moral and Legal Theory (Posner), 204–205, 207
The Problems of Jurisprudence (Posner), 4, 11, 28, 73–74, 198, 203, 207, 209, 265
The Self as Agent (Macmurray), 8, 71, 75, 274
theory of criminal responsibility, 296
theory of personalism, 4–5, 7, 16, 18, 45–46, 71–72, 76–77, 99, 111, 117, 122, 173, 210, 216, 274, 309
thin theory of the good, 101–102, 106, 237
Thompson v. Oklahoma, 193–194
Towards a Personalist Jurisprudence (Donnelly), 5, 8, 11, 21, 33–34, 71, 76–77, 83, 91, 93–94, 100–102, 108, 116, 123, 216
Tracy, David 11, 83, 93, 105
transcending horizons, 60, 85–86, 95, 106, 110, 259, 279
Tribe, Lawrence, 162–165, 167, 172, 182–184, 186–187
Truth and Method (Gadamer), 246, 249

Tushnet, Mark, 110–111, 259
Twining, William, 37, 50, 73, 89, 146, 265
Two Treatises of Government (Locke), 69, 210
ultimate legitimacy, 10, 17, 22, 98, 127, 150, 308
unenumerated rights, 120, 143, 158, 164, 171–173, 176, 180, 187, 196
Unger, Roberto, 15, 82, 110, 259–260
Universal Declaration of Human Rights, 210, 258
Ury, William 280–281
use of rights, 14, 19, 248, 259–260, 263–264, 267, 270–272, 284–285
utilitarian, 211, 222–224, 236, 294–297, 299
utilitarianism, 210–211, 220
Vacco v. Quill, 164, 171, 176, 182–184
vision, 4, 10, 14, 40, 46–47, 49, 51, 56–57, 60, 65, 75, 83–84, 86, 88–90, 101, 103–104, 113, 117, 129, 132, 135–136, 143, 151, 166–167, 169–170, 172, 180–182, 184, 186–189, 209, 246, 248, 260–261, 263, 269–271, 304, 307
Walnut Street Jail, 155, 192
Warren, Chief Justice Earl, 98, 109, 119, 137, 144–147, 149–151, 242, 247, 257, 307
Warren Court, 31–32, 116, 131, 143, 151, 161
Warren, Elizabeth, 291–292
Washington v. Glucksberg, 171, 176–179, 184, 186
weak rights, 38–40, 46, 70, 108, 208
Wechsler, Herbert, 31, 80, 152, 159
Wellington, Harry, 60, 120, 152, 167
Westbrook, Jay, 291–292
White, James Boyd, 25, 104, 170, 187, 206, 208, 248, 252, 271
White, Justice, 173–174, 176, 190, 194
Wiecek, William, 136–144
Wojtyla, Karol 71, 101, 222
Zimring, Frederick, 298